# Left Strategies in the Covid Pandemic and Its Aftermath

# Left Strategies in the Covid Pandemic and Its Aftermath

Edited by
Walter Baier, Eric Canepa
and Haris Golemis

MERLIN PRESS

transform! Yearbook 2022
Left Strategies in the Covid Pandemic and its Aftermath

English edition published in the UK in 2022 by
The Merlin Press
Central Books Building
Freshwater Road
London RM8 1RX
www.merlinpress.co.uk

Editors: Walter Baier, Eric Canepa, Haris Golemis

Managing Editor: Kimon Markatos

Editorial Board: Walter Baier, Eric Canepa, Haris Golemis,
Dagmar Švendová

transform! europe EUPF, Square de Meeûs 25, 1000 Brussels, Belgium
Partially financed through a subsidy from the European Parliament.

Cover Illustration: Stavroula Drakopoulou

ISSN 1865-3480

ISBN 978-0-85036-782-9

Printed in the UK by Imprint Digital, Exeter

# Contents

## Preface
*Walter Baier, Eric Canepa, Haris Golemis:* Left Strategies in the
 Covid Pandemic and Its Aftermath                              9

## The Covid Pandemic and the Social and Political Left
*Leigh Phillips:* A Programme for a Pandemic Justice Movement  23
*Ricardo Antunes:* Pandemic Capitalism: What Now?              46
*Asbjørn Wahl:* Covid-19 and Working-Class Power               59
*Donatella della Porta:* Contentious Politics in Critical
 Emergency Junctures: The Pandemic and Progressive
 Social Movement Organisations                                 72

## Geopolitical Shifts and Conflicts
*transform! europe Peace Manifesto*: Stop the War!
 An Appeal for a Europe of Peace                               83
*Veronika Sušová-Salminen:* Can We Avert Further Wars?
 The West, Russia, and China in the World of Seismic Shifts    88
*Jan Campbell:* China and Europe in the Foreseeable Future     99
*Silvina Romano, Tamara Lajtman, and Aníbal García Fernández:*
 The Geopolitics of Covid in Latin America                     112

## The Marxist-Christian Dialogue
*Walter Baier:* What Can the Socialist Left Learn From the Pope?  133
*Margareta Gruber:* Without the City of Man There Can Be
 No Paradise on Earth: The Bible Ends with a
 Vision of a Megacity                                          143
*Michael Löwy:* Marxisms and Christianities: Recent Publications  153

## Europe

*Étienne Balibar:* The Eternal Impossibility of a Democratic Europe
and the Tasks of a 'Party of Europe' — 167

*Katerina Anastasiou and Axel Ruppert:* Discuss Security –
Reclaim the Future — 180

*Nidžara Ahmetašević:* Europe – from Fortress to Dungeon — 193

*María Eugenia Rodríguez Palop:* Migrants and Refugees:
Pariahs of Europe — 204

## Social Democratic and Radical Left Political Strategies

*Luciana Castellina and Donald Sassoon:* Social Democracy and the
Radical Left: Old Divisions and the Imperatives
of the New Socio-Ecological Crisis — 217

*Gerassimos Moschonas:* Social Democracy's Electoral and
Ideological Retreat, the European Union, and the
Radical Left's Dilemmas — 236

*Steffen Lehndorff:* From the New Deal of the 1930s
to the Green New Deal of the 2020s — 254

*Loren Balhorn:* Class Struggle for Social Democracy — 265

*Seraphim Seferiades:* 'Populism' as a Cognitive Barrier:
A Political Approach — 278

*Dunja Larise:* Why Is Austro-Marxism Still Worth Studying
in the 21st Century? — 294

## Ecosocialism/Ecofeminism

*Ariel Salleh:* A Relational Logic for The Left –
Interviewed by Haris Golemis — 311

*Michael Löwy:* For an Ecosocialist 'Great Transformation':
Fourteen Theses — 326

*Anna Saave:* Ecofeminism Now — 335

## European Country Reports

*Jana Tsoneva:* Neoliberal Hysteresis:
Lessons from Bulgaria's Abortive Vaccination Campaign — 353

*Mario Candeias:* Decisive Elections and the Future
of the Left in Germany — 366

*Claudia Krieglsteiner:* Pandemic De-Socialisation in Austria — 387

*Francisco Louçã:* Portugal: Time Is Running Out — 400

## Anniversary
*Daniel Finn:* The Contested Legacy of Derry's Bloody Sunday 411
## Authors and Editors 423
## Members and Observers of transform! europe 429

# Preface

The production of this year's volume was overshadowed by the war against Ukraine launched by the Russian Federation in violation of international law, with the terrible destruction, worldwide food disaster, and heightened danger to world peace it has unleashed. It has occurred against a background of longstanding military build-ups, scrapped non-proliferation treaties, and NATO provocation, along with the delayed effects of the 2008-9 financial crisis on a Russian economy devastated by its comprador oligarchy. There is urgent need of a revitalised peace movement grounded in a sturdy systemic critique, while not stuck in an anachronistic East-West 'anti-imperialist' campism, and, as a contribution to this end, we are publishing the **transform! europe network**'s appeal for peace and a European security architecture outside NATO and inclusive of all European countries.

At the same time we are still in the midst of the most serious global pandemic in a century, resulting from the ongoing ecological crisis of capitalist society, but without the kind of healthcare systems and cooperation that would have been needed to adequately respond to it. As Leigh Phillips points out, while the left normally did not have a take on the pandemic particularly distinct from the response of the more effective governments, nor was there any major difference between left and right government responses, the hallmarks of the enacted policies were in fact economic planning, state intervention, and public funding – even in the US, with prior massive government funding of vaccine development and then Trump's Operation Warp Speed – all of which plays directly into what the left has always argued for. The issue of cross-subsidisation across regions arose early on, before vaccine rollout, when in the US uneven access to medical care and equipment led even Republican governors of poor rural states to beg for federal government intervention. The lack of financial incentive for the pharmaceuticals to invest in vaccines that may have to be administered only once (or for that matter any medications not requiring continuous use), which the public intervention in the US was meant to address, has become dramatically obvious now. While left demands for economic planning and bringing medicine into the public sector have suddenly become less utopian on the national level, the challenge is more daunting internationally where the grossly unequal vaccine distribution and WTO-protected patents point to the need for an international polity whose democratic legitimation is accepted by citizens.

Although cautioning against any cooperation with anti-vax conspiracy theorists, Phillips acknowledges the problems of scientific paternalism that sow confusion and mistrust of scientists when they fail to explain the thinking behind their necessarily provisional recommendations, which would better prepare the public for later revisions. Jana Tsoneva looks at the anti-vax sensibility in Bulgaria, which in general conforms to attitudes found in the Global North. Contrary to the liberal press's consensus that anti-vaxxers are uneducated, working-class 'populists' (and its orientalising of the Bulgarian popular classes as representing Ottoman and eastern communist vestiges), Tsoneva instead notes that they mostly consist of middle-class professionals who distrust a dismantled and increasingly profit-oriented healthcare system and have developed a consumerist culture of individual self-management in areas previously thought to be society's responsibility. It is ultimately a self-coping with abandonment that takes the form of a populist neoliberal rebellion against the state. In Western Europe this has penetrated deeply into many left and alternative milieus, taking the form of survivalism, designing one's own life, etc. It is clear that many opponents of Covid vaccination are not against doctors and scientists – they listen to the anti-vaxxers among them – nor against all vaccines. In Bulgaria, precarious governments' fear of endorsing mass inoculations as well as a sensationalist media have confused the public about the vaccine and lockdowns. Tsoneva warns of a return to a pre-20$^{th}$-century distrust of the state.

Decades of neoliberal de-socialisation, as elsewhere in Europe since the Maastricht Treaty, preceded the pandemic's arrival in Austria. The features of this transformation reviewed by Claudia Krieglsteiner are, alongside the individual 'self-responsibilisation' noted by Tsoneva, the enormously increased competitive pressure even affecting grade-school children, with a dramatic rise in mental disorders. What was previously understood as the 'social' (the welfare state) is now denounced as Fordist paternalism. Labour and workplace relations are de-politicised and accepted as merely objective and technical and electoral politics seen as increasingly irrelevant to the really important economic decisions, so that it has become hard for people to recognise themselves as whole people with agency – which left politics must now try to rebuild. In addition, neoliberalism has left much less room for young people to experiment with life, as they are expected to validate themselves in the market early on – and the pandemic lockdowns then added huge gaps in adolescent socialisation.

★ ★ ★

Donatella della Porta tracks the remobilisation of pre-existing movements through the pandemic in Europe, particularly around health rights, and new forms of mutualisation along with the spontaneous individual acts of solidarity disasters typically trigger. The local dimension naturally increased in importance, and the new mutualistic initiatives began to collaborate with more established political organisations.

The Covid pandemic dramatised the ongoing dilemmas of the labour movement worldwide. It first of all laid bare the neoliberal devastation of healthcare systems and spotlighted the plight of its workers. Telework has resulted in overwork and isolation, and trade unions will have to fight to regulate it. Furthermore, north-south solidarity was strained by pandemic policies. On the other hand, the suspension of austerity in the EU showed what government could do. With the exposure of Big Pharma's disinterest in preventive medicine, trade unions could have an opportunity to call for bringing production into the public sector. Asbjørn Wahl points out that historically it was labour militancy during the post-war boom that made gains possible, but that the subsequent social partnership approach of Western trade unions – which was only possible because of union militancy – left them unprepared for the neoliberal offensive. More social dialogue cannot repair the ubiquitous collapse of the class compromise, Wahl cautions. Trade unions have largely come up with perfectly good demands but more politicised unions will be needed to win them.

Ricardo Antunes speaks of a particularly lethal stage of 'viral' or 'pandemic capitalism' – with the greatly accelerated planned obsolescence of use-values and of capital's reproductive cycle and the attendant climate catastrophe, deforestation, etc., triggering increasingly devastating pandemics – all of which is more directly destructive of natural creation than ever before but also makes the necessity of a new mode of life more patently necessary, a question that has even begun to be posed as such by large parts of the population in Latin America.

This new lethality of capitalism, as an existential threat, is discussed by Luciana Castellina and Donald Sassoon in relation to neoliberal globalisation and technical 'governance' of the economy, especially in the EU, which has diminished the power of parliaments and political representation to intervene in essential questions and thus delegitimised them for many young people. Previous struggles around income distribution ought now to be embedded in the overarching existential imperative to change the mode of production and consumption. The challenge is to connect this imperative to working-class bread-and-butter issues, for without this it is hardly possible to simply ask the populations to consume less. The dimension of the needed response to this existential crisis transcends the context of the old social democratic/communist conflict around socialist transition and suggests a new synthesis.

★ ★ ★

The need for a new mode of life, for what Gramsci called an ethico-political change, through overcoming the reification and alienation Marx identified as resulting from value, money, and capital that masks human relations and causes the depredation of nature – all of this has no more effective advocate in today's world than the head of the Catholic Church, Pope Francis, as Walter Baier demonstrates through the astounding utterances contained in Francis's encyclicals, exhortations, and speeches.

In his review of recent publications, Michael Löwy traces the evolution of Marxian socialist attitudes towards religion and Christianity, from regarding it as obscurantist and conservative to recognising its anti-systemic subversive force and its utopian, anticipatory function. The most recent organised encounter between Marxism and Christianity that Löwy chronicles is DIALOP, the Christian-Marxist Dialogue initiated by Pope Francis and members of the Party of the European Left, which has made remarkable strides on the basis of 'consensus with difference', without the need to reduce either vision – the Christian or the Marxian socialist vision – to the other.

In the context of the new social initiative of the church and its current dialogue with the left, the *New Testament*'s final book (*Revelation*) appears in a strikingly new light, as Margareta Gruber explains. Its vision of the future is first of all an urban one, full of people, not a flight from the world but a vision of an urban society, having nothing to do with regressing to a simpler pastoral rural order 'close to nature'. Its principal characteristic is transparency, which can be interpreted as that of the real social relations between human beings, not veiled and reified. By contrast with Marxian socialism this is a reality created by God, but the vision wants people to strive for it. It is a city without gates, with people inhabiting the squares, constantly open for new arrivals. It is in a sense religion brought into the world, with no cultic edifice in it, no Temple, and realised *in* the world to become a 'cultic reality'. It is, essentially, directly human society translated into space.

★ ★ ★

Clearly, the now obvious and disastrous 'metabolic rift' produced by fossil-fuel capitalism requires a rejection of productivism and unlimited growth and ultimately capital accumulation – really a civilisational change, as Castellina stresses – what has for some time now been called *ecosocialism*. Michael Löwy outlines an ecosocialist critique and programme which has arisen in dialogue with a number of other theoretical initiatives, including 'degrowth' and ecofeminism. Indigenous societies, and especially women in them – because of their connection to, consciousness of, and responsibility for, nature and the natural economy – are central to the struggle for ecosocialism, not only logically but in practice in recent years. Moreover, women in the core capitalist countries of the Global North, to the extent that they continue to be responsible for social reproduction outside of wage labour, with the necessary 'externalities' they provide that shore up the whole system, occupy a critical vantage point in the struggle. And youth, as such, regardless of its class location, is a central protagonist due to its anxiety about the future. Industrial workers have, for obvious reasons not been centrally involved but will need to be if breakthroughs are to occur, since urban and rural workers constitute the majority of the population.

Anna Saave develops the concept of 'externalities', that is, people's (re) productive capacities along with natural resources, and other ecological services provided without wage compensation, in distinction to the wage labour that occurs 'inside' the capitalist mode of production, but which makes the latter possible. Externalisation of the former, that is, subsistence work (theorised by Ariel Salleh as three colonies: women, the environment, and subsistence workers in the Global South), conceals the fact that the formal market economy is really indebted to women and the environment. This 'debt' is a concept developed by Salleh, which does not imply monetary repayment of it as a political goal but rather the abolition of the arrangements that produce it. By way of Vandana Shiva, Salleh characterises the circular economy of subsistence labour, which she terms 'meta-industrial labour', that is, the regenerative labour of indigenes, mothers, gatherers, and subsistence workers, whose intimate scale means a small consumption footprint, with knowledge built on trial and error, transmitted inter-generationally, without a mental/manual division – a regenerative activity reconciled with the non-linear timings in nature. For Salleh, the meta-industrial workers, who constitute a majority in the world, are another revolutionary subject, alongside wage workers.

★ ★ ★

In the crisis of Western liberal democracy, with the 2008-9 financial crisis and the eventual end of the US' 'unilateral moment', Veronika Sušová-Salminen recognises an organic crisis of capitalism and the world system. US hegemony is confronted with Russia – a defensive and conservative regional hegemon, which, for reasons having to do with its past, is a globally competitive military power – and China – on the way to becoming the world's dominant economic power in a context in which power is shifting from the Atlantic to Asia. The West, having committed itself to economic austerity and post-democracy now has a problem of domestic illiberal populist movements at the same time as it wages a worldwide campaign against foreign autocracy, almost externalising the problem of its domestic populist right as nothing more than the effect of direct Russian interference. Meanwhile, Russia has perpetrated a unilateral aggression in Ukraine, which, while horrific in its human toll and totally miscalculated in terms of the resistance it would meet on the ground, can, in terms of geopolitical shifts, be seen as a mirroring of the US' history of intervention and a challenge to its position as sole military hegemon. In terms of the EU, after the European project's popularity was endangered in Southern Europe, which was subjected to coercive Europeanisation via austerity, obliterating the promises of convergence, the EU sought to recreate its popularity by focusing on the East in promising convergence to Ukraine and is now trying to counteract its disintegration crisis by building its defence identity.

It is not clear how independently Europe will position itself vis-à-vis the US' declining power and China's ascendancy. As Jan Campbell points out, the war in Ukraine and any weakness of the EU could further enhance China's position in the world. The sanctions on Russia are also likely to strengthen China, not least by diverting Russia's fossil fuels in its direction. And everything points to a world in which the dollar is no longer the global reserve currency.

These geopolitical shifts have been playing out in the Global South, as Silvina Romano, Tamara Lajtman, and Aníbal García point out, in terms of the worldwide distribution of Covid vaccines and Covid protection and containment supplies, with the surprisingly pragmatic approach taken by various countries in the Global South to a mix of Chinese, Russian, and US-EU vaccines and, in Latin America, with incipient though belated attempts at regional coordination and response.

Steffen Lehndorff draws some key lessons from the US New Deal experience for a European Green New Deal. Roosevelt's New Deal originated as a strong initiative from above, then combined with a great deal of mobilisation from below, and his administration had an extraordinary commitment to an aggressive 'positive democratic polarisation'. Despite the immeasurably greater difficulty today of fighting climate change under conditions of international financial-market capitalism, the crucial question remains not whether full change is possible within capitalism but how to set the change in motion now, a societal dynamic inspired by positive and identity-creating reform projects. The only way to know whether capitalism can adapt to the needed deep structural changes is to first achieve them. For Lehndorff, a way in can be large-scale programmes for well-paid healthcare and green jobs in manufacturing as the drivers of change. In any case, as with the New Deal, bold fiscal policies are necessary and the issue of public ownership has to be faced from the start.

In contrast to the huge majority Roosevelt's party was able to garner, the large centre-right and -left parties of government in Europe have become smaller. Ironically, this allows a party to govern, usually in coalition, with lower electoral results than in the past, but since the centre-left's vocation is no longer democratic antagonism and social change, the smaller percentages and coalition governments are not a problem. In his interview with Haris Golemis, Gerassimos Moschonas examines the decline of social democratic parties in Europe and chronicles their transformation by comparing their reaction to the 1929 and 2008-9 financial crises and the 2010-15 debt crisis. In the Great Depression, after first aggravating it by applying orthodox deflationary policies, they were then drawn, at different rates, to Keynesianism, lasting through the 1970s. By 2008 social democratic parties had long since lost the bulk of their industrial working-class base due to technological change, delocalisation, the constraints of globalisation and the EU, and the parties' insufficient differentiation from centre-right policies. Nevertheless, with the lessons learned from 1929 they were immediately poised for a Keynesian response, but one without redistributive policies, although the Party of European Socialists did propose a truly ambitious supranational post-third-way agenda, which was ignored by the national parties. All of this demonstrated that large-scale state intervention in the economy is not incompatible with neoliberalism and that a major financial crisis need not be a game-changer. Since governments and parties of all stripes implemented the Keynesian policies the social democrats had nothing different or better to offer. The EU's architecture is also a major problem in itself, as its supranational non-federal structure and economic governance makes almost any left and radical left programme unfeasible.

★ ★ ★

Outside of the European Union, in the US, with a central bank and no supranational economic governance above it, historical irony has it that – because of its levels of inequality approaching those of developing countries, its underdeveloped social state and low levels of unionisation, creating situations in which there is widespread medical-debt bankruptcies and an average undergraduate college student incurs $40,000 in debt, and with no elite to which the labels 'socialist' or 'social democrat' can attach themselves – a sizable electoral potential for universalist working-class demands has emerged throughout the two Sanders campaigns that could almost appear 'class-reductionist' by some European standards. Due to the still unachieved social democracy in the US and the under-unionisation and consequent hunger for unions one could aptly label the current phenomenon 'class-struggle social democracy'. Loren Balhorn analyses the growth of Democratic Socialists of America, with its inside/outside the Democratic Party strategy and the challenge now to maintain this inchoate connection to a working-class majority and not become the activist subculture it has largely avoided being in recent years.

With the introduction of European citizenship by the Treaty of Maastricht, the European Union took on a republican dimension that is potentially democratic. But besides the truncating of this citizenship through its non-inclusion of all who work in Europe, there is fundamentally no European public political life of citizens. The citizenship indicates a mere passive affiliation due to the limited functions of the European Parliament but also, crucially, the absence of a Europe-wide electoral polity, for the MEPs are representatives voted only by citizens of the national states. But because the EU's constitution stipulates its subordination to a technical financial 'governance', citizenship is passivised, in Étienne Balibar's words. It is a form of state that represents the anti-political statification of society through the market. Neoliberalism and the lack of a European social policy tends to unleash nationalist populism, with the EU representing progress only in 'social' rather than economic issues. But pan-European progressive initiatives hold out some hope.

Collective security is a concern widely shared by the majority of people. Katerina Anastasiou and Axel Ruppert argue that the left must take this seriously, arguing for the right of collective security, that is, security *with* the other, not *from* the other. Security is an issue which the left understandably has shied away from, monopolised as it is by the military-industrial complex, by arms and surveillance equipment producers, and by an EU that has tried to counteract its disintegration crisis by forcing a European identity in the face of a 'threat'. However, the security of the majority involves safety from climate devastation, access to care and food services provided, for the foreseeable future, by immigrants whose security is threatened by unequal rights and an increasingly militarised border regime. Ultimately, a central focus of left security demands must be the transformation and democratisation of our productive and logistic chains and energy supply systems.

María Eugenia Rodríguez Palop and Nidžara Ahmetašević analyse the migration policy and practice of the European Union, both in terms of its incoherent collection of reactive stopgap regulations created at election time – which essentially has instituted the externalisation of border control to the territory of 'third countries' and a focus on the return of human beings, with agreements to speed up expulsions – and the system of detention camps, which gives the public a sense of a dangerous state of emergency caused by a 'refugee crisis' and signals to prospective applicants that they will be staying indefinitely at centres resembling concentration camps. The pandemic created an ideal opportunity for the camp system to be developed quasi-naturally.

★ ★ ★

For some time now the world has seen the growth of what is known as 'populism'. But as Seraphim Seferiades points out, when theorists criticising populism do not take seriously the central causal role of the capitalist crisis and post-democracy but regard currently existing democracies as the only realistically possible ones, they tend to view any attempt to connect the subaltern to an anti-elite critique as populist threats to democracy, to pluralism, to constitutional guarantees, even menacing totalitarianism. Although this criticism is directed at the far right, no clear distinction is made between right populism and the left's appeal to the underdog; functionally, it is a defence of post-democracy. Other theorists more concerned about the effects of the crisis and post-democracy, identify populism principally in caudillo regimes and thus ignore the more diffuse populism inherent in cartel-parties without personalist leadership, with their dishonest claims to promote a favourable investment climate for globalised capitalism and uphold labour rights at the same time. On the other hand, Chantal Mouffe endorses populism's non-class-specific people-against-elites rhetoric and advocates a vague left populism from below, without problematising its ephermerality and tendency to retreat and absorption as in the cases of Syriza and Podemos. By contrast, Seferiades suggests that a transformative left's critical definition of populism would more meaningfully be: a political organisational practice that claims to be popular while it is not and which eliminates the intermediary institutions that make it possible for the subaltern to truly participate.

Both Seferiades and Mario Candeias accept the use of a discursive strategy to lend the subaltern an agonistic and polarising subjectivity aimed against the elites – provided that this is anti-capitalist and democratic rather than plebiscitarian. Candeias specifies an 'organic-popular strategy' as the best remedy for left populism's inadequacies. This would involve a close, daily cooperation with the movements, with concrete structures of solidarity that promote the self-organisation of the many and their participation in social movements for immediate improvements.

Francisco Louçã offers a balance sheet of Portugal's Socialist government, which until 2019 could only come to power with the tolerance of the Left Bloc and the Communists, without the latter being bound by a coalition agreement. Although the left was able to maintain its independence and critique, the government only implemented such policies of economic recovery and employment creation that did not defy the Troika, which after the Greek drama could not risk further confrontation. But a great deal of the recovery was due to unique circumstances: the depreciation of the euro, the low price of oil, economic growth in export target countries, Northern Africa's instability deflecting tourism to Portugal, and the tax revenues and service-sector growth due to a golden visa policy for wealthy foreign pensioners. The left's electoral results dropped drastically in January of this year, raising the question of how a radical left force can play a constructive parliamentary role and be a vehicle for connecting popular struggles at the same time. Candeias raises this question in relation to Die LINKE's achievements in the Berlin tenants' and healthcare movements but also the disastrous results of the 2021 federal elections, looking also at the vulnerabilities of the new federal coalition government, which could indeed favour Die LINKE, if it is able to solve the complex problems that have hamstrung it.

For two years at the end of the First World War, the Austrian Social Democrats were in the unique historical position to effect change within parliamentary democracy in the centre of Europe. Theirs was a large party that arose in an empire and then in the power vacuum left after the latter's collapse had the leeway to enact bold changes although in a country too small to enable control of the supply chains. Soon, due to opposition from the rural areas (and then the hostility of other countries), it only became possible to carry out socialist reforms in the city of Vienna. Austro-Marxism represents a body of theory alternative to both Second International and Communist orthodoxies, particularly as regards the state, the national question, transition and socialisation, the reform/revolution question, political and economic democracy, and much else that is of great relevance today. Dunja Larise traces this development in historical context.

And finally, in this year of Sinn Féin's historic electoral victory in Northern Ireland to become the majority party and the fiftieth anniversary of Derry's Bloody Sunday, we are publishing Daniel Finn's contextualisation of the 30 January 1972 massacre, stressing the importance of the non-armed civic resistance and the complex dynamic between the different parts of the resistance, Stormont, and Westminster. It is at the same time a history of the lessons learned by the British government in shifting away from support for earlier forms of unsustainable local colonial rule and from blatantly visible foreign political control.

★ ★ ★

**The transform! europe network** was established in 2001 during the World Social Forum in Porto Alegre by a small group of intellectuals from six different European countries, representing left research institutions or journals, who wanted to coordinate their research and educational work. Today transform! consists of 39 member organisations and observers from 23 countries.

The network is coordinated by a board of nine members, and its office is located in Vienna. transform! maintains a multilingual website and publishes a continuously growing number of reports, analyses, and discussion papers on issues related to the process of European integration.

We would like to thank all those who have collaborated in producing this volume: our authors, the members of our editorial board, our translators, and especially our publisher, The Merlin Press.

*Walter Baier, Eric Canepa, and Haris Golemis*

# The Covid Pandemic and the Social and Political Left

**Download** our e-publications at the website
**www.transform-network.net/publications**

Sign up for transform! europe's monthly newsletter in one of five languages (English, French, German, Greek, and Spanish) to find out about the activities of the transform! network and current events.

www.transform-network.net

facebook.com/transformeurope   @transform_ntwrk

# A Programme for a Pandemic Justice Movement

## Leigh Phillips

The left has not had a good pandemic.

Higher or lower levels of success in reducing mortality and morbidity from Covid-19 generally do not map well to whether a government hailed from the right or the left. Millions died regardless of whether a leader was a social democrat or a conservative, a green or a liberal.

One might respond to this claim by countering that all such governments, even those of the centre-left and left were hopelessly neoliberalised. None of these were *really* governments of the left. But this excuse is less convincing than it might at first appear. To the extent that the left outside government, perhaps more critical of neoliberalism than the left inside government, *did* have any recommendations for policies that might indeed have slashed deaths and rates of transmission, infection and illness, we were for the most part unable to mount arguments or social pressure sufficient to affect how the pandemic has been handled. And much of the extra-parliamentary left just did not have much to say that was very different from that of the left in government in any case (at least in the Global North; the struggle in the Global South is, as we will see, a different story).

The left for the most part just simply did not matter.

Of course, the right has not had a good pandemic either. And in the face of this bi-partisan impotence and incompetence, and the raft of failures of all governments the world over, more people have so far died due to the pandemic than in any war or famine since the Second World War.

In March 2022, the first peer-reviewed study of global excess deaths due to Covid-19 estimated the figure to be 18.2 million souls as of the end of 2021, some three times greater than official statistics of recorded deaths had reported.[1] Published in *The Lancet* – the prestigious British medical journal – the paper's tally broadly matched that of modelling work with a slightly different methodology performed by *The Economist*, which placed the figure at 20.1 million.² (And these numbers do not include those many millions more laid low by how the virus ravaged, or continues to ravage, their bodies.)

It's difficult sometimes to get one's head wrapped around figures with so many zeroes. But for comparison, during the First World War, roughly 20 million were killed – 9.7 million military personnel and 10 million civilians.³ While that war was not the responsibility of the left, for over a century the left has lamented our inability to stop it. Today, we must also lament our inability to do much to inhibit the effects of the Covid pandemic. It is our left's First World War.

One might reasonably conclude in the face of such horror, especially if one is of a pessimistic bent, that if the left cannot do much to alter the course of a holocaust, then what is the point of our existence?

But we must recognise that to a considerable extent, we did not really know any more about what is to be done than any government figure of any other political flavour. In the era of modern infectious disease medicine, the left had not faced down a global pandemic before. There did exist a left at the time of the Spanish Flu pandemic of 1918, but this hit before science had fully developed a germ theory of disease. That was largely a reflection of humanity's sheer defencelessness in the face of an 'Act of God', not an avoidable policy failure. So Covid *is* our first rodeo.

If our ignorance at the start of a phenomenon the left had never confronted before is to some extent forgivable, two years into the pandemic, we do now have a fuller understanding of what went wrong and what worked. Despite the overall catastrophe, there were also some remarkable successes, most crucially the public-sector-driven development of vaccines in mere months instead of the years or decades that it normally takes. And while the successes and failures have not typically mapped well to whether the left or the right was in government, there is nevertheless throughout them a *red thread* of a narrative that explains much in retrospect. And this red thread suggests the left now does have a great deal to offer, for the narrative is a story of economic planning, state capacity, freedom, science, equality, and ultimately democracy, topics very dear to the left since its birth in the French Revolution.

Moreover, the Omicron variant of SARS-CoV2 may not have marked the end of the pandemic. This virus may have some surprises waiting in store for us yet. Contrary to the popular belief that viruses always evolve towards avirulence (milder illness), viral evolution theory instead tells us that while this is possible, so is the reverse. We can however be certain that at some point there will be another pandemic, from some other pathogen. And as deadly as Covid-19 has been, humanity got off much more lightly than infectious disease researchers had expected. Public health officials prior to 2019 had been girding themselves for a zoonotic spillover of something much more deadly, perhaps a novel flu virus, with case fatality rates far higher than that of SARS-CoV2. And that much deadlier pandemic that they feared *will* arrive one day.

It is time to correct the left's failure. We have a lot of experience with global pandemics now. We have learnt a great deal. We are not the naïfs of 2019 anymore. There are about a dozen key policies and broader political transformations that we now know must be undertaken both in order to better combat the still ongoing Covid pandemic, to be far better prepared in the face of any new pandemics and other threats from infectious disease that will always be with us so long as pathogens and humans exist, and ultimately to reduce the incidence of such threats. With all this experience, we can also see how, not least from the gross inequality of vaccine apartheid, we remain woefully unprepared for the deadlier pandemic that is on its way, either this decade or another one, and that governments have not learnt the lessons of Covid-19.

We also should now have a decent idea not just of the optimum policies, but of the sort of structures we need on the left to be built to be able to convince and impose. And here, there is some inspiration that can be derived from yet another issue of planet-wide resonance: climate change.

With the Covid pandemic having slaughtered as many as a World War, posing a far greater threat to humanity than any of the floods, wildfires, heatwaves or storms so far delivered by global warming, we must begin to build a Pandemic Justice Movement at least as militant as the Climate Justice Movement.

One might initially think this is a poor model. In the face of heat domes, polar vortices, local temperatures in more and more places spiking past 40°C and toward even 50°C, and average global temperatures inexorably rising year after year, the climate movement at first glance appears to not have enjoyed much success either. The most recent UN climate conference, Conference of Parties 26 (COP26), eked out little increased ambition in action or targets, not least on the front of climate finance for the developing world.

But while we are right to highlight such insufficiencies and errors, an excessive focus on them would be looking at the glass as being half empty. At the turn of the millennium, business-as-usual greenhouse gas emissions put the world on track for an increase in temperatures of 4 or 5°C above pre-industrial levels by the end of the century. Global emissions were increasing about 3 per cent a year, with a 31 per cent growth between 2001 and 2010, and China was building a new coal plant every three days. Today, clean energy costs have plummeted, beating even the most optimistic scenarios. Meanwhile, coal use is in decline and emissions rose just one per cent per year over the last decade, with a plateau projected in the next few years just off the back of current policies (let alone pledges of enhanced action). The UN Environment Programme, Climate Action Tracker, and the International Energy Agency now put likely warming under those same current policies at 2.6 or 2.7°C, dropping to 2.3 or 2.4°C if 2030 commitments are kept[4] – within striking range of the globally agreed target of 2°C, and down to 1.8°C if existing net-zero pledges are kept, not much above the more ambitious goal of 1.5°C.

Pressure on decision makers needs to continue to be applied, of course; action remains insufficient and too sluggish; and some sectors such as cement production even still lack a commercialised clean alternative. But there has been a tremendous turnaround from business as usual two decades ago, and this very real progress would never have happened without the building of a climate justice movement in every country on the planet.

Now we have to do the same with pandemics and infectious diseases – a threat to humanity now perhaps greater even than climate change, and, if anything, more pressing. Such a movement at the global level builds on the critical work already being done along these lines by such campaigns in the Global South and their allies in the Global North such as South Africa's Health Justice Initiative, the People's Vaccine Alliance, and Global Justice Now, and takes inspiration from heroic public health struggles of the past by such HIV/AIDS activist groups as ACT-UP, the Treatment Action Group, and the Treatment Action Campaign.

What follows is a first pass at what such a movement should be fighting for, building on what has been learnt these last two years – a set of demands around which we can organise. And just as climate justice is a hydra of a problem, a multi-headed beast of sometimes staggering complexity, so will pandemic justice be. While some climate activists focus on clean electricity, others are more active around transportation or heating. Others still campaign around agriculture and industrial emissions. Likewise with pandemic justice, there will be battles around intellectual property, technology transfer, economic planning, outbreak monitoring infrastructure, sick pay, long-term care facilities, civil liberties, the role of public health officials, supply chains, housing, and even democratisation of global institutions. Pandemic justice will be every bit as challenging to market rule as climate justice, and perhaps even more so.

This set of demands is not intended to be definitive, but rather an initial sketch to try to get the conversation going. Hopefully others can continue the conversation, adding parts that have been overlooked and correcting those parts that are incorrect or insufficient. We should all be humble in the knowledge that Covid has repeatedly wrong-footed every single one of us who has made any over-confident predictions or unwavering assertions. There are many secrets Covid and other infectious diseases have yet to reveal. There is only one thing here (and indeed in all things) that we can be certain of: that somewhere our understanding is wrong.

## Global demands

### 1. End vaccine apartheid

We should start with the most immediate and urgent of concerns: an end to the inequality of vaccination between the Global North and South often referred to as 'vaccine apartheid'. As of the time of writing in spring 2022, while 64 per cent of the world population had received at least one dose of a Covid-19 vaccine, just 14.4 per cent of people in low-income countries had received at least one dose.[5]

This is first of all a matter of grotesque injustice, but vaccine apartheid also represents a grave threat to all humanity. The unvaccinated, whether as a result of such inequality or through choice, remain a reservoir from which new variants of concern can emerge. This is because every time the virus is passed on and replicates, it mutates. Any reduction in transmission reduces the likelihood of new variants of concern emerging.

Even with the increased transmissibility and partial resistance to vaccines of the heavily mutated Omicron variant, vaccination still reduces transmission rates, along with substantially reduced rates of infection, illness, hospitalisation, and death. Even a single vaccine dose is sufficient to cut down the likelihood of household transmission by 40-50%, according to a pair of 2021 UK studies.[6] These papers focused on the Alpha variant that dominated at the time they were carried out, but subsequent studies on the Delta variant noted that the reduction in transmission was less pronounced but still effective. A January 2022 European CDC study during the time of Omicron found a continued reduction in transmission of the vaccinated compared to the unvaccinated, and of the boosted compared to those with just two doses – although the reduction in transmission is not as pronounced as for Delta and Alpha. The principle behind the reduced transmission is the same: vaccination reduces infection rates and someone who does not get infected cannot pass on the virus. (And the notion that vaccines offer a binary – either they prevent infection or they do not, either they prevent transmission or not – must be combated: instead, they provide a spectrum of protection.)

Thus while the primary aim of vaccination is preventing illness and death, it remains the case that no one is safe until everyone is safe. Ending vaccine apartheid is in everyone's interest. A 2021 IMF proposal to vaccinate the world placed the cost at $50 billion, a hefty sum to be sure, but still far less than the more than $12 trillion that the pandemic will have cost the global economy according to the IMF.

Defenders of the current global intellectual property regime have argued that vaccine apartheid was not the cause of Omicron, as South Africa has been facing troubles with vaccine hesitancy and now enjoys supplies of vaccine surplus to need. But while there has been a slight uptick in vaccine hesitancy in the Global South over the course of the pandemic, a multi-year survey of attitudes towards vaccines around the world produced by the Vaccine Confidence Project published in 2020 in *The Lancet* found that support for vaccines in the developing world, including in South Africa, is typically far, far higher than exists in the Global North.[7] The three countries prior to the pandemic with the largest proportion of the population that believe vaccines are safe were Uganda (87%), Bangladesh (85%), and Liberia (83%). Meanwhile as of 2015 at the start of the period of the survey, it was France and Japan that tied for lowest levels of confidence, at just 9 per cent. In South Africa, vaccine hesitancy is primarily a phenomenon amongst well-off whites. According to an August 2021 survey from the Human Sciences Research Council and researchers at the University of Johannesburg, some 75 per cent of all black adults wanted a Covid jab compared to just 52 per cent of white adults.[8]

Moreover, phylogenetic tracking tells us that the variant emerged at some point between mid-2020 and November 2021. As South Africa was only able to launch its vaccination operations in May of last year, this timeline for the emergence of Omicron includes a number of months when vaccines could have been distributed in the country but were not. This is not knock-down evidence that vaccine apartheid caused the new variant, but rather that it remains the case that increased distribution would have reduced its likelihood, just as ending vaccine apartheid will reduce the likelihood of further variants of concern.

Essential to this is for the patents on Covid-19 vaccines to be temporarily waived, as was first proposed by India and South Africa in 2020 and is permitted under the Trade-Related Aspects of Intellectual Property Rights at the World Trade Organisation (WTO) – a position currently opposed by the European Union. While the US under President Joe Biden formally backs a TRIPS waiver, the administration has done little to force the issue.

The opponents of such a waiver argue that even were one to be introduced, this would not resolve challenges with technology transfer and manufacturing capacity – not just for the vaccines themselves, but the variety of specialised inputs they require. 'Patents are not the problem', they say, rolling their eyes at the simpletons fixated on intellectual property, and declare that IP waivers would undermine innovation precisely at a moment when we need more innovation than ever. The private pharmaceutical and related firms require some sort of compensation, otherwise they cannot produce new drugs and other medical interventions.

The reality is that the bulk of Covid vaccine innovation and development of the mRNA platform was performed by university or government laboratories, funded primarily by taxpayers. In the face of a global pandemic, the possibility of selling billions of doses of vaccines and other therapeutics certainly appears at first glance to reduce the financial risk of the colossal expenditure of development, clinical trials, and production. But in the face of uncertainty as to whether the pandemic would fizzle out or be constrained to a limited geography as happened with the SARS and MERS pandemics that remained restricted to a few spots in Asia, pharmaceutical firms dithered. It took the publicly owned Biomedical Advanced Research and Development Authority (BARDA), an agency of the US Department of Health and Human Services, to throw billions at vaccine development in the form of direct funding and advance purchase agreements to get the ball rolling. This preference for government shepherding the development of vaccines over leaving it to the anarchy of the market was later formalised through the Trump administration's Operation Warp Speed. Contrary to claims that the vaccines were a triumph of capitalism, the truth is that they were a triumph of economic planning.

In addition, vaccine licences have been awarded to just a handful of vaccine manufacturers, mainly in rich and middle-income countries, but the number of manufacturers who could in principle be producing doses is far greater, particularly with respect to conventional vaccine platforms beyond mRNA technology. And while vaccine supplies as of 2022 have now been more substantial, access to the formulations for new variants remains inequitable.

But even the idea that the Global South is insufficiently developed to be able to handle mRNA vaccines has been disproven by the WHO's establishment of an mRNA 'hub' in South Africa, in partnership with a number of other organisations including the African CDC.[9] The aim is to develop a tech transfer training centre where mRNA technology is developed at the level necessary for mass manufacture, and then for that technology to be transferred to other producers in low- and middle-income countries –

the 'spokes' to South Africa's hub. Backed by the WHO, scientists in the country are successfully reverse-engineering the Moderna mRNA vaccine and platform. (Meanwhile, not only is Moderna refusing to participate, but it has filed patents in South Africa on what it claims is its technology.)

Resolving this problem requires that we push on four fronts. First, we must press Western governments to back a *full* TRIPS waiver. Leaked press reports in March 2022[10] suggested that the EU, US, India, and South Africa were close to a compromise, but this would only permit those developing countries that have exported under 10 per cent of the world's Covid vaccine doses in 2021 to produce more vaccines without the permission of the patent owner. The compromise also, appallingly, excludes non-vaccine therapeutics and diagnostics.

Second, we must press these same Global North governments to simply spend whatever it takes to scale up globally distributed vaccine and vaccine input production. We have a rough idea of the cost already from the IMF's $50 billion assessment. This should be peanuts for the developed world.

Third, there must be continued use of state superintending of private investment along the lines of the Trump and later Biden administrations' use of the Korean-War-era Defense Production Act (DPA), or the locally relevant legislation. This allowed the government to override private firm decision-making to ensure adequate production and, crucially, distribution of personal protection equipment (PPE), ventilators, diagnostic materials, and other essential medical material. This was done to bring an end to the domestic anarchy of market allocation on the basis of who could pay the highest price, and redirect production and distribution on the basis of need. There are roughly 9,000 specialised inputs required for vaccine manufacturing, according to the International Federation of Pharmaceutical Manufacturers and Associations, from bioreactor bags to adjuvants and phials, with production concentrated in the US and Europe. The same state shepherding of production must now occur on the basis of global need, not merely in service of transcending *American* bottlenecks and injustices.

Finally, all those states concerned must compel their domestic owners of intellectual property to take part in the WHO's technology transfer platforms, Covid-19 Technology Access Pool (C-TAP), and the mRNA transfer hub in particular, again without IP constraint. The reason for the lethargy or even intransigence here is the same as for vaccine IP: the greater the spread of vaccine know-how, the greater the chance of puncturing their intellectual monopoly.

*The very regime of intellectual property is not fit for purpose in the age of pandemics. Intellectual property rights within the realm of public health must be abolished.*

## 2. Economic planning to shepherd essential production of vaccines, therapeutics, diagnostics, medical equipment, and all necessary inputs

Vaccines are far from the only essential items whose inequitable distribution is the product of an irrational intellectual property regime. And inegalitarian access to therapeutics, diagnostics, and medical equipment also allows the Covid and any future pandemics to spread further than otherwise would happen, again giving pathogens the opportunity to mutate and evade what protections we have.

As of March 2022, the UN-backed Medicines Patent Pool looked set to unveil an agreement with some 35 companies in low- and middle-income countries to manufacture a generic version of Paxlovid, the Pfizer-produced anti-viral treatment (two drugs, nirmatrelvir and ritonavir, taken orally in combination), and distribute it across a total of 95 such countries – some 53 per cent of the world's population. The treatment, a partner to rather than replacement for the vaccines, reduces the risk of hospitalisation and death by nearly 90 per cent.

The *voluntary* royalty-free licensing agreement is a breakthrough, but it only lasts as long as the pandemic lasts, a vague end-date. After which, middle income countries must pay a 5-10 per cent royalty. Moreover, some upper-middle income countries, such as Argentina, Brazil, China, and Thailand, where there is already considerable generic production capacity, are excluded. (Also, if Pfizer is able to share its IP, data, and know-how for manufacture with a drug, why does the firm continue to resist doing the same for its vaccine?) Further, while ritonavir is part of the two-pill combination, that particular drug had become off-patent by the date of the treatment's development.[11] Pfizer should not be seeking any new monopolies on this drug at all.

Throughout the pandemic, similar IP protections and prioritisation of profit over need have limited the availability of diagnostic tools, ventilators, specialised fridges, even supplies of oxygen to the have-nots. And the challenge here is far from limited to a split between the Global North and South. Similar inequalities exist within developed nations between urban and rural regions, between rich and poor, and between centres of greater and lesser population density. Prior to the advent of the vaccines and the Trump and Biden administration's invocation of the Defense Production Act taking investment, production, and distribution decisions out of the hands of private actors, many smaller US 'flyover' states, even those with Republican governors, were begging the federal government to intervene when even medical supplies that had been paid for were re-routed to jurisdictions that had outbid them.

Thus we on the left need to be very clear about the explanation for pandemic inequalities. While racism undoubtedly exacerbates the situation, the problem is fundamentally a result of the profit motive. 'Colonialism' does not explain why a mostly white Montana or Wyoming struggled to access ventilators. If we focus only on demands such as 'Decolonize Vaccines', this is a slogan easily capturable by the very corporations responsible for medical inequality by, say, appointing this or that person of colour to a senior position, without ever doing anything that would threaten their bottom line. Let us remember that a co-founder of Moderna is a Lebanese-Armenian and the CEO of Moderna's partner, BioNTech, is a Turkish immigrant.

Ultimately, there should be pharmaceutical, medical equipment, and related manufacturing hubs throughout the world that are situated outside the private sector. An additional reason that these would have to be publicly owned and supported by government supervision of supply chains is that in the future, once the current pandemic is over, such a significant expansion of manufacturing capacity may need to sit largely idle for years until the next emergency, like fire fighters sitting in their fire halls waiting for the next fire. No private company has an interest in investing in manufacturing capacity that could be left idle for up to years at a time.

Above all, the pharmaceutical industry needs to be taken out of the private sector entirely. When many countries (outside the United States) socialised or part-socialised their health systems – because we knew that if left to the market, this would produce grotesque inequalities and undermine the health even of the wealthy – in Canada we only ever did half the job. To nationalise hospitals and collectivise insurance provision while leaving Big Pharma untouched was to leave this key pillar of public health beholden to the amoral whims of the profit motive.

Long before the pandemic, clinicians, infectious disease researchers, microbiologists, and public health officials had repeatedly warned of the rise of anti-microbial resistance amongst bacteria and fungi, a phenomenon popularly known as 'superbugs'. Tuberculosis, that ancient enemy of humanity once thought all but vanquished, has returned, resistant to many and in some cases most antibiotics. Gonorrhoea likewise has evolved to enjoy resistance to the 'last line' of antibiotics – the dread 'super-gonorrhoea'.[12] From the press, many will have also heard of MRSA, or methicillin-resistant Staphylococcus aureus, and resistant forms of Clostridium difficile (C. difficile), but we are increasingly seeing similar challenges with many, many other pathogens as well.

Researchers and specialists warn that we are perhaps a couple decades away from having to return to a pre-antibiotic era. Much of modern medicine depends upon a background of anti-microbial protection. Anything that involves piercing the skin, from surgery down to an injection and insertion of catheters would see much greater risk of infection, and when infections happen, there is less and less that can be done. Organ transplants, chemotherapy, hip replacements and even care for premature babies becomes much more difficult, even impossible. It is such a threat to our way of life that the UK's chief medical officer, Sally Davies, once described anti-microbial resistance as posing as great a catastrophic threat to humanity as climate change, adding that 'we will find ourselves in a health system not dissimilar to the early 19th century'.[13]

Overprescription of antibiotics and other antimicrobial drugs has contributed to the problem, as has excessive use of these in farming, both of animals and plants (in the latter case, the contribution is primarily to anti-fungal resistance). But fundamentally the problem is that anti-microbial drugs will kill off the pathogens that are susceptible to them, and those that remain will have mutations that make them less susceptible. These latter will go on to reproduce more than the former, and eventually dominate. This is just evolution. Thus, there is an unending arms race between humanity and pathogens. We need to constantly develop new antimicrobial drugs, or come up with other methods of treatment, or the bugs will out-gun us.

The researchers that warn of the rise of drug resistance also tell us repeatedly in the scientific literature that the problem is fundamentally that antimicrobial drugs, like vaccines, suffer from what they politely call 'insufficient market incentive'. A patient with an infection will take a course of antibiotics (or other antimicrobials) for a few weeks, or perhaps a few months in the case of TB, but then if the drug is working, the infection is supposed to have cleared up. The patient no longer needs to buy the drug off anyone. A drug company has a much greater incentive to produce therapeutics for patients with chronic diseases, for which they have to take a drug every day, perhaps for the rest of their lives. And so for the last three or four decades most major pharmaceutical companies have largely got out of the business of research, development, and production of antimicrobials. Some research still goes on, but primarily by university or government labs, which do not have the capacity or funds to engage in clinical trials or to do their own manufacturing.

Much the same insufficient market incentive held back development of anti-coronavirus drugs despite the warnings of the 2003 SARS and 2014 MERS epidemics.[14] During the last Ebola epidemic in west Africa, Anthony Fauci, the head of the US' National Institute of Allergy and Infectious Diseases, repeatedly told the press that there had actually been substantial advances in Ebola therapy research, including a number of candidate vaccines that had proven effective in non-human primates, but the drug companies were just not interested in taking it any further.

'We have a candidate, we put it in monkeys and it looks good, but the incentive on the part of the pharmaceutical companies to develop a vaccine that treats little outbreaks every thirty or forty years – well, that's not much incentive', he told *Scientific American*.[15]

And the same challenge faces what public health officials call 'neglected tropical diseases' or NTDs, those that affect parts of the world insufficiently developed for firms to be able to make any money from providing the relevant medical interventions.[16] These might as well be called 'unprofitable tropical diseases'.

Many Western governments recognise the problem, at least with respect to anti-microbial resistance that affects their own populations, and have developed a range of strategies that they hope will correct the market failure, such as trying to incentivise pharmaceutical companies to do the necessary research and development.[17] Perhaps they might win a large prize, or be awarded fast-track regulatory assessment for another one of their drugs.

A more elegant, and just solution, is simply to take the pharmaceutical industry into the public sector, and deploy the postal service model: just as profitable postal routes and destinations cross-subsidise the unprofitable ones, profitable drugs would cross-subsidise those that are unprofitable.

*To end disparities in access to pandemic-related therapeutics, diagnostics, and medical equipment, we must achieve an economy at both the domestic and international level that is comfortable with a range of forms of economic planning of the medical sector, not just economic planning related to health insurance and hospitals.*

## 3. Democratise global institutions

Much of the above discussion represents a politic that involves a fairly muscular, if still otherwise conventionally social democratic, economic planning. While ideologically, the political right, centre, and right of left in the neoliberal era found such interventionism rebarbative, since the global financial crisis and especially during the pandemic, we have seen much more willingness on the part of actors across the political spectrum to throw out market fundamentalism in the face of emergency. The Trump and Biden administrations' willingness to repeatedly make use of the Defense Production Act is evidence alone that an openness to economic planning is back. This is certainly only on a case-by-case and temporary basis, and is often implemented in the interest of elite preservation rather than the general good (i.e., similar to the short-term bank nationalisations and socialisation of private debt during the eurozone crisis). But taking this opening to economic planning and making it more comprehensively applicable is an eminently realistic 'radicalism' that the left can absolutely achieve. This is not at all utopian.

Much more utopian is the other assumption upon which much of this programme rests: economic planning in the public good *across borders*. And not just regionally or continentally, but worldwide. If pharmaceutical firms are taken into the public sector (and they must be), voters in those states will rightfully ask why their polity is responsible for a global public service. One can get around this problem by some sort of fiscal transfers from other countries without pharmaceutical industries. But now we find ourselves in the realm not just of cross-border economic planning, but also cross-border taxation. From the American Revolution to the eurozone crisis and Brexit, it is clear that taxation without representation is a non-starter. The socialisation of pharmaceutical production thus depends for its legitimacy upon some sort of global democratic order, in which decision-makers are accountable to citizens via elections.

We run into the same issue with another key requirement of adequate, future-oriented pandemic justice: the establishment of global pandemic surveillance infrastructure. This involves multiple global sites, especially in locations that have been frequent sites of zoonotic spillover, and thus not infrequently in the developing world, with the necessary sampling and genetic sequencing apparatus, clinics, training, and equipment to monitor for outbreaks. The billionaire philanthropist Bill Gates has been lobbying for the creation of such a network at a cost of 'a few tens of billions'.[18] While he has thrown a few million of his own money at the problem, he also recognises that this must fundamentally be a government driven initiative, with neither the private nor philanthropic sector capable of delivering it at the scale necessary. Even more thorny, for it to work, such a surveillance system should be able to function and share its findings across borders even when domestic governments are reluctant to do so. That is, such a network has a veto over national sovereignty, thus, of a democratic country, over how the domestic majority has voted. This is acceptable to voters if that higher level itself is democratic, but, as we saw when the unelected European Central Bank and Eurogroup overruled the democratic will of the people of Greece during the eurozone crisis with respect to fiscal policy, if that higher level is not democratic, it will not be tolerated for long. And rightly so. The problem with a king is not that he is a *bad* king, but that he is any sort of king at all.

One of the challenges that the WHO has faced during this and other pandemics is that the absence of such extra-national powers, coupled to having to beg for funding, permits capture by whoever is the most generous funder. This global organisation with no real global power also produces an obsequiousness to governments who are manifestly failing with respect to public health, on the basis that any criticisms might result in the exclusion of the WHO from their territory, which would be even worse.

Truly we live in an era where humanity is increasingly facing challenges that are planetary in scale, from pandemics to climate change, from trade to war, and that thus require decision-making at that same scale, yet remain trapped with the barest scaffolding of global governance infrastructure in the form of hundreds of treaties and cross-border organisations that have no true democratic accountability. It is the world-historic job of this generation to rise to these challenges and build that global democracy.

This is of course the biggest task that one could imagine! Nothing less than global democracy?

And yet other forces less amenable to democracy and far more amenable to governance in the interest of elites are already proposing and even building transnational infrastructure. Two former UK prime ministers at the start of the pandemic argued for the creation of a global executive, built out of the G20, to take charge during the pandemic. Then last June, some 25 prime ministers and presidents, including of France, Germany, the UK, and Spain, issued a call for a 'pandemic treaty' to build a new, more robust global health infrastructure for future pandemic preparedness and response. Thus, the argument that such structures be built is not as utopian as they may once have seemed. But many of those calling for such global architectures have themselves regularly undermined public health imperatives in the name of profit.

*L'internationale* is being built, but not by the working class.

Thus the role for the left now is to demand that such global pandemic infrastructure be democratic. We must develop our own independent idea of what all this would look like.

## Domestic demands

As this essay is intended for a pan-European audience, it has focused on beginning to sketch out what the transnational demands of a pandemic justice movement might be. There is a raft of demands specific to the domestic arena as well, but these vary very widely, depending on the country and even sub-national region (for public health policies, especially in federal states, are set at the state or provincial, not national level).

Nevertheless, we can sketch out some points of commonality here as well.

**4.** *Rebuild state capacity; reverse 'Deloitte-ification' of the state*
While having the left or the right in government does not map well to better pandemic outcomes, the maintenance of what political scientists term 'state capacity' – in simple terms, the ability of states to 'do stuff' – *does* map well to better outcomes. There has been a four-decade-long neoliberal hollowing out of the Western state that has rendered governments increasingly incapable of performing a number of even basic tasks.

In those places where neoliberal gutting of state capacity did not take hold as firmly, or was reversed, as in East Asian nations such as South Korea and Taiwan, we can observe far superior outcomes on a range of metrics.

Key examples of the collapse of state capacity would include the repeated struggles that multiple jurisdictions faced when ordering a government department to develop a test-and-trace system, or to procure PPE, as well as Canada's laggardly vaccine roll-out when despite having purchased more doses per capita than any other nation, because the state had long since privatised domestic vaccine manufacturing capacity, for many months in early 2021, the country had one of the lowest vaccination rates in the developed world, worse even than many middle income nations.

In the UK, as a result of privatisation of key state responsibilities, the medical supply stockpile had run down. In the 2010s, the procurement division of the public National Health Service (NHS) had been transformed into a quasi-private entity, Supply Chain Coordination Ltd under the supervision of management consultancy Deloitte. While this firm 'managed' procurement, the actual carrying out of procurement was outsourced yet again to a mishmash of eleven different companies, themselves middlemen or 'brokers', not actual manufacturers of the relevant medical equipment. These brokers repeatedly failed to deliver on their promises, resulting in an ignoble PPE crisis in which nurses had to fashion protective gowns out of garbage bags and to fashion full-face snorkel masks from diving shops into medical face masks.

The UK's PPE debacle is noteworthy as an example of this widespread phenomenon because it so clearly illustrates what political scientist George Hoare calls the 'Deloitte-ification' of the state, where various tasks, agencies and even departments of government have been spun out to a network of consultancies that hoover up public revenues with little in return. As I wrote in a recent essay on the phenomenon: 'A minister dials a knob, pulls a lever on the great machine of state, but, like the placebo "close door" buttons on elevators, these knobs and levers are not actually connected to anything. Nothing happens. The placebo state – with its army of revolving door consultant-bureaucrats that move back and forth between civil service and consultant-land – only offers the illusion of control.'¹⁹

This means that one of the key tasks for the left should we come to power anywhere, is not just a reversal of privatisation of public services, although that clearly must be a main priority too, but a reversal of this Deloitte-ification of the state. This rebuilding of state capacity is not a campaign that is easy to fit on a picket sign or banner, but it is nevertheless absolutely essential, no matter how unsexy it is.

## 5. *Fight anti-vax nonsense, the causes of anti-vax nonsense, and scientific paternalism as well*

The situation with respect to attitudes to vaccination has to change as well. For far too long, parts of the left have abetted anti-vaxxer beliefs and the superstition of 'alternative medicine' both as a result of the epistemic relativism of the postmodern academy, and, perhaps more understandably, in reaction to the very real crimes of Big Pharma. In the wake of the opioid crisis in North America driven by the villainy of Purdue Pharma and others, the lack of trust in vaccines is entirely forgivable. Forgivable, but wrong. Much of the credit to why the vaccines were developed and trialled in under a year, an absolutely heroic marvel of science, in fact comes down to the pivot away from a markets-as-usual approach and the use of economic planning to mobilise as many researchers and firms as possible, as well as a very socialist spirit of data sharing and cooperation amongst scientists, freed of careerism in the face of a threat to the whole of humanity. Historically, the side-effects of any vaccines that have been deployed show up within the first couple of months. It is well past a couple of months now, covering a sample size of billions of people – many orders of magnitude larger than the sample sizes of clinical trials. Moreover, all the other medical interventions that anti-vaxxers *do* trust are also produced by profit-motivated companies, yet they are happy to be subject to those therapies. If it is rational to be suspicious of profit-driven medicine, then it is irrational to think that vaccines are the only risk. And the snake-oil salesmen of alternative medicine are *also* in the business of sales maximisation. As the great British debunker of medical frauds, Ben Goldacre, puts it: 'Just because Big Pharma is shit doesn't mean that magic beans cure cancer.'

Moreover, in recent decades, especially in Europe, sections of the green left have opposed genetic engineering, successfully achieving a de facto ban on GMOs at the European Union level. There is nothing wrong with being suspicious of how a profit-seeking enterprise might deploy a given technology, but this must be applied to all technologies. Instead, some on the left argue that genetic engineering is 'unnatural' or scientific hubris, independent of markets. Even a public-spirited deployment would 'go against nature'. Such arguments exchange a legitimate, socialist critique of markets for technophobia and anti-modernism, modes of thought historically more associated with the counter-Enlightenment opponents of the French Revolution. And this unscientific fear of a process that the rest of nature itself regularly performs, that humans have engaged in since the dawn of agriculture – and that about whose safety there is as much of a consensus amongst scientists as there is consensus regarding the reality of anthropogenic global warming – has also fanned the flames of vaccine hesitancy as genetic engineering played a role in the development of aspects of some of the vaccine platforms. There is some irony here that it is the green left, historically the defenders of climate science against the anti-science and climate-sceptic 'merchants of doubt', who this time take on the part of the fear-mongers.

Even stranger are claims that mRNA vaccines could alter your DNA. This is simply not how the relationship between these two biomolecules works. The 'm' in mRNA stands for 'messenger'; and it acts as a messenger between your chromosomes and the protein factories in your cells. In the case of the vaccines, the mRNA acts again as a messenger, telling your cells how to make the infamous spike protein of the virus so that your immune system can recognise the virus when it invades the body. That is all. It cannot combine with your DNA.

The left, historically the great defender of science, must be both tough on anti-vax nonsense and tough on the causes of anti-vax nonsense. Even as we fight for a world of public health relieved of the profit motive, there is a second front in this war: that of obscurantism and woo.

Perhaps there is even a third front: That of scientism, the paternalist assumption by some scientists and other experts that the public cannot be told the complete truth, for they would not be able to understand. Not infrequently during the pandemic, public health officials made over-confident declarations about what the public must do, as this was what The Science tells us, only for The Science to change its directives radically just months or even weeks later. In many jurisdictions we were commanded that we should absolutely not wear masks only to be later commanded that we would be selfish to do otherwise. It was conspiracist and Sinophobic to wonder whether the pandemic might have been the result of a lab leak in China until it wasn't. And, perhaps most egregiously, the language used by many public health officials gave the impression that vaccines prevented infection, transmission, illness and death instead of what is actually the case, that they *reduce* the likelihood of infection, transmission, illness and death but cannot prevent them completely.

Science is not a discovery of facts that are true for all time, but instead at each moment only our best current understanding, an understanding about which the only certainty we have is that some part of that understanding is incorrect and will be corrected at some point in the future.

If experts state their uncertainties openly, trusting people to understand, this reduces the popular backlash when what is incorrect reveals itself. Everyone would already be prepared for things to be corrected.

Relatedly, in the effort to crack down on pandemic misinformation, our online masters at Google, Facebook, Twitter and the like have taken to being the arbiters of what is true and false, what is scientific and what is fake news. Understandably many feel a need to be able to minimise the vast amount of conspiracism, malevolent online actors, and sheer nonsense available on the internet, but such algorithmic censorship not only is an affront to free speech; it also undermines the very struggle against misinformation. Imagine if at the beginning of the pandemic, anyone who argued in favour of the use of masks had been censored by Google. How would we have learnt that we were in fact supposed to use them to combat what had turned out to be a primarily airborne virus? In supporting such censorship ostensibly in the service of scientific rationality, we undermine scientific rationality. As the motto of The Royal Society states, 'Nullius in verba', or 'Take nobody's word for it'. Moreover, as we open the door to such censorship, how long will it be before the ideas of the left are considered fake news, misinformation, malicious falsehoods? We are turkeys voting for Christmas if we support such censorship. The only successful way to combat bad ideas is with good ones.

## 6. *Defend civil liberties*

This defence of freedom of speech, even of the anti-vaxxers and pandemic conspiracists, is part of a wider imperative: a defence of civil liberties.

One of the challenges that the left has faced with respect to a unified approach to pandemic policies is the aforementioned spectrum of variation between and within states. For example, what may be experienced in one location as a very oppressive set of restrictions on the freedoms of movement of association and termed a 'lockdown' may not have been experienced to the same degree or even at all in a jurisdiction with a more open approach, even though in that latter jurisdiction, pandemic rules or recommendations may still have been popularly termed the 'lockdown'. Where I live, the public health orders have leaned toward recommendations rather than rules backed up by threats of fines or imprisonment, trusting the public to do what is right, along with encouragement to get outside and exercise, but other jurisdictions have had strict curfews, bans on meeting in parks, quarantine camps and far worse. Multiple reports from civil liberties associations, rightly historically identified with the left, have detailed how Covid has been used by governments both authoritarian and ostensibly democratic as an excuse to curtail civil rights. Most people are familiar with the draconian conditions in the one-party state of the People's Republic of China, but it was the liberal democracy of Fortress Australia that to its great shame refused to allow the repatriation of thousands of its own citizens, at one point leaving almost 40,000 of them stranded overseas.[20]

There must be room to be able to critique such measures without being accused of being an anti-vaxxer or a Covid denialist. And even in my relatively liberal Corona Shangri-la, there remained many incidents of state overreach. I may have been able to go to a bar or restaurant throughout much of the pandemic, barring a few months at the beginning, but with the advent of vaccine passports, thousands of homeless people with limited access to smartphones and with an understandable suspicion of healthcare systems that have repeatedly treated them appallingly ended up even more cut off from the rest of society than they already were.

And it must be recognised how insufferable for most people the restrictions enacted even in the generally civil-liberties-respecting jurisdictions were, let alone those imposed in the more heavy-handed locations. We are social animals, after all. Solely viewing every other person as a potential vector of disease only reinforces the individualist atomisation that is the anti-social foundation of neoliberalism.

Along these lines, we should also be able to recognise how profoundly destructive school closures and distance learning have been for pupils' education, socialisation, and mental health, however necessary they were to reduce transmission of the virus. One also has to be careful that a very reasonable call to wear masks to minimise transmission does not work to undermine trust in the effectiveness of vaccines. Moving forward, we have to come up with solutions that aim to minimise these problems, from generous spending on ventilation systems to being creative with outdoor schooling – with a social unionism of the teachers' unions and those representing childcare workers at the forefront of this conversation.

But even as we raise the banner of civil liberties and rigorously critique the anti-social outcomes of some public-health protection measures, we should be careful not to fall into the trap of sympathising with or even organising alongside those who have embraced anti-science, anti-vaccination, paranoid, conspiracist and individualist agendas indifferent to the well-being of others.

This is the libertarianism of fools. Indeed precisely because we want to be able to forcefully push back against state overreach, civil-liberties clampdowns, unscientific virtue-signalling, and neoliberal atomisation without being confused with the sadly great many lunatics and reactionaries, it is absolutely necessary to distance ourselves from the latter.

## A miscellany of other measures

Other demands, again depending on the situation locally, might include taking long-term care out of the private sector, ensuring adequate paid sick leave for all, and, as the pandemic was experienced very differently by essential workers exposed daily to the virus, and those, often more middle-class individuals, who could work from home, generous bonuses should be paid to the former, those heroes who kept society running while the rest of us were baking sourdough or learning a foreign language.

Open Science and Open Data, the free sharing of scientific information, are also key requirements that the left is uniquely well suited to put forth, arguing for taking all scientific journals into the public sector and making their wares available to all for free. Looking to more biotechnologically ambitious demands, generous funding, and then use of economic planning to shepherd through to commercialisation of universal flu and universal coronavirus vaccines – those that protect against all flu viruses and coronaviruses, not just particular strains, and thus eradicating the threat they pose – will be yet another fight within the territory of science: once again, unless such vaccines need to be taken annually, they too would face the problem of insufficient market incentive, for once everyone was vaccinated, there would be very little need for new doses for anyone other than children.

We certainly want to keep up the pressure against deforestation and much stricter regulation of animal agriculture, particularly poultry and pork farming, so as to reduce the chances of zoonotic spillovers. Many agribusinesses will push back against the sort of advanced ventilation system filtration required to sharply reduce the chances of pathogen transmission due to their potentially significant costs and thus threat to profits, so this is another likely site of struggle.[21] But we should be careful not to believe that if deforestation and animal agriculture were to halt tomorrow this would mean an end to infectious disease, epidemics, and pandemics. We can only dial down their likelihood, not eliminate them entirely. We should also remember that increased international trade, travel, and immigration – which make all our lives so much richer – also increase the threat of pandemics, as do population-dense cities, which offer multiple carbon emissions reduction benefits from reduced need for heating to lower transportation requirements.

We would not want to turn back the clock on cities and the positive aspects of globalisation. We want to hold on to the marvels of modernity while stripping it of its horrors, not retreat to some romantic agrarian Eden that never was.

There will undoubtedly be other demands that could make up the backbone of a pandemic justice movement but which I have overlooked. This is, as mentioned, a sketch of what its demands could be. There will also be a necessary discussion on the best tactics and strategy to build it. Already South Africa's Health Justice Initiative, Global Justice Now in the UK, and ACT-UP in the United States have organised demonstrations, die-ins, and other protests and direct actions focused on international meetings and the offices of major pharmaceutical companies. Nurses' unions and those of other healthcare workers in many countries have repeatedly taken industrial action over working conditions under Covid and represent a very powerful pinch-point within global health. But such discussions of tactics, strategy, and who is most likely to form the shock troops of such a movement could fill another lengthy essay.

Ultimately there is a great deal that the left – holding on to its classical values of equality, civil liberties, mutual aid, scientific rationality, progress, and planning rather than markets – has to offer with respect to this pandemic, the next one, and all the other infectious diseases we continue to struggle with, even if so far we have not performed at our best under Covid. And if we are clear on those values and the set of demands that flow from them, we will be able to build the pandemic justice movement that is so essential and will break the back of this gravest of threats to humanity.

No one is safe until we're all safe.

NOTES

1   'Estimating excess mortality due to the COVID-19 pandemic: a systematic analysis of COVID-19-related mortality, 2020–21', *The Lancet*, 10 March 2022, <https://www.thelancet.com/journals/lancet/article/PIIS0140-6736(21)02796-3/fulltext>.
2   'The pandemic's true death toll: Our daily estimate of excess deaths around the world', *The Economist*, updated 1 April 2022, <https://www.economist.com/graphic-detail/coronavirus-excess-deaths-estimates>.
3   Reperes, World War I Casualties, <http://www.centre-robert-schuman.org/userfiles/files/REPERES%20%E2%80%93%20module%201-1%20-%20explanatory%20notes%20%E2%80%93%20World%20War%20I%20casualties%20%E2%80%93%20EN.pdf>.
4   Zeke Hausfather, 'Flattening the Curve of Future Emissions', The Breakthrough Institute, 11 August 2021, <https://thebreakthrough.org/issues/energy/flattening-the-curve-of-future-emissions>.

5   'Coronavirus (COVID-19) Vaccinations', Our World in Data, <https://ourworldindata.org/covid-vaccinations>.

6   Chris Stokel-Walker, 'What Do We Know About Covid Vaccines and Preventing Transmission?', *BMJ* 2022, <https://www.bmj.com/content/376/bmj.o298>.

7   'Mapping global trends in vaccine confidence and investigating barriers to vaccine uptake: a large-scale retrospective temporal modeling study', *The Lancet*, 26 September 2020, <https://www.thelancet.com/journals/lancet/article/PIIS0140-6736(20)31558-0/fulltext>.

8   Human Sciences Research Council, Survey shows that acceptance of vaccines is increasing but challenges remain, 17 August 2021, <http://www.hsrc.ac.za/en/media-briefs/dces/survey-shows-acceptance-of-vaccines>.

9   World Health Organization, 'South Africa's mRNA hub progress is foundation for self-reliance', 11 February 2022, <https://www.who.int/news/item/11-02-2022-south-africa-s-mrna-hub-progress-is-foundation-for-self-reliance>.

10  Asleigh Furlong, Compromise reached on COVID-19 vaccine intellectual property rights waiver, *Politico* 15 March 2022, <https://www.politico.eu/article/compromise-reached-on-covid-19-vaccine-intellectual-property-rights-waiver/>.

11  Doctors Without Borders, 'MSF response to license between Pfizer and Medicines Patent Pool for new COVID-19 treatment Paxlovid', 16 November 2021, <https://msfaccess.org/msf-response-license-between-pfizer-and-medicines-patent-pool-new-covid-19-treatment-paxlovid>.

12  World Health Organization, 'What's "Super" about Super Gonorrhea?: A Q&A with WHO's Dr. Teodora Wi', <https://www.who.int/campaigns/world-antimicrobial-awareness-week/2018/features-from-around-the-world/super-gonorrhoea-q-a-with-dr.-teodora-wi>.

13  Sarah Boseley, 'New wave of "superbugs" poses dire threat, says chief medical officer', *The Guardian*, 11 March 2013, <https://www.theguardian.com/society/2013/mar/11/superbugs-antibiotics-bacterial-diseases-infections>.

14  Leigh Phillips, 'The Free Market Isn't Up to the Coronavirus Challenge', *Jacobin* 4 February 2020, <https://www.jacobinmag.com/2020/02/coronavirus-outbreak-free-market-pharmaceutical-industry >.

15  Dina Fine Maron, 'Cross-Border Ebola Outbreak a First for Deadly Virus', *Scientific American*, 30 July 2014, <https://www.scientificamerican.com/article/cross-border-ebola-outbreak-a-first-for-deadly-virus/>.

16  Centers for Disease Control and Prevention, 'Neglected Tropical Diseases', <https://www.cdc.gov/globalhealth/ntd/diseases/index.html>.

17  European Medicines Agency, 'Antimacrobial Resistance', <https://www.ema.europa.eu/en/human-regulatory/overview/public-health-threats/antimicrobial-resistance>.

18  Will Davies, Global Surveillance Sysems Needed to Fight Pandemics: NEF WRAP, *Bloomberg*, 18 November, 2021, <https://www.bloomberg.com/news/articles/2021-11-18/global-surveillance-systems-needed-to-fight-pandemics-nef-wrap>.

19  Leigh Phillips, 'Neoliberal State Failure Is Slowing Down Vaccine Distribution', *Jacobin*, 21 April 2021, <https://www.jacobinmag.com/2021/04/neoliberal-state-failure-covid-19-vaccine-distribution>.

20   ABC.net Australia, 'More than 38,000 Australians stranded overseas due to COVID-19, with dozens of flights planned for August', 30 July 2021, <https://www.abc.net.au/news/2021-07-30/stranded-australians-covid19-flights-international-repatriation/100337702>.
21   Atmosphere, 'Mitigation Strategies of Air Pollutants for Mechanical Ventilated Livestock and Poultry Housing – A Review', <https://mdpi-res.com/d_attachment/atmosphere/atmosphere-13-00452/article_deploy/atmosphere-13-00452.pdf>.

# Pandemic Capitalism: What Now?

## Ricardo Antunes

Within the left there is unanimity that it was not the Covid-19 pandemic which created the world we are now living in. Unemployment, the destruction of nature, the extreme-right, neo-fascism, neo-Nazism, xenophobia, homophobia, racism, sexism, and many other ills all existed before the outbreak of the global pandemic. What Covid-19 did was to lay bare this previous horrendous scenario and to expand and exasperate it to its limits.

The causes of the above tendencies can be found in the outbreak of capital's *structural crisis* in 1973, following intense struggles that took place in several parts of the world in 1968 – a year when the capitalist world almost melted down. From then on there was an intensification of the erosion, devastation, and increasingly precarious condition of labour, nature, racialised groups, indigenous peoples, youth, etc.

It is as if all of capital's demons came out of their bottles, boosted and unrestrained, to consolidate capital's antisocial metabolism[1] as a system that is increasingly expansionist and irredeemably destructive and uncontrollable. Climate change, with its terrible human and social consequences, is more than emblematic of the tragedy in which our contemporary world finds itself.

All this was aggravated by the strong impact the 2008-2009 crisis had on the working class, increasing the levels of misery in almost all parts of the world and resulting in more social inequality, unemployment, underemployment, informality, and precariousness.

Therefore, if the social world before the pandemic already exhibited an immense mass of unemployed, informal, subcontracted, precarious, and intermittent workers, with the outbreak of the new Covid-19 pandemic this destructive setting was substantially aggravated.[2]

Therefore, the confluence, simultaneity, and interrelation between the economic crisis, social inequality, and the pandemic, on the basis of an already very critical previous condition, intensified it even further, especially in the countries of the Global South at the periphery of capitalism, where the consequences are even more acute and brutal. We need, however, also to emphasise that this tragedy also struck the so-called advanced capitalist countries, in the Global North.

In the United States, for instance, we could see a multitude of homeless workers, sleeping on sidewalks, public squares, and parking lots, with social-distancing boxes painted on the pavement – each worker with her very small space out in the open. More than 30 million people in the country filed claims for unemployment benefits in the first months of the pandemic, as the complete failure of the healthcare system of the richest country in the world was plain to see. Following Trump's thwarting of the minor reform represented by Obama Care, the traditionally weak US health system almost collapsed, which resulted in the US becoming the world's leading country in deaths caused by Covid-19 throughout 2020.[3]

In countries of the Global South, the striking examples of India, Mexico, Brazil, and South Africa have exposed the brutality of the reality prior to the pandemic. Super-exploitation of labour and high levels of precariousness and unemployment facilitated a disastrous spread of Covid-19, especially in the most impoverished populations – the working classes of the periphery – resulting in intensified mortality among poor black women, indigenous communities, and immigrants. It is no coincidence, therefore, that in the African continent – marked by centuries of colonial, imperialist domination – dependence, exploitation, poverty, and the degradation of life were intensified during the pandemic. We only need recall that, at the end of 2021, the continent had fully vaccinated less than 8% of its population, which aggravated the isolation and suffering of its people even more.

Particularly in relation to labour, the pandemic put a definitive end to the thesis of an '*end of work*', whose erroneousness became glaringly evident during the lockdown. Without capital's use of global labour power, the creation of value and the private appropriation of wealth were reduced and even obstructed. This was the reason for capitalism's despair – *without living labour there is no valorisation of capital* – which is precisely why the global bourgeoisies pressed for the return of production.

As capital cannot dispense with labour, it tries to relatively and absolutely increase the exploitation of the working class, although in different and uneven ways, resulting, for instance, in an intensified exploitation of women's labour and in the deepening of the uneven social-gender-racial-ethnic division of labour.[4]

Iside Gjergji's critical analysis of *torture* in capitalist society[5] has shown that these destructive forms hit what she calls '*class-bodies*' with greater severity. Something similar is happening now during the pandemic, considering that the highest levels of Covid-19 transmission occur in the *bodies* of the *class-that-lives-from-labour*,[6] particularly in the *class-bodies* of women, black, and indigenous peoples, immigrants, refugees, LGBTQIA+, etc.

The pandemic did not emerge and spread at the margins or outside *capital's order of social metabolic reproduction*, but is a result and consequence of the system's destruction of nature – as a limitless growth economy based on fossil fuels, the burning of forests, mineral extraction, etc. Therefore, rather than being a 'natural' phenomenon it is a tragic consequence of 'capital's order',[7] which in its endless drive to valorise capital, increasingly expands and accumulates wealth, destroying human labour power and nature.

This tendency, greatly aggravated today, led István Mészáros to develop a thesis central to his analysis of the *decreasing rate of utilisation of use values* in commodities within capital's order.[8] As capital increasingly depends on endless selling of either material or immaterial commodities to generate more value and wealth in order to reproduce itself, a relentless *tendency to decrease commodities' use values* reduces their lifespan – through purposeful obsolescence, etc. – with the aim of accelerating capital's reproductive cycle. The result, therefore, is greater predation of nature. Despite all the richest countries' *blah blah* in meetings like COP26 in Glasgow (2021), what is evident is their incapacity to offer a way out of this uncontrolled process of environmental destruction.

Taking into account climate change, pollution of rivers and oceans, production of agrochemicals and transgenic crops, burning of forests, the war industry, and agribusiness, we could venture to say that, in addition to its well-known *destructiveness*, capitalism under the pandemic has also made its *lethality* plain for all to see. We can therefore say that we have entered the age of *pandemic* or *viral capitalism*.[9] If no real limits are set to this *antisocial metabolic order*, humanity will increasingly find itself at points of no return, thus making its own extinction ever more possible.

Only in 1918, during the so-called Spanish Flu, which spread worldwide and killed more than 50 million people, did we face a similar situation. With the Covid-19 pandemic at the end of capitalism's supposed 'golden years', we entered a world in which *'experimenta in corpore vili'* (experiments on a worthless body) like those of anatomists on frogs, were formally made'.[10]

Latin America was not immune to this simultaneous economic, social, political, and health crisis. At the end of 2019, even before the outbreak of the pandemic, around 40% of Brazil's working class was in the informal sector, making it an easy prey to the coronavirus. It is no accident that the high levels of Covid-19 transmission led to the illness and death particularly of black, female, indigenous, and immigrant populations.[11]

The consequences therefore are deep and nefarious, as we will see in what follows. It was amidst this global health tragedy that Brazil witnessed a situation so severe that its present and future existence became much more precarious. In its recent history (which seemed to develop positively in the first years of the twenty-first century), Brazil had to face a simultaneous double tragedy: the outbreak of the pandemic and the emergence of neo-fascism.

## The recent example of Brazil: between reform and counter-revolution

At the beginning of this century, the future seemed to open up for Brazil. Having just elected Luiz Inácio da Silva (Lula) as President in 2002, the country appeared to have entered a new auspicious phase, with the electoral victory of its main labour leadership, with more than 53 million votes for the Partido dos Trabalhadores (Worker's Party – PT), the premier left-wing party in Latin America.

Brazil, however, was not the same country it was in the 1980s. Since the 1989 election of Fernando Collor, an immense process of 'neoliberal desertification' was molecularly disintegrating Brazil's economic, social, political, and ideological structures. A slow and persistent process of *transformism*[12] had already deeply marked Lula and the PT. The more their political praxis envisioned electoral victories, the more they moved away from the whole of the working class, which they had represented so well in the past. Little by little, then, the PT abandoned a more class-oriented and anti-capitalist political activism and directed its efforts to institutional and electoral battles – at no small price, as we shall see.

When Lula won the presidential elections in 2002, he did so through a broad front, choosing as his vice-president José Alencar, a representative of Brazil's high bourgeoisie. Born as one of the most important labour parties in Brazil, the PT was, step by step, transforming itself into a kind of 'party of order', inside the Brazilian left.[13]

It is true that it was especially in Lula's two terms in office that we had the implementation of social policies benefiting popular sectors, which boasted an expansive cycle of economic growth able to greatly boost employment. At the same time, however, we need to realise that Lula's political actions did not challenge the foundations of neoliberal economic policies. Instead, they added a social tone to them. In office the PT managed to combine Keynesian-style state intervention with the basic foundations of neoliberalism – even if slightly mitigated. We can thus say that Lula's two terms embodied a version of social liberalism. Combining an economic and social policy that had more elements of *continuity* than *break* with neoliberalism, the PT in power implemented cross-class policies, which were much better than the ones put forward in the explicit neoliberal years of Fernando Henrique Cardoso (FHC, 1995-2003).

How, then, did Lula manage to become so popular during his two terms in office?

This was due to the fact that especially in Lula's second mandate (2007-2011) there was significant economic growth during a favourable economic climate. It occurred in the context of Lula's defence, ever since the beginning of his political career, of an economic policy based on the expansion of the internal market, in view of the extremely low level of the working class's consumption (and therefore the possibility of its expansion).

It is worth mentioning that in office Lula heavily sponsored production of commodities, such as iron, ethanol, soya, etc. mainly for export to an international market in which there was intense demand for these products at the time. In the same way, Lula implemented policies to boost industrial production, reducing taxes on automobiles, household appliances, and in the building industries, in order to gain strong support from different fractions of the bourgeoisie.

In this sense, since Lula always respected the 'primary surpluses' demanded by neoliberal policies, we can say that the main difference in relation to FHC's neoliberalism was the implementation of one particular, broad welfare policy programme. Known as *Bolsa Família* (Family Allowance), this programme had a broad social reach and reduced, although it did not eliminate, the high levels of extreme poverty that characterised Brazilian capitalism. Alongside this, the minimum wage was always at a higher level than that enforced by FHC.

However, it is necessary to emphasise that there were no strong land, urban, and financial reforms. Such measures would indeed have been able to begin dismantling some of the pillars of Brazilian capitalism. Without them, the gains achieved during the PT terms were subsequently destroyed one by one, first by Temer and now by Bolsonaro. If Lula succeeded in implementing a reconciliation of capital and labour, Dilma Rousseff was not as lucky. Her second term ended prematurely with the 2016 coup d'état that resulted in her impeachment and the abrupt end of the PT governments.[14]

With the crisis coming to Brazil, whose first signs could already be seen in 2013, the broad support the PT had from the bourgeois and popular class fractions gradually crumbled. The June 2013 protests were a clear signal that the cross-class support for previous PT governments was beginning to disintegrate.

Already during the presidential elections of 2014, a significant sector of the high bourgeoisie, which up to that point had given solid support to the PT, began showing signs of dissatisfaction, demanding the implementation of more neoliberal fiscal adjustments policies. The more Dilma's government implemented these adjustments, the more pressure came from bourgeois fractions, and this eroded the PT's working-class support, which used to guarantee the party a strong popular and social base.

The final debacle came with Operação Lava Jato, an investigation process aimed almost exclusively at punishing crimes of corruption ascribed to the PT. The investigations had strong support from media conglomerates, while right-wing and extreme right-wing groups intensified their political campaign 'against corruption' and asked for 'the return of military dictatorship'.

The judiciary and especially the parliament, whose putschist traditions go back to the 1964 military coup, provided an appearance of 'legality' for Dilma's impeachment. One thinks of Marx who said in the mid-nineteenth century that the French Parliament had been humiliated and lost what remained of the respect the people formerly had for it.[15]

In this sense, in August 2016, combining a *judicialisation of politics* and a *politicisation of justice*, the Brazilian Parliament approved the impeachment of Dilma Rousseff and her replacement by Michel Temer, one of the architects of the 2016 coup and at the time Rousseff's vice-president, who had been appointed by Lula. Once again the impossibility of reconciliation between capital and labour became evident, and in the absence of structural reforms the first phase of the counter-revolution in Brazil was launched.

As recent experiments in Honduras and Paraguay showed, Latin America was already witnessing a new type of coup d'état in which parliamentary action replaced the classic military coup so frequent in the history of the continent. The path was open for the 2018 election of Jair Bolsonaro, a former military man.

This brings us then to the second phase of the *pre-emptive counter-revolution*,[16] which can occur even when there is no risk of revolution. The aim was to reorganise bourgeois domination in Brazil, combining a form of autocratic politics with a reactionary and ultraliberal ideology. The counter-revolution has been led by the extreme right and by fascist groups, taking Brazil back to a dark age.[17] It is important to recall, as well, that, besides the specifically Brazilian crisis involving Temer's coup, Bolsonaro's election in 2018 was also the result of an international conjuncture of counter-revolution that boosted the expansion of the extreme right, especially since the electoral victory of Trump in the United States.

We can say that Bolsonaro, the former captain expelled from the Army due to his lack of discipline, is a kind of neofascist with clear Bonapartist traits. Thus, he is a political personality who does not originate directly from the bourgeois classes, but represents them faithfully, although in order to do so he has to *appear* to be above the classes.

In his electoral campaign Bolsonaro thus presented himself as the only candidate 'against the system', while being in fact a vulgar gendarme of the ruling class. His neofascist traits are expressed in his ceaseless striving to remain in power, and in threats of coups and dictatorship. It is, therefore, an autocratic government that is heavily militarised – there are more than 6,000 military people in civilian posts within the federal bureaucracy. On the other hand, the bourgeoisie, seeing all its traditional candidates failing, demanded that Bolsonaro commit himself to an ultraliberal, predatory, and regressive economic policy. This was the only request from the dominant classes in exchange for supporting Bolsonaro.

Bolsonaro is a kind of *caveman Trump*;[18] there is no parallel in the recent history of the Republic. For all this, it seems accurate to understand him as an expression of 'the scum of bourgeois society' that finally formed 'the holy phalanx of order', and 'the hero Krapülinski' who installed 'himself in the Tuileries as the "saviour of society"'.[19] Thus I define his government as a *government of a lumpen-kind*.[20]

The consequences of Bolsonaro's destructive actions are well known internationally: the devastation of labour and nature, climate and pandemic denialism, xenophobia, racism, sexism, homophobia, putschism, the vindication of dictatorships, etc. – the most nefarious outlooks of the contemporary world find expression in Bolsonaro's actions. The closest counterpart to his mixture of autocratic government and primitive neoliberal policies in Latin American history is Pinochet's military dictatorship, the aberration that first introduced neoliberalism to the world.

In particular, regarding the destruction of workers' rights, won throughout more than a century of struggles, we are witnessing their total devastation; precariousness, unemployment, informality, sporadic platform work, poverty, and hunger are the main characteristics of the working class's daily life after almost three years of Bolsonaro's misrule.

In terms of the annihilation of nature, Brazilian policies permitting the use of agrochemicals have expanded substantially; government policy to carry out the burning of forests and the devastation of Amazonia is expanding non-stop; illegal logging and mineral extraction are growing everywhere in the country – all this to fulfil the needs of a predatory bourgeoisie whose thirst for accumulation seems limitless.

Bolsonaro's pandemic policies encapsulate these devastations, greatly intensified after 2018. Governed by a denialist view that might well be called genocidal – especially against indigenous peoples and the poor living in the major urban peripheries – Brazil had, by the end of 2021, more than 600,000 dead, mainly due to the lack of vaccines and medical care. The first recorded death in Rio was emblematic: a 63-year-old black domestic worker infected by coronavirus transmitted by her employer who had just returned from Italy – a country known at the time for its high levels of Covid-19 transmission. This is just one of many examples of class, gender, and race discrimination that resulted in thousands of deaths of poor, black people living in peripheries and indigenous communities where the mortality rates were the highest.

The vaccination boycott policies were abandoned more than a year after the pandemic began, when the Brazilian Congress created a parliamentary inquiry to investigate the government's Covid-19 measures. As a consequence, Bolsonaro was accused of several crimes and of being responsible for thousands of deaths and millions of infections.

Principally responsible for this carnage in Brazil was the neofascist government's defence of the economy and capital against life; it was taken to its limits by Bolsonaro, with his government making it difficult for broad sectors of the working class to go into lockdown. This was also one of the reasons why the working class had the highest mortality rates – a situation aggravated by informality, uberisation, outsourcing, and unemployment; stripped of their rights these workers most directly suffer the consequences of pandemic capitalism.

Taking all this into account, a substantive transformation in Brazil will only be possible through sharp social and political confrontation, capable of aggregating a variety of popular forces, urban and rural, organised in social movements, trade unions, left-wing parties, etc. These working-class sites of resistance and struggle have to decisively abandon any prioritising of institutional action and instead prioritise extra-parliamentary praxis, strengthening and expanding experiences of organisation and self-organisation in anti-racist social movements, in LGBTQIA+ and feminist rebellions, in the struggles in the periphery, in indigenous communities, in the anti-capitalist environmental movements, in youth rebellions, etc., all of them opposing the combination of exploitation and oppression. Only a strong social and political class movement can defeat Brazilian capitalism – one of the biggest economies in the world with a horrendous level of inequality. And if this is a reality not only in Brazil, India, South Africa, and Mexico, but in several parts of the world, we have no alternative but to *invent* a *new way of life*.

## Inventing a new way of life: where to begin?

The paramount question posed by the project of inventing a new way of life is the following: Is the class that lives from labour destined to remain paralysed and a prisoner of a social reproduction system in its most destructive and lethal phase? Is there no alternative?

From my perspective, the pandemic was so severe that large parts of the population have begun to question how this antisocial metabolic system might be overcome, a system that has proven incapable of preserving what is most fundamental to humanity: *life itself*. Several social sectors seem to be perceiving that the pandemic laid bare and exasperated the destructive and lethal dynamic of contemporary societies.

Just as in the great social revolutions in France and Russia, the present level of destruction is creating an imperative for profound and radical transformation. This compels us to find *in the present* the necessary conditions to prefigure a new way of life – as occurred in 1789, under the command of an embryonic bourgeoisie, or in 1917 boosted by the emergent proletariat. Among the conditions that made these two revolutions possible were the longstanding ills of, respectively, French feudalism and Czarist Russia.

The point of departure for the urgently needed invention of a *new way of life* that humanises and emancipates social being is located in daily life, where the most vital questions moving humanity are posed.

On this central issue, I recall Lukács's fundamental intervention in *The Ontology of Social Being*, when he said that 'whilst in normal everyday life each decision that is not completely routine is taken in an atmosphere of innumerable ifs and buts, [...] in revolutionary situations and their preparatory processes, this negative infinity of particular questions is condensed into few central questions that, however, are presented for the majority of people as problems that point to the destiny of their lives, that, in contrast to "normal" everyday life, assume the quality of a question formulated with clarity that must be answered with clarity'.[21]

As in in 1789 and 1917, it is therefore urgent to understand what these 'central questions' are regarding the roots of the ills caused by capital's social metabolic order.

In contemporary capitalism, characterised by a lethal destructiveness, as we have seen, it is possible to perceive that we are entering an extraordinary phase of our history, in which all that seems solid can 'melt into air'. Furthermore, if humanity, which depends on its labour to survive, proves incapable of reinventing a *new way of life*, we would then be closer to extinction than we have ever been.

We can therefore summarise our formulation as follows: for a process of social revolution to flourish in the twenty-first century, it is necessary from the start to prefigure a world, in its totality – from centre to periphery (and from periphery to centre) – without pre-established hierarchies. This is a first step for understanding *what* the vital questions of our time are.

We think there are, as starting points, three essential axes. In sum, it is necessary to eliminate the basic scourges characterising contemporary capitalism. To do so, we urgently need to *simultaneously* end the degradation of labour, the destruction of nature, and gender, racial, and ethnic oppressions. These scourges are taking the class that lives from labour to levels of dehumanisation, exploitation, and spoliation previously unseen in the history of capitalism.

Even if ending these scourges does not eliminate many others, our hypothesis is that they are vital and central *starting points* capable of activating humanity and prefiguring a radical transformation of society. In this way a complex process of social revolution can begin, which, however, can only be realised if it is anchored in and spurred on by questions emerging from everyday life itself.

Regarding the absolute priority of halting the destruction of nature at the limits of its capacity to support human life, the pandemic offered us some immediate insights: it was the cities in lockdown that, for a moment, managed to reduce the global levels of lethal pollution. Without cars circulating, without pollutants from industrial production, without nefarious agribusinesses we could see that air-pollution levels were significantly reduced in several cities, due to a partial stoppage of production.

This made clear that an effective environmental recovery compels us to an *immediate* reduction and subsequent elimination of destructive production and consumption, both fundamental to capital accumulation. This is precisely why humanity, if it wants to fight for the recovery of nature, has to directly oppose capital.

At the same time, to wrest back labour's dignity is essential, since worldwide there are hundreds of millions of workers without work or in precarious employment, which makes a meaningful life impossible. A striking example is immigrant labour, wandering globally in search of any work just to barely survive.

The combined challenge can be summed up in this way: it is imperative to redesign the world of work, making the labouring act something oriented by the production of *socially useful goods*, instead of guided by the creation of more wealth for capital. The working class could then enjoy shorter working hours and recover labour as a *vital and free activity, self-determined and based on disposable time*. This leads us to struggle for the elimination of *wage* and *alienated labour*, which in producing and reproducing capital, is breaking down humanity.

Looked at from the opposite direction: labour that structures a human community can only flourish by de-structuring capital.[22] It is a work that must aim to preserve human life and nature (inorganic and organic nature and human nature), blocking the private and limitless accumulation of capital and wealth and the devastation of nature. Therefore, we must effectively design a *new* and truly *social metabolic order* in order to defeat the expansionist, uncontrollable, and destructive imperatives of capital's system.[23]

If to these basic starting points we add the third vital complex – that is, the achievement of *substantive equality* in terms of gender, ethnicity, and race[24] – we will be in a position possibly to *simultaneously* and decisively advance in the struggle against racism, homophobia, xenophobia, sexism, science denialism and, in this way, socially advance *beyond capital*.

The fusing of working-class struggles with social movements, anti-racist, feminist/anti-patriarchal, and anti-capitalist rebellions, plus the resistance of indigenous communities, can create a capacity for more effective articulation of all of the battles.

Certainly, one can tax this formulation with utopianism. But the bourgeois revolutions of the eighteenth century, the Haitian Revolution of 1791, the emblematic Paris Commune of 1871, and the socialist revolutions of the twentieth century were 'ahead of their times' in similar ways – as were also the truly sustainable and communal indigenous communities in America and the black communities that rebelled against slavery.

To the reasonable question of the sceptic 'isn't socialism dead?' we can reply by asking how many centuries it took for capitalism to become hegemonic. Counting the time from primitive accumulation up to the Industrial Revolution, we see that it took capital three centuries to eliminate the feudal order.

So, taking the Paris Commune of 1871 as a milestone, we might say that attempts at socialist revolution were defeated during these first 150 years but, considering the timeframe of the transition from feudalism to capitalism, it will not be surprising if we need at least another century and a half to build a new way of life beyond capital.

NOTES

1   István Mészáros, *Beyond Capital: Towards a Theory of Transition*, New York: Monthly Review Press, 1995.
2   In this article I readdress a set of theses and formulations presented in the e-book Ricardo Antunes, *Coronavírus: o Trabalho Sob Fogo Cruzado*, São Paulo: Boitempo,

2020; published also in Italy as *Capitalismo virale. Pandemia e trasformazioni del Lavoro*, Rome: Castelvecchi, 2021.
3   Antunes, *Coronavírus*.
4   Antunes, *Coronavírus*.
5   Iside Gjergji, *Sociologia della tortura. Immagine e pratica del supplizio postmoderno*, Venice: Edizioni Ca' Foscari - Digital Publishing, 2019.
6   See Ricardo Antunes, *Farewell to Work? Essays on the World of Work's Metamorphoses and Centrality (Studies in Critical Social Science No. 148)*, Leiden: Brill; and Ricardo Antunes, *The Meanings of Work: Essay on the Affirmation and Negation of Work* (Historical Materialism Book Series, vol. 43), Chicago: Haymarket, 2013.
7   See Mészáros's distinction between capital and capitalism in *Beyond Capital*, chapter 15.
8   See Mészáros.
9   See Antunes, *Coronavírus*.
10  Karl Marx, *Capital*, vol. 1: 'The Process of Production of Capital,.." in Karl Marx and Frederick Engels, *Collected Works*, vol. 35, New York: International, 1996, p. 460.
11  See Antunes, *Coronavírus*.
12  Antonio Gramsci, *Prison Notebooks*, vol. 1, New York: Columbia University Press, 1992, p. 137.
13  See Ricardo Antunes, *O Privilégio da Servidão: o novo proletariado de serviços na era digital*, São Paulo Boitempo, 2018; published in Italy as *La Politica della Caverna: La controrivoluzione di Bolsnonaro*, Rome: Castelvecchi, 2019. On the Party of Order, see Karl Marx, '*The Eighteenth Brumaire of Louis Bonaparte*, in *Karl Marx and Fredrick Engels, Collected Works*, vol. 11, New York: International, 2010.
14  See Antunes, *O Privilégio da Servidão* (Italian edition: *La Politica della Caverna*).
15  Marx, *The Eighteenth Brumaire*.
16  Florestan Fernandes, *A Revolução Burguesa no Brasil*, São Paulo: Zahar, 1975.
17  Antunes, *La Politica della Caverna*.
18  I used this expression in *La Politica della Caverna*.
19  Karl Marx, *The Eighteenth Brumaire of Louis Bonaparte*, in Karl Marx and Frederick Engels, *Collected Works*, vol. 11, New York: International, 1978, pp. 99-198, here p. 112: 'During the June days all classes and parties had united in the Party of Order against the proletarian class as the Party of Anarchy, of socialism, of communism. They had "saved" society from "the enemies of society". They had given out the watch-words of the old society, "property, family, religion, order", to their army as passwords and had proclaimed to the counter-revolutionary crusaders: "By this sign thou shalt conquer!" From this moment, as soon as one of the numerous parties which had gathered under this sign against the June insurgents seeks to hold the revolutionary battlefield in its own class interest, it goes down before the cry: "Property, family, religion, order." Society is saved just as often as the circle of its rulers contracts, as a more exclusive interest is maintained against a wider one. Every demand of the simplest bourgeois financial reform, of the most ordinary liberalism, of the most formal republicanism, of the most shallow democracy, is simultaneously castigated as an "attempt on society" and stigmatised as "socialism". And, finally, the high priests of "religion and order" themselves are driven with kicks from their Pythian tripods, hauled out of their beds in the darkness of night, put in prison-vans, thrown into dungeons or sent into exile; their temple is razed to the ground, their

mouths are sealed, their pens broken, their law torn to pieces in the name of religion, of property, of the family, of order. Bourgeois fanatics for order are shot down on their balconies by mobs of drunken soldiers, their domestic sanctuaries profaned, their houses bombarded for amusement — in the name of property, of the family, of religion and of order. Finally, the scum of bourgeois society forms the holy phalanx of order and the hero Krapülinski installs himself in the Tuileries as the "saviour of society".' With Krapülinski, a character in Heine's poem 'Zwei Ritter', Marx alludes to Louis Bonaparte.

20  Antunes, *La Politica de la Caverna.*

21  György Lukács, *Ontologia dell'Essere Sociale II,* vol. 2 Rome: Riuniti, 1981, 506. The quote appears in the chapter 'The Ideal Moment and Ideology' which is not included in the abridged English edition. For a discussion of it, see Antunes, *The Meanings of Work*, p. 145.

22  Antunes, *The Meanings of Work*, especially chapter 1.

23  Kohei Saito has shown the *ontological indissociability of social being and nature* in Marx's work and the alienation of both under capital. He has also commented on Mészáros's groundbreaking formulations on this topic. See Kohei Saito, *Karl Marx's Ecosocialism: Capital, Nature, and the Unfinished Critique of Political Economy*, New York: Monthly Review Press, 2017; and 'Marx's Theory of Metabolism in the Age of Global Ecological Crisis', *Historical Materialism* 28,2 (2020), 3-24.

24  Mészáros, *Beyond Capital*, p. 187.

# Covid-19 and Working-Class Power

## Asbjørn Wahl

Covid-19 has reminded us of how vulnerable we are on the planet earth, but also of how disrespectfully we behave, since the spread of the pandemic has to do with the way we live, produce, and exploit our existing resources. We do not yet really know how it will all end, not least because the developing world has been left behind by the rich world when it comes to treatment and vaccination against the virus. The unbridled pursuit of profit by Big Pharma and the lack of international solidarity from the North to the South have been among the most depressing aspects of the pandemic so far.

The economic and social effects of the pandemic have been dramatic. In addition to the illness itself, fatal for many, job loss, suspension of work contracts, and deteriorating working conditions have become the order of the day for millions of workers. Precariousness and all kinds of job insecurity have increased. Low-income countries have been the most affected, particularly in the health, transport, and retail sectors. In Europe, Italy, Spain, and France have been among the hardest hit. The International Labour Organization estimates that in Europe the total number of hours worked fell by about 18% in the second quarter of 2020 compared to the last quarter of 2019, which is the equivalent of more than 40 million full-time jobs.[1]

Covid-19 is not the only crisis we have experienced in recent times. Over the last few decades, we have actually had many of them – economic, social, political, environmental, and food crises. The Covid-19 pandemic has come on top of those. A lot of the crises are overlapping, and they have many of the same root causes, going to the core of our economic system. Capitalism has been in crisis mode more or less continuously since the 1970s, with the worst recent effects seen during the global financial crisis of 2007-08. Given the central role of capitalism as a driver of the other crises, it is impossible for us to fight these crises separately.

Workers and trade unions have been put under immense pressure during the last 40 years, an era which was also characterised by a continuous neoliberal offensive. The employers have intensified the class struggle, and the trade-union movement has been pushed on to the defensive. The pandemic has presented workers and trade unions with several new challenges. How then can a crisis-ridden trade-union movement on the defensive meet the new challenges from employers and governments, when we hopefully move into a post-Covid era? It is time to attempt an assessment, but let us first take a further look at some important developments which will continue to have effect after the pandemic.

## Farewell to austerity?

The EU was in deep crisis for many years before the pandemic. With strict austerity policy in place for decades, cuts in public health and privatisation of hospitals and other health services were carried out in most countries, which reduced the governments' ability to deal with the pandemic, while creating a higher risk of infection for health workers. Spain's centre-left government even took the step of re-nationalising hospitals in order to provide better treatment for the country's patients. The failure of the neoliberal policy model was thus clearly demonstrated during the pandemic. As Ingar Solty has pointed out: 'It is clear that people in Italy are dying not because Covid-19 is so lethal, but because the neoliberalisation of healthcare and the EU's austerity measures are literally killing them.'[2]

In addition, the financial and economic crisis resulted in high unemployment, low wages, an extensive precarisation of working and living conditions, and a great increase in social inequality in all EU countries. The pandemic deepened the crisis, with dramatic consequences. Alfredo Saad-Filho summarised this development, as follows:

> The pandemic hit after four decades of neoliberalism had depleted state capacities in the name of the 'superior efficiency' of the market, fostered deindustrialization through the 'globalization' of production and built fragile financial structures secured by magical thinking and state guarantees, all in the name of short-term profitability. [...] Neoliberalism was quickly shown to have hollowed out, fragmented and in part privatized health systems in several countries, while it also created a precarious and impoverished working class.[3]

However, during the pandemic we also learned that what we had been told was impossible could nevertheless be done. Through the suspension of the Stability and Growth Pact and the debt criteria of the Fiscal Compact the EU and governments were able to pump liquidity into the financial sector. The states provided support packages for workers who lost their jobs or were sent home in order to reduce spreading the virus, although informal and gig workers were excluded in many countries – and businesses were the chief recipients. Programmes like the European Recovery Fund, the NextGenerationEU, the European Unemployment Reinsurance Scheme (EURS), and the Multiannual Financial Framework (MFF) are all meant to contribute to the recovery – but this time in a way different from austerity.

We have even seen elements of a planned economy during the pandemic, where factories are being ordered to produce socially necessary products like respirators, hospital beds, protective masks, gloves, and other health equipment – rather than cars, clothing, chemicals, etc. These examples of demand-side economics (Keynesianism) and planned economy can be good ideas to have in store in the event we are ever able to bring a left-wing government to power. Of course, these examples do not mean that neoliberalism is dead; this would be a misunderstanding. Their aim is to save the capitalist system from a potentially existential crisis, and the EU and our governments will surely push for a return to *'normal'* as soon as circumstances change. Only our ability to resist will decide how far they will succeed in doing so.

## Teleworking

Teleworking, or working from home, is not really new, but it expanded greatly during the pandemic. Millions of people across Europe have been working from home, although this has only been possible for about a third of all workers. Others, such as nurses and transport workers, had to go to work or they did not have the space or equipment at home to do their job. The Deputy General Secretary of the European Trade Union Confederation (ETUC), Esther Lynch, notes that:

> A *European Working Conditions Survey* found that those working regularly from home were twice as likely to work 48 hours or more a week than those working at their employer's premises – and six times more likely to work in their free time. According to European Parliament research, long-range managerial monitoring and demand for constant availability can create psychosocial health risks, stress and isolation.[4]

> A 2020 *European Foundation for the Improvement of Living and Working Conditions* (Eurofound) study found that only few countries had implemented regulations to protect teleworkers' well-being. The ETUC and European employers' *Framework Agreement on Telework* establishes some principles

and red lines, including equal pay and employment conditions and normal working hours. Teleworkers are entitled to reimbursement of additional expenses such as equipment, Wi-Fi, and the increased cost of home utilities. Thus, the struggle around regulating working hours as well as working conditions in telework, as well as enforcing existing regulations, will be important for trade unions after the pandemic.

## Big Pharma

In combating the pandemic, vaccine distribution has been disastrous. The vaccine nationalism that we have seen in the rich world is depressing and has devastating consequences for poor countries and ultimately for the whole world, with many in poor countries remaining without protection probably until well into 2024. The collapse of international solidarity that we have seen between North and South is simply tragic. Nor has the trade union movement been able to take the lead in this fight, at least not in a way that goes beyond the level of statements, something which is as revealing as it is outrageous.

The aggressive profit-seeking of the pharmaceutical industry is a part of their inhuman business model. This despite their having benefited from publicly-funded university research, government subsidies, and of course profits on sales (difficult to quantify, since companies insist on secrecy in contracts with governments). For example, South Africa is paying twice the price per shot that the European Union pays, apparently because South Africa did not subsidise development of the vaccine. According to CNN Business, at least nine new billionaires have been created by Covid-19 vaccines.[5]

A temporary TRIPS (*WTO agreement on Trade-Related Aspects of Intellectual Property Rights*) waiver proposed by South Africa and India and now supported by more than 100 other countries, has been met with resistance from the WTO, the EU, in particular Germany, plus Norway and Switzerland. A majority of the (not so powerful) European Parliament has supported the waiver and the US has expressed support, although without pushing too hard. The brutal fact is that people in the Third World are dying for lack of vaccination. It is a glaring example of the reality of '*profit before people*'. David Harvey got it spot on:

> Corporatist Big Pharma has little or no interest in non-remunerative research on infectious diseases (such as the whole class of corona viruses that have been well-known since the 1960s). Big Pharma rarely invests in prevention. It has little interest in investing in preparedness for a public health crisis. It

loves to design cures. The sicker we are the more they earn. Prevention does not contribute to share-holder value. It might even diminish it.[6]

For a trade-union movement suffering from the extensive deterioration of international solidarity in the last few decades, this could very well be a test case and the basis for the re-establishment of a joint struggle, not only for a waiver, but for a full socialisation of the pharmaceutical industry. An international campaign has already been launched.[7]

## Wishful thinking

If workers and unions want more influence in their workplaces as well as in society, they have to mobilise and fight for a shift in the balance of power. Wishful thinking does not work. Currently, trade unions are on the losing side and the situation is dramatic. The *International Trade Union Confederation* (ITUC) issues an annual *Global Rights Index*, whose most recent edition documents a strong anti-worker agenda globally. In a recent article,[8] ITUC General Secretary Sharan Burrow describes the disastrous situation as follows:

- 87% of countries surveyed have violated the right to strike;
- 79% of countries have violated the right to collective bargaining;
- 74% of countries exclude workers from the right to establish and join a trade union at all;
- a new worrying trend is a rise in surveillance of workers and attacks on their right to privacy.

This list tells a lot about the battlefield we are facing. The *Index* shows how far some governments and employers have gone to exploit the Covid-19 pandemic to attack the rights of workers. Most of these countries are admittedly developing countries, but also countries like Belgium, Hungary and Slovakia have seen their ratings worsen. 'It tells a shocking story,' Sharan Burrow says, and I am afraid she is right. But the question remains: how is she and the ITUC going to stop, or at least reduce, this disastrous development? Addressing a UN Economic and Social Council meeting, she indicated what is needed:

> We need a new model of global governance to redress the current imbalance of power and uneven distribution of wealth at international level. A truly inclusive multilateral system where social partners are on board and have a say will make the difference and pave the way to global resilience.[9]

Given the actual situation with trade unions on the defensive all over the world, this is far from being an easy task to solve. At any rate, the first step is to put the real problems openly and honestly on the table for discussion.

## Defensive unions

This could be a useful way to start the discussion of how trade unions should meet the challenges of the post-Covid era. How should they meet the attacks from the employers? How do they build power, and how can they shift the balance of power in favour of workers and unions? Many people say that nothing will be the same after the pandemic. Perhaps this is true, but will things be better or worse? It is not easy to say, but this is no reason to rely on either a poorly justified optimism or a correspondingly unfounded pessimism. We should try to avoid wishful thinking and rather analyse and assess the situation as seen from a workers' or a trade-union perspective. The problems and weaknesses of the trade-union movement, however, go back much further than the Covid era – so let us take a look at the last decades and try to identify the most important barriers.

I assume that there is reasonably broad agreement that the trade-union movement is on the defensive, and that this has been the case for quite a while – long before the pandemic. Ever since the beginning of the neoliberal offensive around 1980 we have experienced an enormous shift in the balance of power from labour to capital. Neoliberalism won hegemony under the leadership of Margaret Thatcher and Ronald Reagan, and this hegemony was used to inflict severe defeats on the trade-union and labour movement.

Since then, trade unions have been under immense pressure from strong economic and political forces. Employers have been attacking on all fronts, and the ongoing pandemic has been used as an excuse for further undermining trade unions, wages, and working conditions. Isn't it proof enough of the crisis we face, that trade-union membership in Europe on average has been reduced by half over the last 40 years? This is an onslaught on trade unions unprecedented in modern times.

## A deep political-ideological crisis

What makes the situation even more serious for the trade-union movement is that the defeats it suffered were not only in relation to industrial actions but they also led to *a deep political-ideological crisis* in the trade-union and labour movements themselves. The unions were simply not prepared for the massive neoliberal offensive and more or less gave in to the other side. This political-ideological crisis must be understood in the light of the *class compromise* and *the social partnership ideology* which have played such crucial roles in Western Europe, particularly after the Second World War.

The origin and history of this ideology go back to the establishment and institutionalisation of the post-war historical class compromise (aka *social contract*) between labour and capital as it developed mainly after the Second World War – with its centre in Western Europe. This compromise, whatever we think of it, was built on trade unions' power which gave workers influence in the workplaces and in society. It was the result of a very specific historic development in the last century in which the trade-union and labour movement was able to threaten the interests of capital through mobilisation and struggles. *Social dialogue* and *bi- and tripartite cooperation* did not cause this development, as many seem to think; rather they were its effects.

That is, the class compromise was not the result of appeals to the employers, but of *teaching the employers a lesson* through a variety of industrial actions. The employers became interested in striking a deal with the workers, not in order to be nice to them but in order to avoid something worse – which to them was socialism of any kind. The class compromise was, in other words, established on the basis of 50 years of tenacious class struggle. It was the shift in power relations during this period, in favour of labour, that gave the trade-union movement influence through tripartite negotiations and social dialogue.

## Breakdown of the class compromise

At present, with power relations having shifted considerably in favour of the employers, the class compromise has either already collapsed or is about to do so across Europe – and in the rest of the world where it has existed in some form. With a weak trade-union and labour movement, very much on the defensive, the employers are no longer interested in class compromise of any kind, not to mention an effective social dialogue. In such a situation, to believe that social dialogue will solve our problems is at best naïve.

The problem is that large sections of the trade-union movement, particularly in Europe, have continued to cling to the social partnership ideology – with social dialogue as its main method of influence – something which, in the current situation, is quite counterproductive. Or, to quote the ETUC General Secretary Luca Visentini at a speech to the EU's Employment, Social Policy, Health and Consumer Affairs Council (EPSCO): 'We appreciate your good words about involvement of social partners, but this is high time to turn nice words into reality.'[10]

What to do, then, if the nice words are not turned into reality and the so-called social partners are not being involved, as is the case most of the time? Is it possible to recalibrate our outlook away from this frustration and towards a mobilisation of social power to confront our adversaries? At any rate, all indications are that it takes more than nice words and social dialogue to come to grips with the fundamental problems of our time, as David Harvey emphasises in arguing that 'the fundamental problems are actually so deep right now that there is no way that we are going to go anywhere without a very strong anti-capitalist movement'.[11]

## The need to reform our unions

In fact, ever more workers are realising that we are in a critical situation, that we have to take new and bold steps towards confronting our adversaries, that we have to reform our unions in order to turn them into more efficient instruments in these struggles and to prepare them better for the confrontations that will come. Sam Gindin underlines that:

> It is not only states that must be transformed but working-class organizations as well. The failure of unions over the past few decades both in organizing and in addressing their members' needs is inseparable from their stubborn commitment to a fragmented, defensive unionism within society as it currently exists, as opposed to a class-struggle trade unionism based on broader solidarities and more ambitiously radical visions. This calls for not just 'better' unions, but for different and more politicized unions.[12]

It is not because they have given up their demands that most trade unions today are weakened, for at the level of statements they are indeed opposing the ongoing neoliberal restructuring of our societies. Programmatically, they are united against privatisation and deregulation of our public services. They agree that people should come before profit in developing our societies. They are united behind a demand for a *just transition* to avoid a climate catastrophe. They are demanding secure jobs, better working conditions, and health and safety at work. All in all, trade unions today have an impressively long list of progressive demands. The problem is that, for many of them, it often stops there. There is a lack of discussions and policies regarding the next step. What do we do after the progressive demands are adopted and made public? How do we reach our goals? Since the actual economic, social, and political developments mainly represent the opposite of our demands, isn't it perhaps time now that we also assess our organisations, our analyses and strategies, our strengths, and weaknesses?

The European trade-union movement is very much engaged in the debate over the kind of Europe that will develop after the pandemic. The ETUC has produced documents and statements lining up its demands for a post-Covid era. In an ETUC note,[13] for example, the Confederation has presented five densely written pages with concrete demands directed to the EU and to the member states. Here too we find an impressive list of progressive demands. Similar documents going in the same direction have been produced by most European and national trade-union organisations. How do we prevent these documents from becoming mere wish lists? What is missing is both a strategy and an identification of agency regarding who is going to carry out the struggle.

## Strategy and agency

One thing is quite clear: unions' comprehensive demands and goals will require deep social and economic transformations, thus obviously involving contradictory class interests. As such, the results will depend on power relations. Thus, broad social alliances will be necessary as well as a massive mobilisation of social forces and mutual solidarity. But as long as large parts of the international trade union movement are stuck in a social-dialogue trap we have a problem.

Judging from my trade-union experience from Norway and Europe, it seems to me that in large parts of the trade-union movement social dialogue has been elevated to the status of an overall strategy to make progress in relation to employers and governments as well as an ideology – a social-partnership ideology that has increasingly been detached from the power relations from which it originally sprang.

My point is not that talking face-to-face with employers is unimportant but rather that this in itself does not give us power. It is the power we represent through our members' ability and willingness to take action that strengthens our position at the negotiating table of the 'dialogue'.

We are criticising unions here for acting as if social dialogue is the primary method of gaining influence in society and in workplaces. Instead of humiliating ourselves by *begging for a seat at the table*, we must direct our resources and policies towards building strong unions with industrial muscle. In today's capitalist society it is quite clear that if you do not represent a potential threat to the employers' interests, you are powerless – with or without social dialogue.

Lockdowns related to Covid-19 have in the short run limited trade unions and other organisations' possibilities for taking action. Industrial actions have therefore been few and far between, although we certainly did see various actions, including wildcat strikes, from groups like care assistants, nurses, ambulance drivers, teachers, laboratory, industrial, and transport workers. Dario Azzellini has studied how class struggles have developed at the global level during the Covid-19 pandemic. He concludes that in spite of problems related to lockdowns, class conflicts have occurred, but they have

> […] tended to start with self-organized workers, with self-organized struggles, grassroots unions with shop-floor organizing, or with new approaches in sections of established unions. […] workers themselves are under more pressure to act, and self-organized struggles from the shop floor can respond faster and in more flexible ways.
>
> In the instances involving the larger, traditional unions, this almost always occurred due to rank-and-file pressure or movements […] The bigger unions mostly avoided actively promoting strikes and struggles on a broad front, or even bringing the subject of general strikes into the discussion at all. Even though conditions differ from country to country, this is not only because conventional unions are often bureaucratized and adhere to the rules of institutionalized industrial action (even if the employers' side does not), hoping to be recognized for mediating between labor and capital. In this regard, 'reliability' in terms of controlling the labor force is as much a part of this as the belief of bearing responsibility for national economies (and their competitiveness). This is especially the case of countries with strongly institutionalized industrial relations, mainly in the global North.[14]

The positive message here is that, for lack of leadership, self-organised workers do organise struggles, and are occasionally also able to pressure larger, traditional unions to take action.

## Demands and struggles

On the question of what sort of society we want coming out of the pandemic, one thing is clear, we do not want a *return to normal*, since the normal was part of the problem. Neither do we need a long wish list of all kinds of things that should have been better in this society. A short list of prioritised demands will do, demands which represent realistic possibilities for which to mobilise and to win – demands with concrete links to workers' everyday realities. Prioritisation must be based on the strength of the actual unions and their ability to mobilise sufficient power to confront our adversaries. The following list could form the basis for a discussion of a revitalisation of trade unions after the pandemic.

- Defend workers' concrete interests through the present crisis (a defensive struggle – including wages and working conditions, collective agreements, labour laws, etc.);
- universal healthcare and upgraded health services;

- an emergency wealth tax for a necessary strengthening of our public services;
- a minimum wage (including platform workers) at the level of a living wage;
- the continuation of the recovery fund *NextGenerationEU*;
- a first step in a radical reduction of working hours;
- international solidarity (we need a redefinition of trade-union internationalism);
- build trade unions, build power.

Of course, the aim must be to move from this defensive, narrow, interest-based struggle to a broader and more ambitious battle over the kind of society we want. This requires moving to more strategic and ambitious demands:

- The Growth and Stability Pact must be abolished – not just suspended;
- no fall-back to the austerity agenda (which is already being advocated by eight EU Member States – among them Austria, the Scandinavian Member States, Latvia, Slovakia, the Netherlands, and the Czech Republic);[15]
- the socialisation of Big Pharma and all health services;
- bringing strategic sectors (like energy, transport, finance) under democratic control and public ownership – also in order to combat climate change;
- putting an end to the free movement of capital and 'free' trade – the introduction of capital controls.

Many trade unions are not prepared for this struggle today. However, even if the Covid-19 pandemic hopefully soon comes to an end, we are still challenged by other crises – including a possible climate catastrophe which calls for workers' mobilisation and struggle. There is an urgent need of action by all trade unions and labour organisations. Why shouldn't we support the clear message proclaimed by the *European Federation of Public Service Unions* (EPSU) at its Executive Committee meeting in November 2020 on the need for co-ordinated actions in the post-pandemic era?

> While major demonstrations are likely to be impossible for some time, joint action will be important and *co-ordinated industrial action* [my emphasis] and other initiatives, including legal action, have to be on the table particularly where trade unions face the same pressures from international institutions, whether the EU, the International Monetary Fund or a new form of Troika.[16]

We should also endorse the statement put forward at one of the digital meetings of the Global Trade Union Assembly (GTUA) which were held between July and September 2021 under the title *Pandemic and Beyond: Workers Organizing for a Public Future*:

> We must use the momentum created by the emergency and the support of the broader population to demand re-nationalisation, re-municipalisation, de-privatisation, re-definition and the sustainable financing of public services as an essential part of ensuring a strong way out of crises and building a new social and economic system based on social and economic justice.[17]

We are living more or less in a state of emergency, but it is a situation which also offers openings and opportunities for trade unions and the political left. However, to move forward we need to shift the balance of power between labour and capital. To that end, we need both to transform our unions and to politicise them.

NOTES

1. ILO Monitor: *COVID-19 and the world of work*, p. 6, sixth edition, <https://www.ilo.org/wcmsp5/groups/public/---dgreports/---dcomm/documents/briefingnote/wcms_755910.pdf>.
2. Ingar Solty, 'The Bio-Economic Pandemic and the Western Working Classes', *The Bullet*, 24 March 2020, <https://socialistproject.ca/2020/03/bioeconomic-pandemic-and-western-working-classes/>.
3. Alfredo Saad-Filho, 'From COVID-19 to the End of Neoliberalism', *Critical Sociology*, 29 May 2020, <https://journals.sagepub.com/doi/full/10.1177/0896920520929966>.
4. Esther Lynch, Making work fit for workers after Covid-19, Social Europe, 24 September 2020, <https://socialeurope.eu/making-work-fit-for-workers-after-covid-19>.
5. Hanna Ziady, 'Covid vaccine profits mint 9 new pharma billionaires', *CNN Business*, 21 May 2021, <https://edition.cnn.com/2021/05/21/businuess/covid-vaccine-billionaires/index.html>.
6. <http://davidharvey.org/2020/03/anti-capitalist-politics-in-the-time-of-covid-19/#more-3209>.
7. 'End the system of private patents! For a pharmaceutical industry under popular control and a free, universal and public vaccination system', <https://www.cadtm.org/End-the-system-of-private-patents>.
8. Sharan Burrow, 'For workers, another year of living dangerously', *Social Europe*, 5 July 2021, <https://socialeurope.eu/for-workers-another-year-of-living-dangerously>.
9. ITUC Press Release, 12 April 2021, <https://www.ituc-csi.org/trade-unions-demands-for-development>.
10. <https://www.etuc.org/en/speech/luca-visentini-speech-informal-epsco-ljubljana-8-july-2021>.

11  Bjarke Skærlund Risager, 'What Is Neoliberalism? (an interview with David Harvey)', *Tribune*, 29 December 2019, <https://tribunemag.co.uk/2019/12/what-is-neoliberalism>.

12  Sam Gindin, 'The Coronavirus and the Crisis This Time', *The Bullet*, 10 April 2020, <https://socialistproject.ca/2020/04/coronavirus-and-the-crisis-this-time/>.

13  <https://www.asktheeu.org/en/request/9226/response/31756/attach/13/Ares%20 2020%202370748%20ETUC%20EU%20Recovery%20Strategy%20for%20the%20 COVID%2019%20outbreak.pdf?cookie_passthrough=1>.

14  Dario Azzellini, 'Class Struggle from Above and from Below during the Covid-19 Pandemic', *Journal of Labor and Society*, August 2021, p. 418-443.

15  Oliver Noyan, 'Post-election Germany: back to austerity or fit for a fiscal union', *Euractive*, 22 September 2021.

16  EPSU, 'Policies for recovery and change in response to the pandemic', p. 15, <https://www.epsu.org/sites/default/files/article/files/EPSU%20Policies%20for%20 recovery%20and%20change%20in%20response%20to%20the%20pandemic%20EC%20 November2020_0.pdf>.

17  <https://slucuny.swoogo.com/gtua2020/534516>.

# Contentious Politics in Critical Emergency Junctures: The Pandemic and Progressive Social Movement Organisations

## Donatella della Porta

On March 2020, after the World Health Organization declared Covid-19 a pandemic and lockdown orders spread all over Europe and beyond, it seemed that the very intense wave of protests that had shaken the world in the fall of 2019, with heightened contestation in arenas as different as Lebanon, Chile, Hong Kong, and Catalonia, were bound to come to a halt. Contrary to these expectations, however, the first stages of the pandemic have been rich in struggles as the health crisis and the other related emergencies triggered intense resistance, with a remobilisation of organisations from previous movements and the emergence of new ones on issues such as social rights, gender rights, and environmental rights, often combined in a call for global health rights.[1]

Contentious politics spread very quickly with various forms of protest addressing the many and dramatic crises triggered by the spread of the virus. While mass media tended to focus on the protests by radical right groups and Covid-deniers, on the progressive side forms of contentious politics multiplied around the increasingly dramatic social problems of the right to housing, income, and education, but also around demands for participation and against repression. While these protests built upon previous moments of global contention – ranging from the global justice movement to the anti-austerity mobilisations but also the resistance to right-wing backlash movements and governments,[2] they also have new features.

Although it did not shut down progressive movements, we would, however, expect that the pandemic would transform them, presenting new challenges as well as new opportunities. In fact, not only has each new wave of protest brought about changes in the forms of action, the organisational models, and the collective framing, but emergency periods also seem to trigger specific dynamics by challenging the assumptions about predictability, and stability on which much theorisation and many strategic choices are based. In this sense, the pandemic, with all its risks and uncertainties, can be read as a moment of 'eventful temporality',[3] which challenges routines and increases the relevance of agency. Thus, previous practices and ideas appear unsuited to address new challenges. In this sense, the Covid-19 pandemic can be read as a critical juncture based on a dramatic emergency.

Moments of emergency – including other health crises, natural disasters, deep economic crises, or wars – have shown that emergencies, while presenting particular challenges also offer opportunities for contentious politics with deep impact on their forms. Since times of emergency are by nature 'understructured and unpredictable', and thus open to contingency, they tend to enhance agency,[4] with a tension between reactive dynamics and emergent norms.

In fact, during the pandemic, progressive social movements have certainly faced challenges connected with the sudden and drastic increase in the suffering of a growing part of the population, the scapegoating of marginal groups, and the shrinking space for collective action. Restrictions on rights to protest, centralisation of power, increasing censorship, and frequent deployment of the military in the streets have certainly shrunk the opportunities for contentious politics. The corona pandemic has been considered

> a social and economic shock as well as a political crisis and a psychological trauma. There was an abrupt end to mobility as, one by one, states imposed lockdowns and quarantines with the result that normal life ceased. Death not life dominated the media for months [...] What at first seemed possible only in a dictatorship became an increasingly accepted way to respond to the danger posed by the coronavirus.[5]

States of emergency have clearly affected political opportunities for social movements, reducing the space for citizens' participation since, 'while emergency rule entails frenetic decision making, its decisions are rationalized as unchosen and unavoidable in substance and timing'.[6]

However, as we have said, the pandemic also opened some opportunities for collective action-enhancing conflicts over scarce resources. Facing the disruption of everyday life, collective action mobilised around immediate needs, and then politicised the surrounding frameworks through coordinated action. As in other emergencies, the more sacrifices were demanded, the louder the demands for citizens' rights became. In addition, the very perception of the failure of existing institutions opened up opportunities for change, while acting together created solidarity. These unsettled times can trigger, or in any case adapt to, what neo-institutionalists call a critical juncture, defined as '(1) a major episode of institutional innovation, (2) occurring in distinct ways, and (3) generating an enduring legacy'.[7] Pandemic times are indeed periods of 'crisis or strain that existing policies and institutions are ill-suited to resolve' – and therefore different from normal politics, when 'institutional continuity or incremental change can be taken for granted'.[8]

But even before the pandemic, recent times have been characterised as momentous: 'great transformation', 'great recession', as well as 'great regression' have been frequently used expressions to define the period following the financial breakdown of 2008 with the considerable mobilisation of so-called 'movements of the crises'.[9] Especially since the Great Recession of the end of the 2000s, social-movement scholars have looked at protests as momentous events in triggering an intensification of the perception of time,[10] as events that were expected to be routine protests but which instead fuelled major momentous waves of contentious politics. In the language of political activism, 'momentum' is often evoked as motion that challenges existing structures, involving massive support and at great velocity.[11] Thus, as in the case of other extraordinary challenges, we can expect that the pandemic will have 'profound effects on the structuring of strategic action fields across society. This is because such crises undermine all kind of linkages in society and make it difficult for groups to reproduce their power', with 'attribution of new opportunities and threats leading to the appropriation or creation of new organizational vehicles for the purpose of engaging in innovative, contentious interaction with other field actors'.[12] Pandemic times open the possibility of building on specific conditions of forced confinement that, for organisers, present challenges but also opportunities resulting from the pressure to do something and the collective feeling of emerging solidarity that is at times stimulated by disasters.[13]

Research on the first stages of the pandemic singled out the capacity of progressive movements to innovate their repertoire of contention, including disruptive protests, but also to build new forms of mutualism and alternative knowledge-building. These mobilisations have been fuelled by existing social-movement organisations, but also by newly emerged groupings and networks, connecting new concerns about the health emergency with a core discourse of social justice and civil rights. Calls for public health and welfare policies were also connected with demands for increased citizens' empowerment. It is precisely these nexuses of protest that seem destined to bring about organisational transformations in progressive contentious politics.

## Grassroots organising in the pandemic as a reconstitution of spaces of sociability

As occurred during the financial crisis that began in 2008,[14] solidarity campaigns grew during the lockdown through a proliferation of initiatives at the local level, arising from the attempt to provide mutual aid among peers as well as in-care activities for the population groups considered to be more in need. Initially groupings of friends and/or neighbours, these initiatives soon started to collaborate with more politicised and structured organisations, among them civil-society organisations that were already involved in solidarity activities and with other social movement organisations present on a certain territory.

At least in the first stages of the pandemic, the importance of the local scale has grown, given the constraints on travelling and meeting with others. In fact, 'social movements start from human needs and our everyday praxis, which already exists but is massively variable'.[15] Faced with immediate needs, 'informal solidarity groups have sprung up to provide such things as cooked hot meals, online vouchers that migrants can use to buy food locally, first aid support and much-needed information on the virus'.[16] As life was disrupted in everyday spaces, responses to the emergency often developed first of all by the affected individuals who acted in solidarity with their neighbours or their peers whom they saw as more in need, providing food and clothes, housing and transportation, medical supplies, and legal assistance:

> ordinary people – those without activist or clearly articulated cooperative political backgrounds and experiences – have shown an empathic response to the suffering of others during the crisis. In such cases, people are motivated to act without having connection to a formal institutional or organisational body. In many cases, involvement begins as simply responding to expressions of need by running errands, empathic listening over the phone or via online connections, or helping to shovel a driveway.[17]

Grassroots forms of mobilisation, often facilitated by digital media, have also developed during labour protests, especially in the least unionised sectors that were often on the frontlines during the pandemic.

Through this grassroots organising, needed collective spaces were reconstituted in innovative ways – for instance, the use of balconies and windows in expressing demands for investment in public health. Balconies and windows became sites of resilience and aggregation at a distance, functioning as a social space for communication, as political and cultural artefacts, and as 'sites of contention'.[18] Especially in the months of the strictest lockdowns, but also in the first reopening as during the Black Lives Matter mobilisation in June-July 2020, protests emerged as self-organised at a very local level, thus indicating the potential for aggregation within physical spaces even during the hardest moments of the first lockdown.

## Networking and alliances in action

Research on the anti-austerity protests has indicated that emergencies are also moments in which intersectional alliances tend to develop out of the very need to provide solutions for urgent problems. During the pandemic the potential for alliance-building emerged in the construction of campaigns around shared concerns, such as housing or health rights. Networks have been built around an idea of solidarity as self-help, which they explicitly contrasted with top-down charity activities, moved mainly by compassion but also around the construction of alternative knowledge, connecting the pandemic to growing social inequalities and environmental exploitation. The conception of the right to health – often framed as the right to care and caring – has provided a master framework for these networks that face the specific needs emphasised by the pandemic.[19] Since the outbreak of the virus, interaction thus spread through intersecting links across different social movement networks with an organisational networking that seems in fact to develop out of the mushrooming of grassroots groups, fuelled by and fuelling a sense of community.

During the pandemic, local groups and grassroots networks born out of emergencies interacted with already existing ones, with some transformations in the organisation of solidarity initiatives. In fact,

> Times of prolonged and profound crisis, like the current pandemic, engender the discovery of a variety of alternative arrangements of protest, mutual aid, solidarity, self-management, self-mobilization and self-organization. The pandemic has introduced a plethora of new technologies for online mobilizations by ordinary people, workers, unions, alliances, and NGOs. […] First, social movements create and reinforce alliances, while building upon existing social and community networks. But also, in practice, movements are about making connections, reinforcing pre-existing associations and solidarities, and reproducing what has already been established as a community's strength in the face of adversity/ies.[20]

With new grassroots groups interacting with more structured ones, the dynamics of organisational appropriation emerged for instance in campaigns around labour issues as strikes grew first spontaneously, which pushed existing unions to then join them.[21]

During the pandemic, there was thus a remobilisation of social-movement organisations that had addressed previous crises, such as the financial crisis and related austerity. In several countries, feminist collectives formed the basis of several organisational innovations in the development of care from below. As *Non una di meno Roma*[22] noted, the new organisational experiences contributed to innovative practices, for instance, around care and caring that became a nexus for several campaigns:

> Care has thus become an experimental field. Moving beyond the enclosed space of the hospital, which, to be sure, is essential at the time of such a sanitary emergency, care has become a matter of diffuse and promiscuous relations, nurtured by networks of intimacy that do not coincide with biological kinship. We need to rethink the forms and the institutions of care beyond heteronormative and patriarchal models that view the individual and the family as the basic units of society.[23]

In addition to the women's groups, environmentalist organisations were pushed by the pandemic challenges to adapt their previous forms of action, expanding their reach and increasing their networking. Especially in the first months of the coronavirus crisis many climate groups made efforts to support local communities and show solidarity with healthcare workers. In particular, environmental groups coordinated with local food banks and supermarkets, delivering supplies to consumers in need or created solidarity funds. In this sense, protests were built upon previous waves of mobilisation, helping to foster further organisational networking.

## Building upon and innovating norms

In sum, the pandemic has seen the development of many activities as organisations assumed many different forms. Pandemic times are certainly challenging for progressive social movements. The many forms of intersectional inequalities risk fragmenting the social bases for progressive politics, while the political positions on the various measures adopted by institutions to contain contagion (from compulsory vaccination to movement restrictions) are still sometimes unclear. At the same time, however, local initiatives all over the world have been able, occasionally, to develop a counter-hegemonic emotional culture against narcissism and individualism.[24]

Covid mutual aid groups mobilised in the thousands,[25] from the bottom up and with major use of new media.[26] Solidarity initiatives created trust and politicised their message,[27] fuelling an alternative sense of community. If the pandemic is a critical juncture, its development implies a series of turning points with the need to quickly adapt strategies and proposals. While we know from historical experiences that moments of emergencies can open opportunities for the development of alternative norms and for citizens' empowerment, they also tell us that this does not come automatically but rather requires broad alliances and innovative thinking.

NOTES

1   Sutapa Chattopadhyay, Lesley Wood, and Laurence Cox, 'Organizing amidst Covid-19', *Interface: a journal for and about social movements* 12,1 (2020), 1-9: 1.
2 · David S. Meyer and Sidney Tarrow (eds), *The Resistance*, Oxford: Oxford University Press, 2019; Donatella della Porta, 'How progressive social movements can save democracy in pandemic times', *Interface: a journal for and about social movements* 12,1 (2020) 355-358.
3   William H. Sewell, 'Three Temporalities: Toward an Eventful Sociology', in Terrence J. McDonald (ed.), *The Historic Turn in the Human Sciences*, Ann Arbor: University of Michigan Press, 1996, pp. 245–80.
4   Mark R. Beissinger, *Nationalist Mobilization and the Collapse of the Soviet State*, Cambridge: Cambridge University Press, 2001; Donatella della Porta, *Where did the Revolution Go?*, Cambridge: Cambridge University Press, 2017.
5   Gerard Delanty, 'Introduction: The Pandemic in Historical and Global Context', in Gerard Delanty (ed.), *Pandemics, Politics and Society – Critical Perspectives on the Covid-19 Crisis*, Berlin: De Gruyter, 2021, p. 1.
6   Jonathan White, 'Emergency Europe after Covid-19', in Delanty, *Pandemics, Politics and Society*, p. 85.
7   David Collier and Gerardo L. Munck, 'Building Blocks and Methodological Challenges: A Framework for Studying Critical Junctures', *Qualitative and Multi-Method Research* 15,1 (2017): 2.
8   Kenneth M. Roberts, *Changing Courses – Party Systems in Latin America's Neoliberal Era*, Cambridge: Cambridge University Press, 2015, p. 65.
9   Donatella della Porta, *Social Movements in Times of Austerity*, Cambridge: Polity Press, 2015; Donatella della Porta and Alice Mattoni (eds), *Spreading Protest: Social Movements in Times of Crisis*, Colchester: ECPR Press, 2014.
10  Donatella della Porta, *Where Did the Revolution Go?: Contentious Politics and the Quality of Democracy*, Cambridge: Cambridge University Press, 2017.
11  Donatella della Porta, *How Social Movements Can Save Democracy: Democratic Innovations from Below*, Cambridge: Polity, 2020.
12  Neil Fligstein and Doug McAdam, *A Theory of Fields*, New York: Oxford University Press, 2015, p. 101.
13  Nicole Curato, *Democracy in Times of Misery*, Oxford: Oxford University Press, 2020.

14   Lorenzo Bosi and Lorenzo Zamponi, *Resistere alla crisi: I percorsi dell'azione sociale diretta*, Bologna, Il Mulino, 2019.
15   Laurence Cox, 'Forms of social movement in the crisis: A view from Ireland', *Interface: a journal for and about social movements* 12,1 (2020): 26.
16   Johanna May Black, Sutapa Chattopadhyay and Riley Chisholm, 'Solidarity in times of social distancing: migrants, mutual aid, and COVID-19', *Interface: a journal for and about social movements* 12,1 (2020): 190.
17   May Black et al.: 182.
18   Carolin Aronis, 'The balconies of Tel-Aviv: Cultural history and Urban Politics', *Israel Studies* 14,3 (2009).
19   Arianna Tassinari, Riccardo Emilio Chesta and Lorenzo Cini, 'Labour conflicts over health and safety in the Italian Covid19 crisis', *Interface: a journal for and about social movements* 12,1 (2020) 128-138.
20   May Black et al.
21   Workers Inquiry Network, *Struggle in a Pandemic A Collection of Contributions on the COVID-19 Crisis*, published by Workers Inquiry Network, Creative Common Licence, 2020, <http://www.intotheblackbox.com/wp-content/uploads/2020/05/Struggle-in-a-Pandemic-FINAL.pdf>; John Krinsky and Hillary Caldwell, 'New York City's movement networks: resilience, reworking, and resistance in a time of distancing and brutality', *Open Democracy*, 2020, <https://www.opendemocracy.net/en/democraciaabierta/new-york-citys-movement-networks-resilience-reworking-and-resistance-in-a-time-of-distancing-and-brutality/>; Jackie Smith, 'Responding to coronavirus pandemic: human rights movement-building to transform global capitalism', *Interface: a journal for and about social movements* 12,1, (2020): 361.
22   The Rome branch of the movement against violence against women, which originated in Argentina in 2015 as 'Ni una de menos'.
23   Non Una Di Meno Roma, 'Life Beyond the Pandemic', *Interface: a journal for and about social movements* 12,1 (2020) 109-114.
24   Tommaso Gravante and Alice Poma, 'Romper con el narcisismo: Emociones y activismo de base durante la pandemia', in Breno Bringel and Geoffrey Pleyers (eds), *Alerta global Políticas, movimientos sociales y futuros en disputa en tiempos de pandemia*, 2020, <http://biblioteca.clacso.edu.ar/clacso/se/20200826014541/Alerta-global.pdf >.
25   Geoffrey Pleyers, 'Echarraiz: futurosalternativos', in Bringel and Pleyers, p. 6.
26   Anastasia Kavada, 'Creating a hyperlocal infrastructure of care: COVID-19 Mutual Aid Groups', Open Democracy, 2020, <https://www.opendemocracy.net/en/openmovements/creating-hyperlocal-infrastructure-care-covid-19-mutual-aid-groups/>.
27   Lesley J. Wood, 'Social movements as essential services', Open Democracy, 2020, <https://www.opendemocracy.net/en/democraciaabierta/social-movements-essentialservices/>.

# Geopolitical Shifts and Conflicts

# MONTHLY REVIEW
## AN INDEPENDENT SOCIALIST MAGAZINE

## MONTHLYREVIEW.ORG
134 W 29th Street, Suite 706 New York, NY 10001

*group solidarity discounts available on our website

transform! europe Peace Manifesto

# Stop the War!
# An Appeal for a Europe of Peace

25 February 2022*

*transform! europe* condemns the attack that Russia, under the governance of Vladimir Putin, has launched against Ukraine. We reject the use of military force against a sovereign state, just as we have previously rejected NATO forces' deployment in countries bordering Russia, and in countries of Asia, Africa, and Europe. **We therefore call for an immediate ceasefire, a stop to the bombing, the withdrawal of Russian troops from Ukrainian soil, and a return to the negotiating table.**

At the same time, we call upon the EU to put maximum effort into reengaging in peace negotiations. In these difficult times, **we stand with the people of Ukraine who are experiencing the Russian attack in full force and whose lives are in danger. We stand in solidarity with the people of Ukraine who are forced to leave their homes**, and we are building networks of solidarity for their support, including providing them with shelter and safety. **We stand with the people in Russia who oppose Putin's war, braving the consequences, as well as the millions of other Europeans who are demanding peace.** The solution to this unjustifiable escalation of military violence is not more violence; the solution is political, based on the principles of common, collective security, concepts which prioritise the well-being of all peoples and the respect of human rights and international law. We join forces with the peace and social movements across the continent to stop this irrational war, we call upon European citizens to take to the streets in the name of peace, and we stand with the people of Ukraine who are forced to leave their homes. **Weapons and wars should belong to the past, the future of Europe and humanity must be peace!**

\* <https://www.transform-network.net/en/blog/article/press-release-stop-the-war-an-appeal-for-a-europe-of-peace/>.

European public opinion, as the Eurobarometer demonstrates in each survey, is overwhelmingly in favour – by more than 85% – of a Europe of peace, human rights, democracy, and without nuclear weapons. This points up the contradiction between people's desires for Europe's future and policy makers' decisions. **The current crisis is an expression of the deep, unresolved contradictions of the European security situation.** Since the end of the Cold War, Europe consists only of capitalist states. There are imperialist contradictions between the states, amplified by their unequal economic and military power.

**We reject any policy that returns us to a policy of blocs and a new Cold War.** We oppose NATO expansion on European soil and its military rhetoric. Europe needs and wants a peaceful path to resolve conflicts.

## NO TO WARMONGERING, YES TO DIPLOMACY

Fighting for peace has been a long tradition in Europe. The radical left has been a pacifist, anti-militarist, and anti-imperialist left since its beginnings. It opposes all chauvinist, racist, neo-colonialist, and war-justifying propaganda of governments, capital, and media. To oppose the creation of enemy images does not mean to approve the policy of a government. We call upon all progressive forces and citizens to raise their voices for de-escalation. We call for an **immediate end of confrontational rhetoric and military action and threats**: By continuing with these tactics, war and military conflict threaten our whole continent and extend the suffering of the peoples of Ukraine. The priority should always be to stop the war.

The peoples of Europe know too well what war and its terrible consequences mean. The EU is currently suffering due to the devastating Covid-19 pandemic and its catastrophic management. We mourn more than 2 million dead over the last two years. The pandemic affects the lives of millions and is reshaping the economies. In this conjunction, **we consider the increase of military expenses, fuelled and justified by the increase of military tensions and warmongering rhetoric, unacceptable**. It is an outrage that during the current lethal pandemic, military expenses increased from 1.63% to 2.2% of the global GDP. Military conflict is not the only challenge to the security of Europe's people. The dire consequences of climate change can already be felt in our continent and both these crises are amplifying structural inequalities in the EU, Europe, and the world. Although not mentioned in most of the international environmental agreements, such as the Paris Climate Agreement, the military-industrial complex is one of the biggest polluters of our planet and war the most devastating strike on nature's integrity. **Valuable resources that could** help eradicate inequalities in the health and social systems of EU countries, as well as promote the renewal and resilience of infrastructure, are spent on the prospect of a prolonged war that would be detrimental to the peoples of the EU and Europe. This has to stop!

## ENDING A NEW COLD WAR TO PREVENT ANY WAR

The opportunity that existed after the end of the Cold War to create a pan-European peace and security system was not seized. On the one hand, NATO continues to exist, tying the security and military policies of 22 of the 27 EU members to the United States; and on the other hand, pan-European and inclusive structures such as the Council of Europe and the Conference on Security and Co-operation in Europe (CSCE) have been marginalised and pushed out of public perception by NATO, the G-7 and the EU itself. **European security policy is in a multiple crisis**. Ukraine is only one of several hotspots where conflict potential is condensing and diplomatic management of individual crises in the acute stage is not sufficient to defuse them. Europe needs a security architecture that fairly considers the interests of all European states. The upcoming 50th anniversary of the CSCE is an opportunity for renewal and a chance to adopt an updated Final Act setting out the cornerstones of European security. In the sense of open diplomacy, peace movements, NGOs, and civil society from all over Europe (and not only the EU) should be involved in the preparation and implementation of the conference not only to shape an accompanying programme, but rather as equal partners.

**Mastering the challenges of the future in peace will only be possible if Europe abandons the Cold War logic of the past and collectively faces the future. The EU needs to start elaborating a new independent security strategy inclusive of its neighbours.** The unbearable costs of war are always paid by the working classes. **The arms industry must no longer enjoy impunity, making millions in revenue while destroying the planet and depriving the youth of their right to a peaceful future.** The youth of Ukraine and Russia are now ripped away from their families and sent to fight in a **war that serves oligarchic interests** and threatens their lives and future. We stand with the families and loved ones of all those drafted into the military because of this irrational war and oppose the patriarchal mindset that invokes violence.

## FOR AN INDEPENDENT EU PEACE AND SECURITY STRATEGY

It is impossible to talk about the strategic autonomy of the EU when the majority of the EU Member States are members of NATO. The development of an EU security policy identity must go hand in hand with the dissolution of NATO and the withdrawal of American troops and especially nuclear weapons. **For an independent EU Peace and Security Strategy and hence a peaceful Europe, the EU must free itself from the security-policy paternalism of the USA. The EU is a global player. It must focus on achieving climate goals, leading a socially just transition from fossil to sustainable energy, realigning its trade policy towards the Global South, and respecting and implementing the UN Refugee Convention in its refugee policy.** The status of neutral and nonaligned members of the EU, as explicitly recognised in the Lisbon Treaty, should be revisited, which expands the EU's diplomatic possibilities of playing a constructive role in the tensions that are now increasing.

We call for a return to international law under the UN as the basis for resolving this conflict. NATO is the only multinational security system that acts on the international stage in violation of the explicit mandate of the Charter of the United Nations. This makes it a threat to peace, as demonstrated by its 'operations', in Europe, Asia, and Africa, which have generated destabilisation, destruction, and setbacks in the full exercise of the social and human rights of people in the areas subjected to intervention.

## EUROPE A NUCLEAR-WEAPON-FREE ZONE

**We demand that all European states join the Treaty on the Prohibition of Nuclear Weapons, as European peoples demand in ample majorities according to any survey that has been conducted on the issue. In addition, we advocate for a nuclear-weapons-free and largely demilitarised zone in the whole of Europe, from the Mediterranean to the Baltic and the Northern Sea as the first step towards a nuclear-weapons-free Europe.**

**We demand that the USA re-enters the Intermediate-Range Nuclear Forces Treaty and that both Russia and the USA refrain from resuming an antagonistic nuclear arms race. A world without nuclear weapons is a safer world for all!**

In short, we call for:

- an immediate stop of the Russian military attack on Ukraine. Respecting the sovereignty of peoples, we reject military action and threats against a sovereign state, as well as any alteration of borders by way of military aggression;
- an immediate stop of warmongering rhetoric and tactics and return to the negotiating table;
- the mediation of the OSCE and the UN in stopping any military action and the deployment of all diplomatic tools within the UN's legal framework, as well as the drafting and implementation of a new peace agreement;
- the EU to take the initiative and propose a broad pan-European conference, including Russia, on peace and collective security, in order to achieve a comprehensive resolution of the crisis in all its dimensions. What was possible during the Cold War at the Helsinki Conference is even more necessary today.
- the EU to resume negotiations on multilateral and comprehensive disarmament, including nuclear and intermediate-range weapons.

We appeal to the people of Europe to stand on strong peace and human rights values, knowing that defending peace is the only way to a sharing world, and that war never resolves conflicts but creates new ones.

# Can We Avert Further Wars?
# The West, Russia, and China in the World of Seismic Shifts

Veronika Sušová-Salminen

In recent years, the international arena has been marked by increasing tension between the great powers, accompanied by growing militarisation – all of this despite the growing climate emergency and Covid-19 pandemic. At present, there are two serious loci of military tension in the world – in the Eastern part of Europe on the borders with Russia and at the Black Sea, and in Asia in the South China Sea. Both places are potential foci of conflict between the great powers with unpredictable but most likely devastating consequences. In the eastern part of Europe, Russia, the USA, and the European Union have failed to create an inclusive security system after the end of the Cold War. The expansion of NATO up to the immediate borders of Russia became an expression of military and security competition between the West and Russia. Now, we can already safely conclude that NATO's enlargement did not bring security to Europe; on the contrary, it has created a spiral of security dilemmas.[1]

In Asia, the rise of China has been in the making during the last four decades. China was able to rebuild its economy and renew its regional as well as global ambitions. During the recent decade, China – a country ruled by its communist party – began to exhibit many of the features of a modern great power, including a growing technological edge and one of the world's major armies and navies. The Belt and Road Initiative has shown very clearly that China has truly global ambitions and interests, which include a new concept of development (which the West abandoned after the Cold War), a new emphasis on geopolitics, which involves infrastructure and resources, and, finally, a clear ambition to boost its economy for the future.

This article seeks to better understand the causes of the crisis in relation to Russia in Europe as well as the rise of China in Asia (and globally) in the context of the global financial crisis in 2007/2008 and its outcomes. The crisis shook the pillars of Western hegemony and sealed already ongoing changes in the political economy of the global system. It undermined the ideological underpinning of Western hegemony, including austerity capitalism and West-centric neoliberal globalisation, and it caused a serious crisis in international institutions and their established practices. Moreover, it cast doubt on the prestige of the US as a global leader with a credible vision for the future, opening the way to what Gramsci called an *interregnum*, which is typified by the dysfunction of established institutions and practices on the one hand, and by increased ideological polarisation and uncertainty on the other hand. Thus, the consequences of the crisis are long-term – the global financial crisis was organic and systemic rather than being just another one of capitalism's conjunctural crises. It means that the dysfunctions and contradictions of the system can themselves be a transformative force for its supersession.[2]

The political responses of the big powers to the economic crisis did not manifest all at once, but when they did they created geopolitical tensions. In 2013, China declared its intention to build a new Silk Road Economic Belt, and at the same time it began the construction of buildings on the disputed territories of the Spratly Islands and the Paracel Islands in the South China Sea. In 2014, China became the biggest world economy in terms of public-private partnerships, surpassing the US economically, with prospects of becoming the biggest economy in the world. This indicator just confirms the general trend towards the new centre of gravity of capitalism located not in the Atlantic world, but in Asia with China at its centre.[3] Russia intervened in Ukraine and annexed Crimea, reinforcing at the same time its strategic military potential vis-à-vis US, and declaring its insubordination to Western hegemony while proclaiming its own national interests and civilisational uniqueness. Both these events can be seen as challenges to the post-Cold War order (or the 'liberal international order', according to some).

The Western reaction to the shifting geography of global capitalism and the global financial crisis was belated and mostly misjudged. It was also complicated by the continuous political crisis at home. In the economic and social policy sphere, the Western democracies largely relied on austerity measures and the socialisation of private debts (while profits remained notoriously privatised). This misinterpretation of the crisis and its impacts brought with it not only grave social impacts but also political implications for Western democracies. The rise of populism in the West suggested that there is something rotten at the core of Western liberal democracies, while at the same time there is an increasing demand for change. The global financial crisis also became the crisis of the democratic system, with the Western establishment refusing to offer any serious programme for substantial change within the neoliberal paradigm that is based on the strategic separation of economy from *democratic* politics.[4] Moreover, the crisis of Western democracy amplified by the global financial crisis was too often seen merely as an external problem, caused by a disobedient Russia.

Instead of reforming the economic and social policies of the bankrupt neoliberal model, the West developed three principal strategies: military expansion – especially through NATO – the ideological contestation of its competitors, and the externalisation of its internal problems. Nevertheless, these strategies must be seen for what they really are – the morbid symptoms of the dying system within the ongoing *interregnum*.

## Expansion, contestation, and externalisation of problems as morbid symptoms

The crisis of relations with Russia cannot be understood outside of the enlargement (in other words, expansion) process of NATO and the EU in Eastern Europe. While Russia perceived the EU enlargement quite neutrally until 2013, the expansion of NATO was seen as a negative process affecting Russian security since the early 1990s.[5] Moreover, the expansion of NATO appeared to be in direct conflict with the spirit of the peaceful end of the Cold War in Europe. From an irritant for a weak Russia in the 1990s, NATO expansion turned into a serious problem seen as a 'threat' to the consolidated Russia of the twenty-first century.[6] The events in Ukraine in 2013/14, which internationalised a domestic political crisis, paved the way for potential NATO membership of Ukraine, which is in the immediate neighbourhood of Russia. They also helped to legitimise NATO's purpose and the increase of its own budget as well as its members' budget lines for defence to as much as 2% of GDP. Furthermore, the Ukrainian slogan 'Revolution of Dignity' also meant a rejection of the Russian-led Eurasian integration programme which was modelled largely on the EU and tried to economically integrate the greater part of post-Soviet space, maintaining Russia's role as a regional hegemon. In this sense, the European Union expansion inevitably clashed with Russian ambitions in the economic sphere.

Nevertheless, the potential danger of Ukraine becoming a member of NATO was much more serious, and it led to the annexation of Crimea (which Russia viewed as the 'unification of Crimea'), intervention in eastern Ukraine, and finally the Russian attack on Ukraine. Despite the patriotic legitimisation of these measures, its real purpose was strategic and security driven. Russian behaviour was unilateral but in fact it was just mirroring the practices of the US, which has quite often exhibited a disrespect for international law while openly (militarily) interfering in the sovereignty of other states or polities to enforce US security or economic interests. In relation to Russia, the US simply reached the tipping point – Russia ceased to respect the specific position of the US as the one and only global hegemon that is allowed to break and enforce the rules at the same time. In fact, Russia claimed its own privileges in this respect.

The crisis in Ukraine opened the whole Pandora's box of problems that have been in the making over the last two decades. They were also often not seen in relation to the global financial crisis as well as to a failed US 'unilateral moment'. First, the domestic political crisis in Ukraine was related to the enormous economic problems of Ukrainian oligarchic capitalism amplified by the local version of the crisis. Second, the EU accession process – in the form of an association agreement which benefited mostly European and Ukrainian capital – together with the change of political regime in Kyiv to one with a strong pro-EU rhetoric and narrative, was a good solution to the actual internal crisis of the European project. In short, while the southern European member states were subjected to coercive Europeanisation with new austerity measures destroying their welfare and public spheres and obliterating the promises of convergence, the pictures from Maidan Square in Kyiv with a sea of EU flags confirmed the attractiveness of very same EU with the very same convergence promises. This was largely how the events in Kyiv have been presented in the European political mainstream. Developments in Ukraine also strengthened the tendency of the EU to project not a seeming 'soft power' but a 'narrow power' in Karl Deutsch's sense. Of narrow power Deutsch says: 'Power in this narrow sense is the priority of output over intake, the ability to talk instead of listen. In a sense, it is the ability to afford not to learn.'[7] In terms of its stated aim, EU policy towards Eastern Europe was completely unsuccessful in Ukraine since it failed to achieve its main proclaimed objectives – to promote stability and peace.

The ideological contestation very quickly became a next strategy to defuse the growing contradictions and problems. More precisely, it became the answer for the crumbling hegemony which is explicitly or implicitly questioned not only by Russia and China, but also from within the Western societies. The conditions of interregnum suggest the co-existence of different and competing hegemonic projects at the same time. One of the key features of this interregnum is that it is rather post-liberal (especially in the Western context where illiberal tendencies, unlike those in Russia or China, are rooted in the experience of liberalism) meaning that classical liberalism is increasingly challenged ideologically by the dissenting movements and structurally by great powers.[8] The Western establishment reacted to this new situation that challenges its sources of status and power with increasing ideological consolidation (which undermines the key principles of liberalism such as diversity of opinion and tolerance) at home. Furthermore, it gradually formulated the new narrative about the battle between democracy and autocracy. Recently, the Biden administration organised a 'summit for democracy' (December 2021) which was aimed at using the democratic narrative in order to legitimise and enforce the leading role of the US in world affairs, especially in view of its competition with China. Once again, actual practice undermined the normative dimension of the US's foreign policy because the real selection of invitees was dictated not by their quality of democracy but by narrower US interests. The inconsistency between rhetoric and reality is nothing unusual for the great powers but in the case of the US it is contextualised by the prolonged crisis of US leadership/hegemony amplified again by the global financial crisis and the Trumpist reaction to it.

This ideological contestation based on the narrative 'democracy versus autocracy' is yet another nostalgic strategy of the West since it helps resurrect ghosts of the Cold War. First, it shows that the West is very comfortable with black-and-white narrative despite its rhetorical adherence to liberalism. Second, nostalgia is often an unmistakable symptom of decline and inability to adapt to new conditions and new challenges. This narrative is largely off-base when it puts Russia and China in the same box, for it lacks strategic depth and misunderstands both countries and their interests.

Finally, the third Western strategy for dealing with current challenges is externalisation of its problems. This helps avoid grappling with these problems because their solution would undermine the position, prestige, and power of the shareholders of neoliberal capitalism. Therefore, the crisis of Western democracy and the populist movements, illiberalism, or social conservative reaction but also the rise of conspiracy theories, distrust and misinformed irrationality in the public sphere are presented not as what they are – that is the consequences of neoliberalism, individualism, and commodification of everything with their destructive effects on the West's society, polity, and welfare. Rather they are seen as something alien, imported, and as such these problems are pushed *outside*. Therefore, it is Russia or China that are sources of 'hybrid threats' for Western democracies rather than oligarchy, rent-seeking, broken welfare and educational systems, and the lost link between representatives and the represented. Thus Donald Trump's election as US president was thought to be possible only because Russia interfered in the

American election process. Or responsibility for practically any dissenting opinion can be very easily and erroneously assigned to Russia and China so that the exchange of opinions is increasingly submitted to the logic of conflict. Furthermore, a new, very dangerous mystification is created – the illusion that geopolitical victory over Russia and China would somehow solve these problems.

These reactions reinforce each other, but they are also instrumentalised in the increasingly pronounced great power competition whose key dynamism, however, is not ideological, but structural – the transformation from a US-led unipolar order to a multipolar world order with increasingly non-Western features.

## Russia and China: What type of challenge?

Russia and China are very different types of actors in the current interregnum. First, Russia can be seen as a post-liberal regional hegemon seeking to enforce its position in post-Soviet space at any cost. Russia's key strategy is defensive and conservative. In terms of economy, education, human capital, innovations, or welfare, Russia does not offer an attractive domestic model or systemic alternative. Economically and demographically, rather, Russia is in decline, which means that Putin's strategy is very much engaged in 'braking' the decline but not in reversing it – for which Russia today lacks sufficient capacity.

Russia wants to maintain its great power status as a key to national survival. To be a great power is nothing less than *the* existential question for Russian political thinking. Therefore, the expansion of Western institutions in its immediate vicinity is read as an effort to undermine its status in its backyard. At the international level, Russia is engaged in what has been called a neo-revisionist strategy: Russia sees the United Nations with its Security Council and international law as a viable platform for a multipolar order. However, Russia challenges the actual implementation of international norms and governance – which have since the end of Cold War been largely based on US unilateralism. As Richard Sakwa suggests: 'Russia's neo-revisionism represents a critique of western practices in defence of the universal proclaimed principles. It is not the principles of international law and governance that Russia condemns but the practices that accompany their implementation.'[9] In short, Russian neo-revisionism challenges US hegemony and its practices rather than the international organisations on which this international system was built. However, it insists on Russia's equal partnership with the US and other European powers, and it also claims its own right to contribute to the definition of the rules. In other words, for

Russia, 'universalist' is not tantamount to 'Western'.

The clash with Russia was permitted because of the failure of the West, or the EU and the US, to integrate Russia into post-Cold War Europe through a shared vision. This is paradoxical because the early integration of Russia into the newly created security system would probably not have drastically challenged either the EU project or Western hegemony as a whole. But in the current situation alienation of Russia and her neo-revisionism do challenge Western hegemony. Here we can argue that Western 'narrow power' contributed to the crisis of relations with Russia turning Moscow – unnecessarily – into a geopolitical rival in Europe.

China is on a very different trajectory. First, despite the communist ideology on which the modern Chinese state is based, its rise is a central effect of its integration into the global capitalist economy. This makes China less of an ideological challenger while it neutralises its potential as a systemic challenger, in comparison with the USSR during the Cold War. But China perhaps unwittingly challenges one of the Western key assumptions – the link between democracy and economic prosperity. Non-Western Communist China is on the rise, which transforms it into an emerging regional hegemon (which it was until the 1800s) and a great power at the global level. In terms of economy and technology, but also of military potential, China can keep pace with the West and, in particular, with the US. Moreover, it has a serious chance of overcoming it in the not-so-distant future. Thus China's potential goes beyond that of regional hegemony.

China's global rise is also historically unique, and this implies a revision of the international system. As Oskar Krejčí puts it:

> China's entry into the globalized world system as a sovereign power represents a geopolitical turning point that changes the entire world order. A period of searching for new rules of world politics and economics has begun. In this situation, the most prestigious models of behaviour of great powers with which Western international political theory works perceive China's growing capabilities as the basis of inevitable international conflicts. Given the fact that these visions have a big impact on the behaviour of the West's power elites, they have an encoded tendency to become a self-fulfilling prophecy.[10]

Meanwhile China represents a rising power with a very specific strategic culture, one which cannot be understood simply by means of Eurocentric assumptions. This is a very important point because although China acts within the Western-dominated international system it has at the same time a unique orientation, which explains its interests, decisions, and aims. It is clear that the 'narrow power' approaches prevalent among Western policy makers and analysts will mislead them in understanding China.

The selective cooperation of Russia and China is not a reflection of similar ideologies, regime preferences, or political cultures. It is much more based on their pragmatic interests, which are security-related, strategic, rather than merely economic.[11] On the other hand, their cooperation is also possible because Moscow and Beijing realise where their weak points or potential sources of conflict are located. This type of pragmatism is something that the Western great powers and Russia failed to practice in their relations after the Cold War. To lump Russia and China together merely as 'autocratic' is a huge mistake that reveals a very dangerous ideological bias. The West's ideological explanation of its thrust against Russia and China is based on the non-differentiation between an economic power and a military great power having its own capacity to use nuclear weapons from the air, the land, and the sea. In short, Western strategy of competing with China and Russia at the same time brings them together and makes them stronger. This is not a rational strategy.

However, Russia and China share quite important characteristics. They are both *outsiders* in the Westphalian (Eurocentric) international system, for both countries were integrated into it at a later stage. To be an outsider means, as Ayşe Zarakol has shown, 'to have an ontologically insecure relationship with the West'.[12] Integration into the Eurocentric international system was accomplished through imported institutions and practices as a composite part of transition to modernity based on the adaptation, imitation, and borrowing of Western models (combining them with domestic characteristics) in the context of outsider states. But hierarchies built into the modern international system still play an important role. Zarakol argues that a state's outsider status means that it will be stigmatised. Such stigmatised states act on the basis of their outsider status; it structures their behaviour in the international system. This is very important for understanding the sources of Russian and perhaps also Chinese conduct. Zarakol puts it neatly: 'Social standards masquerading as objective assessment create and perpetuate power hierarchies, and this is why the stigmatisation framework is particularly apt for describing relations in the modern international system.'[13] In short, these are the key sources of Russia's and China's unequal position, and partial causes of their neo-revisionist critique of the West which also reflects their outsider status.

The West is trying to stigmatise Russia and China by narratives built on the ideas of liberal institutionalism. According to this theory of international relations, peace is achievable through the uniformity of domestic political institutions by creating a world of a kind of democracy defined according to Western criteria and norms. The promotion of democracy is the way in which peace, it is thought, can be achieved in the long term. Cooperation is supposed to be conditioned by the democratic type of regime. Once again, social standards existing in Western societies and historically emerging in European contexts are seen as an objective (neutral) standard for others. The non-Western, or better, hybrid character of Russia's and China's domestic political systems,[14] designed to manage extremely diverse societies and geographically large states with their specific types of political economy, is being weaponised by the West for purposes of geopolitical power struggles. The narrative about the recent clash between democracy and autocracy does not just preserve the existing hierarchies, with Russia and China stigmatised and 'the West' at the top of the pyramid; it is also designed to exclude them from the international system as illegitimate actors despite their structural importance and weight. In this way, domestic regimes have become spaces for geopolitical contestation while the principle of sovereignty and political autonomy (both very Western innovations) is put at serious risk without it being compensated by any viable structures of true global governance.

## Conclusion

For Western hegemony, the global financial crisis had major political and economic impacts. At stake in the crisis was the entire model of neoliberal globalisation which has been the main paradigm of historical development between 1989 and 2008. The crisis helped to radically shift the global political economy and made the systemic contradictions and dysfunctions more visible. The neoliberal hegemonic project's grip was weakened, but it is still alive as an "alternative" within the status quo backed by Western elites and their non-Western allies around the world. However, the shifts in the political economy inevitably brought important political and international changes. In the international system there are currently new imbalances which reflect the increasing importance of China and relative decline of the US.

The 'unilateral moment' of the US has ended with the crushing of US-led financialised capitalism and due to a series of challenging events which interweave political economy with security, geopolitics, and ideological or hegemonic dimensions. The US is challenged by an ascendant China and a disobedient Russia due to the failure of the 'unilateral moment' within the recent interregnum. Russia and China, however, are not identical types of actors with the same importance and identical interests. Their cooperation is largely pragmatic, which is also the crucial attribute for both great powers in successfully managing their differences and the growing asymmetry in their mutual relations. The increasing pressure from the US is forcing Russia and China to deepen their cooperation, a cooperation which, however, does not reflect any commonly pronounced ideological anti-Westernism or the 'autocratic' nature of both countries. It is foremost structurally produced by pressures, imbalances, and changes in the international system. As I argued, the US and its allies in the Western world mostly believe that they can contain Russia and China using old recipes and without any substantial changes at home. This situation is creating very significant tension which might have quite counterproductive effects. Be that as it may, it increases the risks of military conflict at the same time.

There is great need now for an international peace movement, which had historically been one of the pillars of left movements and parties. The left in the EU should use its analytical muscle to provide better understanding of important changes and shifts, promoting dialogue and formulating alternatives. Great power competition—in any of its forms and whatever the 'good' purposes or intentions it is thought to have – must be contained and must be explained to the populations without recourse to simplistic ideological slogans rather than being supported or cheered. This may sound like a simple or even banal task, but simple or banal it is not.

## NOTES

1   About this concept for example: Robert Jervis, Cooperation under the Security Dilemma, in *World Politics* 30,2 (January 1978): 167-214.
2   Milan Babic, Let's talk about interregnum: Gramsci and the Crisis of Liberal World Order, *International Affairs* 96,3 (2020): 767–786.
3   Compare with Andre Gunder Frank, *ReOrient. Global Economy in the Asian Age*, Berkeley-Los Angeles-London: University of California Press, and the Price-Waterhouse-Cooper Report, *The Long View. How will the global economic order change by 2050?*, online at <pwc-world-in-2050-summary-report-feb-2017.pdf>.
4   Quinn Slobodian, *Globalists. The End of Empire and the Birth of Neoliberalism*, Cambridge (Mass.): Harvard University Press, 2018.
5   Andrei P. Tsygankov, The sources of Russia's fear of NATO, in *Communist and Postcommunist Studies*, 2018,1-11.
6   Veronika Sušová-Salminen, *Inclusive European Security? Russia and the EU in the Post-Western World*, epaper: tranform!europe 2017, <https://www.transform-network.net/publications/issue/inclusive-european-security-russia-and-the-eu-in-the-post-western-world/>.
7   Karl Deutsch, *Nerves of Government. Models of Political Communication and Control*, New York: Free Press, 1963, p. 111.
8   Marlene Laruelle, 'Making Sense of Russia's Illiberalism', *Journal of Democracy*, 31,3 (July 2020): 115-129.
9   Richard Sakwa: Russian Neo-Revisionism in *Russian Politics*, 4,1 (2019): 1-21.

10  Oskar Krejčí, *Geopolitika Číny*, Praha: Professional Publishing, 2021, 452-453.
11  Alexander Lukin, *China and Russia: The New Rapprochement*, London: Polity, 2018.
12  Ayşe Zarakol, *After the Defeat. How the East Learned to Live with the West*? Cambridge-New York: Cambridge University Press, 2011, p. 30.
13  Zarakol, *After the Defeat*, p. 64.
14  Compare for example with Ivar Neumann and Einar Wigen, *The Steppe Tradition in International Relations: Russians, Turks and European State Building 4000 BCE-2017 CE*. Cambridge: Cambridge University Press 2018.

# China and Europe in the Foreseeable Future

## Jan Campbell

It is likely that today's political, social, financial, and value transformations, as well as military conflicts in a variety of countries and regions will reinforce the longer-term shifts in international relations that have been underway for more than a decade, and were already amplified by the responses to the Covid-19 pandemic. Post-pandemic, the old props of American world leadership and globalist institutions were already showing increasing signs of wear. However, the Russian war in Ukraine as well as the erosion of the American world order are both likely to continue; and, even more dangerously, a geopolitical interregnum is therefore now in the cards. This indicates a protracted period when the world is neither fully at war nor fully at peace, and where, in place of genuine cooperation, conflict and confrontation become the norm.

While today's military confrontation appears to revive US leadership of the old West, because of its military dominance, in the longer term it is likely to speed up the shift to a post-American world, with China steadily building its own powers and global authority. At this stage of the Ukrainian crisis it seems probable that Beijing will be one of the few winners. By stating its support for Ukrainian state sovereignty, while refusing to join the West's provocative demonisation of Putin and Russia in general, the Chinese approach is more likely to win allies and influence than that of the US, given Washington's dangerous provocations in the build-up to the war, while declaring it had no intention of entering into direct combat.

The outcome of the war is likely to speed up the regionalisation of the world into US-led and Chinese-led blocs. Whether Europe will be an independent region or a junior adjunct to the US remains to be seen. The EU is not able to resolve the dilemma of how much 'strategic autonomy' it can construct, and how much it will remain dependent on the US' declining but still formidable economic, technological, and military power. This uncertainty about the role of European nations within the changing world order is in itself symptomatic of a potentially fluid and shifting global set of international arrangements and of potential regional wars.

In economic and financial terms the world economy's rebalancing towards China and East Asia could gain further momentum as a result of any war and of the weakness of the EU. US efforts to economically 'decouple' China from the West have already been backfiring by reinforcing Beijing's focus on building up its own technological, financial, and productive capabilities, autonomously and through Asian regionalisation. It could well turn out that today's Western actions to 'decouple' Russia also end up enhancing China's position in the world.

Years of ill-considered Western power games and posturing against Moscow and Beijing have been bringing the People's Republic of China (PRC) and the Russian Federation (RF) closer together, despite their lack of ideological affinity. The initial modest Western sanctions imposed on Russia after the Crimean annexation in 2014, and now the much harsher sanctions, have been forcing Russia to turn increasingly to China as an alternative market and financial and trading partner. While this might provide some sort of financial lifeline to Moscow in the short term, in the longer run it is likely to strengthen Chinese regional and Eurasian influence at the expense of the West. Any medium-term diversion of Russian fossil-fuel flows from Europe to China would be an added bonus for Beijing.

## China's economic growth

Last year China's GDP reached over 110 trillion RMB yuan. Continued growth would be growth from a high base. Experience and the latest trends show that it will not be easy for such a big economy to maintain a medium-high growth rate. Western economists say that a 5.5% GDP growth target for this year is quite ambitious.[1]

At a press conference Chinese Premier Li was asked whether a 6% GDP growth target was a bit too modest. He responded that he was aware of the possibility of even faster economic growth because of the previous year's low base but that the 'government still decided to set the growth target at above 6%, in order to leave open possibilities for even faster growth, say, 8%.[2]

The Chinese government set macroeconomic policies, including fiscal, monetary, and employment policies against this 6% GDP growth target. It cut the deficit-to-GDP ratio, steadily lowered the macro leverage ratio and followed the same approach in 2020. The government refused to flood the economy with mass stimulus or excessive money supply. As a result, despite the high inflation worldwide, China's consumer price index rose less than

1% from last year to February this year.

My view is that this has very much to do with the reasonable macroeconomic policies shaped by China's specific national conditions. A comparative study or analysis of macroeconomic policies carried out by think tanks such as transform! europe could be very helpful in this regard.

## Economy, history, and the present

Last year, the PRC successfully achieved its major annual goals and tasks for economic and social development and laid a good foundation for development this year. This year so far has been characterised by new downside pressures, challenges, complexity, and rising uncertainty, all linked to inflation, high prices, sanctions, and the risk of a larger war.

With China's GDP exceeding 100 trillion yuan, a 5.5% increase would generate the amount of output equivalent to the size of a medium economy. Ten years ago, when China's GDP was just over 50 trillion yuan, even a 10% growth would only add some 6 to 7 trillion yuan of output. But this year, even with a lower growth rate, the figure would reach 9 trillion yuan in nominal GDP.

Premier Li used the analogy of climbing a 1,000-metre-high mountain, in which covering 10 % of the height means a distance of 100 metres. But in climbing a 3,000-meter-high mountain, 5 % of the height will already be 150 metres. Moreover, the higher one climbs, the lower the air pressure and oxygen content. So, the growth may look slower now, but it actually carries more weight.

The PRC aims to achieve about 5.5% growth this year to ensure the steady performance of the Chinese economy at a high level. To achieve this goal will not be easy, and it would need the support of a series of macro policies. The government, for example, has lowered the deficit-to-GDP ratio to 2.8 % this year, a decrease of more than 200 billion yuan over last year. At the same time, it plans to beef up government spending this year.[3]

## Strategic and tactical aspects

On 11 March of this year, Premier Li answered several questions as follows:

> We will draw on the savings that we didn't tap into over the last two years, meaning we will use the surplus profits of state-owned financial institutions and state monopoly business operations and funds transferred from the Central Budget Stabilization Fund. In total, government spending this year will rise by no less than 2 trillion yuan. Most of it will be used for tax and fee reductions, particularly tax refund, just like providing oxygen supply for mountain climbers. At the same time, we will roll out a series of supportive

financial and pro-job measures too.

Our policies set for this year are not just aimed at addressing immediate needs. They also take into account long-term development needs. They will not sacrifice future interests and are therefore sustainable. […] China is still faced with a series of challenges, such as climate change, income gap, and debt. We need to forcefully respond to them this year and in a medium-to-long run. The measures required are being worked on. China's modernization is a long process. We need to address issues arising in the course of development through development.[4]

Against the backdrop of China's strategy, it would, in my view, be a worthwhile project to address national and EU strategies, asking how serious they are and comparing their content and context within the EU at least.

## Conflict in Ukraine and the relations between the PRC and Ukraine

In his 11 March press conference, Premier Li stated the following official positions:

1) China is deeply concerned and grieved. We sincerely hope that the situation will ease and peace will return at an early date. China has all along followed an independent foreign policy of peace, and never targets third parties in our bilateral ties. We want to develop cooperation with all countries on the basis of mutual respect and mutual benefit, to bring greater stability to today's world.

2) China follows an independent foreign policy of peace. Regarding the situation in Ukraine, China believes that the sovereignty and territorial integrity of all countries should be respected, the purposes and principles of the UN Charter should be observed, and the legitimate security concerns of all countries should be taken seriously. On that basis, China makes its own assessment, and is prepared to work with the international community to play a positive role for an early return to peace.

3) The high priority now is to prevent the tense situation from escalating or even getting out of control. There is consensus about this among the international community, including the parties concerned. China calls for exercising utmost restraint and preventing a massive humanitarian crisis. China has put forward an initiative for responding to the humanitarian situation in Ukraine. China has provided Ukraine with humanitarian assistance, and will continue to do so.[5]

As of now the main beneficiary of the conflict in Ukraine is the PRC. The second beneficiary would be the US and the biggest loser has to be the EU. As far as the Russian Federation is concerned, the possible benefits of the conflict, at least from the initial calculations of its ruling elite, lie in the fields of its security (for example, in ruling out NATO membership for Ukraine), in its society, in which the aim is to at least partially cleanse it of what it regards as its 'fifth column' (in the press, media and entertainment, in the Ministry of Education, the Foreign Office and also the military and secret services, and in the banking system as well as in the strategic industries), and of sections of the oligarchy that might blur Putin's appeal to the Russian population.

In global terms I would expect an acceleration of the processes of political, cultural, scientific and financial segregation in the world, thus an increased need to know how to conduct a dialogue, what shared values and a shared future mean, and, last but not least, the increasing importance of holistic knowledge and education, including politics.

A useful research project would be a comparative study of official statements (of the UN, of the ministries of foreign affairs, the governments, and militaries of the major economies), media presentations (for foreign and domestic audiences), and public feedback and reactions within the government controls and restrictions recently imposed by the PRC, the European Commission, and selected member states of the EU.

## The policy of the National Institute for Finance and Development (NIFD)

Officially, China's NIFD states that cuts in fees help small businesses and could be followed by tax cuts. On 11 March Premier Li said:

> Our practices in recent years show that tax and fee cuts have worked most directly. I recall that last year I had a conversation with a dozen business representatives in an eastern province. They talked about their corporate difficulties and their hope for more macro policy support from the government. I said that the central government had policies in reserve, yet we need to use them in an integrated way. I gave them three options to pick one they preferred the most. They are, massive investment, which will help them get orders; the second is handing out consumption vouchers to boost consumer spending; and the third is tax and fee reductions for enterprises to stabilize employment and boost investment and consumption. They were only quiet for a moment and almost unanimously chose the third policy option, because they believed it would work most directly in a most equitable and efficient

way. Many reports I have received this year also take tax and fee cuts as the number one aspiration for the government's macro policies. Indeed, fertilizer needs to go to the root. When the root is strong, the plant can grow well.[6]

In contrast to this view, some people and analysts worry that tax and fee reductions have been in place for several years and that with the marginal effect of this policy fading away, the reductions will not work as well as they had.

This year the Chinese government intends to combine tax and fee reductions with massive tax refunds, totalling approximately 2.5 trillion yuan. It must be said that it was through such strong policies that the PRC pulled through very difficult times in 2020. Recently, the government has made some adjustments, and a tax refund will be the policy highlight in 2022. The current VAT code would require tax collection first and tax refunds later for enterprises. This year the government will refund the existing overpaid VAT credits in advance in a lump sum worth 1.5 trillion yuan.

Since 2013, with the reform of VAT, the government has cut taxes by 8.7 trillion yuan. Back in 2013, the PRC's fiscal revenue was about 11 trillion yuan, but by 2020, with the great increase in productivity, fiscal revenue exceeded 20 trillion yuan, nearly double the amount in 2013. In this process, businesses have truly benefited and improved their performance. It is like building a deeper pool to farm more fish. The tax refunds and fee cuts have helped create more sources of tax revenue and nurture business growth.

It seems to me to be a matter of fact that local governments within the PRC face new difficulties in their fiscal revenues, but it is also true that the central government is aware of this. This is indicated by its plan for a 18% increase in transfer payments to local governments, which totals 9.8 trillion yuan, an unusually high amount. As most tax refunds will be financed by the central government, and a certain amount will also be shared by local governments, I believe the policy has a good chance of success.

Priority is to be given to micro and small firms in the refunding of VAT credits because these firms cover a wide range of sectors and provide many jobs. Currently, many of them are financially strapped and are in great difficulty. A similar situation exists in most members states of the EU. In my view, their governments need to follow the old adage: *Getting one concrete thing done is more important than making a thousand promises*.

In terms of Europe, in this light one might well ask what the current state of affairs of the SME sector is in Germany, Italy, and the Czech Republic after two years of Covid-19, and what would the situation of the SME sector be in two years, by the end of 2024, with the current sanction policies. It could be well to study these scenarios using China's policy, methods, and results as a reference.

## Employment

Examples of challenges and useful lessons for the EU drawn from China's experience are:

1) In 2020, during the Covid-19 pandemic, the Chinese government decided not to set a GDP growth target but to set the target of new urban jobs at above 9 million. As a result, over 11 million new urban jobs were created. China's economic growth remained positive, and reached 2.2%. Its economy was the only one among major economies to achieve positive growth.
2) This year we will see a record high increase of new job seekers coming into the PRC's labour force, totalling some 16 million. There will be 10.76 million students graduating from college, another record high.
3) Jobs are needed for some 300 million rural migrant workers. Jobs also need to be provided to relatively young but retired government and administrative employees. And due to business insolvency some people are waiting for re-employment. There is a steady increase in the urban labour force, and new platforms of employment need to be created.
4) Over 200 million people in China are now engaged in flexible employment, which takes multiple forms and covers a wide range of sectors. This kind of employment will long exist not only in a developing country like China. Many of the people in flexible employment are express delivery service providers. The governments should improve policies related to their labour rights and interests as well as social protection.[7]

## The currency issue

I believe that the process of geopolitical segregation is increasing in speed and depth and cannot be stopped or re-directed by peaceful means, and that for the foreseeable future this will lead to the replacement of the USD as the key currency, to trade payments in other currencies like the yuan, rouble, or rupee and the implementation of alternative payment systems using even digital and similar forms of currencies. Examples from the PRC, RF, and elsewhere in the world should therefore be studied in detail. Consequently, it may well be that today's crisis will precipitate the end of the dollar as the world currency.

Ray Dalio, who runs the largest hedge fund in the world, explained in his recent widely praised book, *Principles for Dealing with the Changing World*

*Order*,⁸ that functioning as the global reserve currency is one of the greatest powers a dominant country can exercise. It confers enormous borrowing and buying capacity on the hegemon and ultimately underpins its geopolitical power.

Therefore, it is worth considering the history of the reserve-currency role of the US dollar, as with Britain's pound sterling before it. History demonstrates that this is one of the assets that a declining hegemon is slowest to lose. This is so, in the current case, because so many countries and businesses use the dollar for cross-border activities that it has become enmeshed within international economic operations and hard to disentangle. Hence, for all America's other troubles, not least becoming the world's biggest debtor nation, the dollar in 2019 still made up just over half of global central-bank reserves by currency. The euro, in second place, made up only 20%, and is going to lose a great deal later in 2022, should the western sanction programme continue and at least the RF declare a euro boycott. At the beginning of 2022, the Chinese renminbi, as far as the present author can determine, made up just 2% of global currency reserves

The problem with reserve currency as a hegemonic asset is that it can turn into a source of uncontrollable instability. As the dollar plays a hugely disproportionate role as world money relative to the size of the US economy, it is likely that other countries might see so many dollar holdings as a liability and diversify away into other currencies and hard assets like gold, etc. In addition, nearly all the measures taken by the US government during the last couple of years to weaponise the dollar and try to exert its authority could backfire. Preventing countries from using the dollar for international payments, including Iran and now Russia, sends a warning to other countries, and the freezing of central bank reserves by Washington through decree is already frightening many governments. Currency devaluation could discourage holding dollars, thereby catalysing the dollar's decline as the global reserve currency.

We should look seriously at the fact that the RF and PRC have already been encouraged to devise alternative national and regional payments systems. The Chinese government is making an effort to create a credible central-bank digital currency ahead of others. This would both make China less susceptible to American financial sanctions and offer an alternative for other countries who want to wean themselves off dollar dependency. The West's recent measures to clamp down on Russia's use of its central-bank reserves will eventually motivate other nations to become more serious about moving towards a post-dollar financial world. There should be no doubt that a post-American world order is rapidly taking shape.⁹

## Consequences of the ongoing segregation

Fifty years ago, China and the US broke the ice and started a journey of normalising relations between the two countries. Half a century has passed since then. Despite ups and downs, China-US relations have been moving forward.

The bilateral relations between the European Union and the PRC go back to those established in 1975 between the PRC and the European Community.

China, the US, and the EU are vastly different in terms of social system, history, culture, and stage of development, and disagreements are hardly avoidable. Because global peace and development hinges on cooperation, a dialogue, knowledge of history, and our understanding of our planet's vulnerability. In terms of economy and trade, this cooperation must be based on fair market competition between the US, the EU, and the PRC.

Covid-19 has become an important factor in the segregation process. The pandemic has hit a variety of industries in nearly all countries. In the PRC the services sector was hit hardest, especially contact-based service industries. Many firms in these industries are micro enterprises or SMEs. In general, they are quite weak financially, running on a tight budget and serving transnational companies. In the PRC this means that keeping them afloat is important for maintaining job security in big firms.

The Chinese government has worked out over 40 supportive measures for industries in special difficulty. Tax refunds alone for catering, tourism, passenger transport, and the cultural sector will amount to 180 billion yuan. In addition to fiscal support, the government is encouraging banks to provide loan extensions on a seamless basis for promising businesses; it is urging temporary cuts or exemptions of rental and electricity bills where possible and inviting local governments to extend support. An important aspect of the policy support for industries in distress is not just to tide these industries over, but also to enhance people's quality of life and bring greater vibrancy to the economy.

In the context of Covid-19, the government has issued green lights and opened fast lanes to ensure the normal running of companies and projects in key areas and intends to continue to gain experience and adapt to new developments, gradually restoring the unimpeded flow of goods and personnel in an orderly way.

I believe this is particularly relevant to the EU, which faces the same or similar challenges. Each EU member state would need to provide SMEs with timely help as they play an important leveraging role irrespective of size and represent the backbone of social peace and civic cohesion. At present we can observe that politicians are not acting systematically, aid is hampered by corruption, and hardly any government or anyone in power or those at the receiving end understand that timely support is critical, because it will be too late to 'water a plant once the root is dried out'.

Common prosperity can only be attained through common efforts. As far as the PRC's opening-up policy is concerned, there has been no change in position, and I do not expect a change as there are clear-cut stipulations in China's Foreign Investment Law. Moreover, the government has signed the Regional Comprehensive Economic Partnership Agreement with relevant countries. The agreement has officially come into force this year and creates the world's largest free trade area. It seems to me that no matter how the international environment may change, the PRC will hold to the course of greater openness.

## Meeting basic needs concerns people's daily lives

China's fiscal revenue has reached 20 trillion yuan, but the country still faces fiscal strains. Nevertheless, the PRC has managed to keep fiscal spending on education above 4% of GDP for ten consecutive years. This is by no means easy. Most of the government spending has gone to compulsory education and supported rural areas because the PRC still has 760 million registered as rural population. Therefore increased funding to compulsory education in rural and remote areas should be expected.

The PRC has the world's largest medical insurance system covering some 1.4 billion people, but still with modest benefits. This year, the government will increase its subsidy by 30 yuan per person. It has established a programme of medical insurance for major illnesses, using basic medical insurance funds for the purchase of commercial insurance for major illnesses. In some places, this programme has enabled reimbursement of 300,000 to 500,000 yuan for some illnesses. On average, some 70% of medical bills of rural and urban non-working residents are reimbursable.

The new government will doubtless need to consolidate the outcomes in ending absolute poverty and provide particular support to people who risk falling back into poverty due to illness.

Some 100 million Chinese today move between provinces. Some are elderly people living away from their hometowns with their children in cities. For some the reason is employment or education. They have to deal with much inconvenience due to travel. To reduce this, a new policy will be introduced this year: Although the ID cards in most frequent use in people's daily lives are electronic, the government will also provide alternatives for people who do not use smartphones, especially the elderly. This is an issue also for the EU.

## Taiwan

During Premier Li's 11 March press conference, Taiwan's *ET Today* asked the following:

> Under the situation of further spread of the coronavirus and rising uncertainty and instability in the cross-Strait relations, how will the mainland respond to the situation across the Taiwan Strait, and uphold and promote the well-being of people on both sides of the Strait?
>
> Premier Li's answer:
>
> Our major principles and policies on work related to Taiwan are clear-cut. I have laid them out in the Government Work Report. That is, we are committed to the one-China principle and the 1992 Consensus. We firmly oppose separatist activities seeking 'Taiwan independence' and we will advance the peaceful growth of cross-Strait relations and the reunification of China.

As Taiwan is formally a local issue, and Ukraine a bilateral one in the eyes of the general public, though in reality an issue between the US and RF, it is worth considering that Beijing's tacit support for president Putin during Russia's involvement in Ukraine has not been lost on Europeans, who are viewing the Chinese government with growing scepticism. This matters because 'What we are witnessing now is a major shift when it comes to China's relations with central Europe, and with the EU in general', as Jakub Jakóbowski, senior fellow at the China programme at the Centre for Eastern Studies in Warsaw, has said.[10]

As a matter of fact, the Chinese government has presented itself as neutral in the conflict, but Chinese officials and state media have disseminated pro-Russian disinformation and government censors have cleansed the Chinese internet of pro-Ukraine views. The PRC's abstention from the UN Security Council resolution denouncing Russia's invasion also irked Europeans, who have rallied around Ukraine. This and other issues related to pro-Russian stances have accelerated a shift in Europe toward viewing Beijing not just as a trade partner but also as a security concern. This supports the European Commission position, which labelled the PRC a 'systemic rival' in 2019, and at the same the EU has also emphasised its own strategic autonomy in distancing itself from tougher US policies on China.

Jakóbowski also said: 'For years, China was trying to present itself as a geopolitically transparent actor that has nothing to do with regional security in Europe and is only aiming at cooperation. Now China is certainly becoming a part of the European security landscape, though not directly, but as a Russian enabler.'¹¹ In addition, Didi Kirsten Tatlow, senior fellow at the German Council on Foreign Relations said that 'European officials' and the European public 'see quite clearly that there are similarities between Russia and China'.¹²

Nevertheless, some top European officials still believe that China can play a constructive role in the conflict. Even Josep Borrell said on 4 March that 'Beijing should be the one to mediate between Russia and Ukraine',¹³ a role the Chinese government has also proposed. And Patrik Oksanen, senior fellow at the Stockholm Free World Forum, pointed out that 'China must balance opposing risks in its dealings with Europe and Russia. If they support Russia too much, they will risk having a united West against them.' But 'if they don't support Russia, and Russia collapses and leaves the international arena, then the U.S. could focus its attention on China instead'.¹⁴

The Taiwan issue remains a very serious challenge for the government and people of the PRC. The military involvement of the RF in Ukraine and the reactions of the US, NATO, and the EU doubtless offer very valuable lessons for the Chinese government, the Chinese Communist Party (CPC) at all levels, and the candidates for the new government to be established during the Twentieth Congress of the CPC.

The European left should be asking: What are the Chinese government's priorities, and what does this mean for the European left? What should Europe's priorities be for Europe for the next two years? Should Europeans make more efforts to explore what 'socialism with Chinese characteristics' means in theory and practice?

NOTES

1  <http://www.stats.gov.cn/english/>.
2  <http://english.www.gov.cn/premier/news/202203/12/content_WS622c96d7c6d09c94e48a68ff.html>.
3  Further details at <http://english.www.gov.cn/premier/news/202203/12/content_WS622c96d7c6d09c94e48a68ff.html>.
4  <https://www.fmprc.gov.cn/eng/zxxx_662805/202203/t20220311_10651148.html>.
5  <https://www.fmprc.gov.cn/eng/zxxx_662805/202203/t20220311_10651148.html>.
6  <https://www.fmprc.gov.cn/eng/zxxx_662805/202203/t20220311_10651148.html>.
7  The author of this article is also co-author of a tested (transnational) system of intensive development of individual abilities (SID(I)A). SID(I)A allows development (or even the creation) of a human being able to acquire competences and new habits which would enhance most of the known and less known technologies, including the more natural ones. The programme is described in my book *Consent not needed*,

Prague: Kladno SVK, 2016. The programme was conducted in three or four languages with partial presence, work done at home at a distance, and the collective presentation of results linked to a specific challenge in a company or administration at the end of the programme.

8   Ray Dalio, *Principles for Dealing with the Changing World Order: Why Nations Succeed and Fail*, New York: Simon & Schuster, 2021.
9   See <https://youtu.be/sY4DEyVJtFk>.
10  <https://www.axios.com/europe-skepticism-toward-china-grows-3ef65fe3-d0dd-4b26-8fbc-e1a10f3104ae.html>.
11  <https://www.axios.com/europe-skepticism-toward-china-grows-3ef65fe3-d0dd-4b26-8fbc-e1a10f3104ae.html>.
12  <https://www.axios.com/europe-skepticism-toward-china-grows-3ef65fe3-d0dd-4b26-8fbc-e1a10f3104ae.html>.
13  <https://www.scmp.com/news/china/diplomacy/article/3169407/russias-war-ukraine-it-has-be-china-mediator-eu-foreign-policy>.
14  <https://www.axios.com/europe-skepticism-toward-china-grows-3ef65fe3-d0dd-4b26-8fbc-e1a10f3104ae.html#>.

# The Geopolitics of Covid in Latin America

## Silvina Romano, Tamara Lajtman, and Aníbal García Fernández

Following the end of the Trump presidency,[1] the de-escalation of tensions between the United States and Russia and China that many expected has not come about. Disputes persist as regards the monopolisation of markets, including healthcare and the Covid-19 vaccine, and technological and military deployment and development, cybersecurity, and access to and colonisation of outer space, among other things. In addition to the rapid development of its science and technology sector, China has now begun to play a significant and respected role in international diplomacy. This involves not only specific projects such as the Belt and Road Initiative, the mega trade deal on economic integration in the Asian Pacific, and the Regional Comprehensive Economic Partnership (RCEP), but also a growing involvement and leadership in Western multilateral organisations.[2]

In an effort to reverse declining US hegemony, the Biden administration began with a promise of a return to the multilateralism that Trump had eschewed.[3] One example of efforts to revitalise its leadership is the recent investigation opened against the Managing Director of the IMF for alleged pressuring of staff to manipulate data in favour of China, accusations that were not proven.[4] This reflects the (unilateral) imperialism that has characterised United States foreign policy since the end of the nineteenth century.

On the global geopolitical chessboard, it is evident that core countries have persisted with a traditional Cold War reading of East versus West. This is apparent in the imposition of narratives about the expansion of China and Russia and their use of illegal, abusive, and corrupt practices. Although only occasionally visible and at other times camouflaged within remodelled narratives, such moral liberalism is clearly rooted in traditional anti-communist ideology.[5] In this respect, anti-communist consensus-building by core countries' governments, think tanks, and foundations is undeniably based on prejudices forged during the Cold War.[6] The prevalence of this discourse continues to have an effect on government policy and public opinion.[7] Worse than the instigation of direct aggressive opposition to China and Russia, these narratives are also being recycled in the construction of new enemies. Populism, nationalism, and left-wing radicalism, among others, are positioned in such a way that any associated governments and movements are stigmatised and criminalised, making it extremely difficult to implement a political economic system beyond the boundaries of neoliberal capitalism.[8]

In Latin America and the Caribbean (LAC), the dispute between world powers materialises in tensions between neoliberalism and nationalist, anti-imperialist, and sovereign processes of change, which has had important implications for the balance of power in the region: the Movimiento de Regeneración Nacional government in Mexico, along with the Argentinian and Bolivian governments, as well as Venezuela and Cuba, have shown signs of moving towards regional integration. Since the very beginning of its mandate, the new self-proclaimed Marxist-Leninist[9] government of Peru has been questioned and weakened by both the local establishment and the international community. In this context, during the second annual meeting of the Puebla Group (an alliance of governments, progressives, and the political left) in July 2021 and during the CELAC summit in September 2021, there was a call from progressive governments in the region to renew the political and economic legacy of social justice, to develop more independence from core countries, and to assume greater collective negotiating power in international institutions.[10]

The dispute between traditional and emerging powers arises in attempts to monopolise investment in sectors such as infrastructure, energy, debt financing, and privileged access to markets, where the Covid-19 vaccine represents a bargaining chip and source of pressure. There are at least two elements that are key to understanding the impact of Covid-19 on the region, which have also exacerbated previous problems. First, we can consider the impact of core-periphery relations in the development and distribution of the vaccine. This has included the use of medical supplies and the Covid-19 vaccine as tools of soft power by suppliers, as well as the emergence amongst client countries of an 'everyone for themselves' pragmatism. In some cases, this pragmatism has coexisted within the frameworks of regional organisations' agreements, although slowly and belatedly, and with the caveat that most solutions have excluded Cuba and its successful vaccine production. This situation leads to the second concern, that the recycled and updated anti-communism of 'New Cold War' narratives conceals the long-standing interests of the United States' public and private sectors in the region. These interests are articulated through an institutional network and the personal trajectories of the liberal right-wing and conservatives, the guardians of neoliberalism, who are fervently opposed to any process of real political change that aspires to govern.

## The core-periphery relations of Covid-19

The manufacturing and distribution of Covid-19 supplies and vaccines has exposed the asymmetry of the international system, the reproduction of core-periphery relations, and the centrality of the market in decision-making. As part of this dynamic, since the beginning of the pandemic, countries with the capabilities to develop and distribute Covid-19 supplies and vaccines have used this advantage as an instrument of soft power – in other words, as a bargaining and negotiating chip and even as a means of applying political pressure. From the client country side, in particular those in peripheral spaces, the urgent need to address the health crisis gave rise to an open pragmatism that went beyond political and ideological disputes.

*Asymmetry and business*

The monopolisation of vaccines by core countries was followed by low vaccination rates in some of these countries. In the United States, 66.4% of the population over 12 years old has been vaccinated and almost 718,000 deaths have been recorded since the beginning of the pandemic; more than all the service casualties suffered during all its military invasions. The United States, Canada, Japan, the United Kingdom, and the European Union are now faced with vaccine expiry and the loss of around 241 million doses,[11] even though almost half of the world population has not received a single dose. In Latin America, where only one in four people are vaccinated, more than 2.3 million people have died from Covid-19 and 91.7 million have been infected, representing 46% and 39%, respectively, of world totals by mid-October 2021.[12]

The rampant asymmetry and monopolisation of the manufacturing and distribution of vaccines is explained, in part, by the fact that the Black Rock and Vanguard Groups, two global investment companies, are shareholders in many of the pharmaceutical companies that have developed Covid-19 vaccines. Furthermore, they hold stakes in the main technology companies and have financed members of the United States Congress.

*Vaccines as soft power and pragmatism*

The geopolitical landscape of the Covid-19 vaccine is led by the United States, China, Russia, and India. Collectively, these countries are responsible for most of the 7.5 billion vaccines produced worldwide, up to September 2021.[13]

## Table 1. Black Rock and Vanguard Group Investments

| Company | Black Rock* | Vanguard Group** |
|---|---|---|
| | % of shares | % of shares |
| Apple | 6.3% | 7.2% |
| Alphabet | 6.3% | 7.3% |
| Microsoft | 6.6% | 7.9% |
| Amazon | 5.05% | 5.9% |
| Facebook | 6.4% | 7.4% |
| Berkshire | 7.8% | 9.9% |
| Johnson & Johnson | 6.9% | 8.3% |
| JP Morgan | 6.6% | 7.9% |
| Wells Fargo | 6.5% | 7.2% |
| **Pharmaceutical companies producing Covid-19 vaccines** | | |
| SANOFI | 5.9% | |
| Pfizer | 7.7% | 8.3% |
| AstraZeneca | 4.16% | 2.77% |
| **Election financing and lobbying in the United States** | | |
| 2020 election | $1.7 million | $879, 486 |
| Lobbying in Congress and Senate | $1.8 million | $2.9 million |

Source: 'Mayores accionistas de las empresas más grandes de EEUU', <https://embed.kumu.io/9c0ed5b8af5441b0341875b311e438cb#mayores-accionistas-de-las-empresas-mas-grandes-de-eeuu>; and Open Secrets, 'Black Rock Inc.', disponible en: <https://www.opensecrets.org/orgs/blackrock-inc/summary?id=D000021872>.

\* The founders and main shareholders are Laurance D. Fink, Robert Kapito, Susan Wagner, Barbara Novick, Ben Golub, Ralph Schlosstein, and Hugh R. Frater.
\*\* The founders and main shareholders are Jack Bogle, Mortimer J. Buckley, Gerry O'Reilly, Tim Buckley, and Mortimer J. Buckley.

Russia has focused on the promotion of its vaccine as a means to extend its hegemony and has been accused by Western states of imposing its vaccine ahead of those developed by other laboratories. At the time of writing, the Sputnik V vaccine had been approved in 62 countries, whose 3.2 billion inhabitants account for about 40% of the world population. European countries were quite uncomfortable with this situation. A case in point is the statement by the French Minister of Foreign Affairs that the vaccine was 'more a means of propaganda and aggressive diplomacy than of solidarity and assistance'. Comments by Michał Baranowski of the German Marshall

Fund followed a similar line of argumentation, stating that the Russian strategy was 'neither innocent nor humanitarian. It is part of exactly the same game, of dividing the West, that we see in Moscow's use of military power, cybersecurity, energy security.'[14]

In Latin-American, at least ten countries gave early approval to the Russian vaccine, including Argentina, Bolivia, Guatemala, Guyana, Honduras, Mexico, Nicaragua, Paraguay, Panama, and Venezuela. Access to the vaccine depended on bilateral negotiations without having recourse to collective mechanisms such as the Community of Latin American and Caribbean States (CELAC). Between early and mid-2021, Argentina became the first LAC country to produce test batches of the vaccine, while Venezuela was the first to approve single doses of Sputnik V Light for emergencies, and Mexico developed test packaging for the vaccine. Paraguay, Guatemala, and Honduras, which used to have few links with Russia, signed up as clients almost immediately. In September 2021, Peru reached agreement with the Russian government to construct a domestic manufacturing plant for the production of the vaccine, which at that time had yet to be approved or distributed in the country.[15]

For its part, China has exported 1.1 billion doses of its vaccine to 123 countries (up to 8 October 2021). Of this total, around 110 million doses were purchased by the COVAX initiative (see below for more details). Along with the 2.2 billion doses administered in China itself, this accounts for more than half of the 6 billion doses administered worldwide, up to September 2021.[16]

In terms of LAC, China only donated 2 million doses, while it has sold 388 million, of which 241 million have been delivered. In relation to the donations, 1.5 million Sinovac doses were sent to El Salvador, while 100,000 and 500,000 Sinopharm doses were sent to Bolivia and Venezuela, respectively. Not only has China offered to supply LAC countries with its vaccine, it has also provided loans worth 1 billion dollars to help 13 countries in the region to buy vaccines, including Mexico, Argentina, and Chile.[17] At the same time, China has increased development aid for LAC from 5.1 billion dollars in 2015 to 5.9 billion dollars in 2019. This includes bilateral grants and interest-free loans (48%), Chinese government loans with favourable conditions (21%), and contributions to international organisations (30%).

Events in Mexico provide an interesting example. On 9 March 2021, Mexico announced an agreement for 12 million doses for the Chinese Sinopharm vaccine, as well as an additional agreement with Sinovac to acquire 20 million doses in July 2021. This announcement came one week after the United States refused to provide Mexico with vaccine assistance. Under pressure, the European Union decided to donate 2.5 million AstraZeneca-Oxford doses to Mexico. By October 2021, Mexico had received 136 million doses: Pfizer (34.8 million), Sinovac (20 million), AstraZeneca (54.6 million), Cansino (10 million), Sputnik V (11.9 million), Johnson & Johnson (1.3 million) and Moderna (3.5 million).[18] Honduras is another interesting case because it is a traditionally close ally of the United States and, like the rest of Central America, highly dependent in terms of politics, economics, and security.[19] On 12 May, the President, Juan Orlando Hernández, announced that he was considering opening a commercial office for China as a way of accessing its vaccines. Paraguay had also received doses from Sinopharm through the United Arab Emirates, but only until July 2021 when, as admitted by the Minister for Health, supply was cut for 'geopolitical reasons'.[20]

## The United States, vaccines, and Covid aid

The majority of LAC countries have received vaccines from the United States, although belatedly and in much smaller quantities than expected. The United States announced its first vaccine donation in March 2021, more than a year after the beginning of the pandemic – a consignment of AstraZeneca to Canada and Mexico. At the end of April, President Biden increased the amount of AstraZeneca vaccines promised to a total of 60 million doses to be distributed worldwide, and on 17 May a further 20 million doses of the Pfizer, Moderna, and Johnson & Johnson vaccines. Of these 80 million doses,[21] 60 million were distributed through COVAX, which included 20 million for LAC.[22] The remaining 20 million doses were set aside to cover priority regions, including Argentina, Colombia, Costa Rica, the Dominican Republic, Haiti, Mexico, and Panama. On 10 June, the White House announced the donation of 500 million Pfizer doses through COVAX for low- and middle-income countries, including Bolivia, El Salvador, Honduras, and Nicaragua.[23]

From the beginning of the pandemic to June 2021, the United States Agency for International Development (USAID) allocated around 217 million dollars to the fight against the Covid-19 in the southern hemisphere. Table 2 details the main recipient countries and the agencies that delivered the projects, some of which, like Chemonics, have been linked to efforts to destabilise and interfere in countries' internal affairs.

## Regional response

Faced with the rapid spread of the virus, most countries responded individually. The most compelling example of this is the approach taken within COVAX, a global initiative launched by the World Health Organization (WHO), the

## Table 2. Countries, agencies and pandemic aid

| Country | Amount in dollars | Delivering agencies |
| --- | --- | --- |
| Brazil | 30,084,622 | Escritorio Nacional, International Organization for Migration (IOM), UNICEF, World Vision, Chemonics, Palladium |
| Guatemala | 28,502,039 | Catholic Relief Services (CRS), Medical Teams International, Project Concern International, SCF, Chemonics, Johns Hopkins University (JHU), Palladium, WFP |
| Honduras | 26,400,333 | GOAL, Global Communities, SCF, Chemonics, FHI 360, IOM, PAHO, Palladium, WFP |
| Peru | 24,302,564 | ADRA, Americares, RET, Socios en Salud, SCF, WFP, Chemonics, Prisma, Public Health Institute, Socios en Salud, CEDRO |
| Ecuador | 19,549,089 | Adventist Development and Relief Agency (ADRA), IFRC, UNICEF, WFP, World Vision, Chemonics, FundaciónEsquel, IFRC, JHPIEGO |
| Colombia | 19,347,500 | Abt Associates, IFRC, WFP, Worldwide Relief, Chemonics |
| Haiti | 16,485,478 | CRS, Doctors of the World; International Committee of the Red Cross; Management, Sciences for Health, Inc, IOM, SCF, UNICEF, Caris Foundation International, Chemonics, FHI 360, International Society for Peritoneal, Dialysis, PAHO, Public Health Institute, Spinal Bifida and Hydrocephalous Care Foundation |
| Venezuela | 9,000,000 | Implementing Partners [no specific delivering agency] |
| Bolivia | 6,637,785 | Chemonics, ProSalud, UNICEF |

Source: USAID, 'COVID-19 – Latin American and the Caribbean Response', 29 June 2021, <https://www.usaid.gov/sites/default/files/documents/2021_06_29_USAID_COVID-19_LAC_Response_Fact_Sheet_1_1.pdf>.

## Table 3. COVAX Vaccine distribution programme in Latin America

| Country | Laboratory | Number of doses | Total population |
|---|---|---|---|
| Argentina | AstraZeneca | 2,275,200 | 45,376,763 |
| Bolivia | AstraZeneca | 900,000 | 11,677,406 |
|  | Pfizer | 92,430 |  |
| Brazil | AstraZeneca | 10,672,800 | 210,147,000 |
| Chile | AstraZeneca | 957,600 | 19,107,000 |
| Colombia | AstraZeneca | 2,553,600 | 50,374,000 |
|  | Pfizer | 117,000 |  |
| Costa Rica | AstraZeneca | 254,400 | 5,075,000 |
| Dominican Republic | AstraZeneca | 542,400 | 10,358,000 |
| Ecuador | AstraZeneca | 885,600 | 17,373,662 |
| El Salvador | AstraZeneca | 324,000 | 6,453,553 |
|  | Pfizer | 51,480 |  |
| Guatemala | AstraZeneca | 847,200 | 17,613,000 |
| Haiti | AstraZeneca | 847,200 | 11,263,077 |
| Honduras | AstraZeneca | 496,800 | 9,770,000 |
| México | AstraZeneca | 6,472,800 | 127,576,000 |
| Nicaragua | AstraZeneca | 504,000 | 6,518,478 |
| Panamá | AstraZeneca | 216,000 | 4,219,000 |
| Paraguay | AstraZeneca | 357,600 | 7,252,672 |
| Peru | AstraZeneca | 1,653,600 | 32,510,453 |
|  | Pfizer | 117,000 |  |
| Uruguay | AstraZeneca | 172,800 | 3,461,734 |
| Venezuela | AstraZeneca | 1,425,600 | 28,515,829 |

Source: Arantxa Tirado et. al., 'La vacuna contra el COVID-19 y América Latina', CELAG, 26 February 2021, <https://www.celag.org/la-vacuna-contra-el-covid-19-y-america-latina/>.

Coalition for Epidemic Preparedness Innovations (CEPI) and Gavi (The Vaccine Alliance) to raise millions of dollars in funds to make vaccines available to low-income countries. This mechanism proposed country-by-country rather than multilateral negotiations through regional organisations.

It is highly relevant that CEPI is a global alliance founded by Norway, India, the Bill and Melinda Gates Foundation, the Wellcome Trust (headquartered in the UK), and the World Economic Forum. Gavi was also founded by the Gates Foundation to focus on improving access to vaccines in low-income countries. It is no secret that the Gates's play a leading role in the definition of various WHO policies and lines of action,[24] making COVAX a functional tool for the reproduction of aid within the logic of the philanthropy market.[25]

## Table 4. Responses of the integration organisations at the beginning of the pandemic

| INTEGRATING ORGANISATION | COVID-19 RESPONSE |
|---|---|
| **Pacific Alliance** (made up of Mexico, Colombia, Chile and Peru) neoliberal governments and progressive governments, important alliances with the United States | ■ Launch of the 'COVID challenge' [Reto COVID], a public call (supported by the Inter-American Development Bank) for technological proposals to mitigate the health crisis. 396 proposals were received for the areas of health, community and education, of which 8 projects were selected.<br>■ No specific measures to address the health crisis, such as access to vaccines, etc., were financed. The focus was on 'economic recovery'. |
| **CARICOM** (made up of Trinidad and Tobago, Guyana, Suriname, Bahamas, Haiti, Jamaica, Barbados, Belize, Antigua and Barbuda, Saint Kitts and Nevis, Santa Lucia, Vicente and the Grenadines, Dominica, Granada and Montserrat), important alliance with the United States | ■ Generally speaking, CARICOM was very active, with joint positions and proposals for addressing the pandemic.<br>■ Through the Central American Integration System (SICA), a Regional Contingency Plan to deal with the coronavirus was developed, which would mobilise 1.9 million dollars to address the economic and health-related consequences of the virus. The meeting of Heads of State and Government on 26 March 2020 adopted the declaration 'Central America united against the Coronavirus'.<br>■ Joint position of the bloc to request Covid-19 vaccines from the United States. |

▶

| INTEGRATING ORGANISATION | COVID-19 RESPONSE |
|---|---|
| **ANDEAN COMMUNITY** (made up of Bolivia, Colombia, Ecuador, Peru) neoliberal governments and progressive governments, increasingly close to China | ▪ Approval of '20 decisions' to facilitate commerce, simplify procedures and digitise processes, as well as the enforcement of prevention measures for customs transit and the establishment of a protocol to reduce the risk of infection in rural areas.<br>▪ The Colombian government provided 500,000 US dollars to the Pan American Health Organization (OPS). |
| **MERCOSUR** (made up of Brazil, Paraguay, Uruguay) neoliberal governments and progressive governments, FTA pending with the EU, increasingly close to China | ▪ No joint purchase of vaccines was achieved; at the beginning of the pandemic 16 million dollars were allocated to the crisis. The most important actions taken were through FOCEM, in conjunction with science and technology institutes in different countries. |
| **TMEC** (made up of Canada, the United States, Mexico) | ▪ Between March and October, the United States donated 10.9 million vaccine doses (Moderna, Johnson & Johnson and AstraZeneca).<br>▪ In May 2020, the United States sent 211 respirators and medical materials to Mexico.<br>▪ In January 2021, the Mexican Foreign Minister declared that Mexico would invoke TIMEC's labour chapter so that migrants could receive the Covid-19 vaccine in the United States, but was unsuccessful. |
| **CELAC** | ▪ On 18 September, approval of the 'Plan for self-sufficiency in health matters in Latin America and the Caribbean: Lines of action and proposals' in the framework of the 6th Summit (ECLAC, 2021) |

▶

| INTEGRATING ORGANISATION | COVID-19 RESPONSE |
|---|---|
| ALBA-TCP | ■ Creation of the Vaccine Bank for ALBA-TCP countries, financed by the Bank of Alba (one million US dollars), agreed in the 18th Summit of the Heads of State and Government of the ALBA-TCP.<br>■ In this framework, a meeting was held with representatives of the Russian Direct Investment Fund for the acquisition of the Sputnik V Covid-19 vaccine.<br>■ Medicine Bank to contribute to the improvement of access to medical supplies, rapid tests and PCR tests for the benefit of all countries in the alliance.<br>■ On 29 June 2020 a humanitarian flight was made to connect Antigua and Barbados, St. Kitts and Nevis, and the Republic of Cuba. This permitted the repatriation of 66 scholarship students from Cuba to their countries of origin and the transfer of 41 Cuban doctors to the islands.<br>■ During the Special meeting of the Social Council of ALBA-TCP, the health theme 'United against Covid-19' (19 January 2020) was agreed on to create a humanitarian fund whose purpose was to establish the bank for the acquisition of ALBA vaccines and to create the Medicine Bank. |

Source: Authors' own elaboration

In LAC, each country has a different vaccine plan that depends on bilateral negotiating capacity with third countries. Some countries have only been able to access vaccines leftover following advance purchases by European countries, Israel, Canada, and the United States. The majority stuck to the COVAX system, which, apart from being an individualistic solution, did not manage to deliver the required number of doses.

In spite of the evident pragmatism and the often desperate and unforeseen responses of each government, various regional organisations began to work on collective mechanisms and responses to the pandemic, even if many of these came quite late. The main measures taken through these processes and integrated agreements, during the first year of the pandemic, are outlined in Table 4.

A number of initiatives stand out. For example, at the CELAC summit in September 2021, two lines of action for self-sufficiency in health matters were approved with the support of ECLAC (Economic Commission for Latin America and the Caribbean).[26] Brazil also collaborated in this initiative, even though in 2020 it had suspended its participation in CELAC. Since June 2021, Mexico, which holds the temporary presidency of CELAC, has donated 1.13 million vaccine doses to Paraguay, Belize, Bolivia, Guatemala, El Salvador, and Honduras.[27] The agreement between Mexico and Argentina to produce and package the AstraZeneca vaccine for distribution in Latin America should also be highlighted.[28]

One of the factors that generates discomfort and tensions is the production of vaccines in Cuba. As the only country in the region to develop a coronavirus serum that can be classed as a vaccine, this achievement has to be understood within the context of the enormous barriers and obstacles imposed by the US economic blockade that has been in place since the 1960s. Known as the Abdala vaccine, it was authorised by the Cuban regulator at the beginning of July. There are also two other Cuban vaccines in the final stages of clinical trials: Soberana 02 and Soberana Plus. Vietnam was the first foreign country to approve Abdala, receiving more than a million doses at the end of September 2021. On 21 October, the Venezuelan government announced that it would begin production of the Abdala vaccine. However, the development of vaccines in Cuba has been the target of numerous falsehoods and misrepresentations, ranging from claims that Soberana was really Sputnik, to denunciations of the vaccine's efficacy without supporting data.

The absence of early agreements with Cuba, as well as the invisibilisation of its work in the middle of a multi-faceted crisis generated by the blockade and exacerbated by the pandemic, attests to the depth and persistence of anti-communism within the international community, postures and prejudices that have not dissipated since the fall of Donald Trump. The extreme conditions of the United States' 60-year blockade against Cuba were worsened by the pandemic, contributing to social unrest. Protests against the government, however, were mostly for improved living conditions, which are ultimately impeded by an international community that remains persistently passive to each new sanction imposed by the United States.[29]

## The Cold War narrative as a reproduction of the status quo

In the EU, many experts and political commentators have been issuing warnings along the lines of: 'Russia is still the major threat for NATO. This is understandable considering the geostrategic conditions, but China presents a challenge of a different quality, with its industrial might, vast market with 1.3 billion population, its unique one-party system, and its ability to manage cyberspace and control information as well as its people'.[30] Something similar has been expressed in the United States: 'Russia and China aren't just selling vaccines – they're peddling a value set that undermines international norms'.[31] It has also been claimed that this is provoking a kind of 'vaccine Cold War' by promising to supply various Latin American countries with doses and therefore pressuring Washington to share its supply.[32]

In this respect, it is highly relevant that the Biden administration's first national security measures conserved aspects of the 'competition of great powers'.[33] The declaration of the Commander of the U.S. Southern Command, which operates in Latin America, that Russia and China are a real threat to the democratic values of the continent is also notable. The March 2021 meeting of the Northern and Southern Commands reinforced the notion that China and Russia represent the 'greatest threats' (Department of Defense, 2021): 'This Hemisphere in which we live is under assault. The very democratic principles and values that bind us together are being actively undermined by violent transnational criminal organizations (TCOs) and the PRC and Russia. We are losing our positional advantage in this Hemisphere and immediate action is needed to reverse this trend.'[34]

The worrying thing, in terms of the reproduction of ideology and common-sense values, is what these narratives conceal. Much the same as during the years following the Second World War, the bipolar narrative sustained by the core countries disguises and minimises the asymmetries embedded in the international establishment constructed by the West. In particular, the inequity that capitalism perpetuates through ever greater violence against poor and underdeveloped countries and how, in the name of anti-communism (anti-populism, anti-progressive governments, and so on), this conceals the annihilation of nationalist anti-imperialist processes in peripheral areas. The geopolitics of the Covid-19 vaccine shows the enormous and inherent inequality and inefficiency of the international organisations and the prevalence of markets and corporate interests above human lives. All this attempts to reduce health to a question of morality or simple ideology, where the logic of preferences prevails, as if people were part of a great market, all living under equal conditions and in an ideal world where liberal capitalism lavishes freedom and harmony: 'In the end we did not win the Cold War because we had more guns. We won because our societies, with their freedom and diversity, offered products, education systems, management and governance systems, and a way of life that were more attractive.'[35]

Anti-communism, however, is not just a matter of discourse. The regional right wing, with links to the United States (and European) elite, continues to have a formidable presence in the region. This is maintained through a strong institutional network of political parties, think tanks, and foundations that nourish negative narratives about processes of change and which can profoundly impact decision-making processes.[36] A good example of this kind of activity is the Defense of Democracy in the Americas forum held in Miami, Florida, in May 2021. Organised by the Interamerican Institute for Democracy (IID), the event was attended by prominent conservatives and representatives of the liberal right wing, including: Luis Almagro, General Secretary of the Organization of American States (OAS), which has been accused of supporting the November 2019 Bolivian coup;[37] Carlos Sánchez Berzaín, Director of the IID and an ex-Minister in the Bolivian government of Gonzalo Sánchez de Lozada, who played a leading role in the coup;[38] Lenín Moreno, ex-President of Ecuador, who instigated a witch-hunt against Correism and implemented one of the harshest processes of lawfare in the region, as well as an immediate return to neoliberal measures;[39] Mauricio Macri, ex-president of Argentina, who promoted the criminalisation of the political opposition (in particular that of Cristina Fernández de Kirchner) and quickly reintroduced neoliberalism;[40] representatives of the Inter American Press Association (SIP),[41] an anti-communist information agency established in 1943 that has been counteracting Prensa Latina, the Cuban information agency, since the 1960s; and representatives of the Liberal Foundation (Fundación Libertad), a place where 'young leaders' are trained to operate as government advisors.

The central discussions of the meeting focused on accusations against Venezuela and Nicaragua of undermining 'democracy', claims of violence perpetrated by the left, and the injustice of the political persecution of leaders of the de facto government that took office in Bolivia after the coup. In brief, this kind of meeting, in a hotbed of anti-Castroism and anti-communism like Miami, articulates the personal and institutional trajectories of the region's right wing that are now associated with the most reactionary opposition to progressive political movements in Latin America, in other words: anti-populism.[42]

## Final reflections

Capitalism in the 21st century exhibits an increasing trend towards inequity and unequal development that have prolonged and deepened economic, political, and environmental crises and the fundamental capital/labour and capital/nature contradictions. That the pandemic has deepened the core-periphery asymmetries is evident, not only in the number of infections and Covid-19-associated deaths, but also in the processes of vaccine production, which has been monopolised by a handful of pharmaceutical companies backed by financial capital.

There were also serious faults in the international vaccine distribution process, which was ultimately organised on the basis of special interests. Led by the Bill and Melinda Gates Foundation, the COVAX system did not achieve its objectives, but was certainly functional in terms of the reproduction of philanthro-capitalism. On the other hand, the Latin American and Caribbean countries responded on an individual basis and only after a year or so did regional and multilateral agreements and measures take place. This underscores the weakness of regional processes and the urgent need for the definition of common goals that can reunify our America, beyond sitting governments. A highly relevant fact is that, of the various multilateral mechanisms put in place, ALBA-TCP and CARICOM in the Caribbean – the forgotten Caribbean! – achieved the fastest joint responses. Even if it was achieved somewhat belatedly, it is also important to recall that CELAC approved lines of action for achieving self-sufficiency in health matters by mid-2021.

The geopolitics of Covid-19 has also provided fertile ground for the deployment of soft power that intensifies tensions between the United States and China and Russia. The accusations levelled by the United States against its adversaries in relation to the political and diplomatic instrumentalisation of the vaccines are clearly reminiscent of the Cold War. This makes it plain that the field of dispute is not just commercial, military, or a new arms-space race, but also extends to cybersecuirty and pharmaceuticals. The truth is, in the case of LAC, that the United States only made a belated contribution to the distribution of vaccines in the region and did so under the double standards and fine manners that characterise Democratic governments. These efforts were insufficient to disguise the neoliberal and conservative right-wing network developed in Latin America or to counteract the permanent political turmoil in the region through a search for alternatives to neoliberalism. It also seems inadequate as a means to contain the ever-greater presence of China and Russia. While this reproduction of anti-communist ideology has had some success, the political strategy of the United States is marked by important shortcomings reflected in the rampant inequality and misery that has been generated by Western imperialism, since at least the end of the Second World War.

NOTES

1. For specific data on the impact of Trump's presidency on Latin America, see Silvina Romano, *Trumperialismo: Estados Unidos y la guerra permanente contra América Latina*, Madrid: CELAG-Mármol-Izquierdo, 2020.
2. Andrew Schwartz, 'Confronting the Challenge of Chinese State Capitalism', in Center for Strategic & International Studies, 22 January 2021, <https://www.csis.org/analysis/confronting-challenge-chinese-state-capitalism>.
3. Brett Schaefer, 'Get More Americans Working at the United Nations', in The Heritage Foundation, 24 february 2021, <https://www.heritage.org/global-politics/commentary/get-more-americans-working-the-united-nations>; Daniel Runde, 'A New Approach to Foreign Aid', Center for Strategic and International Studies 27 (December 2020), <https://www.csis.org/analysis/new-approach-foreign-aid>.
4. Guillermo Oglietti, Silvina Romano, and Rafale Britto, 'Kristalina Georgieva y el FMI', CELAG, 9 October 2021, <https://www.celag.org/kristalina-georgieva-y-el-fmi/>.
5. Jodi Dean, 'Anti-Communism is all around us', *Praktyka Teoretyczna*, 1(31), 2019, <https://www.researchgate.net/publication/332959097_Anti-communism_is_All_Around_Us>.
6. Jodi Dean, *The Communist Horizon*, London: Verso, 2012; Edward Said, *Orientalism*, New York: Pantheon, 1978.
7. Noam Chomsky and Edward S. Herman, *Manufacturing Consent – The Political Economy of the Mass Media*, New York: Pantheon, 1988.
8. Silvina Romano and Iban Díaz Parra, *Antipolíticas: neoliberalismo, realismo de izquierda y autonomismo en América Latina*, Ciudad Autónoma de Buenos Aires: Luxemburg, 2018; Álvaro García Linera, *Socialismo comunitario: un horizonte de época*, La Paz: Vicepresidencia del Estado. Presidencia de la Asamblea Legislativa Plurinacional de Bolivia, 2015
9. See Perú Libre, 'Perú Libre: ideario y programa' <http://perulibre.pe/wp-content/uploads/2020/03/ideario-peru-libre.pdf./>.
10. Silvina Romano, Tamara Lajtman, and Aníbal García Fernández, 'Política de Estados Unidos, su impacto en Cuba', CELAG, 23 July 2021, <https://www.celag.org/politica-de-ee-uu-su-impacto-en-cuba/>.
11. BBC, 'Vacunas contra el coronavirus: ¿por qué podrían desperdiciarse 241 millones de dosis?', 22 September 2021, <https://www.bbc.com/mundo/noticias-internacional-58651211>.
12. Milenio, 'América Latina concentra hasta 46% de muertes por covid-19: OPS', 15 October 2021, <https://www.milenio.com/internacional/america-latina-concentra-46-muertes-covid-19-ops>.
13. Airfinity, 'September 2021 snap shot COVID-19 data', 7 September 2021, <https://www.ifpma.org/wp-content/uploads/2021/09/Airfinity_September_2021_Snapshot_COVID-19_Data.pdf>.

14. John Henley, 'Is Russia's Covid Vaccine Anything More Than a Political Weapon?', *The Guardian*, 30 April 2021.
15. Reuters, 'Peru to build plant to make Sputnik V COVID-19 vaccine – President', 6 September 2021, <https://www.reuters.com/world/americas/peru-build-plant-make-sputnik-v-covid-19-vaccine-president-2021-09-07/>.
16. BBC, 'Covid-19 vaccines: Has China made more than other countries combined?', 10 October 2021, <https://www.bbc.com/news/58808889>.
17. Nikkei Asia, 'China's global vaccine gambit', 12 October 2021, <https://asia.nikkei.com/static/vdata/chinavaccine-1/>.
18. SRE, 'Gestión diplomática vacuna COVID', 2021, <https://transparencia.sre.gob.mx/gestion-diplomatica-vacunas-covid/>.
19. Silvina Romano and Camila Vollenweider, '¿Lawfare o lawfear? La guerra judicial y el miedo', CELAG, 16 March 2020: 349-409, <https://www.celag.org/lawfare-o-lawfear-la-guerra-judicial-y-el-miedo/>.
20. Infobae, 'Paraguay denunció que la farmacéutica china Sinopharm canceló la entrega de 750.000 vacunas contra el COVID-19 por razones geopolíticas', 31 July 2021, <https://www.infobae.com/america/america-latina/2021/07/31/paraguay-denuncio-que-la-farmaceutica-china-sinopharm-cancelo-la-entrega-de-750000-dosis-de-la-vacuna-contra-el-covid-19/>.
21. 'Biden boosts vaccine donations, but critics say far more is needed', *Washington Post*, 17 May 2021, <https://www.washingtonpost.com/health/2021/05/17/biden-donates-20-million-vaccine-doses/>.
22. Americas Society/Council of the Americas (AS/COA), 'What Is COVAX and What Does It Mean for Latin America?', 7 June 2021, <https://www.as-coa.org/articles/what-covax-and-what-does-it-mean-latin-america>.
23. White House, 'President Biden Announces Historic Vaccine Donation: Half a Billion Pfizer Vaccines to the World's Lowest-Income Nations', 10 June 2021, <https://www.whitehouse.gov/briefing-room/statements-releases/2021/06/10/fact-sheet-president-biden-announces-historic-vaccine-donation-half-a-billion-pfizer-vaccines-to-the-worlds-lowest-income-nations/>.
24. Jens Martens and Karolin Seitz. *Philantropic power and development. Who shapes the agenda?* Bischöfliches Hilfswerk MISEREOR, Global Policy Forum, EvangelischesWerk für Diakonie und Entwicklung Brot für die Welt – Evangelischer Entwicklungsdienst, Berlin-Bonn-New York, 2015.
25. Gian Carlo Delgado and Silvina Romano, *Medio ambiente, fundaciones privadas y asistencia para el desarrollo en América Latina*, Mexico City: UNAM-CEIICH, 2013, <http://biblioteca.clacso.edu.ar/Mexico/ceiich-unam/20170428030046/pdf_1306.pdf>.
26. ECLAC (Economic Commission for Latin America and the Caribbean), 'Plan for self-sufficiency in health matters in Latin America and the Caribbean: Lines of action and proposals' (LC/TS.2021/115), Santiago Chile, 2021, <https://repositorio.cepal.org/bitstream/handle/11362/47253/1/S2100556_en.pdf>.
27. Expansión, 'México dona 1.1 millones de vacunas a seis países de América Latina', 8 October 2021, <https://politica.expansion.mx/mexico/2021/10/08/mexico-ha-donado-vacunas>.
28. Gobierno de México, 'Gobierno de México anuncia que ya está disponible la vacuna de AstraZeneca producida por México y Argentina', 2021, <https://www.gob.

mx/sre/prensa/gobierno-de-mexico-anuncia-que-ya-esta-disponible-la-vacuna-de-astrazeneca-producida-por-mexico-y-argentina>.

29  Romano, Lajtman, and García, 'Política de Estados Unidos, su impacto en Cuba'.
30  Yoko Iwama, 'Why Should NATO Care About China? A Japanese Perspective', IFRI, 12 March 2021, <https://www.ifri.org/en/publications/editoriaux-de-lifri/lettre-centre-asie/why-should-nato-care-about-china-japanese>.
31  Allison Carragher, 'The "Cold War" Diplomacy Behind Covid-19 Vaccines', Carnegie Europe, 11 March 2021, <https://carnegieeurope.eu/publications/84051>.
32  Genaro Lozano, 'Vaccine Diplomacy: A New Cold War', *Americas Quarterly*, 11 February 2021, <https://www.americasquarterly.org/article/vaccine-diplomacy-a-new-cold-war/>.
33  White House, 'Interim National Security Strategic Guidance', 3 March 2021, <https://www.whitehouse.gov/briefing-room/statements-releases/2021/03/03/interim-national-security-strategic-guidance/>.
34  Craig Faller, 'Statement of Admiral Craig S. Faller, Commander, United States Southern Command', 16 March 2021, <https://www.southcom.mil/Portals/7/Documents/Posture%20Statements/SOUTHCOM%202021%20Posture%20Statement_FINAL.pdf?ver=qVZdqbYBi_-rPgtL2LzDkg%3d%3d>; and Department of Defense, 'USNORTHCOM-USSOUTHCOM Joint Press Briefing', 16 march 2021, <https://www.defense.gov/News/Transcripts/Transcript/Article/2539561/usnorthcom-ussouthcom-joint-press-briefing/>.
35  Iwama, 'Why Should NATO Care About China?'.
36  Karim Fischer and Dieter Plehwe, 'Redes de think tanks e intelectuales de derecha en América Latina'. *Nueva Sociedad* 245, <https://nuso.org/articulo/redes-de-think-tanks-e-intelectuales-de-derecha-en-america-latina/>.
37  See <https://intdemocratic.org/eventos/foro-presidencial-defensa-de-la-democracia-en-las-americas-2/>.
38  Tamara Lajtman, Silvina Romano, Aníbal García Fernández, and Arantxa Tirado, 'EE.UU. y el Golpe de Estado en Bolivia', in Romano et al., *Trumperialismo*.
39  Ava Gómez Daza and Javier Calderón Castillo, 'Lawfare en Ecuador: la vía 'Lenín' al neoliberalismo', in Silvina Romano (ed.), *Lawfare: Guerra judicial y neoliberalismo en América Latina*, Madrid: CELAG-Mármol-Izquierdo Editores, 2019, pp. 85-112.
40  Eugenio Raúl Zaffaroni, Cristina Caamaño, and Valeria Vegh Weis, *Bienvenidos al lawfare!: Manual de pasos básicos para demoler el derecho penal,* Buenos Aires, Capital Intelectual,2021.
41  See Yaifred Ron, 'Los amos de la Sociedad Interamericana de Prensa', en Rebelión, 1 November 2009, <https://rebelion.org/los-amos-de-la-sociedad-interamericana-de-prensa/>.
42  For an example of the power of the right and the Bolivian coup, see Tamara Lajtman, Silvina Romano, Silvina, Aníbal García Fernández, Aníbal, and Arantxa Tirado, 'EE.UU. y el Golpe de Estado en Bolivia', in Romano et al., *Trumperialismo*.

# The Marxist-Christian Dialogue

# Europe as a Common. Exploring Transversal Social Ethics

Time Diagnoses, Vol. 46

edited by Walter Baier,
Cornelia Hildebrandt,
Franz Kronreif,
Luisa Sello

Publisher: LIT
Language: English
ISBN-13: 978-3643912985

To cope with the problems of today's world, we need to enter into a dialogue regardless of political, religious and philosophical beliefs – a transversal dialogue as Pope Francis called for in the private audience, he gave to Alexis Tsipras, Walter Baier and Franz Kronreif in September 2014. This conversation resulted in the DIALOP initiative – a transversal dialogue between Socialists and Christians. Since then, a network of universities and NGOs have been exploring paths of what they call a transversal social ethics. In this book authors from Austria, Belgium, Colombia, France, Germany, Greece, Hungary, Italy, Portugal and the Vatican air their views on topics like social equality, European Unity, democracy, the commons and ecology.

The editors are the steering committee of the initiative DIALOP – transversal dialogue project.

# What Can the Socialist Left Learn From the Pope?

## Walter Baier

For more than twenty years, Christians and Marxists have been engaged in a dialogue that began in Austria but has by now reached the European level. The war in Ukraine particularly underlines the necessity of a transversal dialogue that cuts across the ideological camps which were formed in past centuries.

With the beginning of Francis's pontificate this dialogue took on a new quality: for the first time in history, a man from the Global South is at the head of the Catholic Church; for the first time, the most important theme of the liberation theology that emerged in the 1960s, the Option for the Poor, with its critical socio-political implications, were incorporated into the teachings of the Catholic Church. And this at a historic moment when the threat of a world war waged with weapons of mass destruction and the global environmental crisis are challenging all political and ideological forces to a radical rethinking.

The change at the helm of the Catholic Church has not yet gripped the Church in its entirety. The opposition to the Pope is considerable, and so are the crisis phenomena in the Church, which are the expression of a long-delayed renewal. The change is therefore not irrevocable. Nevertheless, it is an event of world historical significance.

I must say I find that in many respects the Pope's critique of capitalism goes further than the critique expressed by many socialist and communist parties. It was he who, already in 2014 in his address to the participants of the world meeting of the popular movements stated with respect to the ongoing wars in Iraq, Syria, Libya, Yemen, and Ukraine, and the trade war between US and China:

During this meeting, you have also talked about Peace and Ecology. It is logical. There cannot be land, there cannot be housing, there cannot be work if we do not have peace and if we destroy the planet.[1]

And he concluded pointedly:

[…] we are going through World War Three but in instalments since there are economic systems that must make war in order to survive.

Is it legitimate to approach Pope Francis's preaching from a political point of view? I think it is, as the Pope himself called in his encyclical *Fratelli tutti* (2020) for a renewed appreciation of politics as

'a lofty vocation and one of the highest forms of charity' [*Evangelii gaudium*, §205]. […] For whereas individuals can help others in need, when they join together in initiating social processes of fraternity and justice for all, they enter the 'field of charity at its most vast, namely political charity' [Pius XI]. This entails working for a social and political order whose soul is social charity (*Fratelli tutti*, §180).[2]

Five years prior, in *Laudato si'* (2015), Pope Francis's encyclical about the environment, he gave a synthetic critique of what socialists call neoliberal capitalism:

This paradigm leads people to believe that they are free as long as they have the supposed freedom to consume. But those really free are the minority who wield economic and financial power. Amid this confusion, postmodern humanity has not yet achieved a new self-awareness capable of offering guidance and direction, and this lack of identity is a source of anxiety. We have too many means and only a few insubstantial ends (*Laudato si'*, §203).[3]

Indeed, this is the perfect definition of the problem humanity must cope with: anxiety in a world rich in means but poor in ends. The Pope states clearly that the Church does not claim to solve the scientific problems involved, nor does it want to replace politics; but it wants to raise its voice in a necessary honest and transparent dialogue.

## Inequality as the root of social ills

The third document to which I would refer as a relevant source for the dialogue between Marxists and Christians is the Apostolic Exhortation

*Evangelii gaudium,* the first major document that the Pope published – in November 2013. In it he asserts that:

> [...] the Gospel is not merely about our personal relationship with God. Nor should our loving response to God be seen simply as an accumulation of small personal gestures to individuals in need, a kind of 'charity à la carte', or a series of acts aimed solely at easing our conscience. [...] Both Christian preaching and life, then, are meant to have an impact on society (*Evangelii gaudium,* §180).[4]

And in the most unambiguous fashion he adds:

> As long as the problems of the poor are not radically resolved by rejecting the absolute autonomy of markets and financial speculation and by attacking the structural causes of inequality, no solution will be found for the world's problems or, for that matter, to any problems. Inequality is the root of social ills (§202).

At times, the dialogue between Marxists and Christians is burdened by prejudices about each other's motivation: Marxists tend to think that if Christians arrive at conclusions like their own or adopt Marxist analytical tools and vocabulary, this involves an external ingredient added on to belief. Conversely, among Christians there exists the prejudice that the conception Marxists have of human beings rests on a sort of inverted *homo oeconomicus* and that their critique of capitalism is thus ignorant of the individual and spiritual dimension of the person.

Both views are incorrect and tend to neglect the potentials inherent in Christianity and Marxism.

To highlight the humanistic vocation of Marxism, socialists often cite the famous paragraph from the young Marx's *Critique of Hegel's Philosophy of Right* in which he calls for the 'overthrow [of] all relations in which man is a debased, enslaved, abandoned, despicable essence', a categorical imperative which after 1990 became a sort of last moral resort for many socialists. However, the young Marx had already gone beyond an ethical critique of capitalism. In the *Economic Philosophic Manuscripts of 1844,* he wrote:

> The increase in the quantity of objects is therefore accompanied by an extension of the realm of the alien powers to which man is subjected, and every new product represents a new potentiality of mutual swindling and mutual plundering. Man becomes ever poorer as man, his need for money

becomes ever greater if he wants to master the hostile power. [...]

The need for money is therefore the true need produced by the economic system, and it is the only need which the latter produces. [...] Excess and intemperance come to be its true norm.[5]

And

Private property has made us so stupid and one-sided that an object is only ours when we have it — when it exists for us as capital, or when it is directly possessed, eaten, drunk, worn, inhabited, etc., — in short, when it is used by us. Although private property itself again conceives all these direct realisations of possession only as means of life, and the life which they serve as means is the life of private property — labour and conversion into capital.

In the place of all physical and mental senses there has therefore come the sheer estrangement of all these senses, the sense of having. The human being had to be reduced to this absolute poverty in order that he might yield his inner wealth to the outer world.[6]

Let us compare the young Marx to what the Pope said in his address to the participants in the World Meeting of Popular Movements in October of 2014:

An economic system centred on the deity money also needs to plunder nature to sustain consumption at the frenetic level it needs. [...] Brothers and sisters, creation is not a possession that we can dispose of as we wish; much less is it the property of some, of only a few.[7]

While Marx in his day, with remarkable intuition, anticipated the crisis of the capitalist mode of life, for the Pope it is an empirical fact, one with which all of humanity irrespective of faith, nationality, or philosophic or political conviction has to cope.

One can easily multiply the examples illustrating how convergent the Pope's and Marx's perception of the *conditio humana* is here by citing Marx's chief work, *Das Kapital*, which through the theory of commodity fetishism, delineates how, within capitalism, social relations, which in Marxism constitute the essence of the human, appear to people to be alienated and reified as a movement of things. Francis's prophetic preaching on the idolatry of money refers to the same social pathology.

I am not making a case for any syncretism here. Most Marxists are atheists, or at least agnostics, who ground their social ethic in the historically developing social nature of human beings. To be sure, most of them have left behind any atheistic fervour. Nevertheless, within socialist parties the memory remains of how the upper levels of the Catholic hierarchies – which for centuries formed a part of the ruling classes – opposed them as intransigent enemies; and conversely, among Christians the memory persists of the persecutions and suppression they suffered at the hands of ruling communist parties. With this history we must deal consciously and carefully when starting a dialogue. Thus the Pope was right to say that

> [W]e can never move forward without remembering the past; we do not progress without an honest and unclouded memory (*Fratelli tutti*, §249).

## Is he a communist?

About the pandemic the Pope said:

> If everything is connected, it is hard to imagine that this global disaster is unrelated to our way of approaching reality [...] (*Fratelli tutti*, §34).

This means, we can no longer talk of different separate crises, that is, perceiving the ecological, the global social crisis, and the crisis of the economic institutions as distinct matters. We are living through a crisis of the entire mode of production and consumption, in fact of the culture of unbridled capitalism and the corresponding liberal interpretation of the world, which prevails under its auspices. Thus, when the Pope spoke of 'land, work, housing' and of the preservation of peace and nature he could not content himself with modest structural reforms but called for a 'bold cultural revolution' (*Laudato si'*, §114).

And in his address to the participants of the World Meeting of Social Movements in October 2014, he explained:

> It is strange but, if I talk about this, some say that the Pope is communist. They do not understand that love for the poor is at the centre of the Gospel. Land, housing and work, what you struggle for, are sacred rights. To make this claim is nothing unusual; it is the social teaching of the Church.[8]

It is well here to recall Antonio Gramsci, for whom the development of Marxism's 'ethical-cultural dimension' was the essential task of political theory.[9] The fact that we are reaching the planet's ecological limits at a time at which 80% of resources are controlled by 20% of the world's population – and thus experiencing a comprehensive crisis of the capitalist form of life – has to change our view of how to defend the material interests of the working classes in the developed part of the capitalist world. More than at any moment in the history of capitalism, class struggle involves the necessity of a cultural transformation, of what Gramsci called a 'cultural and moral reform' in the privileged part of the world, as there are no borders to shield these areas from the necessary transformation. Nor are there any populist shortcuts for the political left that can spare it from having to accomplish the cultural revolution the Pope is calling for, which involves the transformation of the self.

This is what the story of the Good Samaritan, which the Pope invoked in *Fratelli tutti*, has to say to the left: Individually and collectively and transcending class affiliation and political conviction, we face the alternative of standing on the side of the robber, looking away indifferently, which is tantamount to complicity with him, or standing on the side of the victims.

> Now [When facing this alternative] there are only two kinds of people: those who care for someone who is hurting and those who pass by; those who bend down to help and those who look the other way and hurry off. Here all our distinctions, labels and masks fall away (*Fratelli tutti*, § 70).

And in the dilemma of this choice lies the deepest cause of the now politically reawakened pathologies of ethnic nationalism, xenophobia, and racism, particularly in the privileged parts of the capitalist word.

> For Christians, this way of thinking and acting is unacceptable (*Fratelli tutti*, § 39).

In other words, what is necessary now is a process described by Gramsci as the 'transition from the merely economic to the ethico-political moment, […] as a catharsis'.[10]

The courage and consistency with which the Pope opposes the neoliberal cultural mainstream is amazing. He denounces

> the manipulation of great words […] like democracy, freedom, justice or unity […] which are bent and shaped to serve as tools for domination, as meaningless tags that can be used to justify any action (*Fratelli tutti*, §14).

He castigates the radical consumerist individualism characteristic of neoliberal culture as the virus most difficult to eliminate, for it makes us believe that everything consists in giving free rein to our own ambitions.

And he debunks the hypocrisy of the mighty:

> War, terrorist attacks, racial or religious persecution, and many other affronts to human dignity are judged differently, depending on how convenient it proves for certain, primarily economic, interests. What is true as long as it is convenient for someone in power stops being true once it becomes inconvenient (*Fratelli tutti*, § 25).

Indeed, he argues

> to claim economic freedom while real conditions bar many people from actual access to it, and while possibilities for employment continue to shrink, is to practise doublespeak [quoting *Laudato si'*, §129]. Words like freedom, democracy or fraternity prove meaningless, for the fact is that 'only when our economic and social system no longer produces even a single victim, a single person cast aside, will we be able to celebrate the feast of universal fraternity' (*Fratelli tutti*, §110).[11]
>
> The solution is not relativism. Under the guise of tolerance, relativism ultimately leaves the interpretation of moral values to those in power, to be defined as they see fit (*Fratelli tutti*, §206).

What makes these sentences particularly powerful is not only the critique of hypocritical narratives itself but the consistency with which the Pope points to the power relations they serve. They remind us of a line from Bertolt Brecht's poem *Praise of the Revolutionary*:

> He interrogates viewpoints by asking 'whom are you benefitting'?

With *Fratelli tutti* the Pope has opened a reform agenda which has the potential to unite the popular movements in the Global South with the progressives parties in the North, a programme which is sometimes called a Green New Deal, sometimes a Marshall Plan for the Third World, or New Thinking in Global Politics. Obviously, realising this agenda requires the transformation of the existing world order of which the main characteristic is colonialism. Conscious of this, the Pope asked:

> Is it realistic to hope that those who are obsessed with maximizing profits will stop to reflect on the environmental damage which they will leave behind for future generations? Where profits alone count, there can be no thinking about the rhythms of nature, its phases of decay and regeneration, or the

complexity of ecosystems which may be gravely upset by human intervention (*Laudato si'*, §190).

And in *Fratelli tutti* he soberly states:

> Global society is suffering from grave structural deficiencies that cannot be resolved by piecemeal solutions or quick fixes (§ 179).
> … the scandal of poverty cannot be addressed by promoting strategies of containment that only tranquilize the poor and render them tame and inoffensive (§189).

This leads us to the question of who the protagonists of change are. At his most explicit, the Pope addressed this when he spoke to the participants of the World Meeting of Popular Movements, the same movements with which the radical left met in the World Social Forum in Porto Alegre nearly two decades ago. Here he turned explicitly to the poor not only as the victims of an unjust world order but as protagonists in creating a better one, the 'social poets' (*Fratelli tutti*, § 169) of a new world as he calls the popular movements.

> You are not satisfied with empty promises, with alibis or excuses. Nor do you wait with arms crossed for NGOs to help, for welfare schemes or paternalistic solutions that never arrive […]. You want to be protagonists. You get organized, study, work, issue demands and, above all, practice that very special solidarity that exists among those who suffer.[12]

Marxist-inspired socialism has something to contribute here. In the already cited *Economic-Philosophical Manuscripts*, the young Marx outlined the road map of his future research, aimed at grasping the:

> intrinsic connection between private property, avarice, the separation of labour, capital and landed property; the connection of exchange and competition, of value and the devaluation of men, of monopoly and competition, etc. — we have to grasp this whole estrangement connected with the money system.[13]

And he concluded, still in a preliminary way in 1844 that:

The worker becomes an ever cheaper commodity the more commodities he creates. The devaluation of the world of men is in direct proportion to the increasing value of the world of things. Labour produces not only commodities: it produces itself and the worker as a commodity — and this at the same rate at which it produces commodities in general.[14]

Twenty years later, in *Das Kapital*, Marx showed how labour from being an expression of life turns, in its value-creating form, into a factor that generates a power standing opposed to the workers, a power dominating them through the ever greater accumulation of capital, which in the end makes a section of the potentially working population superfluous, creating an industrial reserve army which now exists on a world scale, living precariously and deprived of rights, and dependent on the movement of capital and its fluctuations.

In other words, and this is my main point here: The particular characteristic of the Marxist view is that it perceives the poor not only as disadvantaged by the distribution of material wealth but also as the creators of all wealth and thus as its legitimate owners.

★ ★ ★

To conclude, in at least that part of the capitalist world still privileged by its prosperity Christians and socialists/communists find themselves in the position of critical minorities, opposing neoliberal, consumerist, individualist culture. Both agree with Pope Francis when he explained that,

> the so-called 'end of history' is still far away, since the conditions for a sustainable and peaceful development have not yet been adequately articulated and realized (*Evangelii gaudium*, § 59).

And we Marxists believe that these goals, which humanity can set itself, are achievable. There is a saying that the night is darkest just before the dawn. Or as the Pope put it:

> One of the more serious temptations which stifles boldness and zeal is a defeatism which turns us into querulous and disillusioned pessimists, 'sourpusses'. Nobody can go off to battle unless he is fully convinced of victory beforehand. If we start without confidence, we have already lost half the battle and we bury our talents (*Evangelii gaudium*, § 85).

NOTES

1. 'Address of Pope Francis to the Participants in the World Meeting of Popular Movements', Old Synod Hall, 28 October 2014, <https://www.vatican.va/content/francesco/en/speeches/2014/october/documents/papa-francesco_20141028_incontro-mondiale-movimenti-popolari.html>.
2. *Encyclical Letter 'Fratelli tutti' of the Holy Father Francis on Fraternity and Social Friendship*, <https://www.vatican.va/content/francesco/en/encyclicals/documents/papa-francesco_20201003_enciclica-fratelli-tutti.html>, §180 (quoting *Apostolic Exhortation 'Evangelii Gaudium'* (24 November 2013), 205.
3. *Encyclical Letter 'Laudato Si'' of the Holy Father Francis on Care for Our Common Home,* <https://www.vatican.va/content/francesco/en/encyclicals/documents/papa-francesco_20150524_enciclica-laudato-si.html>.
4. *Apostolic Exhortation 'Evangelii Gaudium' of the Holy Father Francis to the Bishops, Clergy, Consecrated Persons and the Lay Faithful on the Proclamation of the Gospel in Today's World*, <https://www.vatican.va/content/francesco/en/apost_exhortations/documents/papa-francesco_esortazione-ap_20131124_evangelii-gaudium.html >.
5. Karl Marx, *Economic and Philosophical Manuscripts of 1844*, in Karl Marx and Frederick Engels, *Collected Works*, vol. 3, New York: International, 1975, pp. 306-7.
6. Marx, *Economic and Philosophical Manuscripts of 1844*, p. 300.
7. Pope Francis, *Address to Participants in the World Meeting of Popular Movements*.
8. 'Address of Pope Francis to the Participants in the World Meeting of Popular Movements'.
9. Antonio Gramsci: *Gefängnisschriften* [Prison Notebooks], vol. 3, Berlin 1992, p. 500.
10. Gramsci, p. 1259.
11. The Pope is here citing his 'Message for the "Economy of Francesco"' (1 May 2019): *L'Osservatore Romano,* 12 May 2019.
12. Pope Francis, 'Address to Participants in the World Meeting of Popular Movements'.
13. Marx, *Economic and Philosophic Manuscripts of 1844*, p. 271.
14. Marx, *Economic and Philosophic Manuscripts of 1844*, p. 272

# Without the City of Man There Can Be No Paradise on Earth: The Bible Ends with a Vision of a Megacity (*Revelation* 21:1, 22:5)

### Margareta Gruber, OSF

Our age envisions its future as a catastrophe.[1] And there is a book of the Bible that gives catastrophe a name – *Apocalypsis* (Revelation). In modernity the history of this early Christian prophetic text's effect is above all characterised by a fascination with collapse. As Klaus Vondung has shown, it was especially in Germany in the last century that the idea that salvation could come through extermination produced its own apocalypse.[2]

Today there is no more talk of salvation. Today's catastrophe mode is, in Eva Horn's words, 'Future II'.[3] 'The catastrophe is an end, a conclusion, something that will have come.'[4] Worlds without people populate our works of fiction; or it is the last person who will remain, who looks back on what has been. The radical break, the pure otherness of what is to be is not the 'new' that will come to humanity but 'naked' catastrophe – the world's end without a new beginning.[5] Added to this is the 'dull, subterranean feeling [...] that the continuation of the present is precisely what leads to that future which we fear',[6] and thus that 'the actual catastrophe is the continuation of the Now, the progression of all the present tendencies'.[7]

The present has bid farewell to the biblical concept that through catastrophe in its apocalyptic form, thus through destruction and judgment and struggle, the new, salvation, will come to humankind; that is, the future is that which human beings make – or are to be blamed for.

'As never before', in the words of the Parisian theologian and Jesuit Christoph Theobald, '"humanitas" has to become something that humanity wishes for; which presupposes that it does not despair of its future.'[8] But from where can the strength for this task come? For this I would like to shed new light on the Bible's vision of the end, specifically in the book that has given 'apocalypse' its name: the *Revelation of John*, which was written at the end of the first century after Christ in Asian Turkey.

> Then I saw a new heaven and a new earth; for the first heaven and the first earth had passed away, and the sea was no more. And I saw the holy city, the new Jerusalem, coming down out of heaven from God, prepared as a bride adorned for her husband. And I heard a loud voice from the throne saying,
>
> 'See, the home of God is among mortals.
> He will dwell with them;
> they will be his peoples,
> and God himself will be with them;
> he will wipe every tear from their eyes.
> Death will be no more;
> mourning and crying and pain will be no more,
> for the first things have passed away.'
>
> And the one who was seated on the throne said, 'See, I am making all things new' (*Revelation* 21:1-5).

The final vision of the Bible – the new city. The Judeo-Christian Holy Scripture begins in the *Book of Genesis* with a creation poem and the Garden of Eden and ends with John's *Revelation* (*Apocalypse*) with the vision of a city, an urban space of peace for the peoples, illuminated by God's splendour. This contains a provocation but at the same time great potential for hope and consolation.

## The apocalyptic point zero

It is always cities in which human beings imagine their future, and at the same time every idea of the future is rooted in the present.[9] 'The history of future cities is a chronicle of the hopes and dreams, horrors, and anxieties of the time in which they were imagined. They are the architectural and urban construction of ourselves, fraught with the contradictions and encoded with the concerns of the present.'[10]

First, the historical query: In which present is the visionary of Patmos's image of the future rooted? His text grew out of the apocalyptic movement of ancient Judaism, which, from the perspective of a political situation experienced as oppressive and hopeless, expected a radical end of the present age through God's intervention. Between a present seen as hopeless and the new, which would come, stood God's judgment, the final disempowerment of evil; through this, God would implement justice in history. The images and concepts used by the ancient apocalyptic genre and forms of thought are those of rupture and destruction of cosmic dimension, of wars, natural catastrophes, plagues, and famine, such as live on today in popular apocalyptical scenarios. But what then is to come is the dawning of a new and lasting order bestowed by God; in John's revelation this comes in the form of a new city, the heavenly Jerusalem. In contrast to the early Jewish apocalyptical literature, which hoped for salvation in the (near) future, the early Christian apocalypse assumes that the liberating turning point has already occurred with the resurrection of the crucified Jesus of Nazareth. The discontinuity and destruction that typifies apocalyptic thinking is understood from the perspective of the catastrophic 'point zero' in the cross and resurrection of Jesus. The new epoch has already dawned and is asserting itself in history. This is the theme of John's revelation.

## The heavenly Jerusalem: a new urban world

What is it then that the visionary sees? The heavenly city is a megacity of God, gigantically big, magnificent, sumptuous, and light-filled, with God's throne in the centre, emitting a stream of life and healing, and with a people of God that includes all peoples. It is only the idol worshippers and the cruel who are definitively disempowered and remain excluded. Death and suffering are overcome. The peace promised by the biblical prophets is concretised in this vision of the New City. It is called Jerusalem, although Jerusalem lay in ruins after 70 AC, destroyed by the Romans. However, the vision does not relinquish it but shows it as newly descended on earth from God. The programme is not a flight from the world but a new vision of an urban society. It is about neither a vision of the beyond nor a prediction of the world's end. It is about a vision of present and future urban spaces of peace from the perspective of the consummation that is to come to the earthly world from God. The New Jerusalem is a hope for humanity that has become architecture.

## Not a restored paradise but a redeemed and liberated culture

Let us repeat a very central point: The 'new earth' is an *urban* world; that which people often call paradise or heaven, the symbol as such of the 'beyond', is depicted as a city in the (new) earth. In the eyes of ancient readers an ideal Hellenistic polis arises here with right-angled streets on the square-grid model of the ancient Hippodamian system. The signal is clear – the images of the heavenly city were also intended as political theology.

In contrast to popular conceptions of the new Creation, God's new world is precisely not the restored mythological primal state of Paradise but an urban space, a redeemed culture. This means that the whole history of humanity with its cultural achievements, which in the Jewish and Christian understanding is a history of God with people, will enter into this consummation. We can then imagine how the beauty of a Mozart requiem will co-exist in this city with the beauty of a Koran recitation, just to symbolically mention two classical expressions of religious-artistic beauty, both in metamorphosed form and no longer in competition with one another. The Bible thus ends not with a vacation brochure picturing a beach and palm trees for exhausted city dwellers but with a powerful intellectual and spiritual provocation. The book wants to show something that contains an objective like a blueprint of humanity's living space that continues to be earthly.

The great size of the city is of surreal proportions – a cube of 12,000 stadiums, that is, 2,200 kilometres (21:15-17). The dimensions of this megacity of God would cover the whole surface of the Roman Empire at the time of John! Its sumptuousness also exceeds all that exists. Marble, the ideal building material of an imperial city, is not even mentioned. Instead, the city is built with pearls and gems. It is characterised by beauty and transparency, not wealth and security.

Polis automatically also implies citizenship, thus social order as an essential element of culture. There is thus a system of rule in the New Jerusalem, but for inhabitants of the Hellenistic cities in the Roman Empire this is carried to an absurd point. 'All "citizens" of the city are […] "rulers", but without there being "subjects" ruled by them.'[11] 'Rule' by the 'slaves' of God consists in the vision of the face of God (22,4), thus in the knowledge or recognition of God. In this the prophecy of peace is fulfilled from the Jewish perspective.

Is it a utopia? To the extent that it represents an alternative social order, which relates critically to a current situation and calls on people to work for its realisation, it can be called a utopia. The heavenly Jerusalem, however, is understood not as something fictitious/utopian but prophetic/utopian as an announcement of God's action. It is God who will complete the finiteness of creation. The heavenly Jerusalem is a gift that people receive from God, not the result of historical developments or human strivings. And yet the vision wants to liberate and motivate precisely this kind of striving.

## People as space – a new spatial contract

Where are people within the heavenly Jerusalem? It would appear to be uninhabited. Nor are there houses for people in this city, no self-contained living spaces, only streets and gates as the biblical and oriental sites of communication. All is movement in light, free and unimpeded, anxiety-free encounter and exchange in its streets of 'pure gold like clear glass' (21:21). The New Jerusalem does not indicate a space for people but shows people as space.[12] A new kind of boundary-crossing relationship is imagined as a new kind of communally inhabited space – spatial and personal categories are reciprocally visualised and so produce a vision of peace. The wealth of peoples and cultures is brought into this city. There is no longer night, and so without this threat the city no longer has need of exclusion or boundaries and does not close its gates (21:24-26). This means that all nations have a right of residence there: 'Everyone is born there' (Psalm 87:5). In the first century this was understood as a rejection of Rome's global dominance and all claims to power that do not seek the will of God. Today we read the 'theology of gates' against the background of the refugee flows towards Europe via the Mediterranean but also the flight of millions from the country to the city, which is especially taking place in Asian countries. God's megacity is an 'arrival city'[13] in the literal sense, a city of hospitable arrival that can afford to keep its gates open! This 'theology of walls', whose gates become portals of hospitality, is prophetic, especially today, 'in times of many fences and walls even amongst the poor of the periphery, in times of migration without identity documents, human trafficking, etc.'[14]

The New Jerusalem incorporates a new spatial contract, just as city and space planners today are demanding and seeking to practice in view of the increasing political division and growing economic inequality. *How will we live together?* This is the burning issue in a world of compressed cities in which people, despite increasing individualisation, are longing to connect with each other and with other species in digital and real space. 'How will we live together?' is thus the theme of the 2021 exhibit in Venice, Biennale Architettura. Hashim Sarkis, its curator, has formulated this quest: 'A spatial contract could constitute a social contract. We are looking for a spatial contract that is at once universal and inclusive, an expanded contract for peoples and species to coexist and thrive in their plurality.'[15] An – even only virtual – visit to the world exhibition works as a fascinating commentary on the biblical utopia, conceived and realised by architects, engineers, craftspeople, artists, politicians, and citizens from the whole world. It demonstrates the currentness of the heavenly city and its spatial utopia. The wealth of creativity, concern, responsibility, and pragmatic optimism displayed by the world exhibition is a comforting counterpoint to many futuristic scenarios that are stuck in the apocalyptic alarmism of catastrophe. And so, in Venice I found a concretisation of the spirit of Pope Francis's encyclical *Fratelli tutti* – the sought after collectivity became the city, the urban living space within ecological responsibility.

## Everything is the Temple – a theology of public space

The most important element that the observer sees in this city is what he/she does not see: 'I did not see a temple in the city, because the Lord God Almighty and the Lamb are its temple' (21:22). God too no longer has a 'house', for his 'throne' is on a square in the middle of the city – or, more precisely, the whole city is the square in whose midst is the throne. The vision is not of a space for God but God as space. This does not mean a negation of the cult but its radicalisation: places gain their importance through relations; it is about a new kind of encounter and communication with God through a new communication among people. Politically, this points to the necessity of participation; God as the eschatological space of peace is a 'space of the inclusion of diversity as richness and fullness of life'.[16]

This theology of public space in *Revelation* is perhaps the most important thing it has to say to us today. On this I would like to quote the Brazilian liberation theologian Luíz Carlos Susin at length:

> Our conceptual world is populated with public squares that are linked to the Temple and the established powers: the city hall square, the church square, the parade ground. In the eschatological city, it is exactly the symbolism of the square that takes the place of the Temple [...]. The system and the heart of the city are shifted – the square is the place for everyone, for the whole 'polis', in an inclusive, welcoming, and hospitable way offered by the victims and the poor. The square belongs to everyone and has room for everyone [...]. When we realise that today it is the financial centres that are the powerful, fearsome temples that never forgive and exact blood from the debtors, and 'shopping centres' the enthralling temples that lure people into debt, that private and state credit cards are the mediators between the alluring and the frightening aspects of the numinous, which lead from joyous consumerism to unpayable debt, and if we further take into account all of today's required backup procedures and segregation and victimisation measures, we can then gauge the meaning that the substitution of the Temple by the square has. In our narration the eschatological square is the place in which the people are no longer subjugated to these sanctified powers and where they can freely circulate, take up relationships and live together with others, and experience acceptance and recognition as human beings. The particular time for this experience is the Sabbath, the time of citizenship par excellence, when families and friends can move around the squares unhurriedly with more happiness, more playfulness, and selflessness in their bodies and relationships, so that every stranger becomes a potential friend.[17]

We hear in these words of a Latin American theologian a new poetry of the city that inspires a new praxis of peace.[18] In his utopian theology, the German theologian Friedrich-Wilhelm Marquardt pointedly emphasises the category of space.[19] The new Jerusalem promises the common living space of human beings and God, which was lost with Paradise, in the context of the city as a human life form. This means that without the human city there can be no Paradise.[20] Thus, people's concrete yearning for a habitable living space is kept alive, and those spaces remain in sight whose shaping within the 'old cities' (Marquardt) of the 'old earth' have been and still are given to us.

## Religion in public space

Having lived for four years in the 'earthly' Jerusalem, where religion naturally controls public space and often dominates it in conflict with the country's secular society, I have become more sensitive to the increasingly palpable need to once again publicly carry out a religious discourse. These discourses are often associated with violence, for instance in the case of the cartoon dispute. The public square runs the risk of becoming a symbol of terror instead of being the symbol of the movement towards more openness as during the so-called Arab Spring. In the earthly Jerusalem this applies even to the holy site itself, the so-called Temple Mount or al-Haram asch-Sharif and, below it, to the square in front of the Wailing Wall, where the encounter of the religions repeatedly erupts into violence. The privatisation of religious experience, as occurred in the West after the Enlightenment, and then determining the Western debate around secularisation, is alien to Judaism – as well as to Islam. The goal of God's covenant project from the Jewish point of view is that the earth – the collective, the public – be filled with the knowledge of God: 'They shall not hurt nor destroy in all my holy mountain; for the earth shall be full of the knowledge of the Lord, as the waters cover the sea' (Isaiah, 11:9). In this way the promise of peace is fulfilled.[21] The conflicts in the earthly Jerusalem repeatedly showed me that it is a mistake to want to create peace between peoples and cultures by facilitating the disappearance of religion from public space, not to mention by coercing this. On the contrary, we can observe in the Middle East how the suppression of religion regularly produces new spirals of violence. But the question is increasingly posed for Western societies as well: How can religion find its way (back) into public space without violent confrontation?

In the face of these urgent questions – urgent too for successful cultural cohabitation in Europe – the prophetic vision becomes particularly suggestive: The new city of peace no longer needs the Temple, because its sacrifices have been abolished. From the Christian perspective, Christ the

Lamb's offering of his life is the one 'sacrifice' that unmasks the sacrifice-mechanism and its spirals of violence and overcomes it.[22] Instead of the public cult of sacrifice what would seem to be suggested here is, in a sense, a 'cultic secularity', paradoxically a secular space for all peoples illumined by the worship of God. Marquardt calls this the 'eschatological secularity of the city':[23] 'It will be the opposite of any sort of renunciation of God, any indifference and neutrality towards him.'[24] Instead, it will be grounded 'in the humanity and earthliness of God as an original citizen of this city with the right of access to it'.[25]

## Healing the wounded imagination

The visionary author of the book is completely aware of the city's ambivalence. Therefore, John's *Revelation* is the tale of two cities: Babylon and Jerusalem. With its wealth, Babylon signifies the attraction exerted by Hellenistic culture, the temptation to assimilate, which the visionary strongly condemns. It also stands for the violence with which the Roman Empire ran over its subjected peoples. It is conceivable that the Jewish seer and writer John, or his first readership that fled from Palestine, had a vision in mind of the atrocities of the suppressed Jewish revolt. But now these Christians had arrived in the heart of the Empire, in its eastern cities with their emperor cult and were fighting for their identity as a minority. To this the ascetically inclined prophet counterposed his uncompromising message: move away! (18:4). For him Babylon/Rome is the embodiment of human hubris, a city, a culture that destroys itself with its avariciousness, with its insatiable drive to oppress. The depiction of the dystopian anti-civilisation (Babylon) and its fall – the collapse of its worldwide economic empire[26] – represents both a prophetic warning and a critical potential against the forces of a dehumanised culture. To this the *Book of Revelation* counterposes the vision of the Heavenly Jerusalem as the consummation of the *humanum*, which is inconceivable without non-human Creation but encompasses it. The subversive significance of this urban space of peace, which comes from heaven but arises on earth, the theology of its precious walls, open gates, joyfully peopled squares, and the absence of a temple only becomes discernible against the backdrop of the dystopian counter-images of our time. These make us aware of how this New World, which seems to be so effortless and easygoing, is far from being taken for granted.

What applies to the prophetic warning of catastrophe, however, also applies to the prophetic promise of salvation: The quality of life of God's new world is tied to a turnaround made by people; the vision reveals what is working against this and thus what is straining and endangering peace in the earthly cities. But in the Bible it is not the final destruction or an uninhabitable, pale green, post-apocalyptic world that has the last word but hope, for which the light-flooded, gem-coloured, heavenly polis stands. Whoever exposes her/himself to this vision will experience prophetically an expansion of his or her concepts, wishes, and desires for spaces of peace.

The hope for this perfected form of human culture resists the temptation to nihilist despair or escapism and leads to a new ethos that finds expression in concrete actions. This is the path indicated by Pope Francis in his encyclical *Laudato si'* on 'care for our common home' or the reciprocal relation between the human being and his/her environment.

NOTES

1. Eva Horn, *Zukunft als Katastrophe*, Frankfurt a.M.: Fischer, 2014.
2. Klaus Vondung, *Die Apokalypse in Deutschland*, Munich: dtv, 1988.
3. Horn, *Zukunft*, p. 12.
4. Horn, *Zukunft*, p. 15.
5. Horn, *Zukunft*, p. 27.
6. Horn, *Zukunft*, p. 20
7. Horn, *Zukunft*, p. 17. Walter Benjamin expresses a similar conception in *The Arcades Project*: Walter Benjamin, *Das Passagen-Werk,* in *Gesammelte Schriften*, vol V ed. Rolf Tiedemann and Hermann Schweppenhäuser, with the collaboration of Theodor W. Adorno and Gershom Scholem, Frankfurt a.M.: Suhrkamp, 1982, p. 592: 'That things are "status quo" is the catastrophe.' And: 'Marx says that revolutions are the locomotive of world history. But perhaps it is quite otherwise. Perhaps revolutions are an attempt by the passengers on this train – namely, the human race – to activate the emergency brake.' Walter Benjamin, *One-Way Street and Other Writings*, transl. Edmund Jephcott and Kingsley Shorter, London: New Left Books, 1979, p. 402.
8. Christoph Theobald, *Christum als Stil. Für ein zeitgemäßes Glaubensverständnis*, Freiburg i.Br.: Herder, 2018, p. 200.
9. Horn, *Zukunft*, p. 31.
10. Liam Young, 'The end of the end of the world', in Liam Young (ed.), *Planet City*, Melbourne: Uro Publications, 2020, p. 34.
11. Martin Ebner, *Die Stadt als Lebensraum der ersten Christen. Das Urchristentum in seiner Umwelt*, vol. I, Göttingen: Vandenhoeck & Ruprecht, 2012, p. 65.
12. See, appropriately, the title of Robert H. Gundry's article 'The New Jerusalem. People as Place, Not Place for People', *Novum Testamentum* 29,3 (1987), 254-264.
13. See Doug Saunders, *Arrival Cities: How the Largest Migration in History is Reshaping Our World*, London: Windmill, 2011.
14. Luíz Carlos Susin, 'Die Stadt, die Gott will. Ein Platz und ein Tisch für alle', in Margit Eckholt and Stefan Silber (eds), *Glauben in Mega-Cities. Transformationsprozesse in lateinamerikanischen Großstädten und ihre Auswirkungen auf die Pastoral* (Forum Weltkirche und Frieden, vol. 14), Mainz: Grünewald, 2014, pp. 275-87, 280.
15. Hashim Sarkis, 'How will we live together? Biennale Architettura 2021', Venice 2021, pp. 24-31, here 29.

16  Susin, 'Die Stadt', p. 287.
17  Susin, 'Die Stadt', 278f.
18  See Margit Eckholt, 'Poesie der Stadt. Wie sieht die neue Stadt aus?', in Eckholt and Silber, *Glauben in Mega-Cities*, pp. 302-23.
19  Friedrich-Wilhelm Marquardt, *Eia, wärn wir da. Eine theologische Utopie*, Gütersloh: Kaiser, 1997; reprint: Kamen: Hartmut Spenner, 2021.
20  See Michael Alban Grimm, 'Lebensraum in Gottes Stadt. Jerusalem als Symbolsystem der Eschatologie', *Jerusalemer Theologisches Forum* 11 (2007), 153.
21  I owe much here to conversation with Alick Isaacs who is engaged in arduous talks with the religious settlers' movement. See Alick Isaacs, *A Prophetic Peace. Judaism, Religion and Politics*, Bloomington IN: Indiana University Press, 2011.
22  For more on this see René Girard, *Das Ende der Gewalt. Analyse des Menschheitsverhängnisses*, Freiburg: Herder, 2009.
23  Marquardt, *Eia, wärn wir da*, p. 259.
24  Marquardt, *Eia, wärn wir da*, p. 259.
25  Marquardt, *Eia, wärn wir da*, p. 259.
26  One thinks of the vivid imagery of kings, merchants, and ship captains bewailing its destruction (*Revelation* 18:9-19).

# Marxisms and Christianities: Recent Publications

## Michael Löwy

The first socialists in nineteenth-century Europe – Saint-Simon and his disciples, Cabet and the French communists, and Wilhelm Weitling, the founder of the League of the Just in Germany – were religious and identified with the Christian heritage. It is only with Marx and Engels that a non-religious, or even atheist, socialism arose. The foundational text of this turning point is the article published by Marx in 1844 in the *Deutsch-französische Jahrbücher*.

The first unabridged French translation of the *Annales franco-allemandes (Deutsch-französische Jahrbücher)* has just been published; it includes not only Marx's and Engels's writings but the entire journal, which makes it possible to situate these texts in their historical and intellectual context. As we know, this publication, which appeared in Paris in February 1844 under the direction of Arnold Ruge and Karl Marx, had originally been a project aimed at building a Franco-German philosophical and political alliance. At the beginning of the project, the Young Hegelians chose Paris both to evade German censorship and establish cooperation between French democrats and socialists. But the latter – Lamennais, Étienne Cabet, Pierre Leroux, and Louis Blanc – politely refused this invitation, put off by the *atheism* of the Germans.

Besides Marx and Engels, the authors were Arnold Ruge, Johann Jacoby, Moses Hess, Lazarus Bernays, Heinrich Heine, and Georg Herwegh. It is striking that the majority of these authors are of *Jewish origin*. This is true of Marx, Hess, Jacoby, Bernays, and Heine – five of the eight participants! Admittedly, Marx and Bernays came from converted families and had no contact with Jewish tradition; they were 'Non-Jewish Jews', to use the famous phrase of Isaac Deutscher, an aspect that the editors of the new edition have not highlighted. To a certain extent, the *Jährbücher* are an episode in the long history of left-wing radicalism among Jewish intellectuals, which began in the nineteenth century and reached its zenith in the twentieth.

It is in the Introduction to the 'Contribution to the Critique of Hegel's Philosophy of Right', one of two articles Marx contributed to the journal, that the little phrase appears which was to sanction the divorce between Marxism and religious faith: 'religion is the opium of the people'. Considered by partisans or adversaries as a kind of résumé of the Marxist conception of religion, this ironic formula is by no means unique to Marx; we find it, with some different nuances, before him in Moses Hess, Henrich Heine, Bruno Bauer, and many other authors of the period. Moreover, the concept of religion that Marx had at the beginning of 1844 was neo-Hegelian (as in Feuerbach) and ahistorical – religion as alienation of the human essence. It is only later, starting with *The German Ideology* (1846), that a specifically Marxist analysis of religion appears, as one of the forms of ideology, to be seen in relation to social classes and historical conditions.

★ ★ ★

In fact, Marx was little preoccupied with religious phenomena. It was his friend Friedrich Engels who would give a closer look at the historic development of Christianity, notably in his book on the social and religious wars in Germany at the time of the Reformation. Nicos Foufas's short book is the first analysis in French of this 'classic' text of Friedrich Engels, *The Peasant War in Germany* (1850). It comprises a series of articles published by Engels in the *Neue Rheinische Zeitung: Politisch-ökonomische Revue*, which was edited by the two friends in London where they were in exile after the defeat of the 1848-49 revolution in Germany.

Foufas sheds light on the radical novelty of this work, which in fact represent the first attempt – and one of the most successful – to apply historical materialism to a historic event, the uprising of the peasants in the Holy Roman Empire in 1524-25. Engels's study, Foufas observes, is quite original for its attempt at explaining religious conflicts as class conflicts but also because he does not reduce religion to an obscurantist and conservative factor – but understands it as capable, under certain historical conditions, of expressing subversive aspirations. This was true of various heretical movements in the Middle Ages and, in particular, of the sixteenth-century peasant revolt where religious faith, in the form of the revolutionary theology of the preacher Thomas Müntzer, was to play a decisive role. If Engels found it necessary to write about this event in the context of the years 1848-50 this was because it had been the most important revolutionary uprising in the history of Germany.

The principal weakness, in my opinion, of Engels's analysis is that it sees certain religious beliefs as a simple 'reflection' or even 'mask' of class interests. Nevertheless, in certain passages, which Foufas does not cite, Engels goes beyond this sort of socio-economic reductionism. Referring to Müntzer's communism, Engels wrote:

> Muenzer's political doctrine followed his revolutionary religious conceptions very closely, and as his theology reached far beyond the current conceptions of his time, so his political doctrine went beyond existing social and political conditions. [...] His programme, less a compilation of the demands of the then existing plebeians than a genius's anticipation of the conditions for the emancipation of the proletarian element that had just begun to develop among the plebeians, [...].*

What is suggested in this astonishing paragraph is not only the protest and even revolutionary function of a religious movement but also its anticipatory dimension, its utopian function. This is the polar opposite of the theory of 'reflection'; far from being the simple 'expression' of existing conditions, Müntzer's political-religious doctrine appears as a 'genial anticipation' of future communist aspirations. Here we find a new path unexplored by Engels but which later would be richly elaborated by Ernst Bloch, starting with his essay on Thomas Müntzer's youth and going through his magnum opus, *The Principle of Hope*.

★ ★ ★

Ernst Bloch represents a major turning point in the history of Marxist reflections on religion; he is the first whose goal is less 'the critique of religious alienation' – even if this aspect is not absent in his writings – than the recuperation of the *'Utopian surplus'* of religious traditions, notably Christianity. His *religious atheism* is situated within a unique philosophical position, opposed just as much to institutional theologies as it is to vulgar materialism.

No one is better qualified to treat this subject than the Franco-German Arno Münster, a Bloch disciple and biographer and author of several remarkable essays on Bloch's thought. Münster's *Socialisme et religion au XXe siècle* is somewhat disorganised – with the chapters following neither chronological nor thematic order, resulting in a certain amount of repetition. The first part is a historical précis of the relation between socialism and religion, from Auguste Blanqui to the USSR, passing trough Jean Jaurès (but without Marx!) and is inevitably rather schematic. But his analysis of

---
\* Frederick Engels, 'The Peasant War in Germany', Karl Marx and Frederick Engels, *Collected Works*, vol. 10, New York: International Publishers, 1978, p. 422.

Bloch's philosophy of religion is a very important contribution to the debate on Marxism and religion.

As Münster recalls, Bloch became a Marxist in 1921 under the influence of his friend Georg Lukács; as a fellow traveller in the communist movement, Bloch went into exile in 1933 following the Nazis' coming to power, first to France and then to the United States. Returning to Europe after the war, he settled in the German Democratic Republic where he became a semi-official philosopher from 1949 to 1956. His opposition to the Soviet invasion of Hungary led to his condemnation as a 'revisionist' and the prohibiting of his teaching activities. When the wall was built in 1961 he decided to move to Tübingen in the German Federal Republic where he became a Marxist dissident with a large following among the rebellious youth of 1968.

The philosophy of religion is present in four states in the oeuvre of the German Jewish philosopher Bloch:

1) His youthful work *The Spirit of Utopia* (1918), especially the final chapter with the surprising title 'Karl Marx, death, and the apocalypse'; but also in the excursus 'Symbol: the Jews'.
2) The book *Thomas Müntzer als Theologe der Revolution* [Thomas Müntzer as Theologian of the Revolution] (1921), his first communist book, which profoundly enriches the Marxist approach to religion.
3) Chapter 53, volume III, of his magnum opus *The Principle of Hope*, dedicated to the three major monotheist religions from the point of view of what they bring to the utopia of the Not-Yet-Being.
4) *Atheism in Christianity* (1968), a materialist exegesis of the Bible, which provoked much polemic and controversy – especially on the part of Christian theologians.

Hostile to what he called 'vulgar and impoverished atheism', but also to conservative theologies of all confessions, Bloch was fascinated by Messianism, the Apocalypse, eschatology, the Kabbalah, mysticism, heresies; he was enthusiastic about the prophet Amos, Jesus of Nazareth, Joachim de Flore, Meister Eckhart, Jan Hus, Thomas Müntzer, Wilhelm Weitling, and Dostoyevsky. But it was Karl Marx and Friedrich Engels who supplied him with the connecting thread – class struggles, revolutionary praxis, and communist utopia.

As Arno Münster has shown with considerable intelligence and sensitivity, Bloch's religious atheism is seen above all in his critical, heterodox, and materialist reading of the Bible, in which he looks for its utopian, subversive, and emancipatory elements. A reading 'through the eyes of the

Communist Manifesto was to lead him to a critical dialogue with the most advanced representatives of Protestant theology: Rudolf Bultmann, Albert Schweitzer, Jürgen Moltmann, and above all his friend the Christian socialist and anti-fascist German Paul Tillich who was also in exile in the United States. Of course, Christian theologians could not accept Bloch's central and provocative proposition, namely that 'only an atheist can be a good Christian and only a Christian a good atheist'.

With Moltmann, also a Christian socialist, the bone of contention was to be the categorical rejection by Bloch of Paul's and Luther's 'theology of the cross', which, in Bloch's eyes, leads to an acceptance of suffering as human destiny. One of the Protestant theologians, Carl-Heinz Ratschow, a professor at the University of Marburg, even dedicated, in 1972, an entire book to a discussion of Bloch's heretical theses. Despite his sympathy for Bloch he rejected his Marxist engagement, opposing to Bloch's hope founded in combat, Christian hope based on certitude. Ratschow also went on to reject, as one might expect, Bloch's polemical interpretation of the 'Book of Job' as being a revolt against a God guilty of tolerating the injustice of the world.

Finally, the most positive reception of Bloch was that of the Latin-American liberation theologians (especially Gustavo Gutiérrez); without accepting his atheism, they fully shared the wager that appears in the conclusion of his 1968 book: 'the union of revolution and Christianity in the Peasant War will not be the last such'.

★ ★ ★

If Marxist thinkers are interested in Christianity, are there not also Christians attracted by Marxism? Certainly, one can find many examples throughout modern history. A recent book published in the United States recounts a rather astonishing example – a young Catholic woman, Grace Carlson (1906-1992), who 'converted' to Marxism, becoming one of the principal leaders of the Socialist Workers Party, the Trotskyist organisation affiliated with the Fourth International.

Donna T. Haverty-Stacke's book is a very well documented biography of Carlson's unusual spiritual and political trajectory. Born into a working-class Catholic family of Irish origin, raised by the Sisters of St. Joseph, the young Grace Holmes was interested in the condition of workers, but through the prism of *Rerum novarum* and the Church's social doctrine. As a student at the University of Minnesota she mobilised, together with her husband Gilbert Carlson and her sister Dorothy, in support of a major workers' strike in Minneapolis in 1934, which was led – something very exceptional for the time – by Trotskyist activists. All three of them began to take part in political meetings, which they did not see as incompatible with their religious faith – they could go to Mass and to a socialist meeting on the same Sunday. In the years that followed, the two sisters became increasingly closer to the Trotskyists, and in 1936 they joined this dissident communist current, which was to found the Socialist Workers Party in 1937, invoking the heritage of Marx, Lenin, and Trotsky. At about 1938 Grace stopped being a practicing Catholic, which caused the separation (but not divorce) from her husband Gilbert Carlson.

What were the motivations of what the author calls a 'conversion'? She offers an interesting hypothesis: the *elective affinity* – in the Weberian sense of the term – between Grace's Catholic workers' consciousness and the SWP's workerist socialism. But this hunch is not developed in the book.

In 1942 Grace was to become the only woman in the SWP leadership, the National Committee; after spending a year in prison (1945) charged with 'attempting to forcibly overthrow the government of the United States', she became the SWP candidate for vice-president of the US, the presidential candidate being Farrell Dobbs, one of the leaders of the 1934 strike.

In 1952, however, a second conversion occurred with Grace Carlson deciding to leave the party and return to the Catholic Church – which also led her to reunite with her husband Gilbert but to break with her sister Dorothy who remained in the party, with her companion Ray Dunne, and her numerous socialist friends with whom she had built a network of 'sorority'. James P. Cannon, SWP founder and principal leader, who had become Grace's personal friend, tried to explain to her that the Catholic Church was 'the most reactionary and obscurantist force in the entire world', but without great success.

Her perplexed Marxist friends tried to explain this turnaround by exhaustion in the face of repression and the McCarthyist witch-hunt, but for Grace it meant something else: a spiritual turning point, a need for God. I changed, she said, my attitude towards religion but not my political attitude – 'I have remained a Marxist in my way'. She was taken under the wing of the Sisters of St Joseph and would teach at the School of Nursing at St Mary's Hospital – not without cooperating with Slant, a Christian Marxist group in England, and denouncing the War in Vietnam.

★ ★ ★

In the case of Grace Carlson what was involved was a singular and personal itinerary. What would be found a generation later in Latin America had quite different dimensions – an entire social movement, especially among the Catholic youth, was to appropriate certain Marxist concepts and formulate a new Christian vision, a socialist one. This movement, arising in Brazil at the beginning of the 1960s – after the Cuban Revolution but before the Second Vatican Council – would take different forms, one of which was the formation in 1962 by activists of the Christian University Youth of a socialist/humanist political party, Ação popular (Popular Action – AP). It was only much later, in 1981, that liberation theology was to develop out of this socio-political experience, not only in Brazil but throughout Latin America.

One of the most striking episodes of this convergence between Catholicism and Marxism was the engagement, at around 1968 to 1970, of a group of Dominican friars from the Convent of Perdizes in São Paulo with the armed resistance to the military dictatorship established in 1964 in Brazil. The recent book by Leneide Duarte-Plon and Clarisse Mereiles is a biography of Friar Tito de Alencar, one of the Dominicans who paid for his social and political engagement with his life.

As an activist of the Christian Student Youth, who entered the Dominican Order in 1966, Tito shared with the other friars at the Convent of São Paulo an admiration for Che Guevara and Camilo Torres and the desire to associate Christ and Marx in the struggle for the liberation of the Brazilian people. Tito was close to AP, which was hegemonic within the student movement, and he contributed to the clandestine organisation in 1968 of the Congress of the National Union of Students in the village of Ibiuna. Like all the delegates he was arrested by the police on this occasion but soon freed.

As a result of the hardening of the military dictatorship in 1968 and the impossibility of any legal protest, the most radical wing of the anti-dictatorship opposition took up arms from this moment on. The main organisation of armed struggle against the regime was the National Liberation Action (ALN) founded by a dissident Communist leader Carlos Marighella. A group of young Dominicans – Frei Betto, Yvo Lesbaupin, Fernando Brito, and others – engaged with the ALN without taking up arms themselves but by providing logistical support. Although not one of those who collaborated directly with Marighella and his comrades, Tito de Alencar solidarised with their engagement. Like them, he believed that the Gospel contains a radical critique of capitalist society; and like them he believed in the need for revolution. As he was to write later on, 'the revolution is the struggle for a new world, a form of earthly Messianism in which it is possible for Christians and Marxists to meet'.

During the night of 4 November 1969, the Commissar of Police Sérgio Paranhos Fleury invaded the Convent of Perdizes and arrested several Dominicans, Friar Tito among them. The majority were tortured and their confessions allowed the police to set a trap for Marighella and assassinate him. Tito had no contact with the ALN and responded in the negative to all questions. He was twice subjected to torture (by electric shock) at the end of 1969 and the beginning of 1970, first by Fleury and then in the offices of the army's intelligence services – called by military people 'the unit of hell'. To escape his executioners, he attempted suicide with a razor blade. Interned at the Military Hospital he received the visit of the Cardinal of São Paulo, Dom Agnelo Rossi, a conservative figure who showed solidarity with the military and refused to denounce the torture of the Dominicans. Finally sent to an 'ordinary' prison, Tito wrote an account of his sufferings, which was published in the US magazine *Look* and distributed in Brazil by resistance activists, with considerable impact. Finally, Pope Paul VI condemned 'a major country that applies inhuman methods of interrogation' and replaced Dom Rossi with Paulo Evaristo Arns, the new Cardinal of São Paulo, known for his engagement for and defence of human rights and his opposition to torture.

Some months later, the revolutionaries kidnapped the Swiss ambassador and released him in exchange for the liberation of 70 prisoners, among them Frei Tito. The young Dominican hesitated to accept, so foreign to him was the idea of leaving his country. The 70 were banished from the country and forbidden to return. After a brief stay in Chile Frei Tito took up residence with the Dominicans of the Convent of Saint-Jacques in Paris. Exile was very painful to him. 'It is very hard to live far from one's country and the revolutionary struggle. One has to bear exile as one bears torture.' He participated in campaigns denouncing the crimes of the dictatorship and began to study theology and the classics of Marxism. 'I accept the Marxist analysis of class struggle. For those who want to change the structures of society, Marx is indispensable. But the vision I as a Christian have of the world is different from the Marxist vision of the world.' The French Dominican Paul Blanquart known for his options 'to the left of Christ', described him as 'the most engaged and most revolutionary of Dominicans'.

However, as time went on Tito showed increasingly disturbing signs of psychological imbalance. He believed he was being followed and persecuted by his torturer, Commissar Fleury. It was suggested in 1973 that he move to a more tranquil spot: the Dominican Convent of Arbresle. He became friends with the Dominican friar Xavier Plassat, who tried to help him, and he received psychiatric treatment from Dr. Jean-Claude Rolland. To no avail. After the coup d'état in Chile in September 1973 he became ever more distraught, convinced that Fleury was still persecuting him and that the Dominicans, or the aides at the psychiatric hospital were his accomplices.

Finally, desperate and at the end of his tether, on 8 August 1974 he chose suicide by hanging.

His Dominican friend, Friar Xavier Plassat ended by settling in Brazil where he became organiser of the campaign against slave labour of the Pastoral Land Commission; in his account, 'my work here is an inheritance left me by Tito'.

★ ★ ★

As we know, the Vatican, under John Paul II and Ratzinger, rejected liberation theology as an 'error' due especially to its 'indiscriminate' use of Marxist concepts. With the election of Bergoglio, Pope Francis, coming from Argentina, a new period seems to be opening up. Not only was Gustavo Gutiérrez received at the Vatican but the Pope, on the occasion of a meeting in 2014 with Alexis Tsipras and Walter Baier, two representatives of the Party of the European Left, endorsed the idea of a dialogue between Marxists and Christians and suggested that its focus be a transversal social ethic. Dialogues of this type did take place after the war in certain European countries (in France, Italy, and Germany), but an initiative under the auspices of the Vatican is without precedent.

For this dialogue the Pope delegated Archbishop Angelo Vincenzo Zani, Secretary of the Congregation for Catholic Education, as well as a member of the Focolari movement, a lay network founded by Chiara Lubich in post-war Italy. The book *Europe as a Common* is the first publication to result from this attempt to explore a 'transversal social ethic'. Two of its editors, Franz Kronreif and Luisa Sello, belong to the Focolari, and two of the other editors, Walter Baier (former General Secretary of the Austrian Communist Party) and Cornelia Hildebrandt (of the Rosa Luxemburg Stiftung in Berlin) represent transform! the network of research foundations connected to the Party of the European Left.

The dialogue was first held in the premises of the Sophia University Institute of the Focolari movement, located in the village of Loppiano near Florence, where the participants were welcomed by the Belgian sociologist Bernard Callebaut. Other symposia took place at Castelgondolfo – the summer residence of the Pope! – and in Vienna. But in September 2018 a joint summer school was held at the University of the Aegean located on the island of Syros, seat of a traditional Catholic community. Most of the documents brought together in *Europe as a Common* (which is the first volume of a projected series) are presentations made during the encounter. In the process, the students, who came from each of the two sides of the dialogue, together prepared a document, 'The Manifesto of Hermoupolis', also included in the volume.

In their introduction, Baier, Hildebrandt, Kronreif, and Sello point out that the aim of the dialogue is not mutual conversion, nor creating a syncretism, but the search for what is common without ignoring fundamental differences. Three opening interventions serve as a point of departure:

Franz Kronreif, of the Focolari, speaks of a 'consensus within difference' and proposes that the initial points of reference of the dialogue be Pope Francis's Encyclical *Laudato Si'* and Walter Benjamin's 'Theses on the Philosophy of History'. Walter Baier, of the transform! network, pointed to the need for a self-critical reflection on the part of Marxists on the crimes committed in the name of socialism in the USSR; and he finds in the writings of Karl Polanyi the elements for a convergence between socialism and Christianity. Finally, Archbishop Zani, in a greeting to the 2018 summer school, pays homage to the ideals of justice, fraternity, and solidarity of the young participants of the meeting.

During the course of the dialogues and debates of the summer school, we saw encounters between quite different points of view, for example between economist Léonce Bekemans, Jean Monnet Chair at the University of Padua and convinced partisan of the 'actually existing' European Union, and Luciana Castellina, former European communist MEP, who dreams of 'another Europe' not subordinated to the capitalist markets. In certain cases, however, the discussants were able to redact a common document, as did Cornelia Hildebrandt and Pál Tóth, professor at the Sophia University Institute, on 'A Non-Violent Strategy in a Plural World'. The same occurred with the contribution of Petra Steinmair-Pösel, a theologian connected to the Focolari, in collaboration with Michael Brie, of the Rosa Luxemburg Stiftung of Berlin, on 'The Commons – Our Common Terrain?'.

*Europe as a Common* also contains contributions by Piero Coda, Rector of the Sophia University Institute; Bernard Callebaut, sociologist from the same institution; Spyros Syropoulos, professor at the University of the Aegean; Alberto Lo Presti, of LUMSA University (Libera Università Maria Santissima Assunta) in Rome; José Manuel Pureza, professor at the University of Coimbra and deputy of the Left Bloc in Portugal's parliament; the Islamic theologian Adnane Mokrani – who pleaded for 'a secular state as a religious necessity'; the social psychologist Thomas Stucke; the Colombian political scientist Javier Andrés Baquero who recounts his experience in the 'green' administration of the city of Bogotá; and the author of the present article. The ensemble of persons who bore witness to the plurality of the perspectives engaged in this 'transversal' initiative was completed by an address by Pope Francis on 'The Preferential Option for the Poor as the Key

Criterion of Christian Authenticity' (19 August 2020).

What conclusions can be drawn from this rather uneven bibliographical itinerary taking us from the young Marx to the Pontifex maximus Bergoglio? The only conclusion is that the relation between Marxists and Christians remains an open book whose next chapters will be written less on the basis of the holy scriptures of each tradition but rather in response to the ecological, social, and ethical challenges of the twenty-first century.

BIBLIOGRAPHY

Friedrich ENGELS and Karl MARX *Annales franco-allemandes*, complete French edition prepared by Alix Bouffard and Pauline Clochec, translated by Jean-Christophe Angaut, Victor Beguin, Alix Bouffard, Jean-Michel Buée, Pauline Clochec, Clément Fradin, Michelle L'Homme, and Jean Quétier, presentation and annotation by Pauline Clochec, in the series GEME (Grande Édition Marx et Engels), Paris: Éditions Sociales, 2020, 328 pp.

Nicos Foufas, *Friedrich Engels et la Guerre des Paysans Allemands* (in the series Ouverture Philosophique), Paris : L'Harmattan, 2020, 117 pp.

Arno Münster, *Socialisme et religion au XXe Siècle. Judaisme, Christianisme et athéisme dans la philosophie de la religion d'Ernst Bloch* (in the series Ouverture Philosophique), Paris : L'Harmattan, 2018, 175 pp.

Donna T. Haverty-Stacke, *The Fierce Life of Grace Holmes Carlson,* New York: New York University Press, 2021, 289 pp.

Leneide Duarte-Plon and Clarisse Meireles, *Tito de Alencar (1945-1974). Un dominicain brésilien martyr de la dictature,* Paris (in the series Signes des Temps): Éditions Karthala, 2020, translated from Portuguese by the authors, preface by Vladimir Safatle, foreword by Xavier Plassat, 308 pp.; (original Portuguese edition: Clarisse Meireles and Leneide Duarte-Plon, *Um Homem Torturado: Nos Passos de Frei Tito de Alencar*, Rio de Janeiro: Editora Civilização Brasileira, 2014).

Walter Baier, Cornelia Hildebrandt, Franz Kronreif, and Luisa Sello (eds), *Europe as a Common. Exploring Transversal Social Ethics,* Zurich: LIT Verlag, 2021, vol. I (Time Diagnoses, vol. 46), 267 pp.

Europe

# The Eternal Impossibility of a Democratic Europe and the Tasks of a 'Party of Europe'[1]

Étienne Balibar

In a previous work of mine, *Europe, crise et fin?*,[2] I have had recourse (by way of Zygmunt Bauman) to the Gramscian notion of *interregnum* to characterise the political situation of Europe; it designates the period of uncertainty (which can be very long) between an old institution or project and the crystallisation of a new one able to 'resolve' the contradictions. However, I fear that this formulation, despite its deliberate methodological pessimism, is still inhabited by the *a priori* idea that only a refoundation (accompanied by the emergence of an *active* 'citizenship') can reduce the discrepancy between current structures – 'amplified' and 'deepened' severalfold but still arising out of the system of division of powers established by the Treaty of Maastricht – and the needs of a world undergoing a speed-up metamorphosis. *Nothing could be less sure.* So, in the absence of a refoundation is the 'end' inevitable? *This is no surer.* Given mutual interdependencies, which involve all of the population and all of our countries' activities, and the solidarities that unite Europe's ruling caste, we could just as well imagine another possibility – I once baptised this the 'Roman-Germanic model' (after the example of the Holy Roman Empire which lingered on for several centuries after the dissolution of its principle of government), that is, an organism bereft of historical initiative but which continues indefinitely to live from its own conflicts. Another possibility, however, would be that the end of the European Union as a result of violent events, for example social and ethnic tensions aggravated by a climate or health catastrophe, which will force this system to come face to face with the evidence of its illegitimacy. Nobody can predict anything, but I believe that one must forswear drawing from the fact that something *irreversible* has taken place the conclusion that there will sooner or later be *progress* or *progression*.

From these impressions and extrapolations I derive no resignation to immobility, either in terms of analysis or of actual project. The reason is simple: For a long time, and now more than ever, I have been convinced that *we have no choice* as European citizens. I do not see how any of the problems of civilisation or of cooperation in the globalised world in which we live can be faced by Europe's peoples outside of a common political structure. Inversely, I do not believe that any political practice can be effective today in each of our national spaces, down to the level of the smallest territories, if it is not *at the same time* a politics that aims to implement Europe's resources, and thus a politics *for the purpose of* constructing a Political Europe as its own means. This applies to the organisation of trade and management of the debt. It applies to security and diplomacy. It applies to energy transition and climate regulations just as it applies to the transformation of the labour statute, the struggle against precarity, or the reform of public services. More than ever now it is from the *European point of view* that I want to reflect on the evolution and conditions of politics, above all *democratic* politics. Our task, in spite of everything, as intellectuals and 'activists' in the broadest sense of the term, is to bring alive the *party of Europe*, to spell out not just its programme but first and above all the articulation of the *possibilities* and *obstacles*, or the prospects of change and the aporias it would have to tackle. What good are intellectuals if not for this?

★ ★ ★

In this spirit I would now like to reconsider some *strategic contradictions* of the European construct in so far as it is at once blocked and uninterrupted, never obsolete and always disappointing. I will do so in the form of three constellations of interdependent problems, which I will provisionally designate as follows: first, the node of *citizenship*, of the *constitution* and of *democracy*; then that of *democracy* (once again), of *political* practice, and of *nationalism*; and finally that of the Europe of *nations*, of *cosmopolitanism*, and *postcolonialism* or the *altermondialiste* Europe. What can be shown each time is the difficulty of a policy that goes in circles between the need to remove certain obstacles and the impossibility of doing so without already having, in reality, discovered the means of going beyond, of anticipating what 'has to' follow but is not predetermined. What I hope, obviously, is that the act of *displaying* this circularity will also permit the demystification of its apparent inevitability and will let us see that it involves spaces where initiatives could arise as well as a political sense of what is specifically 'European'.

Let us begin with the node of the three notions that seem to exclusively involve political theory: *citizenship, constitution, democracy*. I am not going to launch into a long conceptual disquisition, except to emphasise again that at the centre of all reflections on the 'crisis' of the European construct there is necessarily the ensemble of contradictions concerning the definition and practical realisation of the idea of *European citizenship* (one of the innovations of the Treaty of Maastricht) that, jumping beyond a mere alliance or confederation of states, has led to the emergence of the Union's 'republican' dimension, that is, the idea of a *political entity* seen as the expression of the will of its members[3] – who as a consequence can potentially orient and control the Union's government. This means that it is at least potentially democratic, expressing a collective 'power' that is not necessarily always used maximally but whose constitution makes it possible to intensify it or claim it. However, the fact is not only that this strong kind of citizenship only exists on paper but that, above all, as soon as it is proclaimed it is systematically neutralised and thwarted – often in the name of 'respecting national sovereignty' but while exaggerating the constraints of the relation of subsidiarity. At which point we come to another preoccupation: While many of us think that building the forces of a European citizenship is not possible without a *remobilisation* of the very idea, historically, of citizenship and of the figure of the 'citizen', endowing it with new powers and modes of collective action, we are nevertheless obliged to imagine this eventual mutation not on the basis of an established acquisition but of a historical regression that disseminates all sorts of harmful influences in the self-conception of the people involved. This means that citizenship manifests itself to us in the form of a struggle between antagonistic tendencies and forces. We simultaneously need resistance, insurrection, and conversion.

How is citizenship, in Europe and by the very fact of contemporary Europe, a truncated and contradictory status that is reduced to impotence? It contains a superposition of at least four types of limitations: this citizenship *does not include the totality* of individuals who, in an organic sense, live, work, create, and serve others or 'provide care' for them within the territory in which it is defined but leaves out the numerous aliens or 'métèques'; it is *progressive* in relation to the national citizenships from the point of view of the guarantee of certain personal rights but *regressive* in regard to other 'social' dimensions of citizenship that democratic theory today considers to be equally fundamental, and outright *repressive* from the point of view of economic citizenship; it is essentially an indirect citizenship from the point of view of representation since the deliberative and executive organ (The Council of the European Union) is made up of representatives of the population (sometimes with three levels of indirect representation), and the European Parliament only has a partial and symbolic right of control over community administration and decisions – and thus, in effect, it confers no real power on citizens; and finally it *does not express* its objectives and issues of concern within a 'political life' composed of public debates and conflicts that extend across borders and confront conflicting options. Under these conditions, it is no surprise that citizenship is essentially 'passive' (that is, it corresponds to an *affiliation*, with its conditions and exclusions, its rights and benefits, and not to an individual and collective *participation* in the implementation of policy) and that it generates *passivity*, indeed an apathy which is sometimes interrupted but is on the whole growing. This then is the *circle* I mentioned: There is no possibility of the crystallisation of 'objective conditions' and real needs tending toward the emergence or development of a European political entity if the 'subjective conditions' are completely absent. But this absence expresses the condition of the subjects themselves whose capacity to think and express a common will, the capacity even to *have different opinions* and to publicly express their differences, is constantly destroyed or hindered.

This situation, as has been said in various quarters, is rooted in the present constitutional order of Europe, provided we understand this in a sense that is both 'formal' and 'material'. And, needless to say, this order does not act alone; it produces these negative effects by dint of historic circumstances and relations of power, of which we could paradoxically say that a constant in the latter is that they always put at the forefront the importance of the construction of Europe while simultaneously erecting obstacles to the democratisation that is a condition for accomplishing it – which goes for the circumstances of the Cold War as well as those of the (partial) reunification of the continent after 1989 or for those of the 2007-2008 financial crisis and its aftermath. The effect the shock of the climate crisis will have remains to be seen. However, even if it is not the sole determinant, the factor of the formal and material constitutional structure shapes many of the forms and limits within which the political processes materialise – or do not. What then is the nature of this regime in which the rules, the government practices, the division of powers and the real preponderance of certain economic and social forces (and of the states that incarnate them) all compete to produce the same result of 'passivising' citizenship? It would be tautological to simply call it oligarchical. Therefore we need to detail the way in which it organises the monopoly of decisions on the part of 'experts' who themselves are closely tied to a managerial class straddling public service and the management of corporations. This is what allows us to verify a sociology of the European 'political class', its bureaucracy, and its careers. But what seems to me most interesting is to freshly pose the question of the relation that the European Union's 'constitution' has to the original process of *statification of the market*. In this connection there is a misleading effect of the 1989-1993 turning point and subsequent years that saw the emergence of a political superstructure of Europe in an enlarged framework, and which seemed to mark a break with what remained as the original sin of the European construction – its subjugation to strictly (geo)economic objectives that are inevitably dominated by the interests of capital (and the dominant capitalist nations) in the name of sacrosanct 'competitiveness'. From this there follows the permanent tendency to judge the gaps and democratic deficits of European governance in terms of incompletion, of abortion, or regression in relation to the ideal of a *constituting of the political* as a 'sovereign' *collective subject* in Europe, whereas what is probably involved is the emergence of a *constitutionalism of a new type*, whose strengths and weaknesses need to be evaluated in its own terms. And certainly today's 'organised European Single Market' is no longer the same as that of the 'little Europe' of the 1950s nor even that of the Franco-German condominium and the 'Great Commission' of Mansholt and Delors in the 1970s and 1980s, but it remains the bedrock of the institutional structure (as demonstrated again in the Brexit negotiations). It is above all a market that – notably through the bias of the monetary and budgetary order – has gained the capacity to set the norms of existence of individuals in a great many domains, by imposing duties, laws, and values on them. Yet political theorists have always tended to think that state and market operate through inverse logics, which although they may be complementary, cannot be fused. They are not prepared to admit the existence of what Carlos Herrera calls a 'statism of the market'.[4] They are thus not ready to suppose that behind the unprecedented extension of 'governance by numbers' (in Alain Supiot's expression), which a priori discredits direct and indirect expressions of the will of citizens, there lies hidden in reality a mutation of the concept of sovereignty, a self-reproducing correlation of political power and economic power whose instrument par excellence is a reciprocal autonomisation of *decision-making bodies*, apparently contrary to any political rationality, but functional in relation to the *systematic prevalence* of a certain regime of economic power and radically exclusive of participatory and even representative democracy. The overwhelming symbol of this is the antithesis between the omnipotence of the ECB and the insignificance of the European Parliament. This is what Sandro Mezzadra calls the 'disarticulation of constitutional circles'.[5] It produces a concealment of the mechanisms of decision-making that goes far beyond the habitual preference of bureaucracies for the removal of their actions from public control but seems to recreate the ancient form of *arcana imperii* or state secrecy. Or perhaps it is a matter of transforming the 'invisible hand' of the market into the invisibilisation of the institutional 'hand' that guarantees its omnipotence. Hence the nearly insurmountable difficulty of creating a European *public sphere*, despite the at times heroic efforts of certain activists. What then is this system, which one never tires of describing in the words of Jacques Delors as a 'non-identified political object'? It is not a *non-state*; it is a genuine *form of state*, or the *anti-political* statification of society through the market. The question arises of knowing whether it is viable, or under what conditions it is, and what the conditions are on which it can run aground. The question also arises, as the development of other continents demonstrate, of knowing whether it is not an avant-garde but an exception in the world (and in 'globalisation', in the way that the Covid crisis is in the course of pushing forward).

★ ★ ★

I have gone in this direction in order to relaunch a discussion that seems latent all around us, but there is something unilateral about it. If we think of the contradictions and paradoxes of the 'rump democracy' in which we live today, we could better refer to *several tendencies* in mutual conflict whose power-balance is not determined once and for all. There is first of all the one I just indicated – the putting into place of a form of statification not conceived as a progressive 'overtaking' of the nation-state, even if it comprises elements of public power subordinating and relativising that of nations, but as a mechanism of monetisation, of judicialisation, of the promotion and geopolitical protection of a market of capitalists, workers, and consumers that implies the homogenisation of modes of life and the circulation of populations. It is striking to compare this to the regulatory idea which has not ceased to inspire Jürgen Habermas in his critique of Europe's development (the 'postdemokratischer Exekutivföderalismus' of which he has been speaking since 2012) – that of a transition between the old national 'sovereignism' and a 'cosmopolitical' constitution in formation. Yet we have cosmopolitanism not becoming one with a republicanism or liberalism in the classic sense but with an authoritarianism of a new type – which guides our imagination in another direction: Is the European Union not the realisation of a new type of state formation, proper to 'neoliberalism', *inverting* the tendencies of the 'social' state, which would not have been possible without a historic *democratic momentum* at least in a part of the world – particularly those which institutionalised 'social democratic' policies and seemed to prefigure a 'great transformation' of capitalism (Polanyi)? The fact that this inversion of the tendency had been made possible by a displacement of the loci of power to outside the national framework (towards 'Brussels'), all the while exerting a constraint on nations that is at once internal and external, could represent the condition of its possibility and perhaps its limit as well.

But there is also another tendency, on which the partisans of a political and democratic Europe insist more or less optimistically – the tendency to the transformation of the existing European institutions themselves, comparable to a *change of regime in Europe*. This is repeatedly expressed, as much through proposals to refound the treaties (especially in connection with the need for democratically implemented fiscal and budgetary reforms) as through the exigencies of European civil society – right now, for example, in the convergence of demands addressed to Europe that it implement its own commitments to reduce carbon energy – as well as by the resistance of civil society – and here we should not forget the mobilisations that accompanied the 'negative' referenda leading to the abandonment of the project for a Constitution in 2005 despite the ambivalence of these votes;[6] but here we should also count the trans-European polls in favour of one or another sort of 'universal basic income'. Certainly, these demands tend to circumvent electoral procedures rather than to use them, which is in particular a way of making oneself independent of the political class incrusted in the system. However, we cannot exclude the possibility that these demands are contributing to regenerate the very principle of representation, which, in the history of democratic systems, has never functioned in *isolation* from other forms of democracy – but under the condition that this kind of buttressing can only occur in a *European framework*, which leads us again to the *political circle* we evoked at the beginning. For it also could be that the movement restricts itself, or folds into, the space of national politics – in which case the chances are good that it will transform itself into *populist* agitation. In fact there is a *third tendency*: that which articulates or even identifies the defence or demand for democratic and thus 'popular' powers, and the critique of neoliberal governance with nationalism or sovereignism – as in Leipzig in 1989 when *We Are The People* (*demos*) metamorphosed into *We Are One People* (ethnos).

This third tendency is the most difficult to define because it involves the question of nationalism, and at a deeper level of the 'nation form' and its transformation in Europe, a question that is as vital as it is confused. But this question is not only an *obstacle* to the emergence of a supranational political arena, more difficult to enter for 'grassroots' politics than for 'higher-level' politics; it is a *blind spot* for the idea of Europe, which has been built on its denial. This means that either one assumes the obsolescence of the nation form as a 'law of history' or a backlash of globalisation – or one writes off its defence as mere conservatism and reaction. Or, still again, one retreats, accepting that the 'party of Europe' must manoeuvre through shaky compromises with nationalist sovereignism. This is what we have to work through in our minds and in the politics around us.

Without going into all the aspects of the problem, I would emphasise *three points* of analysis and diagnosis that seems to me to be the most delicate. First, contrary to the conviction of many partisans of a supranational public power, we have to take seriously and verify the 'Milward theorem' according to which the development of communitarian structures – by a 'trick of history' – leading finally to the creation of the EU did not weaken or delegitimise the nation-states in Europe, but 'preserved' them or even 'saved' them from their difficulties.[7] But how should we interpret this? In my view, this preservation does not only have to do with the fact that the European construct, while 'extracting' from national sovereignty the functions that it wanted to gather outside and above it, refrained from formally calling it into question. Rather, it has to do with the fact that – with the governing of social policies having been entrusted to the nation-states whose 'social contract' they constituted ever since the advent of the *welfare state* – the protection and extension of social rights appeared inseparable from the nation form and its expression in a state that 'belonged' to the citizens at the same time as they 'belonged' to it. This *co-belonging* remained compatible with the statism of the market up to the neoliberal turn of the 1980s. At that moment, doubtless for lack of the adoption of a European social policy, the overseeing of nation-states by a communitarian authority stopped functioning as a protection and was transformed into a mechanism of disintegration and accentuation of social cleavages, which were more or less violent according to the very unequal place the nation-states occupy within the European 'system' (for example, Germany in comparison to Greece).

Which brings us to the second point: Social democracy and political democracy are not independent, and less so than ever in the historical period that we could call 'post-socialist' in which we now find ourselves. But the question that is particularly urgent now is whether one can *dissociate* the questions of the future of democracy on a European scale from the national scale simply because the institutional frameworks are formally separate. I am convinced that it is not possible, and so I have continuously argued against the scheme of 'communicating vessels' which holds that one *preserves* the chances for internal democracy by *preventing* the instruments of public life from being transferred to the supranational scale, or inversely that one loses a possible 'federal democracy' to the extent that democracy is confined to the national level (especially when conceived in terms of a 'sovereign people'). While de-democratisation is the dominant tendency at the level of the Union, even if it is not admitted as such, it is completely repudiated at the national level – except of course in the case of the new 'illiberal' regimes. But in reality it is at work everywhere today, both as a result of the increasingly authoritarian practices of government and of the disaffection of an increasing number of citizens (especially *young citizens*) from the electoral games they see as void of real issues, that is, not offering real alternatives. Nevertheless, if it is relatively easy to show how the transition to 'post-democracy' in the national spaces and the establishment of what one could call 'preventative counter-democracy' at the European scale mutually reinforce one another in a *negative* spiral, it is much more difficult to *positively* demonstrate that the 'restoration' (and extension) of democratic practices at the level of the 'historic' peoples and at the level of the 'European people' that encompasses them has to *go hand in hand*, by mutually reinforcing each other. I do not renounce the idea that I at one time put forward: Europe will only be able to establish its legitimacy if it represents, in a 'virtuous circle', not a regression but an *increase* of rights of citizens in all domains, which also means an *increase* in their *powers* to govern themselves, including at the national scale. But to succeed there is need of forces and ideas, of affects to set this in motion, crossing frontiers and resisting 'populist' arguments that declare the incompatibility of the two developments.

Which brings us to the question of *populism*. That this term forms the concentrate of all the ambivalences of current politics does not in my view justify avoiding an examination of it. Rather it is what makes it necessary. From one end to the other of its usages there are, historically, transfers or passages, as well as grey zones of uncertainty as to the future of one or another extra-parliamentary manifestation. The position that I would defend is that 'populism' is the framework of an antagonism and that to struggle at once against the *neutralisation of politics* and against its *rerouting or its channelling* towards anti-democratic objectives, it is essential that this antagonism appear in full daylight, at the centre of political life, even that it *goes to extremes*, which of course also poses the question of knowing how one can prevent it from degenerating into violence. But it is not by trying to 'circumscribe' the danger of xenophobic populisms that are on the rise today everywhere in Europe, much less by appropriating their 'security' and 'identitarian' preoccupations, that we will escape a repeat of the political catastrophes that plunged Europe, almost a century ago, into darkness and horror. On the contrary, one can do so by making the *confrontation* with open or (more often) camouflaged neofascism the obligatory gateway of a politics of 'commonality' that reaffirms the goals of solidarity in all of the historic space of the European nations; in other terms – once again a situation of circularity – it is by not recoiling in the face of a fundamental conflict that makes the *idea of community* the battleground of today's world. We have to agree that there is no politics, either as a form of collective life or as a system of institutions, without 'communitarianism' in the broad sense. But not all communitarianisms are the same, and above all their conception and their experience incessantly bring forces into conflict that pull humanity towards opposing destinies: liberty and equality, or the exclusion and hierarchisation of individuals and groups. Solidarity or racism. To ensure that this dilemma, which is permanent, comes today to closely overlap a choice for or against *European citizenship* as the counterpart of *national historical particularities*, with the sharing of sovereignty that this implies, this would be the touchstone of a viable 'post-national' project open to its own transformations.

★ ★ ★

I will come now to some remarks concerning the *third* node of strategic contradictions that I indicated – that which combines the questions of nationalism, of cosmopolitanism, and the postcolonial condition of Europe. This constellation clearly comprises two major correlative aspects: that of the forms in which the history of colonisation and its 'reversal' in the contemporary world, with its new migratory flows and phenomena of cultural 'hybridisation', shape the self-conception of Europeans, and that of the place that the European construct inevitably occupies in the game of world politics. These two aspects are never separable, which, at least in principle, makes it possible to maintain that the existence of an active European citizenship is one of the conditions that would allow Europe, although irremediably 'provincialised',[8] to contribute to the world's future and more profoundly to what I am tempted to call a *politics of the human species* – which would be the culmination of the cosmopolitical idea under conditions of globalisation; and, reciprocally, a Europe that actively intervenes in the 'democratisation' of relations between the world's populations, of which the dismantling of systemic racism is obviously a critical component; and also a Europe that can understand the need for and value of organising itself as a solidary political entity. Once again, however, we are plunged into a circularity from which it will not be easy to exit. Without going into the lineage of the problem or the discussion of specifically 'geopolitical' factors, I would offer two more points for reflection.

The first turns around the problem of *hospitality*, the touchstone of the cosmopolitical conception of Kantian origin whose central axiom is the injunction to *not treat strangers like enemies*, which is also a way of *preserving* the possibility of being alien. Today it is focused, in an increasingly conflictual and dramatic way, on the problem of welcoming refugees and immigrants, wrongly presented as a 'migratory problem'. The exploitation of this problem through xenophobic discourse persists, and it weighs ever more heavily on the political life of each country, as well as the tendency of governments (with rare exceptions) to appropriate populist rhetoric in this area and thus to disseminate this rhetoric. There is no point in pretending that this discourse has not by now gained a very strong foothold among citizens of the popular classes (even if it is biased to think that the 'working class' as such has become racist and that the other classes are not touched by it). More seriously, under pressure of the governments claiming they have a mandate from public opinion, Europe has implemented a policy of fortification of land and sea frontiers such as to block the arrival of immigrants, which is essentially an ultra-violent policy of pushing people towards zones of extreme poverty and death – this began with the Schengen conventions, subsequently completed by those of Dublin, then by the agreements on 'sub-contracting' and remunerating neighbouring countries (Turkey, Libya, and Morocco) to intern and hunt down applicants, and finally by the establishment of a militarised maritime police force (Frontex) and the prohibition or punishment of sea rescue operations organised by NGOs and collectives of human rights activists. Europe continues to prevaricate and divide itself over the asylum policy that it periodically says it wants to 'define', while in practice it is organising concentration camps (as in Greece), it is hunting down exiles wandering from one territory or 'jungle' (in Calais) to another, and it is knowingly *letting* passengers of skiffs *die* who are risking the journey to its shores. International humanitarian law is being flouted in the name of an imaginary security, crimes against humanity have been verified, and one can argue that this is genocide. Thus Europe is not able to be solidary but it can organise itself to throw out or eliminate the undesirable foreigner. It is the dark side of its 'unity'. This raises a political problem, a juridical problem, but also a moral problem.

Once more it would be erroneous and unjust to only see the most sombre side of the problem, even if it seems to be preponderant. In reality there is a choice, not only of principles but of effective policies. The German decision in 2015 to open the country's borders to the Syrian refugees, a decision made by Chancellor Merkel against a part of her own majority and in the face of the anger of other European leaders, went beyond the point of honour or of evangelical charity; it showed the existence of a solution that is viable (witness the integration of the great majority of refugees in Germany). I had imprudently hailed it as an 'enlargement of the European Union',[9] which was not the case, but it remains possible (and necessary) to wage a campaign against the policies of rejection and elimination, which today are symbolised by Danish and Hungarian legislation and which other countries (like France) silently practice, on condition that the *sharing of responsibilities and burdens*, loftily proclaimed in other domains, be put back on the agenda, indeed constitutionally imposed. This idea can be defended on the level of economic utility and demographic rationality, on that of human rights and labour rights, and on that of geopolitical coherence (for the increase of climate catastrophes will have as its inevitable consequence an international problem of assistance to disaster-stricken populations, which cannot be fixed by the unilateral closing of borders). But above all on the level of *values*, in the name of which an 'autonomy' of European policy can be asserted in the increasing confrontation of hegemonic blocs and an *ideal* be formulated for European citizens of which their community is the bearer. History shows, in fact, that a *foundation* that at the same time creates a collective consciousness of legitimacy cannot be forged, at least in modern times, on the basis of egoism or an ethnic or civilisational particularism, but requires a universalist project.

The content of the latter, however, has become problematic by dint of the violent history of which Europe and its relations with the rest of the world are the result, and even the product. While projecting itself into the future it cannot abstract from its past and the self-representations which flowed from this both internally and in the eyes of others. There is the same division on this point, certainly, which we have seen in connection with solidarity with and exclusion of foreigners, and again the issue is one of aspects of a single problem but with inequalities that need to be taken into account. Colonial expansion, followed by decolonisation, was only truly constitutive of national formation in a part of the continent, and one could maintain that it does not involve the nations of Eastern Europe (which were instead themselves 'colonised' at different times). It is, however, not only the construction of the racial and cultural *other*, which has been a pan-European project over several centuries, but one could maintain that the history of the twentieth century (particularly that of the ideological division of Europe and its 'reunification' after the end of communism) has had the effect of *sharing* the heritage of colonisation, and by the same token collectivising the problem of 'multicultural' society that it poses. We have to admit that the memorialisation and the teaching of history require different approaches between one end and the other of the European continent, but we also maintain that Europe's nations have to *collectively* determine the idea that they will have of their place in the world and their participation in world culture. Clearly, there is no space here to argue this in detail, but I will still pose as a hypothesis that *a 'creole world'* (what Edouard Glissant called *'le tout-monde'*) is *one of the possible outcomes.*[10] It is not the easiest (quite the contrary) but neither is it the most improbable of outcomes, since a historical social formation having absorbed within it the inputs and personalities of the whole world – no doubt by oppressing them, exploiting them, and disregarding them – also possesses the means to repurpose all this. The models for it will be proposed by activists as much as by intellectuals and artists but also just as much by *common people*, who in their daily lives experience what certain anthropologists have called a 'cosmopolitanism from below', and together confront the same difficulties of existence, the same problems of the future. Here it would obviously involve a reversing of the heritage of colonialism to become an affirmative power of political and cultural (not just economic and technological) 'globalisation', which could only occur at the price of many conflicts and also dramas. What is at stake is very clear – the capacity of European peoples and their citizens to resist marginalisation and decline. For which they need the assistance and contributions of others, *their others*.

NOTES

1 This article is an abridged version of my Afterword to the collective volume *Une Europe politique: obstacles et possibles,* edited by Carlos Miguel Herrera and Ninon Grangé, Paris: Kimé, 2021. It is reproduced here with the kind permission of the editors and the publisher.
2 Étienne Balibar, *Europe, crise et fin?*, Lormont: Éditions Le Bord de l'eau, 2016.
3 See the work of Ulrike Guérot, in particular her *Why Europe Should Become a Republic!: A Political Utopia* (English edition), Bonn: Dietz Nachf., 2019.
4 In his contribution to the above-cited collective volume.
5 In his contribution to the above-cited collective volume.
6 The Greek 2015 referendum – which led to Jean-Claude Juncker's famous declaration 'There can be no democratic choice against the European treaties' – itself contained a certain ambivalence, for we should never forget that what it called for was the maintenance of Greece in the Union (against the threats of 'Grexit') under the condition of a recognition of Greece's rights and vital interests. The reason for Greece's stigmatisation lies essentially in the imperious need to prevent the spread of such a demand to other countries.
7 I am referring here to the thesis presented by the English historian Alan Milward in *The European Rescue of the Nation-State*, London: Routledge, 1992.
8 It is well to recall that the intentionally provocative title of Dipesh Chakrabarty's book, *Provincializing Europe: Postcolonial Thought and Historical Difference* (Princeton: Princeton University Press, 2000) does not mean Europe becoming the dependent 'province' of a metropolis or a capital but its (re)becoming a province of the world among other provinces and equal to them.
9 Étienne Balibar, 'Europe et réfugiés: l'élargissement', in *Europe, crise et fin ?*
10 See Édouard Glissant and Patrick Chamoiseau, *Manifestes*, (preface by Patrick Chamoiseau, Postface d'Edwy Plenel), Paris: La Découverte, 2021.

# Discuss Security – Reclaim the Future

## Katerina Anastasiou and Axel Ruppert

Current debates and policies on security have been largely hegemonised by the political right, with repressive and discriminating policies justified in the name of security. The term 'security' is closely tied to nationalism and often framed in terms of protecting the nation against the 'other'. In today's world, the prevailing security concepts are aimed at ensuring profits for private capital and for the most part offer oppressive, violent, military, and 'law and order' solutions to economic-, social-, racial-, climate-, and gender-justice issues. Referring to security can be toxic, ranging from foreign policy and border-control decisions to law-and-order practices within the European Union (EU) countries. Therefore, caution and careful examination are needed in addressing the term. At the same time, security, or the right to live one's life in safety, is a basic need and an urgent necessity for those affected by war, violent conflict, police brutality, hate crimes, domestic violence, or precarity. Providing security also means preventing the devastation caused by the climate crisis and offering protection from its consequences, ensuring material security in terms of access to quality food, water, housing, energy, healthcare, education, etc., and enabling prospects for a common liveable future. The United Nations 'human security' concept also goes in this direction, although it wears silk gloves in dealing with the systemic causes rooted in capitalist profit-driven modes of production.

In today's world, security has been commodified. This commodification has made security a tradable service, thus transforming a basic need into a lucrative market. The profiteers of the dominant security discourse are those who trade on this market, namely the actors of the military-industrial complex. According to the SIPRI yearbook,[1] in 2020 two trillion US dollars were spent on the military. Today's paradox in a nutshell is that those who create the instruments of repression and war – the arms and security industry – are the very ones who are promising to reinstate security through their merchandise. To be able to continue doing so, and to constantly increase their profit margins, these actors devote substantial sums of money[2] and make great efforts to shape the political discourse in a way that serves their interests – even if pushing their interests means the devastation of people and nature by propagating and ultimately fuelling war.

This article draws on the experience of a series of workshops we co-organised and facilitated for transform! europe and the Rosa-Luxemburg-Stiftung Brussels Office in 2020-21 where we discussed security and its conception and manifestations in contemporary politics, in an effort to stimulate discussion around a security concept for the left and foster its development. The workshops hosted people from left and progressive institutes and foundations, peace-, feminist-, ecology-, and anti-racist movements, as well as left and progressive parties, thus representing a diversity of left sectors. The necessity of a new left approach that serves the need all people have for safety[3] echoes throughout our effort to articulate an appropriate concept of security. In what follows we elaborate on questions that are central to our approach: Whose security is taken into account? Whose security is at risk? Who profits from insecurity? Who has agency to respond? What is the role of the left? These questions remain relevant in times of crisis and war. We began writing this article two years into a global health security crisis, the Covid-19 pandemic, with the world mourning 6 million dead due to infection. As this article was being completed, Russia's military began its invasion of Ukraine. Our focus here is not this war, which is ongoing, as the full extent of its consequences cannot yet be fully known. Our examples are drawn from wars that have been waged in the past decades, in order to demonstrate the absurd contradiction of war allegedly waged for people's security. We offer an outline of what security concepts could be in a future in which wars are obsolete. Any such concepts must necessarily be human-centred and take into account the globally interdependent conditions that guarantee universal security. We hope to stimulate left thinking that can become counter-paradigms to nationalistic, capital-driven securitisation processes that are shaping today's world in its rush toward a ruinous future.

## Profiting from insecurity with old recipes

Military expenditure has been on the rise even before Putin's war on Ukraine. In 2020 military expenditure reached its highest level since 1988[4] – amidst the first year of the Covid-19 pandemic. The military and the threat of its deployment to achieve the goals of particular states has taken centre stage in current security policies. From the rhetoric of the 'War on Terror' or the 'War on Drugs' to the failed military interventions in Afghanistan and the failing intervention in Mali, waging war is portrayed as a guarantor of security by Europe's governments. Pursuing the path of national security at the cost of the suffering of others has been a feature of the EU member states' foreign and security policies. The EU itself is now increasingly becoming a playing field for ensuring military dominance. Its leadership has been advancing the militarisation and securitisation of the bloc, based on the notion that the European project is under threat and that a 'stronger and autonomous Europe' is needed on the global stage.[5] Joint military capabilities are being developed, commitments to increase military spending are being made, and calls for the EU to make use of its military might are becoming louder. As further social or economic EU integration is rejected or blocked by member states, the aim of this strategy seems to be to demonstrate the EU's ability to act, to integrate right-wing populist actors, and thus to forge a new consensus for Europe. These ongoing developments appear to constitute an attempt at countering the unfolding disintegration crisis facing the Union and forcing a European identity into existence by 'uniting in arms against the common enemy'. However, the rhetorical, structural, and financial shift to military priorities will neither ensure peace nor be able to contain the structural causes of the conflicts to be fought, which have been and will continue to be fuelled not least by the exploitative economy of a neoliberal EU.

At the beginning of the 2000s the strongest European states pledged allegiance to the NATO-driven and US-led 'War on Terror', using security as a pretext, and they thus participated in the extensive destruction in Iraq and Afghanistan that led hundreds of thousands to flee those countries. In late 2021, with the retreat of NATO troops from Afghanistan, it became obvious that the war waged in the previous twenty years had cemented and armed the reactionary forces in the region. In the meanwhile, the arms and security industries in Europe and the US have continued to profit from this insecurity, while the working masses in Europe continue to foot the bill for the carnage. As Julian Assange put it in 2011: 'The goal is to use Afghanistan to wash money out of the tax bases of the United States, out of the tax bases of European countries, through Afghanistan and back into the hands of the transnational security elite.'[6]

The left has always opposed war, since in capitalist societies war is always waged at the expense of the poor and working classes who bear its burdens. Our world today is rapidly changing, and the conflicts of capital interests have evolved with it. The result, derived from a Cold War logic, is a toxic climate that prioritises military capacities over diplomacy. The danger of economic wars (for example with Russia and China) escalating to actual military conflict is very real. The peace and feminist movements are already sounding the alarm and demanding a reorienting of the idea of security towards collective and cooperative human security.[7] We feel, accordingly, that the left should argue for collective security in international relations in a way that recognises our co-dependency and is based on creating cooperation instead of trying to maintain mutual assured destruction in a constant state of confrontation.

Addressing the climate crisis and preventing further global warming and destruction of ecosystems is key in providing security for the many. The current security concepts do not respond to the climate crisis but rather worsen it, since the military industrial complex is a key polluter[8] and also serves in securing resource access in a pattern reflecting contemporary colonialism and capital interests. These concepts are predominantly militaristic and antagonistic, in that one fights for one's interests *against* another party instead of striving for a collective state of security in which both parties feel safe.

## Climate struggle is class struggle – 'everything else is gardening'[9]

Climate change and environmental collapse is reality in many places on earth, yet we are not all equally threatened by its consequences. Today the planet measures a temperature of 1.2°C more than during pre-industrial times, and this warming is accelerating. We are currently on a path to surpass the 1.5°C threshold with devastating consequences for nature and humans[10] and probably irreversible damage. People in the Global South are already suffering the most under the consequences of global warming and will be hit first and hardest by further deteriorating ecosystems due to global warming and the destruction of nature. At the same time, those most affected have contributed the least to the release of carbon emissions and the overproduction and consumption that is driving environmental destruction. Climate change also affects public infrastructure. Floods, wildfires, plagues, pandemics, and infrastructural failure also have impact in the heart of Europe today – and, even on European soil, reproduce social inequities. Apart from the immediate effects of extreme weather phenomena and deteriorating weather patterns, agricultural cycles are also being broken, food and water supply distorted, and the costs of whatever reparation measures are enacted are shouldered by the tax-payers (i.e., through public money) rather than by the polluters (through private capital). The future of the whole planet is in a state of ecological insecurity.

Water scarcity exemplifies the threats to human security deriving from the climate crisis. UNICEF estimates that as early as 2025 half of the world's population could be living in areas facing water scarcity and that by 2040, roughly 1 in 4 children worldwide will be living in areas of extremely high water stress.¹¹ Since the lack of existential resources is a driver of conflicts, the intensifying water scarcity is likely to trigger new and fuel existing conflicts.

Taking a closer look at contemporary wars and violent conflict, it becomes clear that the effects of climate change play a leading role in them. A good deal has been written on how the conflict in Syria has resulted from the pressure of year-long droughts on the rural population.¹² What started as civic unrest and a redistributional revolt, escalated to a full-scale war, with international involvement, and it is still continuing, leaving Syrians in limbo, both those remaining and those fleeing.

As demonstrated by the recent COP26, and by all the UNFCCC meetings before it, the threats posed to humanity due to our Western extractivist economies and their impact on climate and nature are not being taken seriously. COP meetings have evolved into green-washing conferences of industrial lobbies, and global inequalities are also manifested through them – for example, polluters get a seat at the negotiations table, while those suffering the consequences of inaction are not allowed any agency.

In the case of the EU for example, the fossil fuel industry is greenwashing fossil gas as 'natural gas' and disguising its increased extraction as a step towards 'European energy autonomy and security', while in reality it enhances the EU's dependency on questionable regimes in the Middle East and East. The East Med pipeline – a mega pipeline that would carry fossil gas from the disputed waters of the Levantine Basin (Cyprus, Israel and potentially Palestine) to Italy – is a tangible example of how fossil-fuel mining and export processes substantially contribute to the instability of a whole region and its militarisation. When completed, this mega-project will be the biggest and deepest supply pipeline for fossil gas in Europe - yet it is already fuelling tensions between Turkey, Greece, and the Republic of Cyprus, enhancing the role of the United States in the Eastern Mediterranean which has already abandoned the project,¹³ and exacerbating insecurity for everyone by contributing to an increase in carbon emissions and continuing business as usual.

Additionally, the urgent need to provide funds for loss and damages due to climate-change-induced environmental and infrastructural collapse is not being decisively addressed by wealthy nations. On the contrary, we see that developed countries are instead investing in militarised border control, which aims to keep the 'Wretched of the Earth' - the survivors of climate collapse - outside their privileged borders.¹⁴

The verdict of the People's Tribunal vs. the UNFCCC that took place in Glasgow 2021, highlights this discrepancy:

Global military spending – nearly $2 trillion in 2020 alone, amounting to trillions over past decades – must be converted to fund climate justice initiatives. Similarly, the odious and illegitimate debt of poor nations must be identified and cancelled. This would free up significant national revenues to build the infrastructure, services, and supports that will allow billions of people to navigate the climate emergency. The vast sums of money spent on the national security plans of wealthy nations, which aim to shield those nations responsible for the vast majority of pollution from those fleeing climate change-induced catastrophes, must be similarly diverted to support the peoples of the Global South.[15]

It is well known that when it comes to climate change and irreversible ecological damage we are running out of time. The past decades have seen mobilisations that have raised awareness of these dangers. However, solutions that blot out systemic failures and predominantly focus on tech fixes and changing individual behaviour and consumption patterns will not work. Traditional left demands for redistribution of wealth and resource access will also not be enough. What is needed for a future safe from environmental insecurity is the transformation and democratisation of our production and logistic chains and energy supply systems. The climate justice struggle is a global class struggle.

## The EU border - securing privileges

Since 2015 the far-right's narrative of migration, which frames immigrants and refugees as a threat to a supposed European identity, has persisted and become hegemonic in the sphere of migration policy. One could say that there are practically no safe routes either for migrating or fleeing to Europe other than expensive 'golden visas'. Europe's borders have been extensively militarised, and new walls and fences have been erected.[16] The rhetoric that depicts immigrants and refugees as a security problem is fuelled by right-wing and far-right politicians and not least by organisations representing the military industrial complex, which use an alarmist and militaristic rhetoric that is already prominently featured in official EU documents.

Frontex[17] – the EU's border management agency – has been repeatedly, directly and indirectly, involved in illegal pushbacks and accused of complicity in violence against immigrants and refugees. The agency is a key coordinator of inhumane deportations throughout the EU. It cooperates with third countries – regardless of their democratic standing – and is the motor of the EU's externalisation strategy of border control. Bilateral agreements with dictators, failed states, and warlords are signed – selling off Europe's core understanding of human rights – as long as they keep 'the threat' represented by migrants and refugees of all sexes and ages at bay, even at the cost of life. All this makes a journey to Europe a life-threatening endeavour. Over 40,000 people have already lost their lives at sea. 10,000 unaccompanied children are still missing along the Balkan route. Currently, real search-and-rescue missions are mostly undertaken by civil society organisations, which are under heavy scrutiny and often face criminal charges for simply adhering to international law and the principle of the right to life.

Frontex's disproportionate funding has skyrocketed since the establishment of the agency. Its budget has grown by over 7,560% since 2005, with €5.6 billion being reserved for the agency from 2021 to 2027. It has been recruiting an army of border guards who can own and use handguns and aims to deploy 10,000 guards by 2027. The agency can now buy its own equipment – such as ships, helicopters, and drones – benefitting the arms, security, and surveillance companies that have been so influential in shaping the EU's border and defence policies through lobbying.[18]

The EU's border regime is inherently racist as it categorises humans based on their origin into wanted and unwanted persons and strips those who are considered unwanted of their dignity in overcrowded camps along the border. Systemic and systematic racism does not stop at the border. Black Europeans and European people of colour have long been affected by racist crime and institutional racism[19] that endangers them in everyday life and underpins the border regime, while at the same time it reproduces racist stereotypes and the othering of those considered to be 'non-European'.

Security – in terms of being taken care of when sick or in need of daily-life support as well as in terms of having access to basic food supplies – currently depends and will continue to depend on people coming from outside Europe – who are largely working in precarious conditions. It is the left's task to argue for a humane EU asylum and migration policy and at the same time for fair working conditions in the care and food sector. Reliable access to quality care and food depends on the material and physical security of those who provide and produce it. Thus, a fair and humane migration policy should be advocated not only on directly ethical grounds but also in terms of the very material effects that extend the insecurity of migrant populations to the majority of the EU's population. If those who provide care and food are not safe, those who are in need of care and food are not safe.

## Counter-terrorism normalising racism in the name of security

The 9/11 terror attacks and the subsequent 'War on Terror' mark a turning point in the majority of Western states' security strategies. Mass surveillance programmes have been established, the mandates and rights of secret services have been expanded, states of emergency declared, and terrorism has been considered the central threat to national security. The radical Islamist terror attacks in Europe since the 2010s were followed by governments in Western Europe implementing counter-terrorism strategies that disproportionately targeted racialised communities and fuelled existing institutional racism. This includes digital surveillance practices, detention without charges, extradition or citizenship removal, the freezing of bank accounts, and racial profiling with stop-and-search procedures.

The 'Prevent Programme' implemented in the UK is a telling example of how counter-terrorism programmes threaten democratic principles and are extended to areas beyond the traditional purview of the security and intelligence apparatuses.[20] The programme aims at preventing people from sliding into extremism and calls upon public servants, teachers, professors, and health professionals to report 'signs of radicalisation' to the authorities. Subsequent self-censorship, restricted access to services such as mental healthcare, and shrinking space for critical discussions on university campuses are the results. Due to the Islamist terrorist attacks and extensive Islamophobia, Muslim citizens and, especially visibly, Muslim women, face widespread suspicion and thus their free participation in society is directly affected.[21] Over time, the Prevent Programme's target definition has been broadened from targeting 'violent extremism' to targeting 'non-violent extremism' and has thus greatly broadened the potential targets of counter-terrorism measures.

Such programmes show the failure of governments in Europe to address the socio-economic root causes of terrorism. Although the majority of radical Islamist terror attacks were executed by young European citizens, the political right and far right has used them to stigmatise refugees and migrants as security threats. The 'extremism' discourse is not only central to legitimising the militarisation of the European border regime and justifying Europe's failure to uphold fundamental rights, such as the right to claim asylum, but also fails to address the economic inequalities, social problems, and racial injustice that cut across European societies. Thus, programmes like the Prevent Programme do little to actually prevent domestic terrorism threats but rather amplify the very conditions that push Europe's youth to the margins of society.

Far-right radicalism and violence have been on the rise in Europe since

2011 (as exemplified by the Utøya massacre in Norway, the murder of MP Jo Cox in the UK, the murders of Sahzat Lukman and Pavlos Physsas in Greece, and in Germany the deadly attacks in Hanau and Halle as well as the murder of Walter Lübcke, a district president in Hesse). The Covid-19 pandemic is also providing a context for more intense far-right terror and conspiracy tactics. Yet we can observe the unwillingness of police and authorities to address this threat with the same vigour they display in combating Islamist extremism. People of colour in Europe are physically threatened by far-right groups, suffer the consequences of stigmatisation in their everyday lives, and live in a constant state of insecurity. From police controls to unemployment agencies, racial discrimination is the rule rather than the exception for fellow citizens whose appearance does not comply with the conception of a 'White European'. And this systematic racism and discrimination is a threat to the safety of millions living in Europe.

While governments in Europe do not sufficiently invest in measures to prevent extremist radicalisation, such as social work, education, and creating life opportunities for those living in marginalised communities, surveillance programmes are expanded and technological developments used to increase their effectiveness. Across Europe, highly intrusive and rights-violating facial recognition and biometric processing technologies are quietly being introduced, which turn public spaces into areas of unseen and technically sophisticated mass surveillance.[22] While this trend benefits those companies and corporations who are developing and selling the surveillance technology, it is diverting resources away from measures addressing the socio-economic root causes of crime.

The revelations around the Pegasus spyware have laid bare the dystopian scope of surveillance[23] and are a wake-up call for the left, which tends to avoid an extensive discussion of technology. From digital monopolies, big data giants, and fake news factories, to algorithm architecture that is applied by unemployment agencies – individuals are turned into data in automated decision-making processes and new societal boundaries are erected. The left should not fall into the trap of engaging in a good vs. bad technology argument. We should rather critically analyse and publicly discuss who is developing technology, with what motives and under what conditions. Who has control over data and processes and who profits from them. Today's commercialised (digital) technology is produced within patriarchal, neocolonial, capitalist, and environmentally destructive systems and thus prone to reproduce global inequalities structurally, with the consequent insecurity that derives from all those forms of oppression.

## Conclusions

Counteracting poverty, environmental collapse, racism, sexism, and viruses with guns is obviously futile and in fact reproduces the sources of these problems. Yet, those in power choose to react to the contemporary crises humanity faces by investing in law and order, zoning life-sustaining territories by the erection of walls, increasing military spending, and protecting the interests of capital. Their lack of imagination and class bias becomes apparent by their focus on maintaining a system of security that safeguards the privileged few at the cost of the marginalised many, pushing the latter into a state of constant insecurity and the planet further down the spiral of collapse.

In our societies, the word 'security' has become synonymous with the repression apparatus and the military, hence the left does not engage politically with the issue, avoiding it like the plague. It is true that 'security' is hegemonised by the political right in the public discourse, but as we have shown above the left needs to address this question on its own terms, since security - in the sense of feeling safe to go about your life - has become a sacred class privilege. Faced with the challenges of our near future, security, for ever more people, will become less of an abstract concept and increasingly a matter of everyday survival, not least in face of the climate crisis.

The year 2021 has shown once more that climate-change-induced extreme phenomena disproportionally affect the working classes, globally. The vulnerability of the poor manifested itself in the 'heart of capitalism', New York City, this year when thirteen people lost their lives during the floods because their subterranean rental apartments were inundated. Some years ago hurricane Irma battered one of the world's poorest countries, Haiti, destroying homes and taking lives. At the same time Richard Branson, one of the world's richest ten people, took to twitter from his privately owned island nearby to brag about the resilience of his house by tweeting: 'Expecting full force of Hurricane #Irma in about 4 hours, we'll retreat to a concrete wine cellar under the house.'[24]

Arguing from a materialist perspective, Olúfẹ́mi O Táíwò, assistant professor of philosophy at Georgetown University, concludes in his article 'Who gets to feel secure?':

> We will find ourselves, much sooner than we think, asking basic questions about how we're going to secure ourselves and our basic needs. Movements and developments in the natural world will be asking the questions, but our fate will be determined by our collective political answers. We have reasons to be skeptical about the kinds of answers our given power structures will produce [...]. The deciding aspect of politics over the coming century

will be whether or not popular movements can challenge the current elite stranglehold on who and what is secured in society when crisis strikes. The compound COVID-19 and climate crisis simply brings new stakes to the old question of how to fundamentally reshape a social system that is centrally organised around securing the profit, hierarchical prestige and physical safety of the few through the carceral, environmental and economic insecurity of the many.[25]

The left has to ask whose security and safety is served by current power structures, whose security is most at risk, and how this connects to colonial continuities and class struggles. A convincing and holistic approach to security derives from social struggles and serves the need for safety of all, by linking questions of class, climate, migration, militarism, peace, state repression, sexism, and racism. Our series of workshops stressed that we cannot fight climate change without tackling the military industrial complex; that we need to argue for disarmament and for humane living conditions for refugees and their right to flee war zones at the same time; and that we cannot fight social inequality without acknowledging the dangers that climate change poses to the lives of all, but in the first instance to the people of the Global South. Fighting extractivism without dismantling neocolonial power structures is futile. Finally, we cannot envision a safe future in which everyone can develop themselves freely without envisioning a world beyond capitalism. A holistic security concept is necessary and could provide a platform for dynamic common struggles for a future of our global society that is safe and liveable for all and the basis for suitable policy proposals.

To advance on this front, the left needs its own language to talk about security, and it must not shy away from discussions of what kind of security we want and for whom. Talking about war and peace alone leaves a void that is filled by our political opponents. To counter the current hegemonic security policies, the left needs to push for collective security approaches opposed to current policies and structures. While antagonistic security policies seek to provide safety *from* the Other, collective ones aim at generating safety *with* the Other.[26] Collective security means arguing for a form of security that makes us safe because the others are safe. The global distribution of Covid-19 vaccines is illustrating this with full force. As long as the global inequity in vaccine availability persists, people everywhere will be confronted with new variants of the virus spreading around the globe and the prospect of a never-ending pandemic. Arguing from a collective security standpoint allows the left to counter the current antagonistic policies and structures with a viable and convincing alternative that does address the actual security concerns of the many and existing inequities at the same time. Demanding safety in all aspects of life for all people is not utopian but rather a realistic response that takes seriously the material interdependence of the world. Nobody is safe until everybody is safe.

NOTES

1. SIPRI, Press release: 'World military spending rises to almost $2 trillion in 2020', <https://www.sipri.org/media/press-release/2021/world-military-spending-rises-almost-2-trillion-2020>.
2. Vredesactie, 'Securing Profits: How the arms lobby is hijacking Europe's defence policy', <https://www.vredesactie.be/sites/default/files/pdf/Securing_profits_web.pdf>.
3. transform! europe and Rosa-Luxemburg-Stiftung Brussels Office, 'Security and the Left in Europe. Towards a New Left Concept of Security', <https://www.transform-network.net/fileadmin/user_upload/left_and_security_report-sc2.pdf>.
4. SIPRI, 'Trends in World Military Expenditure, 2020', <https://sipri.org/sites/default/files/2021-04/fs_2104_milex_0.pdf>.
5. European Commission, 'A Global Strategy for the European Union's Foreign and Security Policy', <https://eeas.europa.eu/archives/docs/top_stories/pdf/eugs_review_web.pdf>.
6. WikiLeaks, Twitter, <https://twitter.com/wikileaks/status/1427929346262642688>.
7. WILPF, 'Feminist criticism of current security practices', <https://www.wilpf.de/feminist-criticism-of-current-security-practices/>.
8. CEOBS, 'Environmental CSR reporting by the arms industry', <https://ceobs.org/environmental-csr-reporting-by-the-arms-industry/>.
9. Paraphrasing Chico Mendez: 'Environmentalism without class struggle is just gardening.'
10. IPCC, Special Report 'Global Warming of 1.5 °C', <https://www.ipcc.ch/sr15/>.
11. UNICEF. 'Water scarcity. Addressing the growing lack of available water to meet children's needs', <https://www.unicef.org/wash/water-scarcity>.
12. Deutsche Welle, 'How climate change paved the way to war in Syria', <https://www.dw.com/en/how-climate-change-paved-the-way-to-war-in-syria/a-56711650>.
13. 'The Gastivists Stop East Med campaign', <https://stopeastmed.org/>.
14. Nick Buxton, *A primer on climate security*, TNI, <https://www.tni.org/en/publication/primer-on-climate-security>.
15. 'The Verdict of The People's Tribunal: People and Nature vs. the UNFCCC', Systemic Alternatives, <https://systemicalternatives.org/2021/11/16/the-verdict-of-the-peoples-tribunal-people-and-nature-vs-the-unfccc/>.
16. Transnational Institute, 'The business of building walls', <https://www.tni.org/files/publication-downloads/buildingwalls-executive-summary-web.pdf>.
17. 'Abolish Frontex', <https://abolishfrontex.org/frontex/>.
18. <https://www.tni.org/en/publication/global-climate-wall>.
19. *Racist crime and institutional racism in Europe: ENAR Shadow Report 2014-18*, <https://www.enar-eu.org/IMG/pdf/shadowreport2018_final.pdf>.

20 Transnational Institute, 'What kind of security policy better serves democracy?', <https://www.tni.org/en/article/what-kind-of-security-policy-better-serves-democracy>.
21 'Boy, 11, referred to Prevent for wanting to give "alms to the oppressed"', *The Guardian*, 27 June 2021, <https://www.theguardian.com/uk-news/2021/jun/27/boy-11-referred-to-prevent-for-wanting-to-give-alms-to-the-oppressed>.
22 'ReclaimYourFace', <https://reclaimyourface.eu/>.
23 'What is Pegasus spyware and how does it hack phones?', 18 July 2021, <https://www.theguardian.com/news/2021/jul/18/what-is-pegasus-spyware-and-how-does-it-hack-phones>.
24 Richard Branson. Twitter, <https://twitter.com/richardbranson/status/905415713225146368>.
25 Olúfẹ́mi O. Táíwò, 'Who gets to feel secure?', <https://aeon.co/essays/on-liberty-security-and-our-system-of-racial-capitalism>.
26 Táíwò, 'Who gets to feel secure?'.

# Europe – from Fortress to Dungeon

## Nidžara Ahmetašević

When the Moria camp on the island of Lesbos in Greece was destroyed by fire in September 2020, in the middle of the Covid-19 pandemic, Ylva Johansen, the Commissioner for Home Affairs of the European Commission (EC), stated there would be no further new Morias.[1] Over the next couple of days and weeks, people who were at the Moria Reception Identification Centre – often referred to as a 'hell'[2] – were transferred to other camps around Greece, or to the location nearby where the new Moria was situated and where they are living more than one year later. Some people were moved to camps on the mainland, including camp Diavata, which was described by a resident as a prison. 'At night, when I look beyond the barbed wire of the camp, I realise how different my life here is from the lives of others out there. I can only look at the beauty of the city lights from afar without knowing how long I will remain here.'[3]

In 2020 and 2021, while the world's attention was focused on the Covid-19 pandemic, authorities all over Europe focused on the continued fortification of borders, increasing security and surveillance, and imposing more limits on freedoms for all. Immigration and immigrants are further criminalised while being pushed into new high-security centres surrounded by double barbed wire fences or walls, in isolated locations. These new facilities are financed by the EU and built by the local authorities with the assistance of the International Organization for Migration (IOM), the main organisation for 'migration management'.

A very similar scenario developed not so far away from Moria, in Bosnia and Herzegovina, where since June 2018, the IOM assumed the leading role in 'migration management'. Part of its task is the creation of 'temporary accommodation centres', as well as assistance to those state security and border protection systems with accommodation centres.

In what follows we will indicate what the situation has been in Greece and Bosnia during the pandemic. Due not only to their geographical position, but also to the fact that they could be considered weak states, both countries have become an important part of the EU's border policies, implemented through a series of agreements, in which 'accommodation centres' play an important part. Poor living conditions, the lack of freedom and rights, and dehumanisation are just some of the characteristics of life in these places, which increasingly resemble concentration camps, while the policy built around all this reminds us of some of the darkest times in world history.[4]

## Greece: Hiding people behind the high walls

*The sense of confinement is becoming oppressive. Our eyes are prevented from seeing the outside world. People pass by the camp in their cars every day and I wonder if they, too, share a similar oppressive sense of being kept in the dark about what goes on in the camp behind the walls. I can see the wall from my window. It is 3 meters high. This image will persist in my mind for all time to come, reminding me that I have been forced to live as a prisoner, behind this wall.*[5]

*Parwan Amiri, a refugee from Afghanistan living in Ritsona Camp, Greece.*

Parwan Amiri, the 17-year-old girl from Afghanistan, arrived over three years ago on the island of Lesbos in Greece with her family hoping to find safe refuge. Unfortunately, they arrived after the EU concluded a deal with Turkey[6] that significantly slowed down the asylum process, leaving tens of thousands of people endlessly trapped in accommodation centres. It was in this situation of uncertainty, living in precarious conditions, that Amiri and her family found themselves at the start of the pandemic in 2020. Soon, they were moved to the mainland, to Ritsona Camp, north of Athens, which in 2021 became the very first centre in Greece to be surrounded by three-metre-high walls. The government announced that walls would be constructed around 24 camps on the mainland. At the same time, facilities on the islands are being replaced with Multi-Purpose Reception and Identification Centres (MPRICs), closed types of facilities with high-security measures. The first was opened in September 2021 on Samos, with a capacity for about 3,000 people. In November, two more were inaugurated on Leros and Kos. Each of the centres includes detention facilities surrounded by three rows of barbed wire and equipped with a sophisticated surveillance system.

At the inauguration ceremony for the centres on Leros and Kos, Margaritis Schinas, the European Commission Vice President, hailed the event as 'a historic day', describing MPRICs as 'another tangible proof of the undivided European solidarity with Greece. The IOM was charged with overseeing the construction and management of these sites in Greece, claiming that everything is done 'in accordance with international standards'.[7] However,

Dunja Mijatović, the Council of Europe's Human Rights Commissioner, disagreed stating that the construction of these centres could 'lead to long-term deprivation of liberty'.⁸

The decision to build MPRICs was made by the EC, which committed 276 million euros for five centres on islands through the European Asylum, Migration and Integration Fund.⁹ In addition, the EU supplied Greece with drones for patrolling from the sky, magnetic gates with integrated thermographic cameras in the camps, x-ray machines and security cameras at the entry and exit points, etc.

The facilities had long ago been planned, but the pandemic made it possible to implement them. Back in 2015, the EU introduced to the world the so-called 'hotspot approach' that was supposed to help with 'managing exceptional migratory flows'.¹⁰ The idea was to create emergency accommodation centres at EU entry points, including the Greek islands. These centres were supposed to serve for the registration of the new arrivals and short-term accommodation. A year later, in 2016, the EU-Turkey agreement was struck to prevent further arrivals, which was not the result. Hot spots were given a new function: keeping people away from the continent. The procedures were slowed down, which soon created bottlenecks in which thousands of people remain trapped for years. Life in hot spots became unbearable, while the centres were becoming overcrowded and dangerous, and living conditions poor. Some activists and researchers claim that the conditions were kept poor intentionally to act as a deterrent to potential new arrivals.

In 2015, the opening of the accommodation centres across Europe came as a response to a situation that could be described as an emergency: the arrival of a significant number of refugees, primarily from war-torn Syria. People were arriving in Europe over the sea from Turkey, and continuing through the Balkan Route, their path to Western Europe. The established centres were supposed to serve the purpose of short-term accommodation, during initial registration and asylum application. In 2016, the EU introduced a set of rules and regulations that eventually slowed down the entire process for the people who were arriving, leading to the closure of the borders and people crammed all over the continent into temporary accommodations. Europe was slowly changing from a fortress into a dungeon.

However, in 2018, the United Nations Refugee Agency (UNHCR) stated that camps in Greece were only intended to provide temporary housing. But just four years later the IOM, which became the leading organisation in maintaining these centres, described them as long-term accommodation sites.¹¹ The concept was further developed during the Covid pandemic, with more attention given to security than to vaccinating people against the virus.

The first official case of a person infected by Covid-19 in Moria was registered on 2 September 2020, and a total lockdown was ordered one day later. The number of infected people continued to rise over the next couple of days, but meanwhile nothing was done to improve living conditions. Before this, the authorities and the EU had disregarded calls coming from health experts and a petition signed by over 35,000 people throughout Europe to evacuate people from the Greek islands.[12] The lockdown included restricting the number of people who could leave the camp to 100 people each hour between 7 a.m. and 7 p.m. or one individual per family at a time. All visitors and NGOs were prohibited from entering the camp for at least 14 days.[13] Similar rules applied in other camps across the country. Local solidarity activists tried, together with people from the camps, to improve conditions by installing hand-washing stations, making and/or distributing masks, and providing Covid information. In May 2021, the Moria Awareness Team, an organised group of Moria residents, issued a public statement pointing out how Covid affects many aspects of people's lives:

> In December last year, a report was published saying that every third refugee in Lesvos had suicidal thoughts, and every fifth refugee had attempted to end their own life. This is also a consequence of the pandemic. Since last year we have been able to exit the camp only on specific days because of Covid-19. This results in us not being able to go to visit an NGO having activities, or to go to the shop to buy food and things like this […]. All in all, because of the situation, then people are forced to spend most of their time on the inside of this fence where we are dependent on so many things that are still not good, and so many of us start to forget what life on the outside is like. This situation is only increasing our mental health problems.[14]

The confirmation of their claims came from the International Rescue Committee (IRC) and other medical organisations. Since Covid lockdown measures were introduced, the IRC has registered a 66 per cent increase in attempted suicides and other self-harming behaviour among people on Lesbos, while depression, post-traumatic stress disorder and other debilitating conditions 'have emerged as by-products of the hopelessness and despair on Europe's eastern borderlands', and they have only increased as a result of the measures.[15] According to the report, 'Research demonstrates how the onset of the Covid-19 pandemic further exacerbated the suffering of already vulnerable asylum seekers and exposed the many flaws in Europe's asylum and reception system.[16] In addition, Doctors Without Borders, noted how children inside the existing camps in Greece are exhibiting 'regressive behaviours such as aggression, withdrawal and secondary enuresis [bedwetting] or [...] delays in cognitive, emotional and social development'.[17] Despite all these warnings, the EU, the IOM, and the Greek government have done little to address these concerns.

## Bosnia and Herzegovina – where there is no functional state

> *They are the focus for the spread of the coronavirus. We have a situation in which the local population do not go out and you cannot see them in the city centre, while 100 to 200 migrants are walking around with no problems. We have to remove them from the streets.*
> Fahrudin Radončić, former Ministry of Security, Bosnia and Herzegovina.[18]

A few days after this statement, on 16 March, the Ministry of Security, responsible for immigration issues, announced that all the 'temporary accommodation centres' in Bosnia Herzegovina (eight at that time), were in lockdown. It meant that a limited number of people were allowed to exit at a given time, and only if they needed to go shopping or see a doctor outside the centres. At the same time, police throughout the country were instructed to remove immigrants from the streets and to move them to the existing centres, which created overcrowding with little possibility of observing any of the preventive measures.[19] As the pandemic progressed, the measures were eased, but life for people in the centres did not change.

In Una-Sana Canton,[20] located in the northwest part of the country close to the border with the EU, restrictions on freedom of movement for immigrants were introduced even before the pandemic, with a lot of criticism of local authorities coming from different sides among international organisations or authorities. The pandemic changed this, allowing the local government in this small corner of the country to legalise the controversial measures and strictly impose their implementation, disguised as corona measures. Nevertheless, even in November 2021, people in centres within this part of Bosnia were obliged to observe the curfew and be behind the gates and wires before 4 p.m., while the police used every opportunity to remove immigrants from public places.

During the lockdown in Sarajevo, the capital city, the police received the order to 'clean the streets' of immigrants and prevent them from moving around, if necessary by force, as a preventive measure. Over the next few months, Sarajevo citizens witnessed the police chase people down on the streets and forcefully take them away, bringing them to one of the two centres in the suburbs, both run by the IOM. Yet the violence that was visible on the streets was of no concern to this or any other organisation involved in providing support to migrants; no international volunteers or organisations said anything about it.

Back in the Bihać area, in Una-Sana Canton, scenarios similar to those of Lesbos were developing. At the beginning of the pandemic, around 1,300 people were accommodated in the Lipa tent centre located in a remote area, away from the city or city infrastructure, and run by the IOM. Food was scarce, as well as bathrooms and access to water, and people had no privacy or possibility of isolating or maintaining physical distance at any given moment. Access to the centre was allowed only for the IOM and its partners, including various local security agencies. At some point, the IOM, under pressure from the public, which demanded more accountability from them, requested that the state take over the centres, but the government showed no interest. The IOM even issued a public warning that they would leave Lipa and stop providing any support due to the authorities' lack of interest in being more engaged. And the IOM did leave Lipa at the end of December 2020. That same night, fire broke out in the camp and almost all the tents were destroyed, leaving people with nothing.[21] The remoteness of the location and the harsh winter prevented them from going to the city. It took days for civil society and the local Red Cross to be able to consolidate forces and act together to provide basic help in the form of food twice a day, some blankets, and warm clothes. The IOM and their partner organisations did not come even when the horrific images were all over the media. Finally, after several weeks, the state authorities came to install new tents, and the IOM showed up again, announcing the establishment of a new facility. Support came from various EU officials, ambassadors, and representatives of western countries, who visited Lipa and promised more donations through the IOM.

Finally, in mid-November 2021, the new Lipa centre was inaugurated in a ceremony similar to those in Samos or Leros and Kos. At the inauguration, the Head of EU Delegation and EU Special Representative Ambassador Johann Sattler said, 'There are many challenges still ahead to achieve sustainable migration management in BiH (Bosnia and Herzegovina),' but we can say that Lipa is a success story of BiH.' And the head of the IOM stated: 'Today we are turning a tragedy into an opportunity.' The Lipa reception facility was constructed with the financial support of the European Union as the main contributor, with 1.7 million euros within the project 'EU Support to Migration and Border Management in Bosnia and Herzegovina' implemented by the IOM in partnership with UNHCR, UNICEF, UNFPA, and the Danish Refugee Council (DRC).[22] Olivér

Várhelyi, the EC Commissioner for Neighbourhood Enlargement, said:

> We will continue to help Western Balkans partners to improve and expand assisted voluntary return programmes. I count on the EU Member States to play their fair part as well, including by using the leverage to promote returns directly from the Western Balkans. It must be clear to everyone that the door to the EU is not open for irregular entry. We remain ready to engage with third countries to facilitate the returns from the Western Balkans [...] I can assure you that the EU will deliver its part, both politically and financially, but we expect equal commitment from your side to address our joint challenges and achieve the goals that are in our mutual interest.[23]

Lipa is surrounded by barbed wire, filled with containers, and has a capacity of 1,500. According to the plans, single men, unaccompanied children, and families (single women are not mentioned) will be placed here, while all the other accommodation centres in the area will be closed.

Bosnia is in a very different position when it comes to the role assigned to it by the EU in 'migration management'. Since the end of the 1992-1995 war, which concluded with the peace agreement,[24] the country has remained a semi-protectorate. In practice, this means that the state has the institutions, but the peace agreement gives ultimate power to the international organisations present in the country.[25] Its structure, imposed by the peace agreement, is weak and dysfunctional, which enables corrupt elites to remain in power.[26] Aware of all this and the fact that the state institutions are blocked due to internal disagreements between political parties,[27] the EU decided in 2018 not to trust the local authorities at any level with 'managing migrations' but to give a free hand to the IOM. However, while disregarding the deteriorating general situation in the country, the IOM and the EU focused on the institutions important to immigration management – namely, the Ministry of Security, the Ministry of Foreign Affairs, and the local authorities. In this way, the IOM helped create a parallel system in which it became impossible to follow what is going on in this particular sphere, or who is accountable for what. In addition, the EU, through the IOM, continued pumping donations into the security and intelligence sector.[28]

Bosnia was not part of the Balkan route until 2018, and little attention was given to the situation in the country when it comes to immigration. At the end of 2017, after the death of Madina Hussiny on the train tracks between Croatia and Serbia,[29] this changed, and the route was diverted away from the Serbian-Croatian to the Bosnian-Croatian border. From June 2018 until November 2021, over 80 million euros were directed toward Bosnia from the EU for 'managing migrations'.[30] An important part of the process was the creation of 'temporary accommodation centres' across the country, all managed by the IOM. The centres were created within the rented private properties, old factories, and, later, old military barracks. Access to these spaces for civil society – including journalists or researchers – remains strictly limited. The public has no information about living conditions inside the centres, which are surrounded by high barbed wire fences and guarded by private security companies hired by the IOM. The public perception is created by the IOM and their partners who hire professional PR agencies. This approach and the removal of people from public visibility allowed the spread of hate propaganda coming from public officials but also from part of the media. Meanwhile, the IOM or their partners are doing little to combat this spread of hate speech. In summer 2020, Edin Ramulic, a Bosnian concentration camp survivor from the last war, wrote a post in his facebook page that 'for refugees in our country, it is much worse than it was for people kept in the concentration camp of Trnopolje'.[31]

## Camps: A system to keep people at a distance

Access to most of the accommodation centres where immigrants and refugees are living in Europe is limited, which the administrators of the centres claim is intended to protect the privacy of residents. Occasionally, when reports and images find their way into the public, people can see places with little or no privacy and unhappy people who are waiting for the moment to leave.

If the state authorities are responsible for the functioning of centres, then it is possible for the public to hold them accountable. In fall of 2021, the Rosa Luxemburg Stiftung published a series of articles based on research conducted during the pandemic in centres located in Germany, concluding that they have 'prison-like characteristics'.[32] Similar reports have come from other EU countries, but also from the UK and Switzerland. If organisations like the IOM are allowed the role they have, nobody is accountable since the centres function outside of any government system. Deaths, deprivation of freedom, lawlessness, violence, and other forms of humiliation and dehumanisation of the people living inside become normalised.

In 2014, the UN Refugee Agency (UNHCR) published a very critical position, pointing out that the very existence of these centres 'creates refugee dependence, distorting local economies, and harbouring security threats', while calling for alternatives to be created.[33] But nothing changed, except that the UNHCR for some reason was replaced by the IOM, which in 2016 became a 'UN-related organisation'. Unlike the UN, which is obliged to adhere to the UN Charter, including the articles related to the respect of human rights, the IOM is a managing organisation whose work is dictated by the donors, being primarily governments, or the EU. The role of the IOM is most visible in less developed countries, or those at the periphery of the EU, as well as weak states, like Greece or Bosnia.

Governments or the organisations involved in the day-to day operation of the centres at the edge of the EU, instead of pushing for faster procedures and open borders, or any other solution, focused on maintaining the overcrowded centres with poor living conditions, using them to deter refugees. Maintaining the centres conveys to the public the sense of a continuous state of emergency caused by the 'refugee crisis' and a false image that those who are running camps are in control of the situation as they try to protect the public. To deter refugees the IOM PR machine pumped the media full of images of many people dying on their way to the EU. The message projected to potential refugees is that those who survive perilous journeys will be staying in centres resembling concentration camps deprived of their freedoms and life. The pandemic was an ideal opportunity to develop this approach still further.

For European officials, the Covid-19 pandemic and the lockdown measures were the perfect moment to introduce harsher measures aimed at stopping immigration and creating a world in which surveillance and containment of the population, for whatever purpose, can be normalised and justified by the state of emergency.

★ ★ ★

Two years after the breakout of the coronavirus, Europe is, as a continent, more militarised, with the movement of people surveilled with new technologies, and borders that are becoming impenetrable.

The cry 'never again' in the face of the Holocaust has long gone unheeded in many parts of the world outside Europe, but with the genocide in Bosnia and now the detention camps in Europe in Moria and the Balkans – with the walls around them, the barbed wire, surveillance, and deprivation of freedom and rights – the demand 'no more Morias' is becoming an ever more urgently felt contemporary way of saying 'never again'.

NOTES

1   <https://www.youtube.com/watch?v=CX49DQsbrzg>.
2   <https://www.theguardian.com/global-development/2020/jan/17/moria-is-a-hell-new-arrivals-describe-life-in-a-greek-refugee-camp>.
3   <https://wearesolomon.com/mag/lab/we-call-it-modernization-reception-centers-for-migrants-will-be-closed-facilities/>.
4   <https://www.hrw.org/news/2016/12/06/impact-externalization-migration-controls-rights-asylum-seekers-and-other-migrants>.
5   <http://birdsofimmigrants.jogspace.net/2021/07/06/letters-to-the-world-from-ritsona-no-21/>.
6   <https://eu.rescue.org/article/what-eu-turkey-deal>.
7   <https://wearesolomon.com/mag/lab/we-call-it-modernization-reception-centers-for-migrants-will-be-closed-facilities/?mc_cid=29f50ff05c&mc_eid=4b61fe2340>.
8   <https://www.thenationalherald.com/greece-opens-two-more-island-refugee-detention-centers/>.
9   <https://www.aljazeera.com/news/2021/5/25/concrete-walls-and-drones-greek-plans-for-refugee-camps-decried>.
10  <https://ec.europa.eu/home-affairs/pages/glossary/hotspot-approach_en>.
11  <https://greece.iom.int/sites/greece/files/July_2019.pdf> and <https://greece.iom.int/improving-greek-reception-system-through-site-management-support-and-targeted-interventions-long-term-accommodation-sites>.
12  <https://www.theguardian.com/world/2020/mar/24/eu-urged-to-evacuate-asylum-seekers-from-cramped-greek-island-camps-coronavirus> and <https://www.theguardian.com/global-development/2020/apr/07/coronavirus-doesnt-respect-barbed-wire-concern-mounts-for-greek-camps>.
13  <https://www.msf.org/greek-police-enforce-unwarranted-and-cruel-quarantine-moria-camp>.
14  <https://www.medico.de/en/this-is-not-disneyland-18200>.
15  <https://www.theguardian.com/global-development/2020/dec/17/thousands-refugees-mental-crisis-years-greek-islands >.
16  <https://www.rescue-uk.org/sites/default/files/document/2389/crueltyofcontainmentreport.pdf>, p. 3.
17  <https://www.infomigrants.net/en/post/34962/greece-msf-criticizes-new-prisonlike-refugee-camps>.
18  <Deutche Welle, Korona zaustavila migrante u BiH. Available at https://www.dw.com/sr/korona-zaustavila-migrante-u-bih/a-52896788>.
19  <https://www.slobodnaevropa.org/a/migranti-ulice-bih-korona-virus/30493247.html>.
20  Bosnia and Herzegovina is divided into two entities: Republika Srpska and the Federation of Bosnia and Herzegovina, along with the district of Brcko, which is independent of both.
21  <https://www.iom.int/news/thousands-migrants-forced-sleep-rough-after-closure-destruction-bosnia-camp>.
22  Additional support was provided by the German Federal Agency for Technical Relief (Techniches Hilfswerk), the Austrian Federal Ministry of Interior, the Austrian Development Agency, the Swiss Government, the Holy See, the Italian Ministry

of Foreign Affairs and International Cooperation, and the Council of Europe Development Bank, <https://europa.ba/?p=73794>.

23  <https://ec.europa.eu/commission/commissioners/2019-2024/varhelyi/announcements/address-commissioner-varhelyi-regional-ministerial-conference-migration-sarajevo-migration-dialogue_en>.
24  <http://www.ohr.int/dayton-peace-agreement/>.
25  <http://www.ohr.int/about-ohr/general-information/>.
26  <https://www.transparency.org/files/content/corruptionqas/Bosnia_overview_of_political_corruption_2014.pdf>; <https://europeanwesternbalkans.com/2021/10/19/key-findings-of-the-2021-european-commission-report-on-bosnia-and-herzegovina/>.
27  <https://kosovotwopointzero.com/en/the-geopolitics-of-the-anticipated-war/>.
28  For one example, see <https://bih.iom.int/pbn/european-union-supports-mobility-and-protection-bih-border-police-and-sipa>.
29  <https://www.refugee.watch/2021/11/19/the-ecthr-confirmed-croatias-responsibility-in-madinas-case/>.
30  <https://www.rosalux.rs/en/dark-side-europeanisation>.
31  <https://kulturasjecanja.org/en/prijedor-camp-trnopolje/>
32  <https://www.rosalux.de/en/news/id/45305?fbclid=IwAR03mbJy_RnVqCF4FtrX8dykSXjZIq64pbMFwIlEceFFu9rhtqW6DqGA-cE>.
33  <https://sswm.info/sites/default/files/reference_attachments/UNHCR%202014%20Policy%20on%20Alternatives%20to%20Camps.pdf >.

# Migrants and Refugees: Pariahs of Europe

## María Eugenia Rodríguez Palop

'[…] no one puts their children in a boat unless the water is safer than the land' – (Warsan Shire, *Home*)

The general framework of the European Union's external migration and asylum policy is established in *The Global Approach to Migration and Mobility*.[1] The Communication was approved in 2011, at a time when the need for a coherent and comprehensive immigration policy was at the centre of the Commission's political agenda. Viewing the human rights of migrants as a crosscutting dimension, international protection and asylum were established as a basic pillar of EU policy, along with legal immigration and mobility, the prevention of irregular immigration, and exposing and combating human trafficking.

Ostensibly committed to the enhancement of solidarity with refugees and displaced persons, the Global Approach to Migration and Mobility focused on strengthening external asylum policy, improving cooperation with relevant third countries, and bolstering their capacities and the protections contained in their asylum systems.

Unfortunately, the policy is hardly worth the paper it is written on. Almost ten years later, the situation is significantly worse and the European Union's position towards migration has hardened.

Ongoing violations of human rights, war, violence, and persecution have forced around 80 million people into displacement. According to a 2021 report of the Comisión Española de Ayudo al Refugiado (CEAR),[2] they represent

> the largest number [of forcibly displaced persons] in history, almost doubling the number recorded only a decade ago. In a world ravaged by the Covid-19 pandemic, 20.7 million refugees remain under the protection of the UNHCR, of which a third are from Syria and a further 45.7 million persons

are displaced within their own countries, mostly in Colombia, Syria, the Democratic Republic of Congo, and Yemen.

Thousands of people are migrating to Europe to flee conflicts, terrorism and persecution.

We should also be aware that many people are migrating because of climate conditions. In 2020, 30.7 million displacements were caused by 'meteorological and climate events (storms, floods, droughts, extreme temperatures, etc.) and geophysical disturbances (earthquakes and volcanic eruptions)'.[3]

In 2019 alone, the European Union gave protected status to 300,000 applicants,[4] but this only represented a minute proportion of those who needed help. 85% of people who sought international protection were given shelter by economically impoverished countries. In 2019, only 17% of refugees were taken in by 'high-income' countries.[5]

In a situation where the protection and reception systems of countries with fewer resources are already overwhelmed, the Covid-19 pandemic has compounded the problem even further. On top of increasing inequality and poverty, lockdowns and border closures have created insurmountable obstacles for those in need of protection. In this context, the particular vulnerability of children and women, who suffer continued setbacks to the little progress that has been made on gender equality, is plainly evident.

The European Parliament's 'Report on the gender perspective in the Covid-19 crisis and post-crisis period', carried out by the Committee on Women's Rights and Gender Equality, states that 'women and girls will be affected disproportionately in the short, medium and long-term and the pandemic has exacerbated existing structural gender inequalities, in particular for girls and women from marginalised groups'. Consequently, the report recommends that Member States guarantee support for migrants 'through access to critical healthcare during the crisis' and 'highlights the need for refugee and reception centres to take due account of women's and girls' needs and risks in view of the known challenges' they face.[6]

Similarly, the 2021 Gender Equality Index, published by the European Institute for Gender Equality, stresses that the restrictions and lockdowns imposed due to the pandemic have increased the risk of violence towards particularly vulnerable groups, such as undocumented migrants and asylum seekers.[7]

Since the height of the 2014–15 migration crisis, the European Union has implemented public policies that have managed to reduce the number of people entering Europe irregularly by 90%,[8] with the exception of the

Canary Islands. However, this is not a figure to be proud of.

Compared to 2019, the number of irregular migrants arriving in Europe fell by 23% in 2020. In part, this was due to the pandemic but was also related to the tightening of border controls and agreements with third countries of origin and transit, in particular those in North and West Africa, which worked to contain the flow of migrants.[9]

The question is: What policies have managed to reduce migration so drastically and what is happening to people who need international protection and to reach safe countries? We should not forget that many migrants find themselves trapped in countries that, far from offering protection, violate their right of access to asylum procedures with full procedural guarantees, along with other fundamental rights. Many migrants become victims of violence and die while attempting to reach safety.

According to the International Organization for Migration (IOM), 1,417 migrants have died or disappeared in the Mediterranean Sea in 2020. 'Amongst all Atlantic and Mediterranean routes to various European Union countries, 1,957 died in 2020, of which 861 deaths (44%) occurred while in transit by sea to Spanish coasts.' In fact, almost half (47%) of migrants who arrive in Europe by sea pass through Spain, the most common route, while 40% arrive through Italy, followed by Greece (11%) and Malta (2%).[10]

## The European Union: surveillance and border control

For decades, the European Union has focused its efforts on financing complex systems for surveillance and control of its frontiers. This has included providing economic support to Member States to secure their borders; entering into cooperation agreements for the policing (i.e., externalisation) of borders with neighbouring countries, such as Morocco, Turkey, and Ukraine; and establishing readmission agreements with countries of origin and transit in order to force the return of undocumented immigrants who manage to enter the European Union.

These controls have increased the profitability of illegal trafficking and organised crime, which encourage migrants to take ever more dangerous routes. From a human-rights perspective, Frontex and Eurosur are failed experiments. The Italian sea operation Mare Nostrum did not prevent tragedies such as Lampedusa, and migrants have not been deterred by the Spanish border surveillance system SIVE, 'joint operations', or by the use of drones. Most seriously, and somewhat predictably, border control without cooperation and without adequate reception and integration policies has proved fatal.

In all this time, nothing has been done to develop a proper European asylum system that overcomes the deficiencies of Member States. On the one hand, the European Asylum Support Office (EASO) has not been given greater importance or powers, and, on the other, Frontex has been given more and more resources, but its purview remains the same. Nothing has been done to help resolve conflicts in affected countries and so reduce the 'push' effect. The reality is that the external dimension of migration policies has not been adequately embedded in the foreign policy framework, nor sufficiently linked to the promotion of security and peace beyond the European Union.

An emblematic example of this folly is the agreement the European Union signed with Turkey. This Agreement violates European and international human-rights laws and puts the lives of many migrants at risk when they are returned to Turkey. With regard to illegal third-country nationals, the Agreement infringes the right of each person to have their case considered individually, as per Directive 2008/115/EC. Consequently, they are not guaranteed full access to the procedures for international protection nor application of the principle of non-refoulement, which requires an evaluation of the situation in the country of origin and of any grounds for believing that the person's life or physical integrity would be in danger if they were returned. Nor does the agreement ensure effective compliance with the obligations established in articles 6, 8, 12, 19 and 24 of Directive 2013/32/EU (common procedures for granting and withdrawing international protection) for applicants for international protection in relation to access to the asylum system, information, legal advisors, procedural guarantees, and special procedures for people who need them.

The definition of Turkey as a 'safe country' implies a prior assessment of the practical application of the law, genuine respect for human rights, and the absence of persecution or serious harm such as would justify international protection. But no guarantees exist — nor have they ever existed — that can ensure Turkey's compliance with these requirements. The situation in Greece is similarly problematic because although Greece respects the right to individual evaluation of cases when processing applications for international protection, the use of accelerated procedures means less time is available for the careful analysis of the circumstances of each individual and for the identification of situations of heightened vulnerability.

In fact, the situation of refugees in Greece is especially dire as they are trapped in camps in 'overcrowded, unsanitary, and unprotected conditions that violate the most basic human rights'.[11] In Greece, even the minimum standards of reception established in European law are not observed, constituting a failure to ensure the guarantees set out in articles 17, 19, 23.2,

24.1, and 25.1 of Directive 2013/33/EU.

Moreover, if a safe third country is one that has ratified the Geneva Convention without geographic restrictions, has an asylum system proscribed in law, and has ratified the European Convention on Human Rights, Turkey could not be classified as one. To begin with, it has no fully established right to asylum and operates a dysfunctional asylum system replete with inequities in access and scope of protection. Furthermore, the geographic limitation of its ratification of the Geneva Convention means that only temporary asylum is available to non-European refugees, while the international community fails to offer anywhere near enough options or places for resettlement. It also must also be emphasised that Turkey has not ratified the 4th Protocol of the European Convention of Human Rights, which prohibits collective expulsions.

Finally, in Greece, the absence of guaranteed individual assessment of applications for international protection, the returning of applicants to Turkey, and the lack of minimum reception standards constitute infringements of articles 18 and 19 of the European Union's Charter of Fundamental Rights. These principles are also enshrined in numerous international treaties such as the Convention Against Torture and Other Cruel, Inhuman or Degrading Treatment or Punishment and the Convention Relating to the Status of Refugees (1951).

The European Agency for Fundamental Rights (FRA) has denounced the pushbacks of immigrants at the European Union's external borders, especially in Bulgaria, Greece, and Spain, and has reminded the relevant authorities that collective expulsions are always illegal.

## The Pact on Migration and Asylum

Against this background, the European Commission introduced the New Pact on Migration and Asylum, which was described by the Commission's Vice-President Margaritis Schinas as 'a house with three floors': on the first floor an 'external dimension – centred around strengthened partnerships with countries of origin and transit', in particular combating human trafficking; a second floor that places 'emphasis on a robust management of the external borders'; and finally 'on the third floor of our theoretical house, we find firm but fair internal rules […] providing for effective solidarity'.[12] The priorities and objectives of the Pact are subdivided into five main areas:[13]

1. Definition of a common framework for asylum and migration management. This new mechanism will comprise 'pre-entry screening including identification, health and security checks, fingerprinting, and registration in the Eurodac database'.

- Establishing fast-tracking procedures at borders and the simplification of asylum and return rules – one of the most controversial aspects of the Pact. In certain circumstances, the person applying for international protection is to be assessed rapidly (when they come from countries whose nationals have less chance of being seen as meriting asylum and therefore have small chances of being accepted, or if they make fraudulent applications or pose a threat to national security).

  This is controversial because, first of all, it will be extremely hard to evaluate these issues rapidly, making it very difficult, for example, to identify possible trafficking victims. Furthermore, the fast-tracked procedure may mean 'a grave risk of diminished procedural guarantees due to the short deadlines established and the possibility of infringing the principle of non-refoulement. Through prolonged detentions, the situation on the Greek islands could become the norm at all the EU's external borders.[14]

  Secondly, it discriminates on the basis of country of origin: Which nationals are considered low risk? How is this assessed and from what perspective?

- A common framework for solidarity and responsibility-sharing in relocations or 'return partnerships'.

- Withdrawal of the 2016 proposal to amend the Dublin Regulation, which will finally be replaced by a regulation on asylum and migration management.

  As CEAR points out,[15] the reform of the European Common Asylum System (CEAS) was already proposed in 2016, but 'none of the documents advanced by CEAS in 2015 and 2016 were approved.[16] Furthermore, the reform of the Regulation on the European Border and Coast Guard Agency (Frontex), adopted by the Council in November 2019, was the only instance in which a definitive agreement was reached between the European Parliament and the Council.'

  No longer is there talk of mandatory quotas but a shift to a system of flexible contributions between the European capitals that may take the form of refugee reception, support for returns through the financing of national flights to third countries, or other forms of operational support. This represents an 'à la carte solidarity' and an ambiguous mechanism for dealing with crisis situations, such as the one that occurred in 2015. While the new system is based on cooperation and on flexible forms of voluntary support, more stringent contributions will be required when individual Member States come under greater pressure.

In brief, Member States have been given the choice between sponsoring repatriations or relocations without taking into account that some countries are highly unequal.

The truth is that the cornerstone of the whole system is the ensuring of returns and on supposed cooperation with countries of origin and transit, and the leading role played by Frontex.[17] This approach weakens any rights- and gender-based focus and does a disservice to the struggle against human trafficking and the protection of the rights of migrants.

2. The second objective relates to the creation of a preparedness and response system for crisis situations, specified in the Migration Preparedness and Crisis Blueprint. This mechanism is supposed to provide a coordinated response and preventative measures, but it must be specified through the Asylum and Migration Management Regulation. It seems remarkable that such an important issue has been postponed and relegated to a draft implementation rule. This is indicative of the lack of political will to address the issue of migration from a rights-based angle.

3. Improving the efficiency of integrated management of the European Union's external border by developing a multi-annual strategic policy.

4. Strengthening the measures to combat migrant smuggling. The Commission has announced 'a new action plan on this issue that will remain in place until 2025, which will strengthen the Employers Sanction Directive in order to deter the employment of irregularly staying persons and promote cooperation with third countries on common security and defence policies'.[18]

5. Bolstering bilateral, regional, and multilateral cooperation with countries of origin and transit in order to improve return policies.

## Migration, systemic inequities, and the Global Compact on Refugees

It seems clear that the Pact on Migration and Asylum is in keeping with the spirit of the 2030 Agenda for Sustainable Development, which states in objective 10.7 that it aims to 'facilitate orderly, safe, and responsible migration and mobility of people, including through implementation of planned and well-managed migration policies'.[19] This Agenda was approved in the middle of the 'refugee crisis' and has a very restrictive focus in terms of migration, as well as rejecting a rights-based approach and uncoupling human mobility from development problems. Furthermore, it is worrying that the only goal that specifically refers to mobility is formulated in terms of control and orderly migrations.

As argued by organisations such as Greenpeace and CEAR, migrations, in particular those caused by climate conditions and disasters,

> are a reflection of a global system based on profoundly unjust relations. In general, the people that have contributed the least to the climate crisis are those who are suffering its worst effects. People living in situations of poverty, those who subsist on agriculture and fishing, and indigenous communities who maintain a profound relationship with their lands, find themselves at the frontline of climate effects. Due to longstanding structural inequalities, women and children are most severely affected. Many of these people do not even have the necessary resources to migrate when faced with imminent risk, remaining trapped in devastated or progressively deteriorating territories.[20]

In fact, with the aim of guaranteeing respect for the human rights of all migrants, the Special Rapporteur on the Human Rights of Migrants has already proposed a parallel agenda to the 2030 Agenda. This report, known as the 2035 Agenda for Facilitating Human Mobility, denounces the oppression of undocumented migrants in border management and the externalisation of borders, i.e., the relocation of border control to the territory of so-called third countries. For this reason the Rapporteur proposes

> a fundamental shift in the way that migration is perceived and framed. Migration itself is a natural part of human existence; it is neither a crime nor a problem, and it has the potential to be a solution. Accordingly, migration governance is not a matter of closing off borders and keeping people out, but one of regulating mobility by opening accessible, regular, safe and affordable migration channels and promoting and celebrating diversity.[21]

The Pact on Migration and Asylum represents a lost opportunity. It was announced shortly after the acquisition of global rights in the Global Compact on Refugees, which 'despite its non-binding nature, created some hope for improvements to the asylum system, the expansion of legal and safe routes, the simplification of family reunification procedures, and the renunciation of the externalisation of borders and return policy as cornerstones of migration policy'.[22] The Compact proposed a path of continuity that has not attempted to address shortcomings and gaps. In reality, 'a restrictive management model has been retained in relation to rights, with an excessive focus on returns and strengthening of controls and the externalisation of borders, which risks the infringement of the principle of non-refoulement and recognised guarantees'.[23]

For example, no agreement has been reached on a safe disembarkation mechanism and subsequent mandatory relocation and, even though search and rescue operations and disembarkation are mentioned in all proposals, these are not financed or coordinated. While it is true that there is a commitment to the non-criminalisation of humanitarian action in the Mediterranean, it should have gone far beyond this, by expressly stating that member states have binding obligations to search and rescue at sea, in accordance with international law.

The European Union's Migration Pact means a reinforcement of the same approaches that have always been adopted: the return of human beings, externalisation of borders, and agreements of readmission in order to speed up expulsions. In short, fewer guarantees in terms of access to the right of asylum and refuge, and no laws or effective proposals guaranteeing legal and safe access routes.

In the words of the Special Rapporteur on the Human Rights of Migrants, countries must 'increase regular channels for migration and the taxation of mobility, through the progressive expansion of visa liberalization' and 'reclaim the mobility market from the smugglers and adopt measures to regularize undocumented migrants'.[24] In short, he asks for the development of a strategic long-term vision, containing specific objectives in accordance with the protection of human rights, and evaluation and accountability mechanisms.

## Conclusion

Europe has been constructed as a fortress within a fortress, as an infinite hierarchy between fragmented citizenships in which a labyrinthine and lethal inequality is meticulously reproduced. 'Welfare chauvinism' and cultural racism have served a privileged few to keep the 'poor and needy' out of their compound. Faced with demands for internal democracy, social justice, and redistribution of wealth, Europe has striven to protect capitalism and the well-being and wealth of a minority.

It could be said that European migration policy is, above all, a policy of border control, a reactive policy that functions on the basis of stopgaps at election times. It has never been based on a common strategy of conflict and post-conflict resolution.

However, on a daily basis, the militarisation of borders corresponds to the brutal economic asymmetries that exist between countries and the conflicts and violence for which Europe is responsible. It collides with the liberalisation of capital and goods, dressed up in the triumphalist rhetoric of mobility, and restrictions on the movement of persons. And their territorialisation also collides with the supposed universality of human rights.

Sadly, the rights that we enjoy as European citizens are a product of a long and costly process of social exclusion and discrimination. The status of others as foreigners, immigrants, the undocumented, those 'without papers', asylum seekers, and the stateless, are the basis of our privileges and only serve to manifest the absurd contradictions in which we live.

The use of citizenship applications turns migrants and refugees into orphans. With no place in the world, these non-citizens have, as Hannah Arendt would say, 'no rights to have rights'. This manner of conceiving the distinction between citizens and foreigners has underpinned many of the practices of social exclusion that we see in everyday life and the rhetoric of 'security' that has been nourished by those same practices.

Expelled, drowned, and sequestered in the concentration camps of our times, the only crime committed by the thousands of people detained in Internment Centres for Foreigners is to have wanted to be part of our world without being one of 'us'; being 'the nobodies' who are not worth the bullet that kills them; being 'the others', 'them', 'those from nowhere'; being those to whom we believe we owe nothing because they are not 'from here', as if our moral and political responsibilities could be determined only on the basis of the borders 'we' have drawn.

## NOTES

1. Communication from the Commission to the European Parliament, The Council, The European Economic and Social Committee and The Committee of the Regions, The Global Approach to Migration and Mobility, <https://eur-lex.europa.eu/legal-content/EN/ALL/?uri=CELEX%3A52011DC0743>.
2. Comisión Española de Ayuda al Refugiado, *NFORME 2021: Las personas refugiadas en España y Europa* <https://www.cear.es/wp-content/uploads/2021/06/Informe-Anual-CEAR-2021.pdf>, p. 8.
3. See Greenpeace, *Huir del clima: Cómo influye la crisis climática en las migraciones humanas*, 6 October 2021,<https://es.greenpeace.org/es/sala-de-prensa/informes/migraciones-climaticas/>.
4. See 'Europe's migration crisis', <https://www.europarl.europa.eu/news/en/headlines/society/20170629STO78631/europe-s-migration-crisis>.
5. Comisión Española de Ayuda al Refugiado, p. 19.
6. <https://www.europarl.europa.eu/doceo/document/A-9-2020-0229_EN.pdf>.
7. *2021 Gender Equality Index*, <https://eige.europa.eu/gender-equality-index/2021>, gender_equality_index_2021_health-1.pdf, p. 19.
8. See European Council, 'Latest news: New EU asylum agency starts its work', <https://www.consilium.europa.eu/en/policies/eu-migration-policy/>.
9. Comisión Española de Ayuda al Refugiado, p. 19.
10. Comisión Española de Ayuda al Refugiado, pp. 42-44.

11    Comisión Española de Ayudo al Refugiado, p. 45.
12    Speech by Vice-President Schinas on the New Pact on Migration and Asylum, <https://ec.europa.eu/commission/presscorner/detail/en/SPEECH_20_1736>.
13    Comisión Española de Ayudo al Refugiado, pp. 48ff.
14    Comisión Española de Ayudo al Refugiado, p. 54.
15    Comisión Española de Ayudo al Refugiado, p. 52.
16    <https://www.consilium.europa.eu/en/policies/eu-migration-policy/>.
17    Comisión Española de Ayudo al Refugiado, pp. 52-53.
18    Comisión Española de Ayudo al Refugiado, pp.53-54.
19    <https://www.un.org/sustainabledevelopment/development-agenda/>.
20    Greenpeace, *Huir del clima*.
21    *Report of the Special Rapporteur on the human rights of migrants on a 2035 agenda for facilitating human mobility*, <https://www.iom.int/sites/g/files/tmzbdl486/files/our_work/ODG/GCM/A_HRC_35_25_EN.pdf>, p. 5.
22    Comisión Española de Ayudo al Refugiado, p. 54.
23    Comisión Española de Ayudo al Refugiado, p. 55.
24    *Report of the Special Rapporteur*, p. 7.

# Social Democratic and Radical Left Political Strategies

## Radical in Diversity. Europe's Left 2010-2020

edited by Amieke Bouma, Cornelia Hildebrandt, Danai Koltsida

Publisher: Merlin Press / Rosa-Luxemburg-Stiftung (November 2021)
Language: English
ISBN-10: 0850367697
ISBN-13: 978-0850367690

What is the role of the radical left in Europe? How can regional groups parties and groups contribute to a common European left?
Scholars and activists from 22 countries explore radical left strategies:
- How best to struggle against chauvinism and right-wing extremism?
- How to respond to economic, financial and migration crises?
- How to combine traditional left interests - social welfare, workers' rights, medical care and education, with new left concerns such as the social inclusion of migrants and the protection of the environment?
- How can left parties contend with new bourgeois and green left-of-center parties?
- And importantly, how to forge a European left that transcends national interests, reigning in corporate interests and promoting social, gender and racial emancipation?

# Social Democracy and the Radical Left: Old Divisions and the Imperatives of the New Socio-Ecological Crisis

A Dialogue Between Luciana Castellina
and Donald Sassoon
Moderated by Haris Golemis

**Haris Golemis:** Let us kick off the dialogue with a note we received from Luciana, in which she feels that there is no place today for the historic conflict between 'reformists' and 'revolutionaries' – or social democracy and Leninism – due to the completely changed characteristics of contemporary capitalism. Luciana, as I understand it, has nevertheless proposed a discussion between the descendants of the two historical traditions, that is, between the new social democracy and what political scientists call the 'radical left', on how to solve the present and future problems of humanity created by the renewed capitalism of our times. Can you start, Luciana?

**Luciana Castellina:** The way I pose the problem is clearly influenced by the history of the Italian Communist Party (PCI), which, as you know, bore many similarities to the social democratic parties – in fact, it was accused of being such a party, something it never accepted, even if it behaved like one. At the same time, others denounced it as an acolyte of the Soviet Union but just wearing a different dress for tactical reasons.

Donald knows very well what kind of special party the PCI was – a giraffe, as Togliatti called it. A strange animal looking down somewhat snobbishly at the other animals, maintaining that it itself had nothing to do with the other communist parties around the world. The question of the difference between social democrats and communists has been quite central in the Italian debate. But, as we know, it has been quite central among all the communist and social democratic party families for a long time. Generally, the imagery of systemic change for the communists would be the storming of the Winter Palace, while for social democrats it was the long road through parliamentary victory. After the Second World War the discussion was different because it was folded into the Cold War, with social democrats being those who were with the United States, and communists supporting the Soviet Union, though not all of them unconditionally.

At any rate, this discussion looks archaic to me today because this 'either-or' difference is no longer something that divides communists and social democrats; instead, both positions appear inside both parts of the left. Today, what both the social democratic and communist party families have in common is that they are in decline. The disappearance of the Soviet Union did not simplify the situation. It was expected that after its demise everyone would become a social democrat, but this didn't happen. Which is not to say that everyone became a communist. What emerged was the deep crisis of the Western systemic model in which we are living, which is deeper than ever before. We were all surprised by this crisis.

In the present situation it is hard to trace the old divide. The Winter Palace? Nobody knows where the Winter Palace is anymore. It's hard to locate it. Where is the power? What is the right strategy? Total state ownership? That doesn't make sense anymore, and especially within the global market resulting from globalisation. Thus, it is hard for social democrats and communists to find a winning strategy today.

Not to mention the new problems that have become central. First of all, the ecological problem, which I think will dominate our future and which is itself also a social problem because its solution has to produce a new kind of society. The social and the ecological cannot be separated. We have arrived at a point where everyone feels that what is needed is a fundamental change and a new model of producing and consuming; there is a sense that we can no longer accept the kind of competitiveness that is crushing social equality. We've arrived at a concentration of power so great that we don't know where it is.

In this context, I have thought of writing an editorial absolving those who have abstained from elections in Italy and elsewhere. Why should people vote for parliaments if parliaments are no longer the institutions that make decisions about the big issues? Decisions are taken at the level of the global market by private actors – such as Bayer buying Monsanto. This kind of decision has far more consequences for our lives than all those taken by our parliaments, which are almost limited to applying private decisions. This means that deliberative – I would even say legislative – power rests with the big multinational corporations, which are completely uncontrolled. The decisions taken by the European Parliament and the national parliaments are always less important. We are witnessing a void in democratic power. And so, the populations are less interested in electoral campaigns today.

I could talk for long about Italy, but I think the sense there is the same as everywhere in terms of what decisions need to be taken in order to respond to the ecological crisis.

So, coming back to what we are discussing here, the real differences between social democrats and communists (or radical leftists) remain but have no longer mainly to do with questions of income distribution, welfare, and so on, as in the post-Second World War years. Instead, the dimension now involved is that of a complete change in the way we consume and produce, which needs to be more related to use-value than to exchange-value, as it is today.

Today people suffer not only from not having a job, but also from the fact that work is increasingly deprived of significance. It's more difficult to fulfil the real needs of the people, which have become more differentiated than they used to be in the past. Contradictions have come onto centre stage that were less emphasised before: gender contradictions, ethnic contradictions, the question of alienated work, of what work really is. All these issues, which once were not important in politics but only in social-science discussions, have now started to become political issues.

Today, the big difference is between those who think the system can go on as it is, and those who think that it would be incapable of ruling the world without engendering protests and violence. It is not that capitalism is collapsing but that it is now incapable of responding to the questions that are on the ground, the most important of which I believe is that of democracy. If we do not respond immediately to the crisis of democracy by finding new forms of representation there is a danger of total disorder, of an ungovernable society. The delegative, purely parliamentary system alone, without the mediation of social organisations that had previously accompanied it, doesn't make sense anymore the way things did when society contained these intermediate institutions.

So, the issue today is not pro or con 'revolution', or whether to have a parliament or not. There has to be a rethinking; but no political party is prepared to do something of the sort.

There is a kind of political research we are obliged to carry out. I think the first step is to find a new form of expression of democracy, for example the idea that Gramsci developed of a prefigurative form of direct democracy, a transitional practice of democracy, in which you manage pieces of society already directly, without simply asking the institutions to do things for you.

I don't think this is an abstract discussion. In Italy, for example, it is not true that there is no politicisation; there are a lot of young people involved in politics, but what they are doing on the ground in this or that part of the city or in a village is not for the purpose of proposing it to the parliament, which will then make the necessary compromises within the institutional framework to resolve any possible problem. It's something they want to experiment with directly, and they do this by going into movements. The new generation up to now has been under the spell of the myth of movements. Now, movements are of course very important, because they have helped alert us to how the world has changed. But movements arise and disappear. They need to find a way to stabilise and organise themselves on the ground in what Gramsci called 'councils', which are part of the management of democracy, carrying out a dialectical confrontation with the institutions. I'm not saying by now 'all power to the soviets', but I am saying that part of what Lenin meant in speaking of soviets is that you have to conquer the ability to manage society – but now in pieces, without thinking of a central power located in a Winter Palace whose conquest would solve everything, because it has been demonstrated that this is impossible.

So, I think this is political work, not just an abstract discussion.

**Donald Sassoon:** Beginning with what Luciana was saying about the end of the distinction between communists and social democrats, I would add that this distinction ended quite a while ago. Quite rightly she points to the Italian Communist Party, but I would add that the other European communist parties in the post-war period were, on the whole, not – and this is not a criticism but a statement of fact – revolutionary parties, in the sense that they were not preparing themselves for an assault on whatever was the equivalent of the Winter Palace. They were trying to find a way of obtaining power in a capitalist society. The issue is that no communist revolution after 1917 occurred in a capitalist country. All the examples we have of countries that called themselves communist were countries which had not been capitalist, which is also the case with the surviving countries still calling themselves communist, although very different from each other. I'm thinking of Cuba on the one hand, China on the other, North Korea, Vietnam, and Laos. Their ways of becoming communist were all completely different and had absolutely very little to do with Lenin's 1917 revolution. Even the relative establishment of communism in Eastern Europe was not due to a revolution but to the might of the Red Army that swept across Eastern Europe. And where they stopped, communism stopped. It is hardly possible to call this a revolution.

The difference in the West, that is, Western Europe – and I'm thinking almost exclusively of the Italians and the French because those parties were the only really strong ones in Western Europe until, to some extent, the end of the dictatorships in Greece, Portugal, and Spain, and even their communisms did not last as major parties for long – was that these parties had pushed for certain reforms, certain regulations of capitalism, particularly forcefully, from the welfare state to the control of the labour market. But these were the kinds of things that had already been foreshadowed by the Second International in 1899, when they began to produce a programme, a manifesto; they asked for universal suffrage including women, an 8-hour day, and so on. To a great extent they were successful because 50 or 60 years later this was achieved nearly everywhere. So, the distinction between social democrats and communists is not really a topic of discussion now. Even the radical leftist parties still in existence in the West – I'm thinking of Die LINKE in Germany or Rifondazione Comunista in Italy – are really ginger groups trying to push the axis of political discussion to the left, which is a perfectly reasonable endeavour. But they're not preparing for a revolution. They do not have a vision of a famous hour x in which the proletariat will take over.

The second point is the state generally of the left now. In the West its condition is so terrible, so disastrous, that to begin to think about achieving a socialist society seems – and I am a pessimist, I must admit – well, extremely unlikely. The traditional left in France, where the communist party used to be very strong and there was also a strong socialist party with Mitterrand, is almost destroyed. The left in Italy, where the PCI was an important party having one-third of the vote – its successor party that is barely even left wing, can barely muster 20%. The experiments of radical left parties gaining power, such as Syriza in Greece, or those which aimed to surpass the social democrats, such as Podemos in Spain, have failed. In Britain, the Labour Party, after the attempt of Corbyn to shift everything to the left, has also failed and for long was trailing Boris Johnson in the polls, despite his disastrous handling of the pandemic and the corruption scandals. Keir Starmer is so colourless that he may not even be able to win the next election. The German SPD, which has won the last election with 25%, was a party that had 40% twenty years ago, and now it has to go into government with other political parties which are not socialist in any way.

So the Western experience is tragic, disastrous. And we should add that the experience of socialists outside Europe has not been particularly good. Apart from Australia and New Zealand, there have been no significant social democratic, socialist parties outside Europe. Almost none in Latin America, except for the short-lived experiment of the Workers' Party (PT) under Lula in Brazil. So, the situation is, to put it mildly, not one which would prompt optimism.

I'd like now to take up another issue that Luciana mentioned. I think, a bit facetiously, she was almost congratulating the people who don't vote, who abstain because why vote for such useless institutions, such as parliaments, and so on. Yet, if 3 or 4 million Americans had abstained instead of voting for Biden, we would have had Trump and things would have been quite difficult. I'm not an admirer of Biden by any means; I think he's just a blah president. But Trump was something quite different; I mean, the election did make a difference, and most of us and the majority of Americans are glad that he's out. So, voting matters, particularly in a day in which many of those who think that parliament is useless vote for right-wing xenophobic parties. These are on the rise nearly everywhere in Western Europe. So not voting, unfortunately, is not a solution either.

Then I want to come to the issue of the day. It's actually been an issue for thirty years now, but it's become so obvious that no one can fail to talk about it, namely the ecological issue. It's one thing, as the ecologists do, to ask governments to do something. And this is all to the good, of course. As you know, I'm far from criticising that. But the wider issue is that in a way the stability and the success of capitalism has been due to its ability to spread consumer society to the masses, which one hundred years ago were completely deprived of it.

One hundred years ago we could say that in the West, say, 20% were essentially well off and 80% were poor; now it's probably the opposite: something like 80% are reasonably well off in the sense that they can have holidays abroad and consume a perfectly satisfactory range of goods. At the same time, a world population of almost 8 billion which also wants to consume accepts that capitalism has been a success. So the real success of capitalism has been its ability to distribute a plethora of consumer goods to this enormous number of people. That means that it is not only capitalism that is causing the ecological crisis, but that people are also causing it through consumption. An obvious policy measure to stem this crisis would be to stop people's excess consumption using the price mechanism, for example by making cars more expensive, making petrol more expensive, making foreign travel and holidays more expensive. Do you think there are politicians around who are ready to go and say 'vote for me and I will make it impossible for you to buy a car, to go abroad, or to eat meat every day', and so on? It's just not possible.

So, the contradiction, unfortunately, is not one which can be resolved easily. That is, we cannot get out of the ecological trap without, at the same time, hitting and hitting hard on the vast majority of people who support the existing system. And, on top of that, since there is something like democracy around, you need their votes. So, paradoxically, the only way to resolve the ecological problem is through some kind of ferocious capitalist dictatorship, which stops people from consuming, except for the top 1%, 10%, or 20%, but this is bringing us back to the nineteenth century, which I think is totally undesirable and extremely unlikely. I have obviously not the slightest idea of how to resolve the issue. I regret to say it, but the very least I can do is to say that this is a very tough problem, which is not going to be resolved by people demonstrating outside COP26, nor is it going to be resolved by the 126 elected or non-elected participants at the meeting. It is an issue that, for thinkers, parties, and politicians, should be at the centre of theory.

**LC:** First of all, I think we should try to understand how we got into this situation. By the beginning of the 1970s, the economic crisis and the discovery of the threat to the planet showed that the industrial model of development, which had been so successful until then especially in the *trente glorieuses*, was becoming impossible to retain, which meant that the compromise between capital and labour, the welfare state, was no longer viable. At this point capital began to attack it, and it has been weakened everywhere. So, the margin that had been available to social democratic policies was no longer there. And so, the difference between communists and social democrats had increasingly less to do with gradualism vs. 'revolution'. And due to the tensions society was becoming harder and harder to govern.

We should always remember 1973, because it was a turning point. It was the first time after the Second World War that there was such a big crisis in the Western economy. We were no longer in the post-war boom and the very positive compromises it made possible. At that time, the Trilateral Commission, consisting of the major economic powers – the US, Japan, and Western Europe – published a document which I think would be good to republish today. A first sign of the crisis was the end of the US dollar's gold backing.

What is interesting about the document, among other things, is that the signatories stated that there was too much democracy in the world. The decade before had been the decade of the Third World coming onto the international political stage with the formation of the Non-Aligned Movement comprised of 120 countries, and with major struggles of workers and students occurring almost everywhere, and so forth.

The document went on to say that the economy cannot be left to politics, to democracy, because its structure was too delicate. And ever since then, the terrible term they adopted, 'governance', has been accepted without discussion, even by the left, instead of talking about government. 'Government' implies popular sovereignty, while 'governance' is something carried out by the boards of banks or other private enterprises. Increasingly, the thinking is that economic matters are essentially technical problems to be solved, and these have to be put in the hands of neutral technocrats. It is not that parliaments are irrelevant; it is that deliberative/legislative power has by now largely been privatised because, through globalisation, big finance and the multinationals have gained such power that their decisions have become far more relevant than most decisions taken in parliaments.

After the 1970s, we began to have politicians and governments that are increasingly 'neutral', which is the reason why the programmes of left and right parties have become almost similar, for instance in the extreme case of Italy, where the country is governed by a banker, Mario Draghi. At the same time and for the years to come, it has become impossible to retain the welfare state. We are all sliding backwards, even in the countries which used to be examples of the welfare compromise – the Nordic countries and Germany. And this tendency keeps growing. Today, the only place where the left is still alive is the United States – there they can struggle to create the welfare state they didn't have in the previous decades. The election of Biden was a very important event, especially because Trump, with whom he has huge differences, is no longer president.

When you consider the current contempt for the social compromises demanded in Europe many years ago – although the demands mostly remained unfulfilled – the crisis has made us face the fact that all the social compromises reached in the democratic economy, the welfare state, etc., are no longer working. Globalisation has put an end to these compromises. And so what's called into question today is much more than just distribution and asking for the return to the welfare state. A general transformation, a major reform, or revolution, is no longer a choice but a condition of survival. It is industrialism itself that must be called into question. This has become the main issue of our times. We cannot go on with industrialisation and competition when competition is so aggressive today that we could even have a war between China and the West simply because of this market competition. The idea of a possible confrontation has almost become acceptable. It's unbelievable, but this is the situation.

When you speak with young people today you can see that, apart from their need to find a job, which is of course central, they are also sceptical about the system, because they feel they are being increasingly deprived of the power to decide about even small things, since everything has been taken over by 'governance', by the technocrats.

The question then becomes: can capitalism, as it is today, solve the new problems? I mean, if we take the ecological problem seriously it is clear that there is a need for a profound change. Another crucial issue is what we can do to save democracy, or rather what remains of democracy, from the existing level of competition. Donald asks what remains of democracy. Of course, it's important that we retain even its vestiges. The point is that young people today don't believe we can do this. If we don't find new forms of democratic expression and bring back to people the sense that they have some power to control what is going on, we will find ourselves with even greater mass disaffection with all the consequences. I know that it is very difficult, it's a very long process, but long processes have to start at some time. We have become used to the idea that when we speak of long processes, these won't start by us – somehow, someone will start them. But no, for a long process to begin, it is we who have to start fighting for a new form of democracy. First, we have to show people that by democracy we don't mean having a politician who comes and says, if you vote for me, I will do such and such. This doesn't make sense anymore; nobody believes it. And it never happens because even the best politician cannot practice what he says since the system is unable to respond to the new problems.

**DS:** But, if I may say, all existing movements ask politicians to do something. An example is the large demonstration in Glasgow, at the time of the COP26 meeting. They are all asking governments to do something, and the same applies to all the lobbies, all the ginger groups. They all share the belief that governments can actually do something. They may be wrong, but this is the basis of their activities. It's not the lack of faith in the state to do things; it's the lack of faith in specific governments to do things, but they want them to do something. In other words, they are acting within the traditional democratic framework. You and I used to do the same thing – we would demonstrate and ask the United States not to send more troops to Vietnam or to stop various activities. In other words, all the effort has always been in trying to direct politics, formal politics, to do something. We did not create any organs of new forms of government.

**LC:** I don't agree with you, Donald, about that. Yes, Greta is asking the politicians to act, as you say, but I think this should be over. One of the valuable lessons of the PCI's experience was that we achieved our greatest results not in government but by staying in the opposition. In this situation, people were made into protagonists, the subject of action fighting to achieve a result without expecting the government to do it. The ecological movement is strong – and I am thankful to Greta and the others for what they're doing – but they must learn that it is not going into the street and asking the prime minister to do something that will achieve the result; rather, they should organise to learn to do what is required; one has to do what one has learned historically to do through *vertenze* – tenacious and constructively waged conflict. I would ask that they change towards this orientation: to fight, not to ask the politicians. We have to organise the people again on the ground – not just for elections and not just demonstrating to ask the politicians to do something, because we've arrived at a point at which what has to be done is unpopular. Even putting forward a modest agenda to answer the ecological challenge is unpopular.

We have to find a way other than demanding that people sacrifice within the system. We have to do it through changing the mode of life, of values, and this is very complicated. So, we are obliged to start a new way of thinking. Before, when we spoke of the end of capitalism, we were dreaming. Meanwhile, we have swept this dream under the carpet, and now we've arrived at a point at which the system can no longer exist without being a horror incapable of compromises, which has by now deeply eroded the welfare state. It is producing what should not be produced, compensating this with the good things one receives from capitalism, which are mainly the consumer goods you find in the supermarket, which are practically all useless. We should produce and offer other things.

**DS:** What other things?

**LS:** Other things that would make sense. Things whose production you can decide on.

**DS:** Let me get this right. People now go to a supermarket and buy food and other things. So, are we telling them not to do it?

**LC:** Look, they don't have to buy all these particular fruits, etc.

**DS:** Ok, so they choose which fruit?

**LC:** We have to struggle to not have these goods produced but others instead. The politicians will answer you that if we do not produce these goods, you will no longer have jobs.

**DS:** I don't understand what the useless goods are.

**LC:** My point is how they are made, how they are transported, and if the agricultural system, which is responsible for more than half of the ecological problem, is going to go on producing in this way.

**DS:** So, we are saying 'don't produce this fruit with chemicals'. I don't want to defend the chemicals, but their justification is that with them everybody can eat bananas and apples. But if you have a different system there would be diminished production of certain things, which means only the rich can buy them. How would you answer to that?

**LS:** There is a serious ecological problem here.

**DS:** Yes.

**LC:** I'm trying to say that change will be very difficult, but there are ways to change the situation, and we have to fight for this, trying to bring the younger generation, people like Greta, together with the trade unions to wage different kinds of struggles. Struggles for not continuing to produce so much steel and to instead produce different things. It's difficult because there is more profit to be made with steel than with other things. This is why, if a society depends on decisions by people who think that whatever creates the highest profits is good then it's the system that has to be changed.

**DS:** But this happens constantly. Elon Musk's electric cars are ecologically much better than the old Fiats and Austins. If there is money in it, they will invest.

**LC:** For a long time, we had one particular experience of capitalism. We were saying that it wasn't good but our reasons for saying this were insufficient. So, the discussion was displaced because for a long time capitalism was delivering a lot of positive things to the populations. But now we have to understand that this capitalism is no longer there.

**DS:** I think the problem is perhaps that we keep talking about capitalism as if it were a monolithic system. I'm trying to say that the capitalist system is made up of competing bits of capitalism and that the way in which it moves forward is by constantly undergoing reorganisation crises. You mentioned the thirty years after 1945 and how this boom, as it were, the boom many of us who are old enough lived through, came to an end – more or less, because naturally capitalism survived perfectly well after 1970. But if you go back through the whole history of capitalism, it is a history of constant crises, of booms and busts. Every bust is an opportunity for capitalism to rejig itself and be born anew. That is its enormous advantage over any other system we can think of. The paradox is that the best years of capitalism, the years 1945 to the early 1970s – *les trente glorieuses* in the famous phrase of the French economist Jean Fourastié – were also the best years for the left; it did exceptionally well in those thirty years, advancing nearly everywhere in

Europe. And, as you mentioned quite rightly, the Italian Communist Party was able to change things from the opposition. Nearly all the regulation and welfare state legislation was very often carried out by non-socialist parties in Europe, by Christian Democrats in Austria, Germany, and Italy, or by parties like the Gaullists in France or the One-Nation Conservatives in Britain. This was done because these parties were afraid of socialist or social democratic parties, and so they instituted the regulation of capitalism and the welfare state.

So, if you like, the achievement of the socialists was not in establishing socialism but in regulating and coercing capitalism in a certain way. The issue we are facing is that this was all done under the aegis of nation-states, that is, by having national states coercing and regulating their own national capitalisms. With globalisation, the power of single nation-states, except for the very big ones like the United States and China, is, as with our European states, too small to control capitalism, and the attempt to have a sort of compact through the European Union has more or less failed. Clearly, the European Union is not going to be able to regulate or control capitalism since, despite all the nonsense of the Eurosceptics, the powers of the European Union are extremely limited. The EU doesn't have fiscal powers; it obviously has no foreign-policy power; and no power over welfare. So, the benefits that the state is supposed to deliver are increasingly weak. It's not just parliament which is weak; it's the machinery of the state in smaller countries – and by small, I mean even Italy, France, Britain, Germany, and so on – which is now weak.

**HG:** In this complicated new world situation, what is your view regarding the future of European integration and what do you believe the left's position should be on it?

**DS:** My belief is one thing, but what is possible is, as usual, something completely different. I'd be in favour of a huge advance in European integration, giving a more democratic Europe greater powers of intervention. But the idea that in the present state of affairs politicians could go around saying 'vote for me and we will help Greece and southern Italy' is a bit pie in the sky. Even within Italy itself, one of the parties, Salvini's Lega Nord, was able to convince nearly a third of voters in northern Italy to support it in order not to give money to southern Italy. And yet this was within the same state! So, the chances for greater integration in Europe, which is what I'd like to see, are very slim. So, we are not getting anywhere, and it is not just the left that is weak; traditional parties as a whole are weak.

I mentioned the fact that a lot of the reforms in the 1950s and 1960s were achieved not by left-wing parties, which were out of power virtually everywhere, but by so-called centrist or centre-right parties – Christian Democrats, the Gaullists, etc. These are in decline as well. The French case is quite significant because both the Gaullists and the Socialists have gone. Instead, we have the not very intelligent banker Macron, who has won against the far-right Marine Le Pen, who in turn was challenged not from the left but from her right. So that she can almost look like a liberal because of the awful Zemmour.

It's the traditional politics in Europe that has declined, but also the quality of the personnel has diminished enormously. Once upon a time in France you had De Gaulle or Mitterrand. In Italy you had the Christian Democrats, intelligent ones like De Gasperi and then Andreotti. In Germany you had Adenauer, but you also had Willy Brandt, and so on. Once we had Churchill and Macmillan, and now we have Boris, a joke. It's a catastrophe. It's getting continually worse in terms of the kind of person who go into politics. In the United States we're all thankful that Biden has been elected. But really, Biden is a second-rate politician. It's just that Trump was so awful that anybody would have been preferable.

So, the present problem is that the old politics is gone, and the old intelligent politicians, who might have been able to reshape their countries, are no longer there. All that is absolutely gone. We are at the point where, as in the very famous phrase of Antonio Gramsci's in 1930, 'The old is dying and the new cannot be born; in this interregnum a great variety of morbid symptoms appear'.

**LC:** Donald, can I ask you, why did all this happen, that suddenly all politicians became stupid?

**DS:** No, alas, it was not suddenly; it happened gradually and slowly. It happened in the course of the last 30 years, since the early 1970s. What happened was that the problems facing them were becoming increasingly difficult to resolve. The situation is much 'easier' when capitalism works, which was the case from 1945 to 1975. At that time, more and more people had jobs and more and more people paid taxes. There was a lot of money that could be spent, and it was possible to regulate capitalism, which continued to thrive. That was wonderful but obviously it couldn't last. And so, the enormous changeover is not so much due to the fact that the politicians became stupid; it is mainly that the system has changed and is producing problems very difficult to solve. And the people who are in charge of public affairs have become less and less able to do so. Thus, they appear to be stupid. I haven't got a clue as to their actual IQ. But we have to face the fact that the problems we are confronting are extremely difficult to solve, and they cannot be solved by saying we need new institutions without explaining what these new institutions would be and, above all, how we can get them.

You were talking before about before the seizure of the Winter Palace. Actually, this seizure didn't accomplish much. The Winter Palace was virtually empty. The Bolsheviks came in and they seized power. The real revolution occurred in the following three years, as they fought a very bitter civil war against the forces of the Whites, not the Liberals, but actually the terrorist or semi-fascist armies. It took them three years during which they started building or developing what they thought was going to be a socialist state. They didn't have a programme before that; they had slogans, like 'all power to the soviets', which didn't mean anything· it was just a propaganda tool. The construction of socialism was a very difficult task even for the communists in the Soviet Union. It was not just because of the three years of civil war, but also because of the reconstruction effort after that. Then it could be done and partially was done on a single-country basis because there was no globalised economy then. In a paradoxical sort of way, it was easier to effect a big change then, as it was also in China after the death of Mao in 1976. China had been transformed, with the establishment of an education system, the promotion of literacy, and so on. Those reforms took place gradually and through a top-down dictatorship. But the real change was achieved gradually with an opening to the rest of the world, something that the Russian post-communists were not able to do.

You – and I – mentioned democracy too many times. Optimism about democracy should also be somehow contained when one thinks of the present furore over Twitter and Facebook, and the social media, with people demanding the social media be controlled because the racists and the fascists are using them, which is all perfectly true. But we are then asking either for the owner of Facebook to control what can and cannot be said or we are asking states to do this. So even this is not an easy problem to resolve. I would also add that in a paradoxical sort of way social media is a democratisation of speech. In the good old days, you went to the pub or the osteria and would complain and say 'I'm fed up with all these immigrants, I'm fed up with this or that'. Now you use Twitter and Facebook. Three billion people are apparently signed up with Facebook. Controlling that is a complete nightmare.

**LC:** But then we agree that it's not because the politicians became stupid but because the system has made it impossible for the politicians to do a series of positive, popular things, which could be done in the past. This is the point. I believe that capitalism of our times is no longer able to offer possibilities of the compromise which had provided some stability to democracy and some sort of justice. Something in the system itself has to be changed because otherwise things will get even worse and more dangerous. So we are more or less in agreement.

**DS:** I entirely agree with you, Luciana. The system needs to be changed. But neither you nor I, nor anyone else, knows how or into what.

**LC:** Well, first, we shouldn't lose too much time fighting for political parties to have more members of parliament, because unfortunately, this kind of representation is becoming ever more distant from what people are thinking – it's difficult to grasp the change that is taking place all over in this respect. We have to understand that we can no longer go on in the same way given the extreme development of industrialism, the market, and globalisation. We can no longer survive as humanity producing the same sort of things and producing them in the same way.

This is a tremendous transformation and impossible to do within capitalism at its current stage, which will continue to lead to ever more undemocratic forms of rule. We've arrived at a stage in which transformation can only be achieved, as usual, by experimenting, struggling, and bargaining. And that is something you won't do in parliament, although of course you can exert pressure for changes. But the left-wing parties have to recognise themselves in trying to struggle for the transformation of the system.

We never thought capitalism would survive forever.

**DS:** It looks like it.

**LC:** It is clear that ecological issues have to be taken seriously. And Covid was very helpful from that point of view because it gave us a couple of years to learn more about these issues and understand the seriousness of climate change. But I agree with you that the 'blah blah' is not enough, that we need a different way of struggling and fighting. And then we have to explain to the people that the problem rests with the market ruling in a way that dictates policies which facilitate more profits. This needs to be understood by everybody, because otherwise we will never do those things that are necessary. What has to be changed is the value system. We have to go back to old Marx who spoke about how life should be liberated from the commodification of everything. We have finally reached a point at which this issue has become fundamental.

**HG:** Luciana, Donald gave his view of Europe and European integration. I am sure that our readers want to also know your position on European integration.

**LC:** I am in favour of European integration but not of present European policy. I am in favour of the existence of Italy but not of the way it is presently governed. I think Europe is absolutely vital because the sort of changes needed can only be done by a larger entity. In the case of Greece it became clear that you cannot apply programmes alone and against a neoliberalism that rules Europe and the world – you would be driven into the sea. Furthermore, the only way to fight against destructive competition among countries is through a larger economic and political entity. And Europe is such an entity. I think that our continent is probably the place where experiments in transformation can be undertaken because of its history of revolutions; due to its past Europe is somewhat better prepared to make a new revolution that is urgently needed.

**HG:** Luciana, you spoke of competition between the US, China, and Europe – I would also add Russia. Do you think that with this competition there is the danger of a kind of Cold War or even real war, as you said before?

**LC:** I am afraid of it.

**DS:** A war is always possible, but unlikely now – given that during the Cold War there wasn't a real war between the Soviet Union, which was powerful, militarily speaking, and armed to the teeth, and the United States, or the West, in a situation in which neither was dependent economically on the other. The Soviet economy was basically a closed economy with Eastern European dependencies, and the West was closed to the Eastern Bloc, including the USSR, except for primary products. The present situation is a very bizarre one because the economy of what used to be the foremost industrial power in the world, namely the United States, is no longer an industrial economy. What is it that the United States makes? It makes ideas. It makes Microsoft, it makes Facebook. It makes this kind of stuff. The material products are made in China; you buy a computer, and the programme is American but the actual computer is made in southern China, very often with foreign capital. If you look at the stock exchange in New York a hundred years ago, all firms were American making products like Ford cars and so on. And America did not export its industrial goods. I mean, very few of us in Europe were buying American refrigerators, American washing machines, American cars. We were buying European washing machines, Italian and German and so on.

The United States had the home market for its own industrial goods, and exported food products and raw materials, and above all ideas: films and music and so on. Now we have this odd situation in which goods are produced in China on the basis (so far) of American or Western know-how. But China, with 1.5 billion people, has enough of a home market, with which it could actually survive perfectly well on its own with just a thriving, expanding capitalism and home market, while the rest of us need its products. And the paradox of the idiocy of American policy now is to set up tariffs on Chinese goods, and all these tariffs do, as the *Financial Times* repeats virtually every day, is to increase the inflationary spiral in the United States because it raises the prices of common consumer goods. So, the United States is more dependent on China than China is on the United States. That was not the case ten years ago, when China really needed the United States, and it's completely different from the period of the Cold War, when neither of the then two superpowers, the US and USSR, depended on the other economically. So, it's a new situation. We should not interpret it with the paradigms of fifty years ago.

**LC:** I can mention another difference from the past, which reinforces your point. Even the way of waging war has changed. In the past a few countries had the nuclear bomb, but now one can carry a nuclear bomb in one's handbag. And one can deploy the weapons with which one can fight a nuclear war having only a small brigade. So even war has changed. It's terrifying.

**DS:** But one should also add that what is less terrifying is that the Americans are obviously completely incompetent in waging wars, in spite of spending more than the next eight countries in defence and in military hardware. They never win a war. They didn't win in Korea, they didn't win in Vietnam, they didn't win, as we know, in Afghanistan. They made a mess in Iraq. They can only win wars when they fight against a tiny dictator, then yes, that dictator can be removed, but otherwise they achieve absolutely nothing. The only function of their enormous spending is to keep up at state expense, i.e., at taxpayers' expense, the famous military-industrial complex which Eisenhower had already decried back in the 1950s.

**LC:** But during the Cold War I felt safer because of the two-power deterrence. Today deterrence is more difficult because weapons are no longer in the hands of one or two big powers; instead, they are spread around. You can have atomic battles now, and that is terrifying. Not a war but battles. I was terrified when I learned from a report published by the British Institute of how mini-atomic weapons are proliferating. This is also a question of democracy.

Which brings us back to the question of the markets and democratic control. If we do not recover some control, if the market decides everything, it's terrifying. I mean, we were talking before about the goods offered in a supermarket. Here I would like to come back to what I was saying before regarding the necessary changes we need to bring about in our times. We should no longer need to use cars in the way we do now. We should learn to plan cities in which one does not need more than a 15-minute walk to reach the places one needs to reach. The mayor of Paris has started to work on this. What I want to say is that there are small things one can start putting into practice now, and these small things add up. I spoke before about the supermarket, which sells a lot of useless things, and this is energy and earth which you consume, but the earth will be unable to yield what we need to eat if we continue with the current system of production.

Now, 40% of our survival problems have to do with the sea. If we throw whatever refuse we want into the sea, and we do so because we don't know what to do with it otherwise, we won't be able to breathe. The extent of the needed changes is enormous. When I say that this is a social problem, I mean that the elite can very well find a place where it can survive and leave the others to die from desertification or food poisoning. So, we have arrived at a point where for the first time in a century and a half there is a question of whether capitalism, the free market, can go on or not. There is a wonderful passage from Marx, which Marcuse used to quote all the time, in which he describes what life in a free society, without capitalist oppression, could be. There he refers to a lot of the values which we have forgotten. Do you think it is normal that people love to be crushed underground instead of figuring out a way to shape cities in a totally different way? Of course, this means that a lot of things we want to do cannot be done anymore.

**DS:** You think I should drive instead of going in the Underground?

**LC**: It's about another way of life, a revolution. You could use another word, but I think that the time for a revolution has returned. Previously revolution was a tool to conquer what others already had. Now we need a different, more difficult revolution, that should be first an internal revolution, which is the aspect Marx spoke of, but which has never been applied. We have to rediscover this aspect. For instance, social, i.e., collective consumption should replace a large part of individual consumption, something which is possible, but of course requires a change in how we live. But it would mean the possibility of saving and protecting the environment. And, of course, it means that there are a lot of entities which won't be able to make profits, as they used to do. So, I think we are now facing something which was emerging slowly for the last thirty years at least, but we never arrived at a point where a looming total disaster required people to embrace the idea of a deep change. And people are not interested in politics as it is now, because it cannot improve their lives.

**DS:** They're not. Most people are not, and most people are not interested in politics.

**LC:** But why should they?

**DS**: Yes, I agree. You are interested, I am interested, but we are a minority.

**LC:** Yes. Well, there are poor young people who are interested in another kind of politics.

**DS:** Yes, but they are not the only ones interested in politics.

**HG:** Well, I think we have come to the end of this interesting exchange of views between two very important European intellectuals, and we thank you very much for this particularly distinguished contribution to the transform! yearbook.

# Social Democracy's Electoral and Ideological Retreat, the European Union, and the Radical Left's Dilemmas

## Gerassimos Moschonas Interviewed by Haris Golemis

**Haris Golemis:** Professor Moschonas, first I want to thank you for having agreed, despite your heavy workload, to be interviewed by transform! on a subject on which you are considered an authority: social democracy. The first question I want to pose concerns the decline over time of the European social democratic parties' influence, as reflected in the electoral results of various countries. Could we describe this as a prolonged crisis of European social democracy?

**Gerassimos Moschonas**: Indeed, there is a long-lasting electoral 'crisis'. This traditionally major party family in electoral terms is no longer as powerful as it was. Social democracy, in the old EU 15, has lost 31.7% of the electoral influence it had in the 1950s and 1960s – from an average 30.9% in that period to 21.4% in the decade 2010-2019.[1] In Europe as a whole, losses are of similar magnitude and exceed 30% of the electoral influence that the social democrats had in the 1950s and 1960s.

This average cumulative loss is no laughing matter. The drop is very sharp, although it is not cataclysmic; hence, it does not mean the 'end' or 'death' of electoral social democracy. Nevertheless, the term 'electoral crisis', which refers to some form of acute but relatively short-lived trend, is not appropriate to the new reality, for the concept of 'stable crisis' simply does not exist. It is rather an oxymoron to call something that lasts for decades 'a crisis'. Social democracy has 'shrunk'. Its size has changed; its electoral status has changed. This creates a new electoral condition, a major shift within the European electoral equilibrium. The resizing is of historic proportions – although this does not mean that social democracy is doomed to disappear.

It is important to note that the process of social democratic electoral decline is highly systematic. It has been confirmed from one decade to the next, as each decade since the 1960s has seen an additional step in the downward dynamic. The precursors of the downward dynamic appeared in the 1970s with the disastrous results of the social democratic parties in Denmark and Norway in the 1973 elections in each of these two countries. They were, in my opinion, emblematic because they signalled a change of trend for anyone who could read numbers.

Of course, in the 1970s and 1980s, the new trend, as is usually the case, did not appear uniformly. There were examples of spectacular defeats coexisting with major successes, contraction with progress, violent decline with rapid recovery of influence, volatility with stability. I could cite examples of parties with remarkable electoral successes in the 1980s: the Social Democratic Party of Germany (SPD), the Dutch Labour Party (PvdA), the Social Democratic Party of Finland (SDP), and most notably the Social Democratic Party of Austria (SPÖ). I would also point to the impressive performance of the Greek, Spanish, and French socialists in the 1980s. In fact, the 1970s and 1980s are decades of transition to a new electoral era for European social democracy. Social democratic overall electoral performance is characterised by a significant increase in volatility and instability, different from country to country, while the trend in Europe is, in the aggregate, mildly downward. Thus, the electoral crisis has been proceeding in a zigzag fashion. However, the electoral weakening has been accelerating, particularly in the decades 2000-2009 and 2010-2019. Significantly, during the period of the debt crisis, from 2010 onwards, the downward momentum has greatly increased rather than being reversed – and not only in the countries of the South.

In conclusion, the social democratic family has well and truly entered another – lower – stage in its electoral influence. Its electoral and political status has changed. In the countries of Central and Eastern Europe, social democracy has even less influence (with exceptions such as Romania and Slovakia). However, it is worth noting that in very recent years (since 2018) social democracy has exhibited a certain degree of electoral stabilisation.

**HG:** An extreme case of this downward trend is 'pasokification', the phenomenon named after the electoral collapse of Greece's PASOK (Panhellenic Socialist Movement) in the January 2015 elections.

**GM**: That's right. I want to point out that the electoral crash of PASOK is an important event not only for Greece. In the 1980s, 1990s, and 2000s, for more than 30 years (before its collapse in 2012-2015), PASOK together with the Spanish PSOE were the most powerful socialist electoral duo in the whole of Europe. This concentration of electoral power in Southern Europe was unprecedented, since historically until then social democratic parties had been strong mainly in Northern Europe. PASOK's influence fell to 4.7% from a very high level (its average score in 2000-2009 was 41.6%).

Two other parties of the social democratic family also experienced electoral collapse: the French Socialist Party (PS) and the Dutch PvdA. Thus, the lowest electoral percentages of the parties that make up the 'pasokification' triplet were : PASOK, 2015: 4.68%, the French PS, 2017: 6.36% and 2022: 1.8% (presidential elections), and the Dutch PvdA, 2017: 5.70% and 2021: 5.73%. However, PASOK (called KINAL (Movement for Change) since 2018) has stabilised (2019: 8.10%) and currently shows an upward dynamic. The PvdA is in very bad shape, despite the excellent percentage (19.1%) it received in the 2019 European elections, and things are going very badly for the French PS.

**HG:** It is obvious that there is a significant decline in social democratic parties' electoral influence. But what about their membership?

**GM**: The decline in party membership is much greater, and it's true that this had preceded the electoral downturn. The electoral decline began after the important weakening of the organisational fabric expressed in the loss of members.

Historically, social democratic parties, despite fluctuations in their electoral percentages, have been institutionalised parties; they have had long-term organisational continuity, at least since the 1920s, a broadly organised base, and this in most cases without changes in the party name (maintaining one's name is a sign of institutional stability). In the West, if my memory serves me correctly, the only party that disappeared from the political map is the Italian Socialist Party, a party with a long but very turbulent history, but which had, after the Second World War, lost its primacy within the left. The PSI was dissolved in 1994 because of the Tangentopoli scandal, but it had already been worn down by both its competition with the Italian Communist Party (PCI) and its participation in governments together with the Christian Democratic Party (DC).

**HG:** Despite the general declining trend of social democracy to which you refer, today many analysts are speaking of its great return. The victory of the SPD in Germany, the electoral success of the socialists in Portugal and in Nordic countries perhaps indicate that something is changing.

**GM:** Indeed, the social democratic parties have had some interesting electoral successes lately. Today, they are governing: in alliance with forces of the left, the Greens, or with the liberals in Germany, in the Scandinavian countries, and in Spain and, in single-party governments, in Portugal, New Zealand,

and Malta (I am not talking about Latin America). And it is true that generally in recent years (since 2018) there is a halt of the downward electoral dynamic of social democracy. However, it is too early to say whether the results really mean a stabilisation or, possibly, a reversal of the downward trend. Good results within three or four years don't necessarily show a change of trend. We must wait a little longer. In any case, the fact that the social democratic parties have become 'smaller' does not prevent them from governing or from winning elections. In countries where social democrats are one of the two big parties it is natural, when the electoral pendulum swings back, to have electoral successes and participate in government.

Let me remind you that towards the end of the 1990s, when twelve out of fifteen governments in the European Union were either single-party social democratic governments or coalition governments with social democratic participation, the great majority of analysts were also speaking of the 'great return' or 'resurrection' of social democracy. But this was not the case. The electoral victories of that decade (and the consequent rise to power of many centre-left parties) took place on the basis of modest electoral performances that did not reverse the overall downward trend.

It is characteristic that in most recent elections held in various European countries, social democratic parties have achieved significant victories but with much lower percentages than in the past: 28.3% for the SAP in Sweden (2018), 25.9% for the Social Democrats in Denmark (2019), 25.7% the SPD in Germany (2021), 26.4% for Labour in Norway (2021), 17.7% for the Social Democratic Party in Finland (2019), and 28% for the PSOE in Spain (2019). In the 1960s these performances would have been seen as heavy defeats. Back then the SAP had a ten-year average of 48.4%, the Danish social democrats 39.1%, the German SPD 39.4%, Norway's Labour Party 45.5%, and the Finish social democrats 23.4%.[2] The Spanish socialists are also far from the average 40.2% of the 2000-2009 period. By contrast, the 41.7% of the PS in Portugal (2022) and the 50% of the Labour Party in New Zealand (2020) are reminiscent of the good old days. I could pay attention to these two results, but I should pay more attention to the relative stabilisation in key northern countries with a strong social democratic tradition. Even if a kind of social democratic 'resurrection' is not confirmed by the data, we do have for the first time in the last three to four years signs of a certain 'upward' electoral stabilisation.

**HG:** What were, in your opinion, the main reasons for the gradual decline of European social democracy?

**GM:** I think it happened for many reasons, but two causes seem most important. The first is the weakening of its natural electoral base, the working class. I'm referring to the working class, not the poor strata. The poor strata now represent a large part of the population, but the working class, especially the industrial working class, as a social and economic actor, with a largely homogeneous identity, has been radically weakened. Both because of the change in the general class structure and social stratification due to wider technological developments, and because a section of industry has relocated outside Europe. The classical working class has not, at least since the 1980s, been a strong 'social player' and the same applies to the trade unions. The shrinking of the core working-class clientele of social democracy and the decreasing propensity of workers to vote for the left have, on the one hand, largely transformed the electoral retreat into a 'class issue' and have, on the other hand, reduced the 'natural' electoral capacity of social democratic parties. It is largely because of this class dealignment that social democracy was electorally reduced.

The second major reason for the weakening of social democratic parties is their dramatically reduced ability to differ politically and programmatically from their competitors, the liberal and right-wing parties. It is telling that class dealignment manifested itself at the same time as social democracy's abandonment of the Keynesian paradigm, that is, when social democracy gradually ceased to be associated with Keynesian policies and the promotion of the welfare state, elements crucial to its post-war identity. Then, especially in the 1970s and 1980s, social democratic parties lost their capacity to represent economic policies different from those of the conservative parties. Moreover, the great strengthening of the power of the EU, from the 1990s onwards, further contributed to the weakening of the left *differentia specifica* of this historical current, making it extremely difficult to promote policies oriented towards the support of the popular strata, the regulation of markets, and the construction of social Europe. The European context has been unfavourable, not only for the implementation of a left-wing reform agenda but also for its very formulation.

The strength of a political party depends on whether its programme appeals to large majorities of society in ways that are different from those of the other parties. Parties exist to differ from each other, not to be identical in their policies. The ability of parties that aim to govern to renew themselves and have ideas that are more innovative than those of their competitors is what allows them to reconstitute and reconstruct their electoral base and thus maintain their electoral strength. But this 'ability to differ' has been severely reduced by globalisation on the one hand and by European integration on the other.

Therefore, the ability to produce superior ideas and policies is not simply a matter for an intelligent staff or a few intellectuals. It is also a matter of the context in which a party operates. In fact, the international, economic, and institutional setting for left-wing political ideas changed dramatically after the 1980s. The social democrats found themselves – and through their own fault (their role, for example, in shaping the neoliberal EU was important) – without a distinct social democratic agenda. Gradually, social democracy lost its ability to promote distinct economic policies. There was a major retreat of economic leftism. In the absence of a credible social democratic project for the future, ideological dynamics and class dynamics converged and created the electoral crisis of social democracy.

**HG:** But this reduction of the capacity for programmatic renewal does not only concern social democracy.

**GB:** Exactly. It is not only the social democratic parties that have seen their capacity for renewal diminished, but also the Christian democratic and conservative parties. The European centre-right has also suffered significant electoral losses. The tendency for all parties of governmental vocation is to become 'smaller'. This tendency allows a party to run a government, usually a coalition government, with electoral percentages lower than in the past.

**HG:** In contrast to the last decades how would you summarise the problem of social democracy in the present time?

**GM:** Although the causes of the decline of social democracy are many, the 'social democratic problem' of the present could be summarised as follows: social democracy gradually lost the battle of positioning itself in the big political arena and failed to carve out a distinct and strong position in the great game of politics and of political ideologies. On strategic issues such as the control of capitalist modernisation, the orientation of globalisation and the EU, the surge in income and wealth inequalities, the fight against corruption in politics, or giving respect and pride to the have-nots – in all these big issues social democracy has failed to articulate in a politically clear and structured manner its own strategic agenda and voice. Its overall positioning is weak, pale, and devoid of political robustness and intellectual force.

Social democracy – from the 1920s onwards – has always been a force that was reconciled with capitalism and the establishment. However, with its policies it aimed, at least in part, to correct capitalism and control the modernising dynamics of the markets, but also to represent social forces that were not part of the establishment. This political, economic, and cultural dualism had in practice become a deep-rooted feature of social democratic logic. This dual, partly contradictory, and undoubtedly ambivalent, identity was the social democratic identity. And although, more often than not, social democracy was close to (or was a central part of) the establishment of each era, this composite identity, the fact that there was a bit of 'Red Rosa' in social democracy, allowed social democratic parties to maintain their majority vocation and to be, in many countries, natural parties of government.. Over the long term, historical social democracy, despite severe contradictions, broken promises, and ideological treason, had – at least, to a considerable extent – a distinct and powerful political identity.

The gradual loss of the ability to be a strong pillar of identity in national party systems imperiled the historical vocation of social democracy as a moderate – but effective – agency for social transformation. The 'typical' social democratic brand has been diluted. This is the reason why studies that focus on quantitative and lexicographic analyses of social democratic programmes and social democratic political discourse make me smile, even though they are intellectually useful. It matters little whether social democracy is (or will be) moving a little to the left or a little to the right on the left-right axis. It matters little whether on issues of cultural liberalism and conservatism it becomes (or will become) a little more libertarian or a little more conservative, or even a little more or less ecological. These moves or choices do not change its place in the great game of politics and ideologies; they do not change its place in the 'big picture.' Important political movements are 'important' precisely because they have a strong and distinctive position within the 'big' political and historical picture as it is formed in each era.

## Economic crises and social democratic programmatic stagnation

**HG:** With the outbreak of the pandemic, one could say that there was not only a change in the alliances of the European social democratic parties with a shift towards the parties of the radical left, but also in their own policies orientated now cautiously towards Keynesianism, with the political will to move away from the institutionalised neoliberalism of the European Commission and the European Central Bank, but also of the national banks of those countries that do not belong to the eurozone. Do you think that this will continue after the end of the pandemic crisis, whenever it happens, or is it a temporary flexibility that is context-specific?

**GM:** Your question, if I broaden it, is about the socio-economic and political-ideological consequences of crises, whether their aftermaths could be different from what preceded them. And whether social democracy will be able, because of the pandemic, to promote ideas and policies that would be more in line with its own historical identity. Let's look at what it did in two previous major crises. First, the 1929 crisis.

After 1929 we had a change in the economic and political paradigm. A real re-foundation, I would say, of the economic and political landscape, with a strengthening of the role of the state, of interest groups, of the position of the working class in the social and political arena, but also the introduction of Keynesian policies. The consequences of the 1929 crisis remained active until at least the 1970s. Thus, the Great Depression turned the previous situation upside down. It acted to a significant extent as a 'great transformer'.

However, in the first phase of that crisis, governments and central banks, in thrall to the economic orthodoxy of the time, instead of taking measures to reduce the destructive potential of the Great Crash, increased it. This was the case with the social democrats who happened to be in power in 1929. The SPD was the main partner in the governing coalition of 1928-1930, with Hilferding, Kautsky's spiritual successor, as finance minister. Caught between rising unemployment, the collapse of investment, fiscal difficulties, memories of the shocking hyperinflation of 1922-1923, and despite the social demands of its electoral base, it chose to promote a 'strict deflationary package'.

The 'social-liberal' economic policy mix of the social democrats of the time[3] – a mix that combined anti-capitalist traditional Marxism with free-trade and deflationary orthodoxy, and, at the same time, a sincere defence of social gains – was, as a response to the crisis, profoundly ineffective. The 'rendezvous with history', alongside the German social democrats, was also missed by Labour in the UK. Ramsay MacDonald, head of the Labour Party's minority government, rejected all proposals, including those of Keynes himself, for alternative policies (a public works programme, an expansionary economic policy, strengthening purchasing power, the implementation of protectionist measures), opting instead for monetary stability, the rationale of balanced budgets, and austerity measures. The Labour prime minister's 'treason' (forming a government with the Conservatives and Liberals in August 1931 under his leadership and without the support of the Labour Party) was indicative of the power of established economic ideas.

Therefore, the good answers for crisis management came too late. And they were the product of ideological and political conflicts in conditions of prolonged deadlock and social despair. I should point out here that the Swedish Social Democrats were the first party in Europe to pursue innovative economic and social policies, partly Keynesian, from 1932 onward, resulting in the near 'disappearance' of unemployment. Since then, this party has dominated the Swedish political scene.

**HG:** For about half a century, if I'm not mistaken.

**GM:** Exactly, until the 1970s. So, unlike the UK, Germany, or France of the Popular Front (1936-1938), and as opposed to the whole history of the left at that time, a social democratic party connected the left identity with economic efficiency as never before.[4] In the 1930s we had a kind of re-foundation of social democracy. It was then that modern social democracy was formed. And it would stay for decades, which was also the case with the ingredients of a new economic policy mix (to which, of course, the New Deal of the Democrats in the US under President Franklin Delano Roosevelt contributed decisively). This first 'coherent' formulation and implementation of the new economic ideas would become the dominant economic ideology after 1945. The new post-war mainstream ideology was called the 'social democratic consensus', although many of those who contributed to its formation and prevalence were not associated with the social democratic parties. The Second World War, was also to contribute decisively to the deepening and consolidation of the new ideas.

In contrast, the great financial crisis of 2008-2009 was a major event within the status quo – it did not substantially modify it. The precedent of the 1929 crisis had acted as a great school, expensive of course, for the bourgeois elites. Thus, now the response to it was handled effectively to a great extent. The decisive management of the crisis, mainly by the US authorities, but also by the European ones (the latter regarding only the period 2008-2009), prevented a plunge into a crisis as catastrophic as in 1929. The policy implemented at the time was a kind of liberal Keynesianism, that is, Keynesianism without redistributive features.[5]

The policies implemented in the 2008-2009 crisis, by limiting its duration and cost, reduced or defused the pressure for major breakthroughs in the state-market relationship. And the social democrats, historically the predominant bearers of Keynesian logic, failed to propose anything different and to highlight their added value, precisely because all governments followed Keynesian forms of policy. A deeper caesura was never attempted, despite the left's expectations and the fiery speeches against unchecked capitalism even by conservative politicians like Nicolas Sarkozy.

This crisis, the most important since that of the interwar period and in my opinion the first major one in a new generation of crises, showed that major financial crises could not be decisive game-changers as the disastrous crisis of 1929 was. Great crises are indeed experienced as cataclysmic events, but they do not always have cataclysmic consequences, as shallow analyses often and naively expect.

But when the financial crisis turned into a debt crisis, from 2010 onwards, and no longer affected the whole of the European Union, but only specific countries, with Greece at the centre, an extremely 'ironic' event occurred. The very same elites — and when I say the same elites I mean almost the same individuals, given that hardly any time elapsed between one crisis and the other — that had adopted Keynesian approaches to deal with the financial crisis, applied extreme austerity policies to deal with the crisis of sovereign debt. So, while the European governments reacted quite effectively in the first phase of the 2008-2009 crisis, in the second phase, which began in 2010, their response was dismal. The austerity mania of the surplus countries and the European institutions — a mania that of course mainly affected the electorates of the indebted countries — was a tragic policy that instead of solving the crisis made it worse. This is the European exception to the general trend towards the effective management of the 2008-2009 crisis and its consequences.

**HG:** Can you please tell us more about how the social democrats dealt with the financial and debt crises?

**GM:** They responded initially by adopting Keynesian policies. In particular, Gordon Brown, the Prime Minister of the Labour Party government in the UK, played an instrumental role in dealing with the financial crisis.

The debt crisis, however, changed things. Even though this second crisis, which quickly turned into a crisis of the entire European edifice, was an opportunity for social democracy to formulate its own plan for the future of the EU. However, it did not seize the opportunity. It failed to renew its reform agenda and to exit the trap of the neoliberal convergence with the centre-right parties.

However, it is worth mentioning the position of the Party of European Socialists (PES), which promoted new ideas, outside the mainstream neoliberal model, on how to deal with the debt crisis. In 2010-2011, the PES formulated the central pillars of a new programmatic agenda. I have called the new programmatic elaborations a 'post-third-way agenda'[6] because their underlying logic, which was focused on the regulation of markets and the rejection of austerity, went beyond the programmatic choices and governmental policies of social democracy in the 1990s and 2000s.

But as far as their implementation is concerned, things went terribly wrong. The socialist parties in government adopted austerity policies — in stark contrast to the PES's programmatic positions to which they had subscribed. Moreover, the need to compromise within the European Council contributed to turning this programmatic success story into a failure of implementation (the U-turn by French President Hollande, and the attitude of the SPD had a decisive influence on this direction). The gap between the economic strategy of socialist governments, which was oriented towards austerity policies, and that of the PES, which was oriented towards growth policies and policies to limit the power of the markets, was enormous. In short, the 'supranational social democratic response to the crisis' failed. This failure showed how much the europarties remain institutions without real power. The PES failed despite its serious programmatic elaborations. When things became tricky, its member parties pursued their own policies. The 'national' predominated over the 'supranational'. This can be a valuable lesson for the future, for European parties are weak institutions with limited influence and power.

**HG:** Then did the social democratic parties follow the same austerity policies as those of the conservative parties?

**GM**: Yes, but they tried to approach it from a different perspective. The social democratic austerity policy is part of a composite fiscal consolidation strategy, according to which safeguarding the fiscal capacity of the state is a prerequisite for social democratic reformism. However, regardless of the intellectual framework and whatever the ideational roots of social democratic austerity, this different perspective did not prevent social democrats from aligning with mainstream ideas and austerity. At the level of government policies, it was the logic of austerity *tout court* that became dominant. The most typical case was that of President Hollande. He was elected in 2012 on the basis of an anti-austerity programme, with a commitment to redress France's public finances, and he was perceived for some time as a 'game changer' within Europe. His shift towards policies of 'social democratic' fiscal consolidation marked the end of hope for a progressive exit from Europe's debt crisis. In the same context, the SPD voted in favour of a constitutional 'debt brake' according to which the structural (not the cyclical) federal deficit was not to exceed 0.35% of GDP starting from 2016. Moreover, the social democrats' support for violent austerity policies imposed on Greece in the post-2010 period made it even harder to distinguish them from right-wing governments. It is also worth noting that Jeroen Dijsselbloem, the Dutch finance minister coming from the Labour Party (PvdA) and former president of the Eurogroup (2013-2018), was one of the most influential figures, together with Wolfgang Schäuble, who were promoting brutal austerity measures.

In summary: First, the PES's post-third-way agenda failed; second, in the immediate post-crisis period national social democratic parties moved, at least rhetorically, towards more left-wing positions in terms of strengthening the welfare state, redistribution and market regulation; and third, these parties adopted austerity policies when in government. Overall, at no point during this turbulent period of the European debt crisis, did national social democratic parties manage to differentiate themselves significantly from the centre-right, nor to send a strong message that social democracy has its own agenda and policies. The electoral defeat of the social democrats simply reflected this failure to formulate a distinct political agenda[7] If social democracy failed to renew itself during the long crisis of 2008-2015, the question arises of what else needs to happen in order for it to overcome its programmatic stagnation?

**HG:** But as far as the post-pandemic crisis is concerned, will the flexibility that the European institutions are exhibiting continue, or is it only temporary?

I referred to previous crises and, in particular to the financial crisis (2008-2009) and the European debt crisis (post-2010), to show that crises are not necessarily agents of great and lasting change. Furthermore, my view is that 2008-2009 showed that large-scale state interventions in the economy are not incompatible with neoliberalism. I believe the same holds true for the pandemic crisis. Will these huge state interventions since 2020, as well as the relaxation of European fiscal rules, be permanent? My answer is no, they will not be. I think that when the pandemic crisis is over and with the increased debt of all EU countries due to the increased public spending, the forces that want to put an end to expansionary policies and to return to fiscal austerity will prevail. This time the transition will be gentler and more relaxed than the one that took place during the last financial crisis. I think that the social democrats have learned their lesson from their failure during the debt crisis and will be more sceptical of austerity policies. This is what their programmes over the last three to four years shows. I don't think they are ready for a confrontation to maintain expansionary policies. It is more likely that they will move, especially in the 'frugal countries', in the direction of fiscal consolidation, although not as harsh as that of the 2010-2015 period. It is no coincidence that the ministry of finance, which in the previous German government was under the social democrat Olaf Scholz, has been taken over in the present government by the hardliner neoliberal Christian Lindner. However, as we speak, the ongoing war in Ukraine makes any forecast precarious.

**HG:** What you just said about the present coalition government under the social democrat Olaf Scholz shows that the 'left' turn after the experience of the 2008-2009 crisis did not change the identity of the SPD as it was formed, or rather distorted, by Schröder in 1998-2005 period. Given Germany's role in the process of European integration, shouldn't we also not expect a substantial change in EU policies?

**GM**: The establishment of the European Union as an institutionally and politically polycentric system makes it difficult to change European policies. All experts agree on this. This is less the case for the US federal system. The economic and social policies of the Obama, Trump, and now Biden administrations show a capacity for change that is not present in the institutionally and politically conservative European system.

## The EU and the radical left's dilemmas

**HG:** In an earlier article of yours in the transform! yearbook, you supported the view that the structure of the EU prohibits any substantial social change that would express the will of a social democratic party in the government of a large country and, much more so, any structural social transformation of a radical left party of a small country. You have already mentioned the case of Hollande, who did not do what he promised during the election campaign. As an old-timer, I remember the excitement in May 1981 created by the election of Mitterrand as President of France and the subsequent formation of the PS-PCF government under Pierre Mauroy on the basis of a 'common programme'. These followed the legislative elections held in June of that year and the triumph of the PS. The common programme was extremely radical from the economic point of view; it provided for wage increases, the nationalisation of large industrial enterprises and utilities, etc. Pressure from Germany and other EU partners, but mainly the outflow of capital which depressed the French franc, forced Mitterrand to a 180-degree turn. I will not mention the well-known case of Syriza, which also accomplished a 180-degree turn in July 2015 with respect to its electoral promises, because Greece, as a small, indebted country with zero influence on policy-making in the EU, left no room for a radical anti-austerity policy unless it exited the EU. So, is the EU an obstacle to left radicalism and can we expect anything more from a left party than a disciplined social democracy which does not challenge the capitalist system?

**GM**: 'In France they turned and turned again', Donald Sassoon wrote with realistic sarcasm in reference to Mitterrand's U-turn.[8] Indeed, the PS has accomplished three major turns in its economic policy. The first is the one you just mentioned, Mitterrand's U-turn shortly after his election to the presidency in 1981. The second was made by Jospin who was elected prime minister in 1997, and the third is Hollande's turn in 2012. Well, all three of these turns have pointed to the influence in European economic policies of the export-led growth model focusing on increasing competitiveness, which in turn has as its main tool a form of austerity. However, the constraints imposed by the EU played an important role in the turnaround of Jospin and Hollande. The French socialists did not change their position just because they were 'reformists'. This takes me to your main and very important point. The EU is a system inherently based on compromise: compromise between different institutional centres, member states, and party families. The European political system is therefore a conservative system, not in the sense of a left-right divide, but in the sense that it is allergic to novel policies, whatever they might be. The EU does not favour new political majorities, it does not favour big policy changes, or political charisma. As a result, the EU shows 'a very high degree of policy stability'.[9] This 'conservative' character of Europe's modus operandi has its raison d'être in the multinational and multistate nature of the regime. The European machine cannot function differently.

Given this general framework, the European Union acts as an obstacle to strategies of social transformation. I consider the Maastricht Treaty and the subsequent creation of the European Union to be a major historical breakthrough blocking the possibility of a left economic transformation in Europe. The renaissance of Europe, especially since the 1990s, is a key economic and political-institutional development which destabilised the historical strategies and repertoires of action of the radical left. In the medium term and perhaps in the long term, the European multi-centred and multi-state system weakens the capacity of the radical left to act as a force for social transformation, even though it favours its electoral potential when it is in opposition. This was not the case in the past when the European Economic Community (EEC) was a looser form of economic integration.

To the preceding I would like to add a point that is not often discussed. If, at the national level, left-wing radicalism can gain access to power, and thus access to the implementation of a part of its policy objectives, at the level of the EU this is much more difficult. Governance at the centre leaves radicalism – almost permanently – outside of all possible coalitions, and without important access to European public powers. This unprecedented and historically unique development not only creates a void of political representation on the left but it also limits the European elites' capacity for renewal, and thus it limits the legitimation of the whole European system.

Thus, the position of anti-EU left-wing currents has got a strong basis. In fact, if a country wants to implement a programme of radical social transformation it will have to leave the European Union. The EU in effect functions as a strategic barrier thwarting the adoption of alternative economic policies championed by radical left parties.

However, there is a serious problem with this otherwise pertinent analysis. The economic impact of the EU is so great, in the way it sets economic rules, that it also affects European countries that are not EU members. Moreover, and most importantly, the European Union is a powerful global entity. The reason why national states and national societies want to be part of the European Union is not only economic. There are other reasons, motives and considerations, often more powerful - such as reasons linked to geopolitical security and the exercise of international influence, those linked to the cultural identity of a nation or to the degree of democratic security of a society – that influence the desire to join or not to join the EU. The EU is strong precisely because it proposes for national states a framework that involves more than the economy. It provides states with a kind of security and the opportunity, real or imagined, for greater political leverage.

If we view the EU strictly in economic terms, we will not understand much about its power and weaknesses. We will also not understand much about the radical left's attitude towards the phenomenon of European unification. Europe's left, historically Eurosceptic, did not become pro-European just by mistake. The great irony of the radical left's European policy is that they gradually accepted European integration just as the latter was acquiring increasingly neoliberal characteristics. The transformation of Europe, after the second half of the 1980s, into a powerful, heavyweight political machine induced national governments to seek inclusion in the EU, and parties on the left to give 'critical support' to this process, in order to avoid, among other reasons, political isolation in the domestic political arena. The composite nature of European integration was therefore a factor that influenced the European left's policy towards the EU.

So, it is not just the economy that counts. In Eastern Europe, confidence in the EU and support for membership have a strong security and identity component. Equally, from Germany and France to Greece and Cyprus or Finland, there is a strong geopolitical rationale behind the support for European integration. The reason why a country joins, or wishes to join, the European Union is therefore a complex phenomenon, something that Eurosceptic or anti-EU currents do not adequately assess, as they mostly stress the economic side of the issue.

All the above shows that the left is facing a dilemma with no easy solution. The EU poses an extremely intractable problem of collective action as much for the left parties that adopt a critical Europeanist stance (especially those belonging to the Party of the European Left), and those that follow a national go-it-alone radical strategy (exit from the Euro, return to national sovereignty).

The pro-European (and today majoritarian) current of the radical left cannot convincingly argue about its ability to promote deep changes within the EU. It therefore risks losing its radical character, as the rigid nature of the European system makes any strategy of 'strong reformism' particularly difficult to implement. The lost European battle and the U-turn of Syriza paint a uniquely representative picture of the difficult relationship between left-wing radicalism and European unification.

On the other hand, the Euro-hostile current of the radical left finds it difficult to argue convincingly for the feasibility of the anti-EU strategy it proposes (which varies from 'social democracy in one country' to 'socialism in one country'). This strategy presupposes a return to national sovereignty with the visible risk of reducing the left to the role of a permanent minority cut off from the 'modern' social strata and without the capacity to influence international developments. Leaving the eurozone poses a difficult-to-manage cost-benefit problem for a party, and those parties on the left (but also on the far right) that support euro exit decisively (not just in words) risk reducing their electoral influence. It is indicative that not only Le Pen and Salvini, but also Mélenchon, have watered down their anti-European stances. Greece again has shown that the proposal of exiting the eurozone, whatever its economic rationality, was not electorally attractive as the average voter does not easily choose a decline in his living standards (even though Greece has lost – during the debt crisis – more than 25% of its GDP) for the prospect of a future medium-term improvement. Many left-wing analysts in Europe have not realised how great fear can be of uncontrollable consequences (and not only economic) and thus not understood the electoral limits of a strategy of transition to a national currency.

Consequently, from the viewpoint of the European radical left, none of the left-wing 'isms' – left-wing Europeanism, left-wing populism, left-wing anti-Europeanism – can provide a politically convincing answer at the moment. This is also true of social democracy: we need only recall Jospin's failure to fulfil his promise of amending the Maastricht Treaty's criteria in an anti-monetarist direction in 1997, the Holland's U-turn or the resignation of the social democrat Lafontaine in 1999. The 'in or out' dilemma, whichever side one opts for, involves no good solutions, only less bad ones. Besides, the 'good' solution may be different for each country.

Economic policies with a 'radical' content would theoretically be possible at the level of the European Union if it had a federal structure. However, this possibility does not exist today as European citizens and national states are against federalism. If we make the heroic assumption that European integration could lead to a federal EU in twenty or thirty years, in theory the parties of the radical left could wait while pursuing, where possible, policies of sectoral radical change at the national level – given the impossibility of promoting an overall change at the European level.

Sectoral radicalism at the national level (with a view to the tax system, the minimum wage, the distribution of wealth, ecological policy issues, etc.) is relatively feasible – just as it is possible to seek a more favourable balance for the left at the European level in the strict sense. But that too, in the light of today's balance of forces is difficult to promote and implement, though, in any case, 'sectoral' radical policies cannot be excluded *in abstracto*. However, policies of total reversal do not seem possible to me, unless the world turns upside down.

In brief, the EU represents a massive shift in the structure of political opportunities. More generally, the new political opportunity structure is inauspicious for any kind of radical project, left, far-right, or radical federalist. In particular, the EU is inhospitable to all the strategic options, social democratic or radical, that have dominated the history of the left. In the long run, this will either change (which is very difficult) or strengthen anti-Europeanism in certain parts of the radical left, or it will affect the raison d'être of radicalism and lead (in fact it already has) to the partial de-radicalisation of radical left parties. I think this is the big picture.

In a certain sense, the radical left, due to the collapse of existing socialism and the constraints of the EU and globalisation, is – like social democracy – losing its place in the great game of ideologies. It is less a strong pillar of identity within party systems than it has been in the past – and this independently of its electoral performances, present or future.

Since 2016, the EU has demonstrated a remarkable capacity for adaptation and evolution. The pandemic crisis has illustrated this. European integration has been accelerated. However, the European system remains a 'slow' conservative system that requires the formation of large and heterogeneous majorities to enable it to function. Large and heterogeneous majorities are an obstacle to the adoption of radical policies. The latter are not consistent with the overall rationale of the system. No matter how much the EU changes, it is unable to significantly improve the political opportunities offered to outsiders and to political parties or movements which are vectors of a more conflictual version of politics. It would be naïve to imagine that, in a foreseeable future, the joint management of sovereignties could be done otherwise. In a sense, the European Union is not just an obstacle to the renewal of the left – it is also an obstacle to the renewal of mainstream parties and of its own heavy structures.

## NOTES

1. Pascal Delwit, '*This is the final fall': An electoral history of European Social Democracy (1870-2019)*, CEVIPOL Working Papers, 1/2021.
2. Gerassimos Moschonas, 'Historical Decline or Change of Scale? The Electoral Dynamics of European Social Democratic Parties, 1950-2009', in James E. Cronin, George W. Ross, and James Shoch (eds), *What's Left of the Left: Democrats and Social Democrats in Challenging Times*, Durham, N. C: Duke University Press, 2011, pp. 50-85.
3. Mario Telò, *Le New Deal européen: la pensée et la politique sociales-démocrates face à la crise des années trente*, Brussels: Editions de l'Université de Bruxelles, 1988.
4. Dimitris Tsarouhas, 'Sweden', in Jean-Michel De Waele, Fabien Escalona, and Mathieu Vieira (eds), *The Palgrave Handbook of Social Democracy in the European Union*. Basingstoke: Palgrave Macmillan, 2013.
5. Jonas Pontusson and Damian Raess, 'How (and Why) Is This Time Different? The Politics of Economic Crisis in Western Europe and the United States', *Annual Review of Political Science*, 15 (2012):13-33.
6. Gerassimos Moschonas, 'Reforming Europe, Renewing Social Democracy? The Party of European Socialists, the Debt Crisis, and the Europarties', in David Bailey, Jean-Michel De Waele, Fabien Escalona, and Mathieu Vieira (eds), *European Social Democracy During the Global Economic Crisis: Renovation or Resignation?*, Manchester: Manchester University Press, 2014, pp. 252-269.
7. Gerassimos Moschonas, 'Economic crises as game-changing events – or not any more? The social democratic response to the financial and sovereign debt crises in the light of the 1929 Crash', in *Progressive Prospects for Turbulent Times. How to Boost Political, Organizational, and Electoral Potential*, forthcoming, Foundation For European Progressive Studies – FEPS.
8. Donald Sassoon, *Morbid Symptoms: An Anatomy of a World in Crisis*, London: Verso, 2021.
9. George Tsebelis, *Veto Players: How Political Institutions Work*, Princeton: Princeton University Press and Russell Sage Foundation, 2002.

# From the New Deal of the 1930s to the Green New Deal of the 2020s[1]

## Steffen Lehndorff

The 1930s US New Deal under President Franklin Delano Roosevelt has become a broadly shared historical point of reference for a 'Green New Deal' of the 2020s,[2] not only in the US, but increasingly in Europe as well, albeit with very different emphases and subtexts. The spectrum ranges from a 'left-wing Green New Deal' in the sense of a 'socio-ecological system change'[3] to the 'Green Deal' of the EU Commission.'[4]

But it is precisely the latter that engenders distrust among some on the left, a distrust based on a distorted view of the 'old' New Deal. Is the Green New Deal not a case of greenwashing to create the illusion that the climate and planet can be saved under capitalist conditions? And wasn't the New Deal of the 1930s ultimately also a project to save capitalism, a project whose positive elements first had to be forced from below, through mass strikes? Not to mention such faults as timidity in countering racism in the US?

It is true that the New Deal did not, to use a popular left expression, 'go far enough'. In fact, it was not aimed at overcoming capitalism. If anything, the New Deal was an attempt 'to rescue capitalism from the capitalists'.[5] That this attempt was both necessary and successful was remarkable enough, but the same can be said of the historical achievements of the European labour movement, such as the welfare state, which the left necessarily repeatedly defends even though it too does not 'go far enough'.

Let us not fool ourselves: If the New Deal had been only one episode among other reforms of twentieth-century capitalism, its attraction would probably not be felt in both the bourgeois and the left spectrum. Therefore, it is worth taking a closer look. *What* was done, and even more importantly, *how* was it put into practice?

It is precisely the 'how' that is particularly relevant today. In view of the looming disasters resulting from climate change today, a powerful societal dynamic must be set in motion in a very short time. This is precisely what the New Deal government, though confronting substantially different challenges, succeeded in doing within a few months. In the following years the momentum of the first 100 days was successfully translated into a farther-reaching reform process. And one aspect must be particularly emphasised today: It was a *democratic* dynamic at a time when millions of people in Europe were cheering Mussolini and Hitler or were awestruck by Stalin.

Naomi Klein neatly sums up the role model of the New Deal of the 1930s and its potential as a model today: 'The media debates that paint the Green New Deal as either impossibly impractical or a recipe for tyranny just reinforce the sense of futility. But here's the good news: The old New Deal faced almost precisely the same kinds of opposition – and it didn't stop it for a minute.'[6]

What were the most important elements of this virtually unparalleled political and societal dynamic, and what lessons can be drawn from them for the political turnaround required to push through the Green New Deal in the 2020s?

## Breaking new ground

When Roosevelt was elected President in November 1932 with 57 per cent of the vote, his promise of a 'New Deal for the American People' had brought the Democratic Party 12 million new voters (a total of 28 million compared to 16 million in 1928). The country was then not only in an economic and social but also in a moral depression. It was a political vacuum, which was described in an internal government report in the following terms: 'The problem is not one of fighting off a "red menace" […] but of fighting off hopelessness; despair; a dangerous feeling of helplessness and dependence.'[7]

In contrast to many European countries, there was no organised fascist mass movement. On the other hand, the labour movement, whether in the form of political parties or trade unions, was weak. In terms of membership numbers, votes, alternative strategies, and political appeal, both the Socialist and Communist parties were of only marginal significance. As to the unions, membership had dropped since the early 1920s to a density rate of 6 per cent, and most unions were traditionalist trade associations whose headquarters had no political impact. The economic boom of the 1920s had 'brought the class struggle to a standstill'.[8] During the crisis, industrial action flared up again in some sectors, which many companies countered with sometimes brutal anti-unionism and so-called 'yellow' unions, but overall strike activity remained at the low level of the pre-crisis years.

It was under these conditions that immediately after taking office in March 1933, the Roosevelt administration began to put the blurry promise of a New Deal into practice with a huge reconstruction programme: The banking sector was stabilised and regulated, and the stock exchange was put under state supervision; the first attempts to establish elementary social standards were launched; with the help of several employment programmes and government agencies that had sprung up, more than six million previously unemployed people were put to work building schools, playgrounds, kindergartens, roads, green spaces, and carrying out reforestation and landscape conservation; 3,000 cultural workers of various disciplines were promoted and brought art to the people; dam systems for the cultivation, irrigation, and electrification of entire regions were created with extensive infrastructure projects.[9] In all these measures, the government ventured into new territory that was completely unknown at the time.

A typical characteristic of the New Deal approach was the undogmatic search for solutions: nothing was excluded from consideration and measures were changed if they proved ineffective. Breaking new ground required strong, resolute government, in other words *democratic leadership*. It is obvious that Roosevelt's role as a charismatic leader was of fundamental importance for this 'experimentalism'.

It was an approach which 'measured results in terms not of conformity to *a priori* models but of concrete impact on people's lives'.[10] This might be hard to accept by some on the left who prefer to stick to invariable theoretical models and allegedly established truths. Not surprisingly, this applied to the US left of the 1930s too. For the general secretary of the (nevertheless very grassroots-activist) Communist Party USA, the New Deal programme was 'the same as that of finance capital the world over. […] In political essence and direction it is the same as Hitler's program.' The Socialist Party, in turn, lurched between differing variants of a somewhat milder sectarianism. One fairly temperate criticism maintained that the objective of the New Deal was simply to establish 'state capitalism', while voices purporting to be more militant described it as 'the apotheosis of opportunism' and 'the greatest fraud among all the utopias'.[11]

Given the self-marginalisation of the political left and the organisational and political weakness of the trade unions it is obvious that the New Deal was not, as many on the left maintain, primarily enforced from 'below'; rather, it was initiated 'from above'. However, the spark of energetic government action, determined as it was to break new ground, very quickly spread to large sections of the population. It encouraged a multiplicity of grassroots movements, which became a major driver behind the powerful reform dynamic in the years 1933 to 1938.

This mutually reinforcing interplay can be illustrated, for example, by the path to legal anchoring of labour standards and by the grassroots involvement in the implementation of major infrastructure projects. Let us start with the latter.

## Flagship projects

Government policy cannot replace progressive social movements. But it can – and must – encourage them. During the years in question, key projects with symbolic power were at the heart of this interplay.

The large-scale infrastructure programmes in particular were highly symbolic. Always supported by an energetic anti-corruption agency, they included thousands of local construction projects as well as large-scale projects for the development of entire regions, in which dam systems were created for electrification, irrigation, and cultivation. The flagship project here was the Tennessee Valley Authority (TVA), whose innovative combination of central planning and decentralised participation increasingly succeeded in establishing electricity supply as a public goal.

Previously, electricity supply in the US had been the exclusive domain of private cartels, which led to steep prices with simultaneous undersupply in regions considered unprofitable. This was now counteracted by state-run utilities. In this process, the federal authorities had many mayors and other local actors on their side. Municipalities established their own utilities that bought electricity from the state-owned power companies, and in many cases secured the support of the majority of the population through referendums. In rural areas, non-profit cooperatives of farmers were founded and connected to the state power grid. In this way, the private cartels were subjected to very effective competitive pressure in all regions.

Of course, the decentralised implementation of federal projects also had important downsides. Particularly noteworthy was racism, especially in the South, where it was not only an integral part of local government but also a crucial constituent of the Democratic Party, which the New Deal had to take into account.

Nevertheless, the everyday experiences of growing parts of the African American population with the New Deal were different. African Americans experienced above average integration in the large employment programmes, and the Department of the Interior for the first time introduced a quota system that required contractors to hire a fair share of their community. Many public projects for the construction of homes, schools, and hospitals were deliberately located in disadvantaged black neighbourhoods. And it is also worth mentioning that for the first time African Americans were appointed to senior positions in government and other public bodies. All this contributed to the overwhelming support in 1936 amongst African Americans for Roosevelt's re-election campaign.

It is obvious that flagship projects such as the TVA and the huge employment programmes cost a great deal of money. This led to major conflicts but also learning processes within the government, which are still relevant today.

## Trial, error, and progress

Very soon the 'experimentalist' approach of the New Dealers involved the question of how to manage public deficit and debt. From 1932 to 1936 federal government expenditure rose from 6.8 to 10.3 per cent of GDP. Revenues did not increase at the same pace, which resulted in considerable public deficits. At this stage, Roosevelt still remained faithful to economic orthodoxy, which could not accept over-indebtedness. Consequently, he reduced some of the employment programmes. This, in turn, gave rise to some vehement protests, both within government and in particular among the unemployed. In response, substantial programmes were taken up again within new institutional frameworks.

What followed was, on the one hand, a zigzagging between pragmatism and relapse. Roosevelt correctly stated that, 'the only way to keep the Government out of the red is to keep the people out of the red. And so we had to balance the budget of the American people […] and to spend money when no one else had money left to spend.'[12] Nevertheless, after his re-election in 1936 he cancelled some of the spending programmes again, which immediately triggered a recession and a painful resurgence of unemployment. The economy only recovered when these expenditure cuts were reversed in spring 1938 after heavy disputes within the administration. Keynes in particular was very critical of this inconsistent expenditure policy.[13] In a personal letter to Roosevelt in February 1938, he wrote, 'a convincing policy […] for promoting large-scale investment […] is an urgent necessity. These things take time. Far too much precious time has passed.' In the end, it was only the preparation for war 'which freed the government from the taboos of a balanced budget'.[14]

Before this, however, a second, equally important learning process was already taking place. Between 1935 and 1937, the first steps were taken towards increasing tax revenue. In three successive pieces of legislation, the tax burden on high incomes, corporate profits, and inheritance was massively increased. These measures were part of a radicalisation of the New Deal whose popularity can be gleaned from the nickname for the 1935 tax measures 'Soak the Rich'. The paradigm shift that this tax legislation instigated marked the beginning of a redistribution policy that was strengthened still further during the Second World War and into the 1950s. The top tax rates eventually reached 91 per cent for income tax, 77 per cent for inheritance, and an average federal tax above 45 per cent on corporate profits.

A similarly contradictory search and learning process can also be observed in another key project and milestone of the New Deal: The route to the legal anchoring of labour standards by the so-called Wagner Act of 1935 and the Fair Labor Standards Act of 1938 was a particularly striking example of the mutually reinforcing interplay of government policy and social pressure for change.

## Readiness for conflict

As early as spring of 1933, the government launched a large-scale attempt to introduce social standards in conjunction with the first employment programmes. A National Recovery Administration (NRA) was established to bring together business organisations, trade unions, and consumer associations to agree on minimum prices, minimum wages, maximum working hours, and the right to collective bargaining and unionisation. This attempt triggered widespread public approval and large demonstrations of support under the banner of the NRA's patriotic Blue Eagle symbol. In fact, a number of agreements – mostly between NRA and employers' associations – were reached with great difficulty. With regard to social standards, however, this attempt soon failed. The bosses of major industrial groups torpedoed their operational implementation, and in 1935 the Supreme Court declared the NRA unconstitutional.

The reactionary boycott policy, however, triggered novel, far-reaching dynamics. First, it proved to the government, as the economist Gardiner Means, a member of the New Deal inner circle, put it, that 'self-regulation by industry doesn't work'.[15] Second, it encouraged massive strike action at the workplace level. In sometimes bloody struggles, especially for the right to collective bargaining and unionisation, the number of strikers rose from 324,000 in 1932 to almost 1.5 million in 1934 and almost 1.9 million in 1937.[16]

It was initially only a few union executives who took advantage of the opportunities offered by the New Deal. These minority unions launched massive organising campaigns, using slogans like: 'The President wants you to join the Union'.[17] The new grassroots unionism ushered in a split of the trade union movement which gave rise to the formation of the powerful Confederation of Industrial Organizations (CIO) which consisted of industry-wide unions that thus broke with the Anglo-Saxon tradition of craft unions. Union membership rose from around two million in 1933 to over ten million by the end of the decade – with union density in manufacturing industries exceeding one third of all workers.

The fierce opposition of powerful economic and political interest groups on the one hand and the new, strengthened labour movement on the other convinced the government to turn towards confrontation. It now aimed at a legally binding anchoring of social and employment standards and at creating the foundations of a welfare state, which was finally enforced by the 1935 and 1938 Acts. In doing so, the Roosevelt administration brought to bear an enormous willingness to engage in conflict. It was not populist campaign bluster when the US president uttered phrases like these in 1936, during his campaign for re-election: 'We know now that Government by organized money is just as dangerous as Government by organized mob. Never before in all our history have these forces been so united against one candidate as they stand today. They are unanimous in their hate for me – and I welcome their hatred' (Roosevelt 1936).[18]

This readiness for conflict shown by the New Dealers resulted in an even greater landslide victory in 1936 than in 1932.

## Diversity as a strength

After initial support for the Roosevelt administration by sections of big business, the wind had soon changed. Supported by 'anti-Bolshevik' campaigns in leading media, politicians (of both parties!) and heads of large corporations formed an 'American Liberty League' against minimum wages, collective bargaining, and the right to unionise. At the same time, a populist current sympathetic to European fascism grew up, calling for 'sharing our wealth' and fighting Roosevelt as a member of the rich East Coast elite while rejecting the advancing trade union movement.

In contrast to standard realpolitik practice, increasing resistance from various sides did not lead to attempts by government to appease and seek compromises. Rather, the government found a way out of the political crisis by being more resolute than in the first phase of the New Deal, as the key projects sketched here demonstrate. The New Dealers went over to what could be called a 'positive and democratic polarisation' policy. One example of this was the formation of a 'Roosevelt Coalition' in preparation for the 1936 presidential elections.

The Women's Division was the most energetic and active part of a grassroots movement within the Democratic Party whose leadership was by no means unanimous in its support for the New Deal. Beyond the party, public and political figures (including prominent Republicans) formed a

'Progressive National Committee'. Numerous mayors of different party affiliations mobilised the populations of large cities for Roosevelt's re-election. An initiative that initially was considered risky but finally proved successful was the formation of a broad-based Good Neighbor League, in which members of the most diverse religious and ethnic minorities, who had traditionally been isolated from each other – Catholics, various Protestant groups, Jewish communities, and prominent individuals – came together. A particularly important element was the winning over of representatives of the African American population, who had traditionally supported the Republicans as Abraham Lincoln's party, provided they had the right and the opportunity to vote at all.

Of great importance also was the active participation of trade unions. Some leaders of the ossified traditional trade unions continued to support the Republicans, but leaders of the newly formed and rapidly growing industrial unions formed a Labor's Non-Partisan League, which – since donations to the Democratic Party from business were now largely absent – made the largest contribution to financing the election campaign and did massive public-relations work.

Last but not least, the role of cultural workers must be emphasised. The promotion of visual arts, music, and theatre in all parts of the country was an integral part of the New Deal programmes. This not only provided cultural workers with a material livelihood but was part of a cultural and moral awakening that also shaped the political climate.

All these initiatives, alliances, and activities contributed to transforming the ethnic, religious, cultural, regional, and social diversity of US society from a parallel existence (often also opposition) between separate 'communities' into a factor of strength. With over 60 per cent of the vote, Roosevelt's landslide victory in 1936, even greater than that of 1932, saw its largest majorities in the working class and among the African American and Jewish populations.

## Tackling the impossible

What can we learn from this today? Of course, the differences between the conditions and challenges then and now are enormous. Having to fight climate change under the conditions of international financial-market capitalism is difficult to compare with a situation in which it was a matter of venturing into uncharted new territory within the nation-state framework in order to find a democratic way out of the deepest economic, social, and political depression to date.

Today we know that in its time the New Deal actually succeeded in 'tempering private ownership by government control'.[19] But will capitalism prove to be just as adaptable to the deep structural and cultural upheavals that must accompany the needed reorientation and also the restrictions that need to be placed on the now dominant model of accumulation? From a Marxist point of view this is doubtful because 'land grabbing', the consumption of nature, is one of the basic laws of the capitalist mode of production.[20] Against this background a Green New Deal, understood as a socio-ecological transformation that meets the requirements of the Paris climate goals, will be the ultimate historic test for capitalism. How adaptable capitalism proves to be in this process over the coming one to two decades we and future generations will not be able to know until everything that is required to save the natural basis of human civilisation has been achieved. What matters are, as mentioned above in connection with the New Deal, 'results in terms not of conformity to *a priori* models but of concrete impact on people's lives'.

The only thing we know for sure is that the process of a Green New Deal can only *begin* under the conditions of present-day capitalism. True, there are good reasons for Birgit Mahnkopf's view that 'social movements and political parties that want to be part of the solution' must 'attempt the "impossible", simply because the "possible" leads to ecological catastrophe'.[21] Nevertheless, the first step is to 'do what is possible here and now to bring about the conditions for such a *change of direction*'.[22] I highlight the words 'change of direction' because this is what the left needs to focus on today. The crucial question for a turn towards stopping climate change is not what is possible or impossible under capitalist conditions, as many on the left prefer to discuss. The crucial question is how the political and societal process of fundamental change can be *set in motion* in the first place.

Hence my plea for a new policy approach that takes up successful major reform experiences of the past. Most certainly, a radical Green New Deal will be, at least as much as the New Deal almost 90 years ago, a conflict-ridden dynamic of searching and discovering taking place within all spheres and at all levels of political struggle. The core of the socio-ecological transformation that now needs to be launched will be – as it was for the New Deal of the 1930s – a societal dynamic inspired by positive and identity-creating reform projects: large-scale socio-political projects that contribute to securing the natural foundations of life and that at the same time offer convincing solutions to everyday problems of existence. A crucial aspect here is the large-scale development of a sustainable public infrastructure. By way of example, large-scale programmes for well-paid 'white jobs' in the care sector and 'green jobs' in manufacturing may become positive drivers of change.

The experience of the 1930s also shows how resolutely the financing of large infrastructure projects must be approached through bold fiscal policy. Moreover, it shows that the question of public ownership arises particularly early in infrastructure policy. Courage in addressing issues of public investment and spending – issues that are central to tackling the climate crisis – is all the more needed here, as Keynes warned as early as 1938 (see above): 'These things take time. Far too much precious time has passed.'

It is only by encouraging and mobilising reform projects that many fears, justified or unjustified, associated with climate policy can be allayed, while making a way of life that preserves the environment more attractive. Such key projects with symbolic power are also of crucial importance because they are the lifeblood of social movements.

In all likelihood, and in contrast to the years from 1933 onwards, a Green New Deal will not come into being except as a result of massive pressure exerted by social movements. However, without governments with fact-based powers of persuasion and a willingness to engage in tough conflicts with lobby organisations, it is difficult to imagine a turnaround towards a socio-ecological transformation. Both then and now, resolute democratic political leadership will be crucial to maintain this, and governments will need societal countervailing power to be able to stay the course – and, if necessary, to be pushed beyond what they originally planned.

It is this mutually reinforcing interplay of government policy and social pressure for change that will prove to be the decisive factor in determining not only how a Green New Deal might be implemented but also whether it will materialise at all. But the heart of the matter is to set such a social reform dynamic in motion in the first place, and in this respect the New Deal of the 1930s offers a wealth of experience. The political left just has to manage not to get lost again in the dead ends of its predecessors and instead use the potential of the New Deal as a source of inspiration and encouragement.

NOTES

1 The present article is based on my booklet 'New Deal means being prepared for conflict – What we today can learn from the New Deal of the 1930s' <https://www.transform-network.net/publications/issue/new-deal-means-being-prepared-for-conflict/> whose publication was supported by transform! europe. It includes a more detailed description of the dynamics of the New Deal and comprehensive references to the information used here.
2 EuroMemo Group, *A Green New Deal for Europe – Opportunities and Challenges – EuroMemo 2020*, Brussels: transform! european network for alternative thinking and political dialogue, 2020.
3 Bernd Riexinger, *System Change. Plädoyer für einen linken Green New Deal. Wie wir den*

*Kampf für eine sozial- und klimagerechte Zukunft gewinnen können*, Hamburg: VSA, 2020.

4   For a critique of the European Commission's Green Deal see David Adler and Paweł Wargan, 'The EU's Green Deal and the Betrayal of a Generation: A Strategy to Fight Back', in Walter Baier, Eric Canepa, and Haris Golemis (eds), *transform yearbook 2021 – Capitalism's Deadly Threat*: 117-29. <https://www.transform-network.net/publications/yearbook/overview/article//transform-europe-yearbook-2021-1/>

5   Arthur M. Schlesinger, Jr., *The Age of Roosevelt, Volume I: The Crisis of the Old Order, 1919-1933*, Boston and New York: Mariner, 2003 (1957).

6   Naomi Klein, 'A message from the future with Alexandria Ocasio-Cortez', <https://theintercept.com/2019/04/17/green-new-deal-short-film-alexandria-ocasio-cortez/?comments=1>.

7   Arthur M. Schlesinger, Jr., *The Age of Roosevelt, Volume II: The Coming of the New Deal, 1933-1935*, Boston and New York: Mariner, 2003 (1958), p. 272.

8   Daniel Guérin, *100 Years of Labor in the USA*, New York: Pathfinder, 1979 (*Le movement ouvrier aux États-Unis*, 1967); German edition, p. 56.

9   For an overview see Lehndorff, '"New Deal" means being prepared for conflict', pp. 16-19.

10  Arthur M. Schlesinger, Jr., *The Age of Roosevelt, Volume III: The Politics of Upheaval, 1935-1936*, Boston and New York: Mariner, 2003 (1960), p. 654.

11  Schlesinger, *The Age of Roosevelt*, vol III, pp. 190, 179.

12  Schlesinger, vol. 3, p. 621.

13  John Maynard Keynes, 'To Franklin Delano Roosevelt, 1 February 1938, Private and personal', in Elizabeth Johnson and Donald Moggridge (eds), *The Collected Writings of John Maynard Keynes*, Volume 21. Cambridge: Cambridge University Press, 2012, pp. 437 f.

14  William E. Leuchtenburg, *Franklin D. Roosevelt and the New Deal 1932-1940*, New York: Harper & Row, 1963, p. 347.

15  Studs Terkel, *Hard Times: An Oral History of the Great Depression*, New York / London: Pantheon, 1986, p. 249.

16  Jürgen Kuczynski, *Die Geschichte der Lage der Arbeiter in den Vereinigten Staaten von Amerika von 1789 bis in die Gegenwart*, Berlin: Die Freie Gewerkschaft Verlag, 1948.

17  Eric Rauchway, *The Great Depression and the New Deal: A Very Short Introduction*, Oxford: Oxford University Press, 2008, p. 94

18  Franklin D. Roosevelt, Address at Madison Square Garden, New York City, 1936, <https://www.presidency.ucsb.edu/documents/address-madison-square-garden-new-york-city-1>.

19  Schlesinger, vol. I, p. 191.

20  On the concept of 'land grabbing' (originally coined by Rosa Luxemburg as 'Landnahme') as an integral part of the socio-ecological 'double crisis' of capitalism and the roots of this concept in the works of Marx and Engels, see Klaus Dörre, *Die Utopie des Sozialismus. Kompass für eine Nachhaltigkeitsrevolution*, Berlin: Mathes & Seitz, 2021. Similarly, John Bellamy Foster in Baier, Canepa, and Golemis (eds), *transform yearbook 2021*, p. 57, refers to Marx's 'ecological critique of capitalism'.

21  Birgit Mahnkopf, 'On the Political Economy of the Ecological Crisis', in Baier et al., *transform! yearbook 2021*, pp. 73-95.

22  Michael Brie and Gabi Zimmer, 'Sagen, was ist! Zur Strategiediskussion der Partei DIE LINKE im Vorfeld der Bundestagswahl 2021', *Sozialismus* 455 (47)10: 2-6.

# Class Struggle for Social Democracy

## Loren Balhorn

Ten years ago, few if any on the European left would have entertained the notion that the United States would soon host an inspiring revival of the socialist movement. In Europe, recent years had witnessed the formation of several substantial democratic socialist parties such as Syriza in Greece or Die LINKE in Germany, and the founding of a new, continent-spanning Party of the European Left in 2004. Barring the electoral collapse of the Partito della Rifondazione Comunista in Italy, Europe's post-communist left appeared to be moving from strength to strength in the 2000s, while a series of social movement mobilisations in the countries most affected by the economic crisis beginning in 2010 stirred hopes of a broader left-wing insurgency across the continent.

The United States, by contrast, appeared inert. Historically a country with a weak workers' movement, hamstrung by a number of institutional and cultural factors,[1] socialists in the US had never achieved the levels of organisational strength they had in Western Europe. The country had witnessed several upsurges in both labour organising as well as socialist political activity over the twentieth century, but by the early 2010s, the left in the US was largely invisible. The percentage of private-sector workers organised in trade unions had dipped below 10 per cent and showed no signs of reversing.[2] The Socialist Party of Eugene V. Debs had long since dissolved, while both the Communist Party as well as the various pretenders to its throne that formed in the wake of 1968 had effectively folded into the Democratic Party. What remained of the political left consisted of a scattering of small irrelevant sects and a broader ecosystem of left-liberal NGOs which were capable of periodically organising large demonstrations, but hardly amounted to a coherent political force.

Whatever political momentum emerged in opposition to the Bush administration's War on Terror in the 2000s was subsequently absorbed into Barack Obama's presidential run, which in turn served to blunt popular anger following the 2008/2009 financial crisis. Incidentally, it was around this time that the right reintroduced the word 'socialism' into public debate, deploying it in its hysterical denunciations of Obama's eminently centrist and pro-capitalist policies, while Bernie Sanders was introduced to a broader national audience for the first time as a result of his left-wing opposition to those same policies.

The explosive emergence of Occupy Wall Street in late 2011 briefly appeared to signal a change in mood, but within a few months the encampments had been cleared and the movement fizzled out, leaving little in its wake in terms of organisational infrastructure. A few new collective publications emerged, including the quarterly magazine *Jacobin*, which would go on to become a leading voice of the emergent left,[3] but for the first half the 2010s the action continued to be in Europe, with the upward trajectory of Podemos and Syriza in particular drawing many American socialists' attention.

## A decade where decades happened

Fast-forward to 2022, and the tables have turned quite dramatically. Parties of the European left took power in one country (Greece) and joined coalitions in several others (Spain, Portugal), but by and large the forces of the left find themselves in a state of general retreat. Some of the most sizeable parties, such as Die LINKE in Germany or Bloco de Esquerda in Portugal, have suffered stunning electoral losses. Pablo Iglesias and Jeremy Corbyn, two of Europe's most well-known socialists, both resigned in the wake of major defeats. Syriza leader Alexis Tsipras, once the darling of the left the world over, may still be in charge of his party, but to what extent it remains a force for socialism is up for debate, to say the least.

Across the Atlantic, by contrast, remarkable advances have been made. Bernie Sanders's 2016 and 2020 presidential runs may not have ended with him in the White House, but they did succeed in making him one of the country's most popular politicians and probably the most recognised socialist on the planet. His once-lonely presence in Washington is now reinforced by a small but growing cohort of young lawmakers, most notably Alexandria Ocasio-Cortez (known as 'AOC' to admirers and detractors alike), whose main talking points – a nationwide living wage, universal health care, and free university tuition – have become popular across wide swathes of the electorate. Together with the dozens of other democratic socialists elected to state and local office in the last five years, they ensure that the movement is a small but growing pole of attraction both in and outside of the Democratic Party for the first time in two generations.

On the organisational front, the US left appears to be making headway at a time when many of its European counterparts have watched their ranks stagnate, if not decline. This trend is most visible in the case of the Democratic Socialists of America (DSA), an organisation founded in 1982 through a merger of elements of both the 'Old' (1930s) as well as 'New' (1960s) Lefts. Though beginning from a much more modest starting point, DSA has seen its membership numbers increase nearly twenty-fold since 2015, from some 5,000 to the low six digits, with over 200 active chapters and 14 thematic working groups. Boosted by its association with high-profile representatives like AOC and Cori Bush, it is now *the* paramount socialist organisation in the country, far outpacing any of its competitors. In terms of absolute numbers, it is the largest socialist group in the country since the heyday of the Communist Party and the most exciting organisational development on the left in decades.

## From theory to practice

Politically, one could argue that DSA exhibits similarities to the leading New Left group of the late 1960s, Students for a Democratic Society (SDS), as Ethan Young did in last year's edition of this yearbook. It is a 'big tent group with room for experimenting and trial-and-error', and boasts a number of 'skilled organisers' but 'no clearly defined political pole in leadership'.[4] Like the New Left, it emerged outside of the organised labour movement and tends to be dominated by young, college-educated activists, reflecting the make-up of the Bernie campaigns from which DSA so successfully recruited. In some branches, particularly in smaller cities where links to trade unions and experienced organisers are weakest, the group's politics lean towards a kind of ultra-leftist posturing, mixing a more 'radical' version of the identity politics that have suffused American liberalism in recent years with shades of anarchism or even the so-called 'Marxism-Leninism' of previous generations.

That said, such political growing pains are to be expected in any rising political movement and should by no means be seen as indicative of the organisation's overall trajectory. The dissolution of several of its most prominent far-left factions and the marginal status of those remaining suggest that, even if DSA has yet to form a cohesive political leadership and profile, transformation into a revolutionary vanguard party is not in the cards. In that sense, DSA is quite different from the New Left of the 1960s and 1970s: while much of that generation's energy ended up directed towards (fruitless) attempts at building mass parties inspired by the Russian and Chinese revolutions, most DSA leaders and organisers appear more interested in developing a strategy informed by their own experiences, rather than those of past generations. Arguably the most important of these experiences, and the one most consequential for DSA's current trajectory was how the organisation has managed to use elections to galvanise support.

Prior to 2015, most of the explicitly socialist left in the US pursued a strategy of building movements and organisations outside and to the left of the Democratic Party, which many derided as a 'graveyard of social movements' that served to absorb and neutralise political protest more than anything else.[5] To the extent that election campaigns were treated as a venue of political activity whatsoever, then only in the form of long-shot, third party candidacies such as Ralph Nader's 2000 presidential bid with the Green Party, or quixotic, perennial campaigns that functioned primarily as vehicles for recruitment rather than genuine attempts to win elections. Campaigning for Democrats, many argued, simply channelled limited time and resources into a party that would only betray the movements. The primary task of socialists was to build independent organisations and mass movements, which would in turn lay the foundation for future growth (and, perhaps, electoral success).

DSA, by contrast, has long cultivated what its leaders called an 'inside-outside' strategy when it came to electoral politics, in line with its founder Michael Harrington's position that the Democrats represented the 'left wing of the possible' in American politics, and thus a vital arena for socialist activity.[6] For decades, neither of these positions could boast much in the way of empirical verification. As its critics happily pointed out, DSA had utterly failed to move the Democratic Party to the left – indeed, the party had lurched further and further to the neoliberal centre since the late 1980s, as it sought to swap out its declining working-class base for the culturally liberal middle classes located in the suburbs. The more radical left had also failed to build any substantial formation outside of the Democrats, but could at least point to the large protests against various free trade agreements in the late 1990s or the Iraq War in 2003 as evidence that such potential existed.

This disagreement continued to constitute a major dividing line between the marginal US left well into the 2010s – that is, until Bernie Sanders announced his first run for president in April 2015. In a matter of months, the hitherto theoretical question of whether the Democratic Party could be utilised as a tool for building a socialist movement became an eminently practical one. While many other socialist organisations stood on the sidelines, cautioning its members about the structural limits of Sanders's campaign, DSA embraced it head-on. This, combined with its decades of experience working with left-wing challengers to the Democratic establishment, put the organisation in an excellent position to seize on the campaign as not only a tool to pressure Hillary Clinton from the left, but to become the natural political home of many Bernie supporters and, thus, the organisation it is today.

The last few years have thus settled the age-old question of whether or not to engage with the Democratic Party (the truth, after all, is always concrete). Socialists who continue to make the case for absolute and immediate independence from the Democrats do so from a position of deep marginality – with the exception of Seattle city councilwoman Kshama Sawant, a leading member of the Trotskyist group Socialist Alternative, no independent socialist campaigns have registered any notable successes. Meanwhile, more and more opponents of the inside-outside strategy have opted to join DSA and try to function as its furthest-left wing – thereby indirectly confirming the failure of strategies based on absolute independence from the Democrats.

## Searching for socialism

Performing well in a few national elections, registering 100,000 members, and becoming a visible nationwide political force in less than ten years may represent an impressive advance for socialists in the US, but at least thus far, developments there could be seen as merely catching up, so to speak, to their European counterparts, where democratic socialist parties have long sat in parliament and exercised varying degrees of influence over politics in their respective country.

Yet precisely because the political system in the US is so different from Western European parliamentary systems and the prospect of forming an independent political party still so far from grasp, learning from the experiences of the European left is not possible in any direct sense. DSA members have instead had to develop their own, home-grown approach to organising, treading a fine line between dissolving into the broader liberal milieu, as some of its predecessors did, and falling back into the kind of abstract propagandism that characterised much of the socialist left in recent decades, and would almost certainly condemn the organisation to political irrelevance. Concretely, they must figure out how to keep one foot within the political mainstream, operating in and around the Democratic Party, while simultaneously building up their own, independent organisation.

What could that look like? One of the more comprehensive proposals was put forward in an essay for the 2018 *Socialist Register* by American political scientist Adam Hilton.[7] Although not referring to the DSA specifically, Hilton's essay on the prospects for 'left challenges inside the Democratic Party' argued that the constraints of the American two-party system obligated the US left to explore new approaches to building working-class organisation. The traditional model adopted by social democrats and communists alike, whereby a group of socialist militants goes about constructing an independent political party to organise and represent the broader working class with the ultimate aim of assuming state power either through elections or revolutionary rupture, was impossible in a system in which parties functioned overwhelmingly as 'electoral devices' allergic to mass-membership involvement.[8]

To move forward, socialists ought to 'divorce the twin tasks traditionally assigned to the working-class party, separating the organization of the proletariat into a class from the imperative to win governmental power'.[9] Even if constructing a 'working-class party' as traditionally conceived was impossible in the medium term, socialists in the US could build political capacity and influence by continuing down the path laid out by Bernie Sanders. By running candidates on the Democratic ballot line while also building an independent organisation outside of that party, the left could cohere 'a geographically rooted network of mass-member civic organizations, oriented toward building a base within working-class communities and labour unions that can also act as an effective independent pressure group on the Democratic Party'.[10]

The Sanders campaign attempted to launch precisely such a network with the political action committee 'Our Revolution', launched in August 2016 as a vehicle to continue the Bernie-inspired insurgency within the Democratic Party. Although Our Revolution continues to operate, it failed to become the network envisioned by Hilton and early Our Revolution staffers and has lost most of its early momentum,[11] further raising the stakes for DSA as the premier organisation carrying on the Bernie legacy. The approach described above, or at least something similar to it, has in many ways become political common sense in the organisation. Particularly in its larger chapters, DSA cultivates a focus on running in winnable local and state elections and ballot initiatives, usually on the Democratic ballot line.

For all of the ire the strategy attracts from the organisation's far-left currents and various 'revolutionary' sects, it appears to be working: according to DSA national director Maria Svart, two-thirds of all DSA-sponsored candidates and initiatives proved successful in the November 2021 electoral cycle.[12] In cities like Chicago and New York, the organisation has elected a number of city councilmembers and constitutes a substantial, albeit minoritarian, current within the local Democratic Party, while in Nevada, where Bernie Sanders won the Democratic primary with over 40% of the vote, DSA supporters even succeeded in taking over the party leadership last year.

DSA's electoral progress is encouraging, but particularly in a situation in which socialists are running for office as the (still fairly negligible) left wing of a much larger capitalist party, it is arguably not, on its own, a viable path to building a nationwide organisation capable of transforming politics anytime soon. This fact is not lost on DSA organisers, who, like most socialist organisations past and present, have also sought to expand the group's influence by intervening in social struggles around the country.

So far, a large part of the group's organising capacity has focused on struggles in the economic sphere, i.e., by supporting strikes and unionisation drives, showing up to picket lines and encouraging its members to join or help found a union in their workplace. How exactly this sort of work should look remains contested. One of the more prominent currents, the Bread & Roses Caucus, aggressively puts forward the 'rank-and-file strategy' associated with veteran socialist Kim Moody and the journal *Labor Notes* – something of a departure for the organisation, which traditionally focused more on building influence within the trade union bureaucracy. Yet regardless of how exactly the labour movement should be built, slogans such as 'every worker deserves a union' and phrases like 'building working-class power' are uncontroversial across the organisation.

This strategic orientation towards elections combined with rebuilding the labour movement distils the logic of what a number of thinkers in and around DSA have termed 'class-struggle social democracy'. The phrase denotes the understanding that social democracy (defined as a robust welfare state and a functioning political democracy) represents the furthest any society has come to realising something resembling socialism, but also (and more importantly), the most plausible medium- to long-term prospect for the US left. Incidentally, one could argue that it also constitutes a more accurate (and honest) description of the programme pursued by the parties of the European Left. Beyond lip-service to a transformational strategy going beyond capitalism, effectively, all socialist forces today find themselves campaigning by and large for social democratic measures and against the neoliberal reforms that have set the terms of political debate for decades. This is as true for socialists campaigning to pass the Protect the Right to Organize Act in Oakland as it is for activists in Berlin trying to re-socialise housing stock that was privatised 20 years ago.

That said, class-struggle social democracy is particularly suited to a country like the US, where forty years of an employers' offensive have rolled back much of what was already a meagre welfare state to begin with, and poverty and social inequality rival those of many developing nations. Material burdens on the working and middle classes that are unimaginable in Europe – such as the medical debt that bankrupts hundreds of thousands of Americans every year, or the $40,000 in student debt that the average American incurs to complete a Bachelor's degree – make the universal social programmes associated with social democracy particularly appealing and urgent. The explosive potential of universal demands was put on full display during the two Sanders campaigns, and has continued to buoy democratic socialism's appeal in the country ever since.

So where does class struggle come in? Precisely because the US electoral system appears so impervious to building third parties, implementing progressive social reforms – what Bernie Sanders called a '21st-century Economic Bill of Rights' – will require massive political confrontation with the ruling elite and thus with capital. Historically, periods of major social reform in the US have also gone hand-in-hand with the growth of trade unions and an uptick in class struggle – the rise of the Congress of the Industrial Organizations in the 1930s, concomitant to the passage of the New Deal, being the most obvious example. The same will almost certainly be true today: to win such a confrontation, the left will need more than elected officials at every level of government. It will require organised power in the workplace capable of waging economic warfare and forcing employers to come to the bargaining table lest their profits cease to flow altogether. What happens when such organisation is not present is evidenced by how quickly Joe Biden, initially hailed by many liberal commentators as a 'transformational' president who would introduce New Deal-esque legislation, folded in the face of opposition from capital, a recalcitrant Republican Party, and centrists within his own ranks.

Winning such battles will not, by itself, open up a socialist perspective in the near or medium term. It does, however, greatly raise the chances of enacting progressive social and environmental legislation that will improve the lives of working-class Americans, shift the balance of forces towards labour, and thus broaden the audience for socialist ideas over time. As Vivek Chibber, editor of the Marxist journal *Catalyst* and an influential thinker around DSA, summarised it several years ago: 'You build a party based in labor, you strengthen the organizational capacity of the class, you take on employers in the workplace and create rings of power in civil society, and you use this social power to push through policy reforms by participating in electoral politics.'[13]

To some, this approach may sound old-fashioned – at worst, perhaps 'class reductionist'. For while departing from the vanguard-oriented approaches of some twentieth-century Marxisms, class-struggle social democracy retains an emphasis on the working class as the crucial agent of social change and the primary focus of left-wing organising. This stands in stark contrast to large parts of the European left, where a number of post-Marxist approaches have become dominant and classical Marxism is often seen as having been overly preoccupied with the fates of white men in heavy industry. With a few exceptions, today's parties of the left talk less about the working class than they do about 'the people' or 'the movements' – necessarily vague formulations that more often than not obscure more than they reveal.

Given the conditions in which DSA operates, however, there is a strong argument to be made that a class-based, universalist approach is the most effective way to build the left today. After all, DSA's rise can only be understood against the backdrop of the 2008/2009 financial crisis and the exploding economic inequality in the years that followed. The slogan that animated the Occupy movement – 'We are the 99 per cent' – continues to encapsulate how many Americans view their place in the social hierarchy, regardless of race or gender. A recent study sponsored by *Jacobin*, YouGov, and the Center for Working-Class Politics entitled 'Commonsense Solidarity'[14] also reached similar conclusions. Based on surveys of voters in key swing states, the study came to the conclusion that working-class voters are highly receptive to social democratic and left-populist messaging particularly when it focuses on 'bread-and-butter', i.e. material, issues, but tend to be turned off by activist rhetoric.

These findings should not be taken as arguments for abandoning issues of racial and gender disparities, however, but rather as a challenge to find ways to incorporate them in a broader, universalist programme that appeals to workers of all races, genders, and identities. It was after all young people – those most likely to be in tune with activist language – who proved most receptive to Sanders's universalist messaging, and continue to identify more positively with socialism than any other age group (47% of those between 25 and 34, according to one prominent poll).[15] For many young Americans, the last decade of social crisis and rebellion has facilitated a kind of positive working-class identification (whether real or imaginary) that is often absent in Western European social movements.

Within the US working class itself, a hesitant but nonetheless undeniable rise in militancy has begun to take shape over the last two years, with the tight labour market giving workers more leverage over employers and inspiring some unions to launch organisation drives at industry leaders like Starbucks and Amazon. The unions are still far from reversing the decline of the last four decades – indeed, union density remains at a historic low – but popular attitudes are beginning to shift in their favour, and the composition of the National Labor Relations Board, which mediates between workers and employers, is the most pro-labour it has been in decades.

Taken together, what this means is that the prospects for (re-)building a socialist current rooted within the organised labour movement are still, to put it diplomatically, dim, but nevertheless incomparably brighter than they were one decade ago. Bernie's unexpected success, the subsequent rise of DSA, and now the uptick in class struggles all go to show that the deep social crisis that plagues American society has made its politics more open and unpredictable. In this situation, the left has a chance, however small, to continue to grow as a factor on the national stage if it succeeds in relating its platform and its activity to the concerns of the majority.

## In it for the long haul

DSA's membership numbers experienced another bump in the beginning of the Covid pandemic[16] and continued to climb throughout the year, fuelled by anger and anxiety about job losses and lack of access to affordable health care in the midst of a public health crisis. Over the last year, however, DSA's growth appears to have stalled. With the election of Joe Biden in November 2020, complete with his calculated rhetorical nods to the Sanders campaign, the political urgency that many felt during the Trump era – as demonstrated not only by DSA's growth, but also the explosion of protest movements like Black Lives Matter – appears to have subsided. As a result, the kinds of organisational leaps the left was capable of making in Sanders's wake are most likely off the table for the foreseeable future.

Democratic socialists in the United States now find themselves in what *Jacobin* publisher Bhaskar Sunkara recently described as political 'purgatory', or, more concretely, 'the end of a period of rapid politicization and settling into one of either gradual decline or slow advance'.[17] For Sunkara, and for many who have been a part of democratic socialism's astonishing rise over the last decade, the challenge of the coming period will be to consolidate and expand the movement's foothold within the working class rather than subsist as a visible, but politically ineffective, activist subculture.

This danger is very real, as indeed the experience of the European left demonstrates. One need only look at the track record of the German party Die LINKE in recent years to see where a national political presence absent a base in the organised workers' movement can lead.[18] A certain level of material infrastructure – elected officials, paid staff, and a left-wing media ecosystem – can facilitate political echo chambers that give the false impression of outsized political influence and encourage sympathisers to take the party's presence for granted. Combined with organisational stagnation, the result can be destructive, inward-looking ideological fights that alienate the left from the broader public and distract from party-building and immediate tactical and strategic decision-making.

DSA is still a small organisation compared to its Western European counterparts, but recent public controversies around issues like DSA International Committee members meeting with officials from the Venezuelan government, or Congressman Jamaal Bowman participating in a trip to Israel sponsored by the liberal lobbyist group J Street, evidence the pull that ideological in-fighting can exert in the absence of tangible forward progress. This is not to imply that debating these questions is somehow illegitimate, but the outsized attention these disputes received and the level of acerbic rhetoric involved, with at least one DSA working group publicly calling for Bowman's expulsion, should serve as a warning.

The difficulties encountered by the left in Europe over the last few years may also offer a more general lesson about the limits of purely oppositional politics for building a socialist majority. The rise of the European left parties in the 2000s was first and foremost in reaction to European social democracy's turn to the right (or at least the neoliberal centre). Whether in Spain, Germany, Portugal, or Scandinavia, democratic socialists performed best when voters saw them as a necessary corrective to a political mainstream in which cutting social spending and curbing the welfare state had become a consensus – which were the conditions in which Bernie Sanders and Jeremy Corbyn rose to prominence in the mid-2010s.

Yet in the last few years, as neoliberal orthodoxy has begun to show cracks and social democrats undertake a cautious pivot to the left, the left has struggled to articulate its political use-value. Should one really 'waste' a vote on a protest party if social democracy stands a real chance of winning the election and enacting even some minimal progressive reforms? For many erstwhile supporters of the left in Portugal and Germany, at least, the answer appears to be 'no'. The infrastructure provided by parliament and a residual core supporter base has kept European left parties from slipping off the radar so far. Nevertheless, it seems clear that merely serving as a parliamentary 'voice of the streets', as it is often put, is not a viable path to political power. To remain politically relevant, the left will have to aim squarely for the broad middle of society in the same way that Bernie did. The precise outline of a socialist programme will inevitably vary between countries and political systems (one can hardly campaign on universal health care in countries where it is already a reality), but it will necessarily entail prioritising broad, bread-and-butter demands that can unite voters across cultural and geographic divides.

For DSA, ways to avoid the subcultural impasse appear a bit more straightforward, simply given how much more restrictive the US political system is. The limits of human biology make another Sanders presidential run in 2024 essentially impossible, and although figures like AOC and Cori Bush show a lot of promise, they are still years if not decades away from being in a position to run for president. Thus, the US left can rule out another mass insurgent campaign like in 2016 and 2020. The organisation will have to adopt a more long-term approach, geared towards building its base in the unions and its capacity to contest elections at the local level. Luckily, it can draw on a wealth of experiences in places like New York, where it is already a political factor to be reckoned with.

In the US as in Europe, socialists are staring down the barrel of a long slog to fortify their positions and cultivate a social base broad enough to unite something approaching a majority. This task will probably take decades – a disconcerting proposition given the pressing ecological and social crises facing humanity, but nevertheless our best shot. A decisive question for DSA, but also for the European left, will be whether it is able to grow beyond its overwhelmingly young, white-collar base in urban cities, and appeal to the millions of working-class people who stand to gain from the socialist agenda, but have yet to embrace it as their own. Whether such a feat is possible is anybody's guess, but would anyone have predicted the events of the last decade ten years ago?

NOTES

1   The question as to why the US has never had a socialist movement comparable to its European counterparts has been discussed exhaustively for over a century, beginning with Werner Sombart's 1906 classic, *Why Is There No Socialism in the United States?*, and is (obviously) beyond the scope of this essay. It is safe to assume, however, that the comparatively high living standards enjoyed by American workers for most of the twentieth century, which played a decisive role in Sombart's analysis, do not suffice to explain the marginalisation of socialism in the US. After all, nearly four decades of wage stagnation, rising poverty rates, and exploding household debt failed to kindle any sort of socialist revival prior to Bernie Sanders's 2015 presidential run – underscoring the significance of this particular 'subjective factor' in the movement's re-emergence.

2   See G. William Domhoff, 'The Rise and Fall of Labor Unions in the U.S.', Chapter 7, *Who Rules America?*, February 2013, <https://whorulesamerica.ucsc.edu/power/history_of_labor_unions.html#Chapter_7>. Despite some flashes of activity in recent years, trade union organisation remains stubbornly low in the US.

3   Founded in 2010, the success of *Jacobin* (at which the author of this article is a contributing editor) mirrors the growing influence of the movement itself. Though it attracted attention early on for its uncharacteristically professional design and heterodox approach to socialist strategy, it was not until Donald Trump's election that the publication's circulation began to explode – reaching 30,000 by his inauguration, according to the magazine's founder, Bhaskar Sunkara. The recent announcement

that Sunkara is to become the next president of *The Nation*, the oldest and largest left-liberal magazine in the US, is further testament to the growing influence of democratic socialism in the country. Of the other radical publications that emerged in and around the Occupy movement, few have survived, and none have reached comparable influence.

4   Ethan Young, 'US Politics in Freefall', *Capitalism's Deadly Threat*, transform! yearbook 2021, London: Merlin, 2021, p. 311.
5   A textbook example of this line of argument, reproduced countless times by socialists over the last century, can be found in an essay by the Marxist academic August H. Nimtz, 'The Graveyard of Progressive Social Movements: The Black Hole of the Democratic Party', *MR Online*, 9 May 2017, <https://mronline.org/2017/05/09/the-graveyard-of-progressive-social-movements/>.
6   The inside-outside strategy is by no means the exclusive property of DSA, but no other group seems to have benefited from it as much as it has in the last seven years. On the continuities between Harrington's vision and DSA today, see Maurice Isserman, 'Michael Harrington, American Socialist', *Jacobin*, 31 July 2019, <https://jacobinmag.com/2019/07/michael-harrington-dsa-democratic-socialism>.
7   Adam Hilton, 'Organized for Democracy? Left Challenges inside the Democratic Party', *Socialist Register 2018: Rethinking Democracy*, 54, edited by Leo Panitch and Greg Albo, London: Merlin, 2017, pp. 99–129. Another noteworthy essay on the topic, with which Hilton engages, is Seth Ackerman, 'A Blueprint for a New Party, *Jacobin* 23 (2016): 101–111.
8   Hilton, p. 108.
9   Hilton, p. 122.
10  Hilton, p. 123.
11  See the account of leading DSA member and former Our Revolution political director David Duhalde, 'Our Revoution Failed to Live Up to Its Potential. But the Bernie Movement Needs a Mass Organization Now', *Jacobin*, 28 April 2020, <https://www.jacobinmag.com/2020/04/our-revolution-bernie-sanders>.
12  Maria Svart, 'Director's Report: We Join DSA to Organize', *Democratic Left*, Winter 2021, <https://democraticleft.dsausa.org/issues/winter-2021/directors-report-we-join-dsa-to-organize/>.
13  Vivek Chibber, 'Our Road to Power', *Jacobin*, 5 December 2017, <https://jacobinmag.com/2017/12/our-road-to-power>.
14  Jared Abbott, et. al., *Commonsense Solidarity: How a working-class coalition can be built, and maintained*, 2021, <https://images.jacobinmag.com/wp-content/uploads/2021/11/08095656/CWCPReport_CommonsenseSolidarity.pdf>.
15  See the most recent Gallup poll: Jeffrey M. Jones, 'Socialism, Capitalism Ratings in U.S. Unchanged', *Gallup News*, 6 December 2021, <https://news.gallup.com/poll/357755/socialism-capitalism-ratings-unchanged.aspx>.
16  Elaine Godfrey, 'Thousands of Americans Have become Socialists since March', *The Atlantic*, 14 May 2020, <https://www.theatlantic.com/politics/archive/2020/05/dsa-growing-during-coronavirus/611599/>.
17  Bhaskar Sunkara, 'The Left in Purgatory', *Jacobin* 44 (2022): 9.
18  For a more thorough discussion of Die LINKE's trajectory, see Loren Balhorn, 'Are These the Last Days of Die Linke?', *Jacobin* 44 (2022): 32–39.

# 'Populism' as a Cognitive Barrier: a Political Approach

## Seraphim Seferiades

Though often described as an 'exogenous' development, it is clear that the Covid pandemic did not just fall from a clear sky. Along with the climate disaster, it reflects systemic irrationalities, exacerbating inequalities and exposing the multiple structural flaws of global capitalism. In this juncture, the left has to come forward with robust transgressive (supra-systemic) alternatives, yet it is hampered by the notion of 'populism' in its twin fashionable – 'right' and 'left'– varieties. I claim not only that the whole conception is problematic but that it poses a threat to the way we think, hence also to the way we act.

'Concepts', wrote Cambridge physicist George Thomson (1892-1975), 'are ideas which receive names. They determine the questions one asks, and the answers one gets.' When, nowadays increasingly, we use the term 'populism' what is it exactly that we have in mind? What sorts of 'ideas' does this concept implement, and how does it purport doing it? The question is crucial, for, whether we realise it or not, when we engage in concept-building, we implement notions of reality that we hold: mental images of the entities, events, or phenomena we deem noteworthy. And this is precisely where normative convictions, ideological beliefs, and value systems enter the picture – as the factors determining which 'realities' are to be perceived and analysed, and for what purpose. But the relationship between the two (concept-informing norms and concept-prescribed observables) is bi-directional. If values determine the empirical reality that a concept delimits as significant, it is also possible to work our way backwards: from the guided observables to the guiding values. We do this not in order to judge them as values, but to assess their *Wertrationalität* (value rationality) - to see whether they are served by the concept in question. But this is not all. For, as we pass from the ideational realm to that of empirical reality - from the pure declaration of a meaning to the challenges of denotative adequacy - we need to see if the concept helps us conduct effective research.

The argument visualised in the figure below indicates the two – plus one – controls or assessments we need to be performing not just for 'populism' but – I would suggest – for all concepts: (a) *Wertrationalität* (value rationality – the normative assessment), i.e., does the concept adequately implement the notion(s) from which it emanates? (b) *Zweckrationalität* (technical rationality) (the practical or technical assessment), i.e., does the concept help us produce sound research conducive to significant results? The dotted line at the bottom (*Rationalität*: assessment of *phronetic potential*),[1] finally, indicates (c) the – hitherto unrealised (hence a dotted line) vision of a phronetic social science,[2] the assessment question being: Is the cognitive result of our research sufficiently robust to help us revisit and/or re-assess the values from which we start?

## Values, Concepts, Research (and Phronetic Social Science)

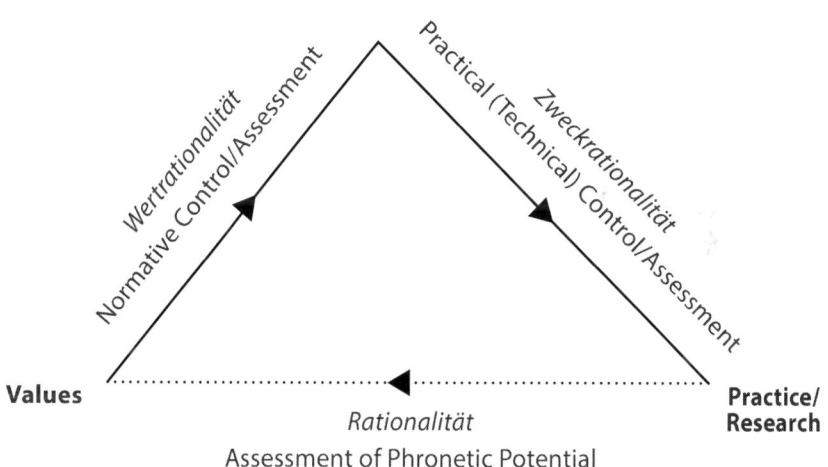

I suggest that, contrary to what is often assumed, there exist two normative motives behind extant conceptualisations of populism (one explicitly welcoming 'populism' as a 'democratic corrective' with a transformative potential, and one which abhors it as a threat to pluralism and democracy), and two major conceptualisations, one Manichean, seeing it as a moralising pitting of an innocuous people against a sinister elite, and another approaching it as a plot by personalist leaders against a largely unorganised social base for the purpose of capturing and exercising power. But the underlying normative motives and the conceptual implications intersect: authors who think of populism as a potential blessing share the same conceptualisation with their normative adversaries; and vice versa, scholars who agree in thinking of it as a threat have fundamental disagreement in terms of the overarching concept.

Examining the conceptualisations for their normative bases, I find all varieties, with the exception of the first, to be quite effective. Things invariably turn sour, however, when we pass to the examination of their technical rationality: the situation here is extremely problematic – which leads me to formulate an alternative conceptualisation, one that will not be just another assertion, but the product of elaborate conceptual reconstruction.

## Populism, the concept: genera and differentiae

In the recently published *Oxford Handbook of Populism*,[3] the editors identify three major conceptualisations and corresponding approaches: the 'ideational', the 'strategic', and the 'cultural'. Let us briefly examine what they consist of.

Introducing the 'ideational' variety, Cas Mudde moves to incorporate a number of similar conceptualisations in the following overarching definition: 'Populism', he claims, is a '[thin] ideology that considers society to be ultimately separated into two homogeneous and antagonistic groups, "the pure people" versus "the corrupt elite," and which argues that politics should be an expression of the volonté générale'.[4] Mudde's take on the issue is inclusive but also bold, as he is surely aware of other similar conceptualisations at the genus level – things like 'populism' as 'a type of political discourse';[5] as a 'mode of identification';[6] or as a 'frame'.[7] Still, he successfully subsumes them under his, because much as one may try to discover the cognitive significance of a protracted debate over whether 'populism' is an ideology, a discourse, or a general political style, the likelihood is that we will be disappointed, for no matter which characterisation we choose, we would still be conceiving of 'populism' as a discursive (hence ideational) construct.

My claim that 'discursive modality' adequately captures the genus most authors have in mind when thinking of 'populism' may at first sight appear inaccurate when we examine the 'strategic' approach suggested by Kurt Weyland. 'Populism', he argues, is 'a political strategy through which a personalistic leader seeks, or exercises government power based on direct, unmediated, uninstitutionalized support from large numbers of mostly unorganized followers'.[8] Weyland's definition is clearly different from Mudde's; however, in my view this is due to the differentiae specificae he adopts (to which I will return), and not so much due to his account of the genus. After all, to acquire their real-life dimensions, personalist strategies and opportunist endeavours must also be articulated in discourse. This said, I appreciate that a major strength of Weyland's approach is his claim that 'populism' is not something one says, but something one does.[9]

The 'cultural' approach formulated by Pierre Ostiguy, finally, suggests that 'populism' is 'the antagonistic, mobilizational flaunting of the "low"' – consisting in utterances that are hostile to the culturally elaborate (and nefarious) 'high' and, hence, deliberately 'improper' with an eye to provoke and shock.[10] Although pitched at a level of abstraction higher than that with which Mudde operates, it is fairly obvious that for Ostiguy, too, 'populism' is a particular variety of discourse.

To fully grasp the intellectual significance of these definitions, however, it is necessary to carefully examine the differentiae specificae they propose.

Considering the literature's staggering size, it is surprising to realise that, for what really matters, there exist just two basic sets of criteria used to delimit 'populism' as a species of the genus (discursive modality). The first, which is by far the dominant one, is that 'populism'– in speech or action, word or deed, as thin ideology, or as frame – exists when someone invokes an all-encompassing and Manichean notion of the 'ethically good' (or 'pure') 'people' against the 'corrupt elites' with an eye to pitting the former against the latter. The second, qualitatively different criterion proposed by the 'strategic' approach involves domination: a conscious project by opportunistic and personalist leaders to attain and/or exercise power by politically exploiting unorganised followers. This is why, whilst they purport to interpret the 'general will', these leaders engage in stratagems such as the abolition of intermediary institutions (between leadership and rank and file) which could impede the schemes they have devised.

## Normative-Cognitive Underpinnings and the *Wertrationalität* Control (V-C)

Although seldom mentioned in the literature, it is not difficult to detect two drastically different attitudes or normative predispositions among the scholars who approach 'populism' in a Manichean fashion. Epitomised by the writings of people like Kriesi and Pappas,[11] Aslanidis,[12] but also by the original formulations of Cas Mudde and Rovira Kaltwasser[13] as well as Ostiguy,[14] the first predisposition is (a) a thinly disguised reproach and condescension towards discourses that look to connect subaltern populations with the construction of related subjectivities; and (b) the idea that such a project constitutes a threat to democracy, since it invariably involves a rejection of pluralism and constitutional guarantees, the emergence of rampant plebiscitarianism, even a menace of totalitarian politics.[15] Whilst the reproach and condescension is all-encompassing and cynically moralising in tone, the claim that 'populism' constitutes a threat to democracy is, for the most part, directed at the extreme right (which constructs subjectivities based on exclusionary appeals to the 'nation'). To the extent, however, that no firm conceptual distinction is made between this and the 'left-wing' version that appeals to the social underdogs, the same sort of anxiety is also felt in the face of left attempts to connect with the subaltern.

What is very telling, however, is that authors in this tradition have very little to say about the state of democracy in the era of capitalist crisis. A detailed scrutiny of this kind of literature is unlikely to turn up any mention of the economic crisis engulfing all political processes, with either very fleeting acknowledgements that something may be amiss in the way representative institutions have been functioning lately or, incredibly, no mention of this at all. It is quite evident that for these scholars the problem is hardly a matter of phenomena such as rising inequalities, shrinking social and political rights, unaccountable executives, etc., but rather, the massive responses that the crisis has provoked. It can be safely concluded, then, that the principal normative imperative guiding and inspiring this scholarship's conceptual and empirical work is the *defence of post-democracy*. At the same time as we criticise this kind of scholarship we must admit that the choice of its *Wertrationalität* is sinisterly brilliant, for the 'cat-dog concept' it proposes,[16] effectively delegitimises all serious criticism of post-democracy: If the 99% slogan of 'Occupy Wall Street' can be assimilated to Hungary's Orbán and the Greek neo-Nazis, then every reader (and citizen) has a duty to defend this battered post-democracy, no further questions asked.

But within the Manichean conceptual universe, there is also a second normative stance, reflected in the work of the Essex School. Unlike their conceptual brethren, scholars in this tradition have been keen to highlight the problematic areas of neoliberal democracy and sensitise their readership to the potentially beneficial aspects of 'left-wing populism' as a democratic corrective. The school's father figure, the late Ernesto Laclau,[17] along with, more recently, Chantal Mouffe have in fact gone so far as to suggest that this 'left-wing' version of populism is in fact a promising strategy - if not *the most* promising strategy – for the left, one that can transform and revitalise its internal dynamics, allowing it to decisively defeat neoliberal orthodoxy. As Mouffe's article dedicated to the experience and trajectory of Jeremy Corbyn's Labour is as good an example as any of this approach's main cognitive coordinates (and normative intentions), it is worth reviewing it in some detail.[18]

Couched in an - unnecessarily - philosophising language, Mouffe suggests that what gave Corbyn's Labour its original boost was that it promoted a new 'agonistic debate'. So far so good. But what were these – allegedly 'new' – elements? They were: 're-nationalization of public services, especially the rail networks, energy providers, the postal service, [...] [bringing an end to the privatisation of] the national health service as well as the education system, the abolition of student fees, and [...] increase spending on the welfare state.' Mention is also made of the intent to 'empower citizens to take part in the management of public services'; the desire 'to build links with social movements'; and the general orientation to uphold the goal of 'equality' versus the ill-conceived 'liberty' of an all-encompassing and domineering market. One wonders, of course, why any of this is fundamentally different from what the left has traditionally advocated. The answer Mouffe and the Essex School provide is that this new 'populist' left establishes 'chains of equivalence between different democratic subjects across [...] society'.

The argument, however, is utterly spurious. Historical research, especially in the context of the 'linguistic turn' in social history, has amply demonstrated that the first mass parties of the left were not addressing themselves to some monolithic 'working class' but to a wide variety of 'popular classes' – establishing the sorts of 'equivalences' the Essex School considers to be benevolently 'populist'. But this is very consequential. Although widespread methodological glibness typically misses this reality, what this conceptualisation does is to assume that 'left-wing populism' and the 'left' are synonymous – two words for one meaning. Since the stipulation of synonymies is one of the main mechanisms through which collective ambiguity is manufactured in the social sciences, it is worth noting something that Giovanni Sartori stressed in his methodological writings – elevating it, moreover, to the status of a cardinal rule: 'Awaiting contrary proof, no word should be used as a synonym for another word'. If no such proof is given, synonymies 'unsettle, without resetting, the semantic field to which the stipulation belongs'.[19]

To wit, if – following the Essex School – we call Corbyn's Labour (but also Syriza, Podemos, and other similar parties and social movements) 'populist', how are we to think of and what are we to call the 'left', let alone the 'radical left'? But reducing 'the left' to 'populism' has the additional shortcoming of whimsically annulling perfectly valid historic characterisations of strands *within* the left – such as 'revolutionism', 'reformism', 'anarchism' and several others. Considering that all these tendencies in one way or another portray the 'people' as 'exploited', 'dominated' or 'oppressed', one fears that this approach threatens us with a cognitive regression to an unbearably abstract generality. The question then arises: *Why is this done?* Which requires that we infer the normative motives behind the conceptualisations in question.

In the above-cited article, Mouffe refers to several new radical left parties and social movements, but what is stunningly absent from her treatment is the party which, employing such discourse and organisational practices, managed to come to power – Syriza. The reason for this absence is glaringly evident: Syriza is the living proof of this strategy's utter failure – precisely the opposite of what Mouffe suggests.

This experience is so theoretically telling because, despite its unquestionable social-movement origins and early characteristics, Syriza subsequently became thoroughly cartelised at a pace which, in terms of its swiftness, may have been historically unprecedented. Coming to power in January 2015, and only after seven short months of haphazard negotiation with the troika institutions (conducted mostly behind the backs of the party organs), the party capitulated to the neoliberal template, reneged on its electoral pledge to end austerity, and crowned the act with the referendum of 5 July 2015 when, overnight, the leading group around party leader Tsipras turned a massive defiant 61.3% 'No!' against the troika proposals into a compliant 'Yes'.

It is thus possible to understand the normative motive guiding the Essex conceptualisation as the defence of a particular political mentality, specifically the one epitomised by Syriza and other like-minded parties. However, instead of the theoretically bombastic but empirically bland idiom used by Laclau and disciples, there exists a far clearer and more concrete term with which to describe it: *reformism* – the old ideology of the Second International, according to which robust and lasting social change can be effected through a class-collaborationist *Burgfriedenspolitik* or, put simply, by playing by the rules of the game. *This* and nothing else is the defining feature of the strategy Laclau and Mouffe have in mind. To capture the historically specific dimension of the contemporary phenomenon, we may call it *new reformism*.

But if, as I claim, these scholars' underlying normative-cognitive motive (conscious or unconscious) is the historical and hoped for salvaging of this strategy, then their chosen *Wertrationalität* works perfectly. All that one needs to do to be convinced of this is to look at the consequences. If the left is reduced to 'establishing chains of equivalence amongst subaltern populations' then (a) new reformism is credited with an undeservedly universal valence; (b) it becomes a sort of TINA for the left; and (c) all debate about different strategies' merits and shortcomings is cancelled.

We see that despite their diametrically opposite cognitive-normative starting points and motives (defence of post-democracy and defence of new reformism) the two Manichean varieties share an impressive *Wertrationalität*. The scholars involved have indeed hit upon a way to effectively promote what they hold dear normatively and deem worthwhile cognitively. But, as I will argue below, the results are precisely the opposite when examined from the perspective of their respective concepts' practical performance.

First, however, we need to consider the *Wertrationalität* of the other major conceptualisation – the 'strategic'. Although in their writings the 'strategic' authors dwell little on the precise nature of the capitalist crisis, they are both well aware of it and intensely concerned about its implications. Moreover, the late Peter Mair[20] – the scholar who introduced the notion of a 'hollowing of western democracy' – also belongs to the same tradition, as he was the one to explicitly link 'populism' with phenomena of party cartelisation and the use of plebiscitarian tactics by unscrupulous leaderships. It is quite clear, then, that the normative-cognitive motive behind this conceptualisation is neither defensive anxiety vis-à-vis post-democracy nor promotion of new reformism as a universally valid strategy for the left. Maintaining that 'populism' is not what populist leaders proclaim but what they do, scholars in this tradition draw our attention to plebiscitarian institutional arrangements and practices in which the rank and file are called upon merely to ratify leadership decisions.

By insisting that 'populism' is just a 'strategy devised by personalist leaders', however, this approach narrows the potential scope of its own cognitive contribution, for fixation on opportunist organisation diverts attention away from the political elements involved, thereby effectively reducing it to mere organisationalism. As a result, 'populism' is reduced to a mere feature of caudillo-type regimes, mostly in historical and contemporary Latin America. By contrast with the Essex School's implicit support for such regimes, this is an appreciable merit, yet it falls short of what the strategic approach could potentially explain. The reduction to organisationalism blinds the 'strategic' approach to Mair's perspicacious suggestion that 'populism' is the very political substance of all cartel parties in post-democracy; and, furthermore, it also prevents these theorists from looking at 'populist' practices amongst parties that lack leadership structures (or executives), in other words, that are not 'personalist' properly speaking. Contemporary Social Democracy is a telling case in point. All in all, if the cognitive-normative goal is to warn against nepotism and the stunning discrepancy between words and deeds in contemporary political projects, the *Wertrationalität* of conceptualising 'populism' as the personalist strategy of individual leaders seems insufficient.

But now we must consider how these conceptualisations' perform at the practical level, examining their capacity to adequately delimit phenomena in research that has practical political cogency. That is, let us examine their *Zweckrationalität*.

## A nightmare of 'Findings' – the *Zweckrationalität* Control (C-R)

Political sociology and social science, as they have developed over the last few decades have tended to delegitimise attempts to judge a scholar's normative-cognitive motives. A political scientist may come across data like those regularly published by Oxfam and Crédit Suisse showing that the world's eight richest billionaires together have the same wealth as the poorest half of the globe's population and think that this is quite unproblematic. Or witness such gigantic failures of political strategy as Syriza's and view them as a wise adaptation to environmental constraints. Such scholars may always defend themselves by claiming that pursuing their preferred normative-cognitive motive is their prerogative. But this defence falls away when we examine their work from the angle of its instrumental rationality. If demonstrating that a concept is cognitively irrelevant is not enough to undermine it, its protracted failure to contribute to sound and cumulative empirical research certainly is. What is the balance sheet for the conceptualisations we have been discussing?

One may begin by enquiring what 'populism' as a concept contributes to our understanding of the contemporary and historical political landscapes. Starting off with the first, punitive variety of the Manichean conception, the main prescription is that research on social movements should be tied to research on the far right. Assuming that the objective is to understand in a way that can be explained, one rarely finds something so aptly captured by Sartori's cat-dog fallacy, resulting from an analytical orientation to pseudo-classes, that is, classes which, because they are conceived at a prohibitively high level of abstraction (at which far too many dissimilar ingredients are filtered out), are given a denotation that is both analytically intractable and cognitively spurious. Explanatory hypotheses that combine social movements and far-right parties may be formulated, of course, but either they will be utterly trivial (for example, when it can be said that both phenomena emerge in times of crisis) or they will have to be continually suspended. As Sartori put it, when our concepts contain 'utterly different animals', verifying explanatory hypotheses about them is practically impossible.[21] But the analytical impasse does not just result from this concept's cancelling out major differences on the flimsy basis of secondary, trivial similarities. Equally fatal is the ambiguity and consequent vagueness of the *differentiarum specificarum* adopted. The idea of pitting virtuous majoritarian collectivities against malevolent minorities is so old and anthropologically rooted that the problem may not become immediately apparent. Upon closer scrutiny, however, one discovers that, as 'appealing to the people' and identifying a sufficiently homogeneous political adversary is a standard practice of practically everyone involved in politics, one is never sure about what is really 'populist', and what is not – a state of affairs bespeaking *undenotativeness*, this fatal error in concept-building.

Take, for instance, Mudde and Rovira Kaltwasser's (2017) recent stock-taking of the literature.[22] By my count, in this short book the authors present no less than seventy analytically bewildering varieties, in all five continents. It is quite evident, however, that the reason they can so easily manipulate their denotata (augmenting or reducing their cases at whim) is not because they really discover politicians, movements, parties, or regimes that invoke 'the people' in a way that is particularly 'populist', but – quite prosaically – because this fits the flow of their – underlying normative – argumentation.

The situation is not very different with the Essex School's theorists of benevolent 'populism'. One regularly discovers that it is being attributed, or not, purely on the basis of normatively charged criteria – when, for instance, the conservative position adopted by the French Communist Party during the explosion of May '68 in France, at the time justified on the grounds that it was necessary so that broad-based coalitions (one might say 'chains of equivalence'!) would not be endangered, is described as resisting the 'populist temptation'.[23] But as the benevolent version flows from the same core concept as the negative version, this must come as no surprise. Nor is the problem solved by this school of thought's – otherwise correct – insistence that we distinguish right-wing populism from its left-wing analogue. Though this partly addresses the cat-dog of analytically combining racism and social movements, the serious problem of ambiguity and vagueness remains. Tsipras and Corbyn (as well as *both* Obama *and* 'Occupy Wall Street') are customarily declared more or less 'populist', but Salvador Allende, Luiz Ignácio Lula da Silva, or the interwar French *Front Populaire* are not. Well, are they? We will never know.

In terms of research, the problem with the strategic approach appears to be the obverse of what it is in the Manichean. The denotation here is not overly extensive, but unduly constrictive – relying exclusively on machinations of opportunist and personalist leaders. The problems this creates have already been highlighted, so there is no need to belabour the point much further. Insistence on the motives of personalist leaders and their internal institutional machinations limits attention to them and them only, at the expense of other research which could highlight organisational plebiscitarianism *in the absence* of such distinctly personalist leaderships. Partly because of this, the approach also tends to de-politicise the populist phenomenon, stripping it of its ideological underpinnings, making it appear as if it were the result of personal whim. Is populism caused simply by the opportunism of some individual leaders? Are there no distinctly political and ideological processes at play that merit research and analysis?

All in all, we see that, in terms of their capacity to adequately delimit 'populism' in a manner that would facilitate significant research, the extant approaches fare rather poorly. What would a more adequate approach be?

## Seeking an Alternative: Populism as Political Deception

Whoever reviews the massive literature on 'populism' is bound, sooner or later, to run into the writings of Nadia Urbinati[24] – which represent an effort at identifying democratic pathologies and suggesting ways of coping with them. Having identified 'populism' as one such pathology, Urbinati suggests that one must distinguish between the 'populist rhetoric' that often contaminates popular social movements, from 'populism' properly speaking – that is, political projects seeking to reshape society according to their world views ('populist power'). Cases in point concerning the former are the Italian Girotondi of 2002, the US Occupy Wall Street of 2011, and the Spanish Indignados of 2013, while the most typical instance of the latter is Hungary's Fidesz.

The reason I think Urbanati's distinction is telling, however, has nothing to do with her own depiction of the cases: she claims, for instance, that the social movements she cites projected an 'anti-representative' discourse (for example in the famous Indignado slogan '¡Que no, que no, que no nos representan!') whereas it is far more reasonable to identify it with an agonistic search for institutional alternatives capable of guaranteeing genuine accountability. Even so, one can still accept her crucial distinction between 'popular' and 'populist': the former is genuine in its concerns and participatory intentions – seeking social justice, a deepening of democracy, and candid democratic accountability; while the latter, which also practices an 'emancipatory' discourse, in essence makes a sham of it, for its real goal is to dissolve actually-existing institutional checks and balances in order to capture and exercise power.

In the same general spirit, equally telling is the notion of 'artificial anti-capitalism' in the context of a broader political project of 'hijacking the left', as suggested by Vassilis Petsinis.[25] The primary lexical definition of 'hijacking' is 'to steal, to rob, to seize', but the broader family of meanings to which it belongs is a glaring foul play. In this sense, for a political project to hijack a discourse is to claim being something that it is not.

One will surely realise the affinities that this notion has with the strategic approach's distinction between what populists say and what they actually do. 'The very essence of populism', exclaims Weyland,[26] is 'the disjuncture between form and substance, style and strategy, rhetoric and reality.' What is distinctive about 'populism' is precisely this sinister 'twist': whereas 'discourse implicitly depicts populism as a bottom-up mass movement, it really rests on a top-down strategy through which [...] [specific populist projects marshal] plebiscitarian support for [their own] [...] goals'. What stands out is, once again, a malignant discrepancy between what is proclaimed and what is done.

Combining these three insights, and in light of my earlier criticism of extant approaches, let me now suggest my own view, that 'populism' is best conceived (both cognitively and practically) as *a species of the genus 'discourse' that claims to be popular while it is not.*

Though, as anyone can tell, this – admittedly terse – definition is devised at a high level of abstraction, I hasten to say that this is as it should be – for, cognitively as well as practically, 'populism' encapsulates a huge variety of human interactions both in the public and the private sphere. As far as the less readily identifiable manifestation of populism in the private sphere is concerned, a populist performing privately is someone who, in an unscrupulously moralising fashion, taps feelings of compassion, kind-heartedness and/or care, to promote his or her self-interested motives. His/her 'populism' of course involves invocation of some 'suffering underdog', but the feature that renders this practice populist is its fake nature. Moving down the ladder of abstraction, one ought to have no problem conceiving populist instances that are distinctly political. Everything that the Manichean-ideational literature (of both varieties) mentions can be of use in this connection, albeit with the proviso that what makes a discourse populist is not its pitting the subaltern against the dominant, but that it simply claims to be doing it while it does not.

It is also crucial to note that, although populism is principally a discursive recourse that is had by forces in opposition, it can also appear in power; the literature in all shapes and forms has duly made note of that. Although this does not change the overall status of the concept I am proposing, it allows us to incorporate the strategic approach's suggestion regarding the need populist formations have to establish organisational plebiscitarianism: schemes that practically annul intermediary structures between the grassroots and the executive and establish plebiscitarian rather than participatory political subjectivities. In this connection the case of ostensibly 'radical left' parties, such as Syriza and Podemos, is worth examining, especially in light of the historically unprecedented swiftness of their transformation from allegedly 'movement parties'[27] into fully blown cartel parties.[28] The point here is that organisational plebiscitarianism is a *consequence* of political populism – precisely because the latter is a bogus doctrine necessitating bogus practice, all those espousing it have, sooner or later, to attempt to conceal their act by undermining the intermediary institutions that could possibly restrain them.

The same also goes for populism's tendency to de-politicise its claims, obliterate the distinction between left and right as outdated, and slide into rhetorical schemes that are crude and inchoate. Accordingly, what really distinguishes the populist invocation of 'the people' is not its comprehensive character but its vagueness; not its establishing 'chains of equivalence', but its concealment of the glaring internal contradictions it contains as a discourse – the fact, for instance, that one cannot *both* promote a 'favourable investment climate' for globalised capitalism *and* uphold labour rights.

One must ask, however, where does the populist impulse originate? Is it just the personal whim of opportunist leaders, or are there roots at once deeper and more political in nature? In light of our protracted failure to seriously examine, analyse, and evaluate political content (discourse, ideology, and strategy), it comes as no surprise that nowadays we find ourselves at a loss when it comes to assessing different political projects. If we begin to do this, however, we will discover that historically speaking (as well as in contemporary incarnations), populism signifies a strategy which a more traditional Marxist jargon would describe as 'class collaborationism': a strategy which, although (a) nominally antagonistic, is nonetheless principally characterised by (b) its penchant to collaborate with sections of the elites (typically behind the backs of the rank and file), and by (c) excluding all the intermediaries (initiatives, movements, and parties) capable of resisting such collaboration. To a large extent this also explains why, as a discourse, it is (d) internally contradictory, inchoate, and/or evasive: because, while, rhetorically, it brandishes an intent to undo privilege, in practice it seeks to share in it.

But the claim that populism comprises deceptive invocations of the popular also needs to be subjected to the value-rationality and instrumental-rationality controls I have applied to all the other approaches examined.

The value-rationality control requires that the analysis I pursue clearly states its cognitive-normative motives. This is quite straightforward. Concurring with the strategic approach, I view populism as a threat: unlike the punitive Manichean view, however, a threat not to post-democracy but to the subaltern populations it claims to represent and whose demands and aspirations it claims a capacity to voice. Clearly at odds with what the Essex School professes, my approach also suggests that popular movements and political initiatives must be on the alert to avoid the political template of 'undoing domination without clashing with the dominant', the combination that generates populism. If this is the cognitive goal, I think that the concept I introduce adequately serves it.

Doubt is, nonetheless, bound to persist regarding the concept's performance within the instrumental rationality dimension. Can we produce sound research on its basis? Or, otherwise put, can we ascertain empirically the existence of populism as phony political opposition? My reply is, that to do so we will have to rely on the – nowadays all too easily forfeited – historical control. History has witnessed several oppositional strategies claiming they could cope with their contemporary adversities – a small minority of them successful, the vast majority not. We need to tap this experience and draw the necessary conclusions. Judging them by their respective outcomes, we must be able to assess which strategy was authentically promoting the interests of those it claimed to represent and which was just a bogus facade. Such an exercise is, of course, bound to be difficult and controversial. But it is only by undertaking it that we will be able to discover and pinpoint discourses, strategies, and organisational practices that have been/are populist: i.e., political projects discursively claiming to express and promote the interests of the subaltern, whilst in practice undermining them. Such analysis is particularly urgent for the left, especially in the context of the contemporary organic crisis of capitalism.

NOTES

1   Stemming from the Aristotelian *phrónesis* (wisdom), phronetic denotes a social science that would involve actively promoting what is rationally good.
2   For a definition of phronetic social science, see <https://www.cambridge.org/core/books/abs/real-social-science/phronetic-social-science-an-idea-whose-time-has-come/72F5DBE22B6D9209BBF008FAAB9549BF>.
3   Cristóbal Rovira Kaltwasser, Paulina Ochoa Espejo, Pierre Ostguy, and Paul Taggart (eds), *The Oxford Handbook of Populism*, Oxford: Oxford University Press, 2017, pp. 27-47.
4   Mudde, 'Populism: An Ideational Approach', in Ochoa et al., *The Oxford Handbook of Populism*, p. 27.
5   Ernesto Laclau, *On Populist Reason*, London: Verso, 2005; David Howarth, 'Populism or Popular Democracy? The UDF, Workerism and the Struggle for Radical Democracy in South Africa', in Francisco Panizza, (ed.), *Populism and the Mirror of Democracy*, London: Verso, 2005, pp. 202-223; Yannis Stavrakakis, 'Antinomies of Formalism: Laclau's Theory of Populism and the Lessons from Religious Populism in Greece', *Journal of Political Ideologies*, 9,3 (2004): 253-267.
6   Francisco Panizza, 'Introduction: Populism and the Mirror of Democracy', in Panizza, *Populism and the Mirror of Democracy*, pp. 1-31.
7   Paris Aslanidis, 'Is Populism an Ideology? A Refutation and a New Perspective', *Political Studies* 64,15 (2015): 88-104.
8   Kurt Weyland, 'Populism: A Political Strategic Approach' in Ochoa et al. *The Oxford Handbook of Populism*, pp. 48-72, 50.
9   Weyland, p. 54.

10   Pierre Ostiguy, 'Populism: A socio-cultural approach', in Ochoa et al. (eds.), *The Oxford Handbook of Populism*, pp. 73-100.
11   Hanspeter Kriesi and Takis S. Pappas, 'Populism in Europe during Crisis', in Kriesi and Pappas (eds), *European Populism in the Shadow of the Great Recession*, Colchester: ECPR Press, 2015, pp. 1-22.
12   Paris Aslanidis, 'Is Populism an Ideology?'; Paris Aslanidis, 'Populist Social Movements of the Great Recession', *Mobilization: An International Quarterly* 21,3 (2016): 301-321.
13   Cas Mudde, 'The Populist Zeitgeist', *Government and Opposition* 39,4 (2004): 147-174; Cas Mudde and Cristóbal Rovira Kaltwasser, 'Populism and (Liberal) Democracy: A Framework for Analysis', in Mudde and Rovira Kaltwasser (eds), *Populism in Europe and the Americas: Threat or Corrective to Democracy?* Cambridge: Cambridge University Press, 2012, pp. 1-26.
14   Pierre Ostiguy, 'The High and Low in Politics: A Two-Dimensional Political Space for Comparative Analysis and Electoral Studies', Kellogg Institute Working Paper No. 360 (2009).
15   Jan-Werner Müller, *What is Populism?* London: Penguin, 2017.
16   Giovanni Sartori pointed to the meaningless results that can derive – by way of parochialism, misclassification, 'degreeism', and conceptual stretching – illustrating this by an assumption that a creature exists called a 'cat-dog' about which two hypotheses are successively tested: all cat-dogs bark and all cat-dogs mew. Giovanni Sartori, 'Comparing and Miscomparing', *Journal of Theoretical Politics* 3,3 (1991): 243-257, for the cat-dog fallacy 247.
17   Laclau, *On Populist Reason*.
18   Chantal Mouffe, 'Corbyn a mis en oeuvre une stratégie populiste de gauche', *Le Vent Se Lève*, 2018, <http://lvsl.fr/chantal-mouffe-corbyn-populisme-gauche>.
19   Giovanni Sartori, 'Guidelines for Concept Analysis' in Giovanni Sartori (ed.), *Social Science Concepts: A Systematic Analysis*, Beverly Hills: SAGE Publications, 1984, pp. 38-39.
20   Peter Mair, 'Partyless Democracy. Solving the Paradox of New Labour?', *New Left Review* 2, March-April 2000: 21-35.
21   Sartori, 'Comparing and Miscomparing': 248.
22   Cas Mudde and Cristóbal Rovira Kaltwasser, *Populism: A Very Short Introduction*, Oxford: Oxford University Press, 2017.
23   See, for example, Ioannis Balampanidis, 'Historicizing the Populist Temptation: The Case of Eurocommunism', in Giorgos Charalambous and Ioannou Gregoris (eds), *Left Radicalism and Populism in Europe*, Abingdon, Oxon: Routledge, 2000, pp. 67-85.
24   Nadia Urbinati, *Democracy Disfigured: Opinion, Truth, and the People*, Cambridge, MA: Harvard University Press, 2014.
25   Vassilis Petsinis, 'Hijacking the Left? The Populist and Radical Right in Two Post-Communist Polities', in Charalambous and Gregoris, *Left Radicalism and Populism in Europe*, pp. 156-180.
26   Weyland, pp. 53-54.
27   Donatella della Porta, Joseba Fernández, Hara Kouki, and Lorenzo Mosca, *Movement Parties Against Austerity*, Cambridge: Polity, 2017..
28   Loukia Kotronaki, 'From the Street to the Parliament: The Topographies of Protest and SYRIZA in the Years of Crisis, 2009-2015', in Nikos Serntedakis and Stavros Tompazos, (eds), *Facets of the Greek Crisis: Contentious Protest Cycle and Institutional*

*Outcomes*, Athens: Gutenberg, 2018, pp. 135-177; Seraphim Seferiades, 'Parties and Movements Without Politics? The "Cartel-Party" Model in the Light of SYRIZA's Experience' in Serntedakis and Tompazos, *Facets of the Greek Crisi*, pp. 178-221.

# Why Is Austro-Marxism Still Worth Studying in the 21st Century?

## Dunja Larise

Socialism has taken different forms in different epochs and countries. These transformations occurred against the backdrop of changing economic and political constellations throughout history. Its foundations were located in Marxist theory to which Austrian socialists contributed significantly, having been in the historical position to effect change within the framework of parliamentary democracy in the immediate aftermath of the First World War.

Their most significant contributions to the development of Marxist theory were made in an era of an increasingly globalised capitalist economy by intellectuals close to the Socialist Democratic Workers' Party of Austria (SDWP), which had been founded in 1889. Until 1910, it was the second largest party in the Parliament of the Austrian half of the Austro-Hungarian Empire, and it participated in parliamentary politics from 1919 until 1934, governing the First Austrian Republic in its formative years 1919 and 1920, enacting several laws to anchor radical political change towards socialism.

A considerable number of important legislative measures that had been in the programme of social democracy for years were implemented in a relatively short period. Examples of such laws were the eight-hour day, paid workers' leave, regulations restricting child labour and night work for women, the introduction of unemployment insurance and improvement of unemployment benefits, the inclusion of all workers and employees in the healthcare system, and protective measures for particular groups of workers such as miners and bakers.

The revolutionary achievements of the period were the introduction of self-management by workers, which was a step toward an economic democracy embodied in the Factory Council Act. This ensured the participation of employees in business and operational management and guaranteed the participation of these bodies in the recruitment and dismissal of workers and the establishment of Chambers of Labour, alongside the Chambers of Commerce. This was an expression of the social equality of workers who gained the right to influence state economic policy and provide expert opinions, reports, and proposals.

During the Belle Époque, Vienna was notorious as the world capital of tuberculosis. The causes included precarious working conditions and malnutrition but above all the catastrophic housing conditions of the workers, who typically shared one bed in three shifts in often dark, cold, and stuffy rooms. Since the SDWP won an overwhelming majority in Vienna's local elections, so-called 'Red Vienna' was able to organise a monumental project of providing social housing which still today can be seen as a model for solving housing problems in big cities around the world. Social housing was financed by progressive taxation of the rich and not by public debt.

But the SDWP was still more ambitious than this, and the attempt was made to socialise key industries with a view, ultimately, to pave the way to a socialist society. These large-scale projects failed essentially due to the political and economic constellations of the period, in which Vienna was a red island within a hostile country. Relations with the federal states were initially very tense. The international position of the young Austrian state after the First World War was one of dependence on loans for the country's economic reconstruction and an even deeper reliance on international chains of supply.

What is the relevance of all this for us today? Given the crushing setbacks experienced by both communism and social democracy in the past 30 years, what is a left strategy, if there is any, to achieve radical social change? How is radical social change to be operated in a global capitalist world and now more than ever dependent on global supply chains? Can radical social change be achieved locally, and could such a local socialist entity realistically survive in the grip of global capitalism? If the change can be made locally, what could this local entity look like? Should it be a nation-state or some other political entity? If the nation-state still has a role to play in future change, do the strategies of social movements or left parties include the conquest of state power or rather the search for other options?

These questions are as relevant today as they were one hundred years ago. Austro-Marxists had to wrestle with them in contexts not so very different from our own. Their successes and failures, but above all the insights and experiences they acquired in the process, are an invaluable source of practical and theoretical tools for the left in the 21st century.

## Radical change, yes, but how exactly?

In the 20th century the idea that radical social change is achievable by taking state power was an accepted commonplace on the left. The differences concerned strategies of how to do it. Classical Marxist theory offers two approaches: the strategy of revolution and gradual reform. The former usually entails violence and bloodshed, but, more to the point, it is a conscious violation of the existing legal order in order to overcome it altogether. The latter means peaceful and gradual change within the framework of the current order. Although any recourse to violence and possible bloodshed sounds repugnant to most present-day leftists, revolution was the first choice for classical Marxism, with gradual reform being considered revisionism, classically in the idea of social reform articulated by Eduard Bernstein, a member of the German Social Democratic Party. Ferdinand Lassalle, the initiator of the social democratic movement in Germany, endeavoured to reconcile these two opposing strategies, fusing them into one. His view was that the means used to achieve radical social change are relatively insignificant and that the contrast between reform and revolution was often overblown.

> Revolution means upheaval, and a revolution has always occurred when, with or without violence – the means are not at all important – *a completely new principle* is put in place of the existing condition. On the other hand, reform occurs when the existing state of affairs is retained and developed to achieve merely more benign or more consistent and fairer circumstances. Again, it does not come down to the means. A reform can be won through insurrection and bloodshed, and a revolution in the greatest peace.[1]

Rosa Luxemburg held against this view, arguing that reforms cannot create a socialist society. She was convinced that revolution was necessary to overthrow capitalism; however, she also believed in the collapse of capitalism due to its economic instability. This idea of an inevitable collapse of capitalism had an enormous influence in revolutionary socialist circles.[2]

While Lassalle still contrasted reform with revolution, Victor Adler, the most prominent first-generation Austro-Marxist (not to be confounded with Max Adler), attempted to soften the original Marxist concept of revolution further. He went beyond Ferdinand Lassalle in seeing any remaining contrast between reform and revolution as insignificant and misleading. Thus, he paves the way for declaring every significant reform a revolution and allowing every revolution to merge into reform.

Every reform is important and worth every effort, *but every reform is worth as much as there is revolution in it. If you ask us revolution or reform?*, our answer is *revolution and reform! Or reform, only for the sake of revolution.*³

Adler occupies a position between Bernsteinian revisionism, which shies away from any thought of the revolutionary use of force, and Bolshevism for which reforms are to be rejected as patching up the existing order; he thus saw himself as standing in the spirit of the *Communist Manifesto*, which considers reforms acceptable only as measures within the immediate transition to a revolution, as preparatory actions leading to it with the proviso that all energies are concentrated on accomplishing it. At the first congress of the Second International, which was held in Paris in 1889, Adler tackled this problem:

In the last hour, when the capitalist social order collapses – and it will collapse on its own, without any help from outside – the fate of the proletariat will be decided according to the degree of intellectual development it will have achieved. We have less influence on the coming of this moment than we are willing to assume and far less than our enemies suspect. But one thing is in our power: to prepare for the moment – be ready, that's all.⁴

The belief in a teleologically unfolding historical process can have two different effects on revolutionary activists. On the one hand, it can help accelerate a revolutionary development by intensifying the will to bring about what necessarily has to come. However, it also often has the opposite effect of inducing people to wait for the inevitable to happen automatically through historical necessity. The tactic of waiting and being ready is hardly very motivating. Hans Kelsen, a liberal leftist who was not directly affiliated with Austro-Marxism, was the first to warn about the potential fatalism hidden within historical teleology: '[…] instead of the highest level of activity, a certain trusting fatalism will take hold'.⁵ However, it would be wrong to depict Victor Adler or the Austrian Social Democrats as fatalists. On another occasion, after the Great War, Adler showed a more differentiated approach:

The difference in the basic conception of the historical situation is that the communists were convinced, as Lenin and Trotsky announced in Russia, that the world revolution must come immediately with this world war, that there could be no recovery of capitalism and the great collapse is inevitable. But we Social Democrats are used to examining things in terms of their economic conditionality. We believed that capitalism would no longer recover directly and unconditionally, but how the world is currently shaped depends on the political and economic circumstances in the various countries. The communists believe that it only depends on the will ... We cannot tie ourselves to a belief because we all wish that capitalism will never again be in a position to rule the world. We Social Democrats say: Even though we would like it to turn out that way, we cannot ignore the facts.[6]

Max Adler, one of the most influential Austromarxists of the second generation, emphasised systemic change circumventing the question of revolutionary violence.

> [...] revolution and evolution are not opposites at all; for the latter relates to the causal connection of the changes, the former to the nature of the same. Opposites are merely revolution and reform (variation), in that the former denotes the change under a break with the previous system, the latter the change within the system.[7]

## Otto Bauer: revolution and state

The two key figures who set the tone for second-generation Austro-Marxism were Otto Bauer and Karl Renner. On Victor Adler's death, Bauer inherited the office of Foreign Minister in the first weeks of the new republic. Throughout the interwar years, from 1918 until 1934, he was the de facto leader of the SDWP in Austria. His ideas about revolution, state power, and democracy underwent a particular evolution through time that reflects the changing circumstances in which Austria found itself between 1918 and 1934. In 1911 Bauer represented a midway position between revolutionaries and revisionists. His realist stance and down-to-earth approach to politics had become one of his most characteristic attributes.

> Marxism is equally hostile to revisionism from the right and revisionism from the left, peaceful reformism and violent syndicalism. It knows that the iron laws of capitalist development cannot be overturned either by socialist ministers or socialist assassins. Its action is instruction, its work educational. It teaches the masses that their misery cannot go away within capitalism, but only with capitalism.[8]

In 1918 the Social Democrats decided to take the lead in the formation of the new republic and govern it within the power vacuum that emerged during the days of the Empire's collapse. They chose to embark on the road of parliamentary democracy and to effect change within that framework.

The Communists, on the other hand, attempted a coup on the very day of the proclamation of the Republic, with the intention of constituting a council republic, an attempt averted by the Social Democrats.

The Communist Party accused the Social Democratic Party of not seizing the historical opportunity when a council republic could have, they claimed, been established in German-Austria, thus betraying the entire people who stood united behind Social Democracy in anticipation of the socialist overthrow. The Social Democrats were vigorously opposed to Communist coup plans and indeed used all their influence and authority with the masses to dissuade them from taking this path.

Otto Bauer explained this position already in 1912: 'The bourgeoisie are opponents of Bolshevism because they fear the temporary victory of the proletariat. I am because I want to spare the proletariat the subsequent defeat.'[9] Much later, in 1934, as fascism took hold in half of Europe, including Austria, he would disparage his and his party's position at the time as pure reformism/revisionism and reformism/revisionism as an illusion.

> The labour movement of all the nations of Austria has been imbued with the spirit of revisionism for more than a decade. We indeed have few conscious revisionists, and only a few have preached the theory of revisionism here. But the peculiar history of Austria has filled us all – including those who profess Marx's theory – with revisionist illusions.[10]

In the context of his retrospective analysis, Bauer repeatedly spoke of the fact that history has refuted the illusions of revisionism. When in 1934 he wrote *Zwischen zwei Weltkriegen? Die Krise der Weltwirtschaft, der Demokratie und des Sozialismus,* his last book to be published during his lifetime, it may well have appeared that the path of participatory democracy had been wrong right from the start and that the Communists may have been right in their revolutionary tendencies. At the same time, however, he resisted calling these revisionist illusions a mere aberration. Instead, he considered revisionism, despite his criticism of it, 'an inevitable and fruitful phase of development between the revolutionary socialism of the age of the bourgeois revolution of the past and the revolutionary age of the proletarian revolution of the future.'[11] Having been a soldier in the Great War, Bauer saw the extreme face of political violence. Like many of his generation, he was loath to see it repeated.

The Social Democrats had chosen to fight for radical social change through the institutions of the state. Nevertheless, by 1926, at the latest, they were well aware of the structural and geopolitical obstacles that impeded them from accomplishing this mission. The Linz Party Congress in 1926 stated that

> The socialist social order cannot be established in a *single*, small country dependent on the capitalist world powers, but only in large *contiguous areas* that meet the requirements of a socialist planned economy. The Social Democratic Workers' Party will therefore, after the conquest of power in its own country, only be able to carry out the socialisation of the means of production concentrated in the property of the capitalists and the big landowners to the extent that the development of the other states has already created the preconditions for it.[12]

Oscar Pollak, an Austrian journalist of the period, summed up the tragic contradiction in the fate of Austrian Social Democracy in the post-war period as the predicament of a big party in a small country.[13]

## Democracy

> The democracy that we have and that is the only possible one in the class state may be termed political democracy; on the other hand, that democracy that we want and that is only possible in a socialist society can be called social democracy.[14]

In direct contrast to liberal democracy, Max Adler, who among Austro-Marxists developed the most elaborate theory of democracy, believed that true democracy can only be economic democracy. For him the real purpose of democracy was not representation but a society based on solidarity. Like Rousseau, Adler does not see democracy as the numerical majority of atomised individuals but rather as a kind of *volonté générale*: 'The principle of democracy is not the majority principle but the idea of the general interest, the common good in which everyone is equally involved, and which all are called upon and entitled to create in the same way.'[15]

Political democracy, as the doctrine of mere legal equality, has its basis in the political theory of liberalism, whose fundamental error, in Adler's view, was to understand society as an aggregation of isolated individuals. Adler opposes the liberal principle of a separation between the political and economic spheres and calls for democratic management of the economy. As in the present-day criticism of liberal democracy, he recognised that more power was directly associated with more wealth. To go beyond mere political democracy, he speaks of the need for self-government and gives the example of the industrial democracy that the English workers demanded, which is closely related to the idea of socialising key industries that the SDWP tried to implement in 1919, in which it eventually failed.

In 1908 Bauer still believed that when the workers became a self-conscious class – and it was the Social Democrats' task to educate them in that direction – the parliament would represent their interests through the workers' parties. But that belief was seriously shattered in the 1930s with the outbreak of the global financial crisis and the concomitant advent of fascism and national socialism.

> Parliament is not an independently acting power that stands above society and shapes it, but it is the means by which the forces working in society make their will into law. […] If parliament does not fulfil the demands of the working class, this is due firstly to the working class not yet constituting the majority of the electorate, and secondly, to the fact that hundreds of thousands of workers are still loyal to the bourgeois parties and have not yet matured to become class conscious. Only capitalist society itself can change the class structure of society; it will gradually make the working class into the majority of the electorate everywhere. But it is our task to educate the workers to be class conscious.[16]

The insight that unfulfilled hope for change could turn workers against parliamentarism and eventually even against the left parties represented in parliamentary democracy, if they were not powerful enough to achieve social change within the parliamentary framework, appeared as early as one year later, in 1909.

> With the rage of disappointed hope, the masses turn away from the hustle and bustle of parliament in disgust, something for which we are, certainly, not to blame. Responsibility, rather, rests with those who could not even get along amongst themselves as they united against us and are now unable to work because they have started to fight each other. But the mistrust of the masses becomes a danger to us too.[17]

At the 1913 party congress, Julius Deutsch worried: 'We must ensure that this dissatisfaction with parliament does not turn into dissatisfaction with the party, that what is directed against parliament does not ultimately turn out to be directed against the party […] Our activity is often prevented by the fact that we stare at Parliament as if hypnotised.'[18]

By 1923 Bauer's early fears that the proletariat might be disappointed with democracy if social changes could not be achieved through parliamentary democracy were partly proven right. Still, he believed that the workers would be loyal to the republic in its crisis.

> The sentiment that swept through the masses in 1920 against the coalition policy was simply the expression of the working class's disappointment that it could not assert its hegemony, its unhappiness that in place of its hegemony a power equilibrium arose. Nevertheless, the relation of the proletariat to the people's republic was radically different from that of the bourgeoisie. When the counter-revolution threatened the people's republic, the proletariat rose to protect it.[19]

15 July 1927 saw a turning point in the balance of power between Social Democracy and the bourgeois camp. By 1931 the workers had long become increasingly dissatisfied with the burdens placed on them by the economic restructuring enforced by the Geneva Protocols, and by the inability of the Social Democrats to redistribute the burden. The straw that broke the camel's back was the exonerating verdict in the case of a murdered worker a few days before 15 July. On this day extensive riots broke out which the SDWP was unable to control. The party's weakness became evident, after which the balance of power shifted in favour of the Conservatives. Conservatism in Austria then took on increasingly authoritarian traits.

In the early 1930s, it became clear that the global financial crisis was having a devastating impact on the trust workers had in Social Democracy and in democracy in general; all hope of achieving socialism waned. As fascism was on the verge of taking hold in Austria, brutally suppressing not only the workers but also basic civic freedoms, Bauer stood up to defend democracy, even in its basic form as a liberal democracy, against fascist dictatorship at any cost.

> Today, the problem no longer stands between capitalism and socialism; this decision cannot be brought about in this country today, but at this moment we are faced with a completely different question. Surrounded by the reactionary states around us, by fascism in the south, south-east, east, and west, it is the immensely difficult, immensely great, but also immensely glorious task of the Austrian proletariat to preserve an island of democratic freedom here.[20]

## Socialisation

The idea of social democracy in Austria was intrinsically connected to socialisation. This was the concept at the core of economic democracy and its main difference from liberal political democracy.

On 14 March 1919, the Constituent National Assembly passed the 'Law on Preparing for Socialisation'.[21] It stipulated that, for public welfare reasons, suitable businesses could be expropriated for the benefit of the state, the federal states, and the municipalities. A state commission for socialisation was entrusted with its preparation. Its first president was Otto Bauer, but its co-president was Ignaz Seipel of the Christian Social Party, the SDWP's coalition partner. Bauer had already developed his characteristic approaches to socialisation in his 1919 work *The Road to Socialism*. He was aware that hasty socialisation would fail not only because of the political balance of power but also because of inadequate economic conditions. Recognising these facts, he concluded: 'The political revolution was the work of a few hours; the social revolution will have to be the result of the bold but also judicious work of many years.'[22] Bauer advocated partial socialisation and turned his focus to enterprises that could be considered ready for socialisation.

Bauer advocated the expropriation of the owners in return for compensation but wanted the costs to be raised by a property levy. He also drafted structures for the organisation of the commonly owned enterprises, recommending a tripartite division of the management of these companies: the workers, employees, and civil servants employed in the company were to be represented by trade unionists, the consumers by representatives of the consumer cooperatives, and the local authorities by government administrators. The net profit from the revenue generated in socialised branches of industry was to be distributed accordingly: one third was to go to the workers and employees employed in the company, one third used for investments, and one third paid to the state. With the change in the international situation and the disappearance of the public pressure to make these concessions, the resistance of the non-socialist parties to the implementation of the socialisation programme stiffened.

The law of 30 May 1919, regulating the procedure for the expropriation of commercial enterprises, remained a mere procedural law with no practical impact due to the resistance of the Christian Social Party and Greater German Association. Thus, the Social Democratic plans for the socialisation of the coal and electricity industries and large agricultural estates remained unrealised. The socialisation programme remained in force *de jure*, but it was soon understood that the financial and credit-policy situation determined the time and circumstances of its implementation.

For Hans Kelsen, the failure of the socialisation project was proof that the Social Democrats had overestimated their power and neglected the real economic facts.[23] However, for Otto Neurath, who advocated full socialisation, the modest successes of the public-service socialisation remained merely a small move forward within 'the structures of social capitalism'.[24]

One of the best analyses of the failure of the socialisation project was published by the Social Democratic economist and Austro-Marxist Käthe Leichter. In her view, socialisation ought to have begun with those branches of the economy that occupied a strategic position. This would have strengthened the kind of political and economic power on whose basis further takeovers could have been accomplished. Unfortunately, this was prevented by foreign takeovers (as in the case of Alpine Montan Company) and the scarcity of Austria's coal deposits. Still, socialisation could also have been initiated with the banks.

> A well-planned socialisation can also – and this has been the dominant notion especially since Hilferding's *Finance Capital* – come from the banks; he who controls banks, controls the economy in the age of finance capital.[25]

However, the banks also suffered a severe blow in the First World War, after which they were creditors of a weak new state, which made it impossible to transfer them to state ownership in 1919. What remained, after production and banking, was consumption, but how could socialisation be carried out in the consumer markets if the state did not dispose of raw materials and semi-finished products, and more importantly, if a large proportion of consumer goods came from abroad? The problem was exacerbated by the collapse of the Monarchy's greater regional market and the simultaneous collapse of the national supply chains.

Leichter believed that socialisation could have worked at that time in a bigger country where the entire supply chain could have been subject to national law. But socialisation was not just about nationalising private companies; that was not an end in itself. It was about planning a transition to a socialist economy. In her view, this was too optimistic. It was a mistake to start socialising immediately, as the most elementary socialist insight indicated that it was impossible to create socialist islands in the capitalist sea.

The issues Leichter raised remain highly relevant today for all who contemplate concrete steps of transforming global capitalism into a new socialist society.

As for the specific Austrian situation in the early 1920s, she thought it preferable not to have regarded the nationalisation of the core private companies as socialisation per se, in order to prevent necessary setbacks and disappointments. One could have started with small steps to experiment with such undertakings. Here, firstly, it would have been possible 'to test the viability of the system in bitter competition with the old established forms of business, to get to know its shortcomings and advantages'. And secondly, it could have accomplished the development of enterprise democracy and thus the use of its organs for future socialisation'.[26]

## Conclusion: Liberal economy, global crisis, and their consequences

The Austro-Marxists were sharp opponents of a laissez-faire economy and were among the first to criticise its most prominent advocates, Ludwig Mises and Friedrich Hayek. Particularly outstanding was the criticism made by Helene and Otto Bauer. In terms of economics, Austro-Marxists were grounded in a brand of Marxian economic orthodoxy that led to errors, especially in defence of a labour theory of value that was even then hard to maintain. On the other hand, they could clearly see through the flaws in the laissez-faire neoclassical model.

Otto Bauer outlined the principle underlying the economic programme of the SDWP as follows:

> We reject the liberal-individualistic doctrine in which the state should not intervene in economic life, and in which it should leave the individual economy[27] to do as it pleases. But we also reject the conservative police-state principle in which the state bureaucracy should regulate the economy of the individual.[28]

The truth is that when the crisis of 1929 struck neither neo-classical orthodoxy nor Marxist economic orthodoxy had the recipe for solving it. In her last writings, Helene Bauer was still sceptical of Keynes's programme of inflationary investment. Unfortunately, the success of his strategy was demonstrated when it was already too late for Austria. However, both Helene and Otto Bauer clearly saw the devastating consequences of a capitalist crisis for the labour movement and peace in Europe. Helene Bauer drew a bitter conclusion that echoes like a warning for the future:

> But the mere fact that when the current crisis broke out in both countries [England and Germany)] the governments had a socialist trademark, sufficed to make the two workers' parties appear co-responsible in the eyes of the masses for everything they were too weak to prevent.[29]

*All citations, except those quoted from English publications, have been translated by the author.*

## NOTES

1. Ferdinand Lassalle, *Gesammelte Reden und Schiften*, ed. by Eduard Bernstein, Berlin: Cassirer, 1919, vol. IV, p. 87.
2. Rosa Luxemburg, *Social Reform or Revolution,* London, Militant Publications, 1986.
3. Victor Adler, 'Marx-Feier 1903' (address given on 16 March 1903), in *Victor Adlers Aufsätze, Reden und Briefe*, Vienna: Wiener Volksbuchhandlung, 1922, vol. 1, p. 167.
4. Victor Adler, in *Protocol of the International Workers' Congress in Paris from 14 to 20 July 1889*, Nuremberg, 1890, p. 45.
5. Hans Kelsen, *Sozialismus und Staat: Eine Untersuchung der politischen Theorie des Marxismus*, Leipzig: Hirschfeld, 1920; new edition: Vienna: Wiener Volksbuchhandlung, 1965, p. 23.
6. Victor Adler, *Victor Adlers Aufsätze, Reden und Briefe*, Vienna: Wiener Volksbuchhandlung, 1922, vol. 4, p. 36.
7. Max Adler, *Die Staatsaufassung des Marxismus. Ein Beitrag zur Unterscheidung von soziologischer und juristischer Methode*, Vienna: Wiener Volksbuchhandlung, 1922, p. 164.
8. Der Innsbrucker Parteitag, *Protokoll über die Verhandlungen des Parteitages der deutschen sozialdemokratischen Arbeiterpartei in Osterreich, vom 19. bis 24. September 1909*, Vienna, 1909, p. 176.
9. Otto Bauer, `Begrabene Hoffnungen´, *Der Kampf*, V,7 (1 April 1912): 289-295.
10. Otto Bauer, *Zwischen zwei Weltkriegen? Die Krise der Weltwirtschaft, der Demokratie und des Sozialismus*, Bratislava: Prager, 1936, p. 250.
11. Bauer, *Zwischen Zwei Weltkriegen*, p. 259.
12. 'Programm der Sozialdemokratischen Arbeiterpartei Deutschösterreichs, beschlossen vom Parteitag zu Linz am 3. November 1926', in Hans-Jörg Sandkühler and Rafael de la Vega (eds), *Austromarxismus – Texte zu 'Ideologie und Klassenkampf'*, Frankfurt: Europäische Verlagsanstalt and Vienna: Europa Verlag, 1970, p. 397.
13. Oskar Pollak, 'Die österreichische Partei und die Internationale', *Der Kampf* XXIV,7-8 (July-August 1931): 331.
14. Max Adler, *Politische oder soziale Demokratie: Ein Beitrag zur sozialistischen Erziehung*, Vienna: SPÖ/Tribüne, 1982, pp. 52-53.
15. Max Adler, *Politische oder soziale Demokratie*, p. 57.
16. Otto Bauer, 'Parlamentarismus und Arbeiterschaft', *Der Kampf* I,11 (1 August 1908): 483.
17. Otto Bauer, 'Die Lehren des Zusammenbruchs', *Der Kampf* II,11 (1 August 1909): 485.
18. Julius Deutsch in *Protocol of the negotiations of the party congress of the German Social Democratic Labor Party in Austria, from October 31 to November 4, 1913*, Vienna 1913, p. 186.
19. Otto Bauer, *The Austrian Revolution*, Walter Baier and Eric Canepa (eds), Eric Canepa (transl.), Chicago: Haymarket, 2021, p. 354.
20. Otto Bauer, Protocol of the Social Democratic Party Congress, held from 13th to 15th November 1932, Vienna, 1932, p. 39.
21. Gesetz über die Vorbereitung der Sozialisierung, *Staatsgesetzblat 1918-1920*, No. 181, p. 410

22  Otto Bauer, *Der Weg zum Sozialismus*, Vienna: Wiener Volksbuchhandlung, 1919, p. 5.
23  Hans Kelsen, `Marx oder Lasalle´ in Hans Kelsen: *Demokratie und Sozialismus*,Vienna: Wiener Volksbuchhandlung and Wissenschaftliche Buchgesellschaft, 1967.
24  Otto Neurath, 'Vollsozialisierung und gemeinwirtschaftliche Anstalten', *Der Kampf* XV,2 (February 1922): 58.
25  Käthe Leichter, *Leben und Werk*, ed. Robert Steiner, Vienna: Europaverlag, 1973, p. 388.
26  Leichter, *Leben und Werk*, p. 391.
27  By 'individual economy' and the 'economy of the individual' Bauer intends everyday economy and trade on a small scale.
28  Otto Bauer, *Sozialdemokratische Agrarpolitik, Erläuterung des Agrarprogramms der Deutsch-Österreichischen Sozialdemokratie*, Vienna: Wiener Volksbuchhandlung, 1926, p. 174; *Protokoll des sozialdemokratischen Parteitages 1926*, Wien 1926.
29  Helene Bauer, 'Im vierten Krisenjahr', *Der Kampf* XXV,12 (December 1932): 493-94.

**The Austrian Revolution**
by Otto Bauer
edited by Walter Baier,
Eric Canepa

Publisher: Haymarket Books
(July 2021)
Language: English
ISBN-10: 1642591629
ISBN-13: 978-1642591620

Otto Bauer's The Austrian Revolution is one of the now largely forgotten gems of the extraordinarily rich literature that Austro-Marxism produced. Thanks to an excellent new translation, this classic work is now available to English-speaking readers in a complete version for the first time. It is one of the classics of Marxist political analysis, only comparable to Marx's The Eighteenth Brumaire of Louis Napoleon or Trotsky's History of the Russian Revolution.

Michael R. Krätke, Lancaster University

# Ecosocialism/Ecofeminism

# A Relational Logic for the Left

Ariel Salleh Interviewed by Haris Golemis

**Haris Golemis:** Professor Salleh, your university lectures, books, articles, interviews, participation at conferences, but also activism in the movements, has established you as one of the world's most eminent ecofeminists. Since not all of our readers are familiar with your work, allow me to begin with a rather predictable question, which I am sure you have answered many times. What exactly is ecofeminism? A strand of feminism or a strand of ecology? An appeal for the connection of social movements, a counter-hegemonic discourse, or a strategic proposal for societal transformation?

**Ariel Salleh**: I guess the first thing to say is that ecofeminism is one among at least six feminist paradigms out there, each having different political inflections.

First you had *liberal feminism,* which has been about women having equal rights alongside men. In eighteenth-century England, Mary Wollstonecraft argued for this, and of course the early twentieth-century suffragette struggle was over women's right to vote. My home state of South Australia actually gave women the vote in 1893 and even refused to join the 1901 Australian Federation unless women's right to stand for parliament was adopted by the new national Constitution. But across the world – from Kabul to Texas – there are wide disparities in the conditions that women endure. Even Switzerland did not have full universal suffrage until quite late in the twentieth century; and in the United States, or wherever abortion remains illegal, it is terribly hard for women to achieve equal opportunity.

When the left and social movement leaders refer to women's emancipation, they usually have liberal feminist reforms in mind, but this leaves the norms of masculinist culture as such unexamined.

In the 1970s, *radical feminism* appeared spontaneously among women in grassroots communities. They claimed men's domination over women to be universal and called for a new society based on matri-centric values like care. *Anarcha-feminism* took a similar line, and both collided with *socialist feminism*, which identified capitalism as the key determinant of women's oppression. Of course, if you see competitive private enterprise as simply the modern face of patriarchalism, there is no incompatibility here. Radical feminism is often confused with *cultural feminism* because each emphasises socio-cultural aspects of domination over economic ones. Then in the 1990s, as French poststructuralism became popular, cultural feminism was captured by the academy and turned to the study of power through discourse analysis. Meanwhile, from the 1980s on, *ecofeminism* had been gaining the attention of activists. It overlapped with the other feminist approaches but was wider and deeper in scope. That is to say, ecofeminist political agency was decolonial and eco-centric from the start. It was a marked paradigm shift from inside the patriarchal capitalist imperium.

To share from my own experience, the idea of an ecological feminism came to me in 1976 while opposing transnational plans for new uranium mines on Australian Indigenous country. Saving First Nation people's livelihoods was a decolonial fight. But pediatrician Dr. Helen Caldicott's lectures on environmental and medical consequences of the nuclear industry left no doubt that we needed to rethink all our socio-ecological relations. The Railway Workers Union, students, churches, and many housewives came on board in our Movement Against Uranium Mining. Just as with climate crisis today, the movement joined different sub-cultures in the conviction that protecting life on earth is the common denominator of all our politics.

This intuition was reinforced as I read the deep ecologists, Arne Naess from Norway and Bill Devall in California. The compassion these philosophers felt for the natural world was genuine and profound. Yet it was oblivious to the violence and exploitation of women and racialised peoples. I challenged the deep ecologists on this in 1984, and an extended debate ensued in the journal *Environmental Ethics*.[1] The ecologists' resistance to an eco-feminist lens led me further towards thinking in terms of transversal relations: how to integrate the political spectrum? Helping to catalyse this synthesis of worker's, indigenous', women's, and ecological politics remains the focus of my work.

You ask: 'Is ecofeminism a strand of feminism or a strand of ecology? An appeal for the connection of social movements, a counter-hegemonic discourse, or a strategic proposal for societal transformation?' It is all these things; but let's take them one by one.

Ecofeminism, at least as I see it, places feminist concerns inside ecology by adopting an *eco-centric ontology*. That is to say, it leaves conventional anthropocentric assumptions behind by acknowledging *humans-as-nature-*

*in-embodied-form*. Note that this is a materialist claim, and best articulated in the classic 1980s ecofeminist statements. At the same time, the ecology movement is subjected to feminist critique in that the 21$^{st}$-century planetary crisis is judged to be an inevitable outcome of culturally masculinist attitudes. This dialectic carries workers and indigenous politics along with it, since capitalism and coloniality are simply modern expressions of an earlier social form of patriarchal domination. Thus, ecofeminism is certainly counter-hegemonic, comprehensively so. It is a strategy for *four-revolutions-in-one:* socialist, decolonial, feminist, and ecological, the last of these being irreducible, our shared ground.

**HG:** As a follow-up to your answer, could you please indicate the points of divergence and convergence between ecofeminism, ecosocialism, and socialist and/or Marxist feminism? Is it not true that all these currents of thought share similar views regarding the injustice, violence, and ecological unsustainability of the global patriarchal capitalist system, as well as the need to overturn it? Do you agree that there needs to be a forum for the exchange of views and the discussion of differences and of points of emphasis among these different traditions for the benefit of the common cause?

**AS:** Yes, we do need to come together and examine these historically given political labels the better to clarify our common cause. Exchanges between movement strands have been happening for decades but without much progress. There was a time when I thought the emergent green parties would achieve this synthesis. But soon enough in every country, new party formations succumbed to the repressive tolerance of electoralism. At the turn of the millennium the World Social Forum held out a promise of global unity, but the movements were too unevenly developed to advance this dialogue. Back when I was an active editor of *Capitalism Nature Socialism*, I started an in-house ecofeminist collective to address this inflexibility, and in 2006 published a set of encounters with ecosocialists.[2] Today, the Global University for Sustainabilty provides an opportunity for transversalism, North-South, East-West. The international offices of the Rosa Luxemburg Stiftung and transform! europe encourage such conversations as well. But ecosocialism continues to be rather weak on feminist analysis; at the same time, Marxist feminism is often weak on ecology. Then again, both would benefit from a respectful encounter with indigenous insights.

An analysis of 'the woman question' should be essential to any democratic politics, but beyond acknowledging women as victims, the Marxist left is uncomfortable discussing patriarchal domination; and its theorists rarely refer to women thinkers. This has become a vicious circle in which ends and means are entangled. It is so important in political organising to acknowledge and neutralise *the sex-gender hegemony* that affects communication styles. Beyond this, conceptual difficulties arise because most of our radical analyses are based on technocratic constructs from sociology or political economy. These disciplines are essential to explaining the structural features of capitalism and coloniality, but they lack tools for teasing out the psycho-cultural dynamics of individual action which oils such structures. If we work exclusively with an abstract structural analysis it turns our materialism into an idealism by disengaging thought from raw experience. In tackling the hegemony of sex-gender, the structural analysis can become a political sanitisation.

The patriarchal capitalist imperium developed over time, and still functions as three systems, embedded one within the other like nested frames. The 5,000-year-old masculinist culture serves as the oldest and broadest frame, always there as a fallback. Then around 500 years ago, market economies and colonialism evolved out of it. But modern productivism remains rooted in, and energised by, its ancient base.

How to explain the persistence of this masculinist stronghold? Feminists often use a psychoanalytic vocabulary to account for the heteropatriarchal norms that pass from generation to generation. Object-relations thinkers like Nancy Chodorow would identify a stage in sex-gender development that was missed in Freud's model of the Oedipal complex. Before father identification can take place, a boy child needs to break from his felt embodiment in the maternal bond.[3] This preconscious move involves a psychological *dissociation* of Self from M/Other, the very first subject/object distinction. At least in Eurocentric history, this sublimated form of 'object relations' got to be collectively shared as a culture built on binaries. In the now globally dominant ontology, the 1/0 structure of dissociation is repeated over and over in the *othering* of everyday commonsense pairs like Man versus Woman, Humanity/Nature, Production/Reproduction, Value/Non-Value, White/Black, North/South.

This sex-gender-based hegemony was consolidated in the Abrahamic religious traditions, then rebranded in Enlightenment science, modern law, and economics. Capitalism is served well by the ancient patriarchal imaginary when women, blacks, and animals are demeaned and resourced as 'closer to nature'. The 21$^{st}$-century planetary crisis is deeply implicated in this worldwide structure of masculinist entitlement. A lot more than money is at stake for the climate denialists.

Research by the ecofeminist historian Carolyn Merchant has shown how these same tensions of disembodiment manifested in the rise of Enlightenment science and England's Royal Society, no less. By order of

King James, midwives and herbalists were hunted down and burned as 'witches'. Then the idea of nature as an 'organism' was replaced by the idea of nature as 'machine'.[4] This preconscious war against the reproductive body was fed by a fantasy of invention and control. By the twentieth century, a powerful military-industrial complex protects the virility of nation-states, and high-tech becomes the soft sell for ongoing coloniality.

Sharing this qualitative historical awareness is essential to movement transversalism. And one path into deep transformation might be consciousness-raising discussions of the kind that women practiced in the early days of Second Wave feminism. This reflexivity is already happening in a decolonial context, as settler activists commit to historical truth telling. However, there is a catch hiding in the preconscious *libidinal* dissociation, denial, and projection that still seals off the core of patriarchal domination.

The hegemonic tendency is to essentialise all our struggles as predicaments of 'humanity'. Climate politics is a case in point. But at least a breakthrough for socialist feminism is occurring with the rising popularity of books on reproductive labour. The significance of the distinction in *production versus reproduction* was ignored by left leadership for almost a half century. Yet by 1972, a wages-for-housework group had emerged around Mariarosa Dalla Costa in Italy.[5] In 1983, Hilkaa Pietilä from Finland took a similar economic critique to the United Nations.[6] Did the reluctant assimilation of such scholarship re-enact the old sex-gender dynamic? In any event, the socialist feminist point has been that free domestic labour provided by women subsidises not only a husband's capacity to gain the wage, but flows on to the generation of surplus-value for the capitalist.

An *embodied materialist* ecofeminist approach to this question of reproductive labour is broader than the usual socialist feminist one. Written in 1986, Maria Mies's analysis expanded on Rosa Luxemburg's pathbreaking world-system perspective. Investigating German colonial impacts in West Africa, Mies observed how local women lost their control of food markets to men, only to be 'civilised' by being put back into the home. At the same time, German women were turned into 'housewife consumers' of cheap African goods.[7] Inspired by her experience of life in the Global South, Mies's *subsistence perspective* anticipated the 21$^{st}$-century political popularity of degrowth, cooperatives, and food sovereignty.

Meanwhile, Vandana Shiva, a former physicist turned mother and conservationist, exposed the disastrous ecological impacts of artificial fertilisers, genetically engineered seed, and pesticides imposed on Indian farmers in the name of development. Shiva's account contrasts these so-called Green Revolution technologies with the circular economy of Indian women forest dwellers, practitioners of a vernacular science that meets human needs and catalyses healthy ecosystems at the same time. I have quoted Shiva on this many, many times, but her account of this labour – what I call ecosystem *holding* – deserves to be heard again.

> It is in managing the integrity of ecological cycles in forestry and agriculture that women's productivity has been most developed and evolved. Women transfer fertility from the forests to the field and to animals. They transfer animal waste as fertilizer for crops and crop by-products to animals as fodder. They work with the forest to bring water to their fields and families. This partnership between women's work and nature's work ensures the sustainability of sustenance.[8]

**HG:** In your work, mainly the classic *Ecofeminism as Politics* (1997/2017), you make extensive use of two concepts, 'meta-industrial class' and 'embodied materialism', which play an important role in your theory. Would you please elaborate on these?[9]

**AS:** Well, what Shiva describes above is a perfect example of *meta-industrial labour*. In our ecofeminist anthology *Eco-Sufficiency* (2009), I distil a dozen or so principles that guide this eco-centric epistemology. In each case, the regenerative labour of indigenes, mothers, gatherers, and subsistence workers reveals methodological features that make 'a good fit' with nature – to borrow indigenous ecologist Jessie Wirrpa's phrase. As you read these, think childcare, or think bioregional governance.

- The consumption footprint is small because local resources are used and monitored with daily care by the provisioner.
- Scale is intimate and hands-on, maximising responsiveness to matter/energy transformations.
- Judgments are built up over time by trial and error, a cradle to grave assessment over an intergenerational time horizon.
- This means that meta-industrial labour is intrinsically precautionary.
- Lines of responsibility are transparent and accountable – far from the tyranny of small decisions that impairs bureaucratised economies.
- As local social structures are less convoluted than modern industrial ones, there is opportunity for synergistic problem solving.
- In domestic and farm settings, multi-criteria decision-making is essential.
- Regenerative work patiently reconciles human time with unpredictable, non-linear timings in nature.

- This is an economic rationality that knows the difference between stocks and flows.
- It is an autonomous and empowering work process, without a division between the worker's mental and manual skills.
- The labour product is not alienated but immediately enjoyed or shared.
- Meta-industrial provisioning is eco-sufficient because it does not externalise costs through debt or entropy.[10]

The idea of an embodied materialism has a number of resonances. One is a pointed allusion to the linear productivism of the left and its neglect of the reproductive sphere. So too, the notion that humans-are-nature-in-embodied form directly challenges the 1/0 dissociation at the foundation of androcentric reason.

The disembodied character of patriarchal knowledge-making has preoccupied me since I was a student in the sociology of knowledge, rebelling against positivism, and later the fashion for post-structuralism. That led me into an MA thesis on varieties of dialectical thought. Certainly, I see meta-industrial labour as dialectical – an empirically grounded cycle of praxis to theory, an intuitive phenomenology, integrated and contextual, a vernacular science, a prefiguration. People working with all their senses, come to a *kinaesthetic awareness* of multiple timings materially embedded in what is handled. Holding labour is about learning to synchronise one's actions with organic growth.

**HG:** Regarding the 'meta-industrial' class, do you believe that this constitutes the 'revolutionary' subject of our era that will transform society, and at what level can this take place: national, regional, or global? What should the relation be between those who belong to this 'new' class and the so-called 'regular' workers and employees in various traditional economic sectors?

**AS:** Globally, meta-industrial labour subsidises the capitalist system by reproducing its workforce for free and keeping its natural resources in good repair; yet this subsumption – *economic and thermodynamic* – is entirely taken for granted.

Look at the 2015 United Nations Sustainable Development Goals. There is no structural analysis here of how poverty and multi-dimensional violence are historically grounded in states and corporate monopolies. Consumerism is to be the driver of development, with GDP as indicator of progress in full defiance of earth's *biophysical limits*. Science is treated as infallible, while other kinds of knowledge are marginalised. Meanwhile, governance is increasingly global and reliant on top-down technocratic models of managerialism.

But your question about the site of movement political contestation being 'national, regional, or global' possibly prioritises the spatial aspects of our politics, rather than the cultural shift that we have been exploring. The latter is a prerequisite of respectful transversal dialogue and organisation. For instance, as distinct from the capitalist logic that contrasts exchange versus use value, meta-industrials protect and create *metabolic value* or flows of life-energy.[11] Thus, while meta-labour does not need capitalism, capitalism cannot do without meta-industrial labour, and that is the global strategic power of localism.

Yes, I do talk about meta-industrial labour as a newly discovered working class, *another revolutionary subject* with its own historical agency. Significantly, the concept is inclusive of the global majority of workers, indigenous, women.[12] That is to say, they/we have the numbers! This perspective also converges with a Franciscan ethic, as well as liberation theology with its celebration of community self-reliance.

**HG:** There was a period when you were a strong proponent of the alter-globalist movement and its organisational structures like the World Social Forum. However, this movement eventually faded away. Why do you think this has happened, and do you see the possibility of its resurgence now when some people think it is more needed than ever?

**AS:** I am still a passionate *alter-global-localist*, and I see this politics renewing itself. A crucial preparation will involve addressing the tragic predicament of regular urban folk, fully dependent on, and locked into, an industrialised economic system that not only violates their own wellbeing, but simultaneously cuts down the metabolism of life-on-earth. I imagine the tension between the conventional hopes of such workers and the vision of those we call meta-industrials had a good bit to do with why World Social Forum enthusiasms faded.

An understanding of humans-as-nature-embodied displaces the false patriarchal dualisms of Humanity/Nature, Economy/Ecology. Thus, while we conventionally discuss debt in dollar terms, an embodied materialist also recognises *debt as a thermodynamic* relation, an extraction of the very life-energies through which we live and labour in biodiversity.

Perhaps the conventional left could enrich its materialist analysis and its social-justice politics, if it considered extractivisms beyond the capitalist theft of surplus value. There is surely a need to enumerate the theft of livelihood resources in the global South; the theft of unpaid embodied labour owed to women for childbearing and domestic care; the intergenerational theft victimising youth worldwide, expected to make their futures in a failing planet. We might add the predatory theft of life taken from other species; and the theft of energy flows now destabilising the earth at large. This *matrix of six debts* corresponds to the formation of political movements – socialist, decolonial, womanist, youth, animal liberation, and ecology. When you look at extractivism in this way, it shows how narrow the focus of left politics has been.

Up to this point, left advocacy of ecological modernisation, green deals, or tech fix solutions to planetary crises is not so terribly different from routine capitalist commodification of the natural environment. If radical politics is to get beyond this barely disguised Eurocentric coloniality then conversations about a transformative politics – say at the Rosa Luxemburg Stiftung or DiEM25 – will examine this dilemma. Time to be done with the old hierarchy of Natures based on dissociation, othering, and denial.

In terms of rebirthing the World Social Forum or its next incarnation, a multitude of vibrant international networks are in daily communication. Think of Ecosocialist Horizons, Degrowth, Via Campesina, Global Tapestry of Alternatives, World Women's March, WoMin, Extinction Rebellion, Fridays for Future, Minding Animals, ETC, Climate Justice Charter, and Water Warriors. Recently, a team of us brought out a compilation of social initiatives written by activists across the world. This book, *Pluriverse* (2019), was dedicated to the Zapatista ideal of 'a world in which many worlds fit.'[13] The idea of a pluriverse is not some wishy-washy liberal pluralist indulgence, as some on the left might charge. On the contrary, taking lessons from the unique cultures of othered peoples is a materialist decision. It opens a way for the affluent global North to discover forms of human provisioning that do not cost the Earth as 21st-century economies do.

As well as affirming indigenous' and women's realities, the limits of our Eurocentric political experience must be shared openly with youth. The wash up from COP26 and aftermath of the Covid pandemic is a fertile time for this re-assessment. We can't let the Oil lobby and Big Pharma, Big Data, and the Davos World Economic Forum get away with their Great Reset.

**HG:** A number of Marxists and Marxist feminists have criticised some ecofeminists for having the romantic idea that the world can change 'outside' the global capitalist system through the construction of 'alternative communities', especially in the Global South. Do you agree with this view?

**AS:** Actually, this very term 'outside of capitalism' is symptomatic of the problem we have, because nothing is outside of capitalism. Everything is joined to everything else in the ecosystem we inhabit. That said, to be democratic in our politics is to acknowledge that the Global South is the majority world; and that the South already has the skills needed to feed and preserve life-on-earth. I would call this realism. The romantics are the ones who believe the world can survive under an ecosocialism with a Green New Deal face. The Marxist metabolic rift notion argued by John Bellamy Foster is invaluable here.[14] In the days when we were all involved with the journal *Organization & Environment,* I suggested that a *prefigurative* notion of metabolic value was already to hand; but though Foster cites my work, he's not put the notion to use.

**HG:** We are in the midst of the deadly Covid-19 pandemic, and nobody knows when it will come to end. How can you explain, from an ecofeminist view, its origin, as well as its differentiated health, economic, class, gender, and regional repercussions? What are your immediate and mid-term proposals for overcoming this multiple crisis?

**AS:** Well, as you know there are competing accounts circulating on the origin of Covid-19. One proposition has it that 'modernising development' via deforestation, agroindustry, and polluting global trade, has violently disturbed the natural habitat of organisms including microbes, now forced to find new living environments among human beings. A second popular hypothesis is based on reports that the US National Institute of Allergy and Infectious Disease (NIAID) led by Dr. Anthony Fauci has been sponsoring genetically manipulated Gain-of-Function research at a facility in Wuhan, China. Certainly, numerous applications for product experimentation with corona-like material have been registered with the US Patent Office over a number of years. However, in the absence of clear information from those involved, one can only speculate on these things. A recent editorial in *The Australian* does this by noting that bio-weapons constructed as a disease virus can be mass produced at .05% of the cost of traditional weapons in terms of damage per kilometre.[15] Whatever the pandemic cause, people were hospitalised in Wuhan in October 2019; and in the same month, Johns Hopkins University and Bill Gates's GAVI vaccine alliance were looking into the practicalities of global pandemic management. It is widely known that there is an overlap of commercial interests between Big Pharma, Big Data, and the US defence sector – and their international networks include government agencies, universities, and mainstream media. A few months after the Covid-19 pandemic started, several of these corporations announced US$500 billion in profits presumably reflecting the link between lockdown directives and public reliance on the internet for everyday communications. In any event, with Big Pharma and Big Data functioning in tandem, state policy and societies at large are being restructured.

In my country, workers such as nurses, orderlies, drivers, and cleaners, mostly recent migrants, have borne the brunt of Covid-19 fatalities. A neoliberal government has become monetarist overnight, borrowing heavily to keep the private sector afloat. A policy to sustain the newly unemployed with weekly Job Seeker installments is ad hoc, on and off, and some businesses have simply pocketed Job Maker payments. Social precarity has followed from government lockdown orders; more women losing jobs than men; and along with the loneliness of home-based telework, domestic violence incidents have doubled. Schools and childcare centres have opened intermittently. Universities have been de-funded due to the loss of overseas students, and a fifth of the country's academic work force has been terminated. Unregulated outsourcing of the service economy as piecework has become the norm. Prices of basic necessities have risen sharply as long-haul supply chains are disrupted. New South Wales, the most populous and worst pandemic-affected state, has faced lockdown suburb by suburb; with failure to mask-up in public attracting a police fine. In the Outback, First Nation communities have been offered army-organised vaccination sessions. Urban youth are persuaded to 'take the jab' with free football tickets.

While there is no agreed vaccination policy across the seven Australian states, a fact that is rattling the Federal constitution, 'the jab' is recommended as compulsory for travel and workplace access – with some state parliaments excepted. People worry about losing their income source if they 'refuse consent'. Seemingly arbitrary pandemic controls, cafe closures, and cell phone surveillance as a condition of supermarket entry, have led to street demonstrations. In Victoria, the unemployed AltRight joined left-wing building workers in rolling protests against mandatory vaccination. Authorities describe them as 'a rabble of louts, gym junkies and anti-vaxers', although some of them are mothers of young children and rarely on the streets. In the above case, the state response was to close down the construction industry for two weeks so the workers lost pay. The class structure is also being hollowed out by financial policy – with super-low bank interest rates for borrowers and stimulus packages for property owners. The result is a real-estate boom that is locking the next generation out of the market. Australian society is in vertical free-fall, and counselling psychologists say they are booked weeks ahead. What needs a close investigation is whether this sociological revolution, as some are calling it, has been an incidental effect of Covid-19, or a planned 'reset', to borrow a term from the World Economic Forum.[16]

As one who served for several years on a Federal government Gene Technology Ethics Committee, I would be cautious about unknown outcomes of a genetically engineered product based on experimental Gain-of-Function technology.¹⁷ It is not possible to determine the biological effects of G-o-F interventions as these evolve in the body over decades.¹⁸ In the first instance, the global response to Covid-19 might have examined the likelihood of herd immunity through natural bodily functions. Instead, government agencies adopted new untested vaccines, approved for use under emergency provisions, often on little more than the word of Big Pharma. Meanwhile, the manufacturers indemnified themselves against prosecution for harm. The collection of Covid-19 statistics has been far from reliable and as the US Centers for Disease Control and Prevention advises, the PCR or polymerase chain reaction diagnostic test should be discontinued because it is giving false positives.¹⁹ Official statistics are counting deaths deemed 'pandemic related' with no postmortem evidence; and there is widespread confusion over how to classify post-vaccination deaths. Unfortunately, public criticism of this Covid-19 crisis management is usually dismissed as 'conspiracy thinking', a judgment applied to investigative journalists as much as to independent-minded medics. Australian politicians raising the 'human rights' aspect of crisis management have been ridiculed on social media and subjected to defamation law. Here, and in Canada I understand, a proposed vaccination passport, which would legislate two levels of citizenship into being, will be tested in court as a violation of established Nuremburg principles.²⁰

Going back to the big picture: Freud in old age fell into a deep depression while contemplating the First World War and then modified his thinking about human nature. In *Civilisation and its Discontents* he conjectured that there must be 'a death drive' innate within the species.²¹ Not only did he blindly *essentialise humanity* with this proposition, he deflected attention from the capacious, always already agency of life-affirming labours. Ecofeminists argue that this sex-gender difference is historical, formed dialectically in the early self/other process of object-relations. But the damage was long done. The left too often refuses to look into patriarchal domination on the basis that it means a descent into 'bourgeois individualist psychology'. For an embodied materialist, individual action is the very stuff that social structures are made of. An avoidance of reflexive politics only serves existing entitlement by default.

Pandemic speak is also contaminated by sex-gender. It does not belong to the logic of life, reproduction, and care. Rather, the political discourse is organised around 'a war footing', 'a statewide blitz', 'need to ramp-up', 'roll out', 'shots', 'hit the target population'. Indeed, where I live, an army general has been appointed to coordinate the crisis response. People fear they are being engineered biologically by Big Pharma, and registered digitally by Big Data for long-term global surveillance. Foucault's theory of the carceral state might have written such a script, for under the shadow of bio-political edicts, the democratic contract is close to broken.[22] I agree with Yanis Varoufakis's comment that the 21st century is heading towards techno-feudalism.[23]

With financialisation disconnected from economic provisioning, perhaps a de-growth based dual-power response is the only option left for 'we the people'? Certainly, it makes good sense to embrace the healing power of *buenvivir* and 'ways of worlding' such as an ecofeminist subsistence alternative, permaculture cooperatives and the like, commoning in whatever ways we can. Already young people on every continent are reaching out for a sane humane ecological future.

**HG:** I would like to thank you again for finding the time in your busy schedule to contribute to our 2022 yearbook. Considering how active and prolific you are, I will end by asking you about the projects – both theoretical and practical – on which you are now working.

**Ariel:** Thank you Haris, I appreciate your interest in these things. At the moment, I am badly overdue on getting a three-volume book to my publisher. This takes a closer look at relations between decolonial, ecosocialist, and ecofeminist movements, growing out of my work from the last decade. My hope is that it can bring movement activists to a deeper transversal appreciation of each other. I am especially writing for youth, on the assumption that those who do not know their history are likely compelled to repeat it!

Aside from my herb garden and support for Friends of the Earth, GeneEthics Network, and Green Left, there is no hands-on activism for me until the writing is done. The climate crisis has ignited worldwide interest in ecofeminism, and in recent months I've joined zoom events with the Catholic University of Lisbon, Political Ecologists in Slovenia, the Global University in Hong Kong, Fridays for Future in Italy, and Australian Earth Law Alliance.[24] My commitment to Nelson Mandela University in South Africa is ongoing but without travel. In 2022, I'll join Jason Hickel and others for a University of Hamburg degrowth workshop, and am advising on the art exhibition *Reclaim* for Palais de Tokyo in Paris. There is a planned Boston College panel with environmental ethicists Baird Caldicott and Michael Zimmerman based on work I did in the 80s. Closer to home, I have an upcoming seminar with Kombu-merri philosopher Mary Graham, and a peace conference at the University of New England. No doubt the AU-UK-US nuclear submarine deal will be high on the agenda.

Activism is always more fun than writing, and I want to get back to working with water. Communities contained by bioregional catchments can practice autonomous relational economies and eco-centric governance. Decentralisation allows a materialist response to climate change, as against the old 1/0 abstraction of counting carbon emissions.[25] We have to learn from First Nations people about *holding* country.[26]

NOTES

1. Ariel Salleh, 'Deeper than Deep Ecology: the ecofeminist connection', *Environmental Ethics*, 6,4 (1984): 335-341.
2. Ariel Salleh, 'Ecosocialist-Ecofeminist Dialogues', *Capitalism Nature Socialism*, 17,4 (2006): 32-124.
3. Nancy Chodorow, *The Reproduction of Mothering,* Berkeley: University of California, 1978.
4. Carolyn Merchant, *The Death of Nature: Women, and the Scientific Revolution*. New York: Harpers, 1980.
5. Mariarosa Dalla Costa and Selma James (eds), *The Power of Women and the Subversion of the Community*. Bristol: Falling Wall Press, 1972.
6. Hilkka Pietila and Kyosti Pulliainen, 'Revival of Non-monetary Economy Makes Economic Growth Unnecessary', *IFDA Dossier*, 1983, No. 35.
7. Maria Mies, *Patriarchy and Accumulation on a World Scale*. London: Zed Books, 1986.
8. Vandana Shiva, *Staying Alive: Women, Ecology, and Development*. London: Zed Books, 1989, p. 45.
9. Ariel Salleh, *Ecofeminism as Politics: Nature, Marx, and the Postmodern*, London: Zed Books, 1997/2017.
10. Ariel Salleh (ed.), *Eco-Sufficiency & Global Justice: Women Write Political Ecology*, London: Pluto Press, 2009, pp. 302-303.
11. Ariel Salleh, 'From Metabolic Rift to Metabolic Value: Reflections on Environmental Sociology and the Alternative Globalization Movement',*Organization &Environment*, 23,2 (2010): 205-219.
12. 2012 'Rio+20 and the Green Economy: Technocrats, Meta-industrials, WSF and Occupy', <http://rio20.net/en/documentos>.
13. Ashish Kothari, Ariel Salleh, Arturo Escobar, Fede Demaria, and Alberto Acosta (eds), *Pluriverse: A Post-Development Dictionary*. New Delhi: Tulika & Authors Up Front, 2019.
14. John Bellamy Foster, 'Marx's Theory of Metabolic Rift', *American Journal of Sociology* 105,2 (1999): 366-405.
15. Editorial: 'Whatever Happened in Wuhan Changed the World', *The Australian,* 21 September 2021, p. 10.
16. Klaus Schwab, *The Fourth Industrial Revolution,* New York: Currency, 2016.
17. The BioScience Resource Network, 'Statement by Scientists, Legal, and Policy Experts:Why We Need your support for a Global Moratorium on the Creation of Potential Pandemic Pathogens (PPPs) Through Gain-of-Function Experiments', 2021, <https://docs.google.com/forms/d/e/1FAIpQLSdLCylWqArvdGSWf9ad42vG4euMikB4aJ5CEiWRD-bZOumfRQ/viewform>.

18  Robert Malone, 'An interview the inventor of the mRNA vaccine', <https://www.utube.com/watch?v=iwPKnOhJRYg>.
19  CDC, 'Lab Alert: Changes to CDC RT-PCR for SARS-Cov-2 Testing', 21 July 2021, <https://www.cdc.gov/csels/dls/locs/2021/07-21- 2021-lab-alert-Changes_CDC_RT-PCR_SARS-CoV-2_Testing_1.html>.
20  Declaration of Canadian Physicians for Science and Truth, 2021, <https://canadianphysicians.org/>.
21  Sigmund Freud, *Civilisation and its Discontents*, in J. Strachey (ed.), *The Complete Psychological Works,* London: Hogarth, 1952.
22  Michel Foucault, *Power: Essential Works 1954-1984*, London: Penguin, 2001.
23  Yanis Varoufakis. 'Techno-Feudalism is Taking Over', *Project Syndicate*, 28 June 2021.
24  Ariel Salleh, Interview with Salvo Torre and Alice dal Gobbo: 'Ecofeminist Thinking on fter Covid19', Fridays for Future, Italy, April 2020, <https://www.youtube.com/watch?v=_vB7QVmZgMs>.
25  Ariel Salleh, 'Editorial: Water and the Complexities of Climate', *International Journal of Water* 5,4 (2010): 285-451.
26  Ariel Salleh, 'An Embodied Materialist Sociology' in Michael Bell, Michael Carolan, Julie Keller, and Katharine Legun (eds.), *The Cambridge Handbook of Environmental Sociology,* Cambridge University Press, 2021.

# For an Ecosocialist 'Great Transformation' – Fourteen Theses

Michael Löwy

I.

In his classic work, *The Great Transformation* (1944), Karl Polanyi described, from a critical perspective, the process through which, in the eighteenth and nineteenth centuries, the substance itself of society was subordinated to the laws of the market. Everything, including labour and land, became a commodity, and was sold in the market for its price. As Marx writes in *Capital*, thanks to free exchange, people were thrown 'beneath the wheels of the Juggernaut of capital'.[1] A Christian socialist, Polanyi called this system the 'satanic mill'. It crushed not only humans but also Nature: 'Nature would be reduced to its elements, neighbourhoods and landscapes defiled, rivers polluted, […] the power to produce food and raw materials destroyed.'[2] 'The dangers to man and nature,' argues Polanyi, 'cannot be neatly separated.'[3]

The process of general commodification described in this classic essay from 1944 has dramatically intensified during the last decades, under the hegemony of neoliberalism. Human beings and the natural environment are subjected, in a systematic and ruthless way, to the requirements of capitalist accumulation and the maximisation of profit.

What we need today is a reverse Great Transformation, breaking the iron grip of the capitalist market over human and natural life, and subordinating production and consumption to the democratic control of society. This is the meaning of the ecosocialist proposal.

Marx and Engels can be considered the forerunners of ecosocialism. In *Capital*, vol. III, Marx wrote that capitalist agriculture provoked an 'irreparable rift in the interdependent process of social metabolism' [*Stoffwechsel*] 'between man and the earth, a metabolism prescribed by the natural laws of life itself.'[4] '[…] all progress in capitalistic agriculture is a progress in the art, not only of robbing the labourer, but of robbing the soil; all progress in increasing the fertility of the soil for a given time, is a progress towards ruining the lasting sources of that fertility.'5 As John Bellamy Foster has shown, Marx and Engels were among the very few authors of the nineteenth century to understand the destructive dynamic of capitalism in relation to nature.

## II.

The ecological crisis is already the most important social and political question of the twenty-first century, and will become even more so in the coming months and years.

The future of the planet, and thus of humanity, will be decided in the coming decades. As the Intergovernmental Panel on Climate Change (IPCC) explains, if the average temperature exceeds that of the pre-industrial period by 1.5°, there is a risk of setting off an irreversible climate change process. The ecological crisis involves several dimensions – species extinction, ocean acidification, air pollution, etc. – but climate change is doubtless the most dramatic threat. What would the consequences be? Just a few examples: the multiplication of megafires such as in Australia, destroying the last remaining large forested areas on the planet; the disappearance of rivers and the desertification of land area; the melting and dislocation of polar ice and rise in sea levels, which could comprise dozens of meters. Yet, just at two meters, vast regions of Bangladesh, India and Thailand, as well as the major cities of human civilisation – Hong Kong, Calcutta, Venice, Amsterdam, Shanghai, London, New York, Rio – will have disappeared under the sea. How high can the temperature reach? At what temperature will human life on this planet be threatened? No one has an answer to these questions.

The process of climate change has already begun, and is getting worse by the year, leading to catastrophic consequences in the next decades. Calculations by certain scientists as to scenarios for the year 2100 are not very useful for two reasons: a) scientifically – because it is impossible to calculate all the feedback effects and make projections for the next century; b) politically – because, so the thinking goes, at the end of the century, all of us, our children and grandchildren will be gone. So who cares?

## III.

These are risks of a scale unprecedented in human history. One would have to go back to the Pliocene, some millions of years ago, to find climate conditions resembling what could become reality in the future due to climate change. Most geologists believe that we have entered a new geological era, the anthropocene, when conditions on the planet have been modified by human activity. The activity that affected climate change began with the eighteenth-century Industrial Revolution, but after 1973, thanks to neoliberalism, there was a qualitative leap. In other words, modern industrial civilisation is responsible for the accumulation of $CO_2$ in the atmosphere, and thus for global warming.

As Leonardo Boff, the well-known Brazilian liberation theologian, has commented:

> The Anthropocene as a new geological era was not introduced by 'humanity' but by the capitalist mode of production, in its political version of a new liberalism, especially in its radical form (the schools of Vienna and Chicago). The absolute majority of humanity is the innocent victim of this system which can lead us to a social-ecological Armageddon. For me this system cannot be reformed, but is so constituted as to lead us to the abyss, at the price of our lives. – Personal letter to the author, 18 December 2021

## IV.

The capitalist system's responsibility for the imminent catastrophe is widely recognised. Pope Francis, in his Encyclical *Laudato S'*,[6] without uttering the word 'capitalism', spoke out against the dominant economic system as responsible both for social injustice and the destruction of our Common Home, that is, Nature. For him, the dramatic ecological problems of our age are a result of 'the mechanisms of today's globalized economy' (§144), a machinery that constitutes a global system, 'a system of commercial relations and ownership which is structurally perverse' (§52).

What are, for Francis, these 'structurally' perverse characteristics? More than anything they are those of a system where 'the limited interests of businesses' (§127) and an instrumental logic understands profits as its only objective. However, 'the principle of the maximization of profits, frequently isolated from other considerations, reflects a misunderstanding of the very concept of the economy. As long as production is increased, little concern is given to whether it is at the cost of future resources or the health of the environment' (§195). This distortion, this ethical and social perversity, is not unique to any one country, but rather characterises a 'global system where priority tends to be given to speculation and the pursuit of financial gain, which fail to take the context into account, let alone the effects on human dignity and the natural environment. Here we see how environmental deterioration and human and ethical degradation are closely linked' (§56).

A slogan universally chanted the world over in ecological demonstrations is 'Change the System, not the Climate!' The attitude shown by the main representatives of this system, advocates of *business as usual* – billionaires, bankers, 'experts', oligarchs, politicians – can be summed up by the phrase attributed to Louis XV: 'After me, the deluge'.

## V.

The systemic nature of the problem is cruelly illustrated by governments' behaviour, acting, with very rare exceptions, in the service of capital accumulation, multinationals, the fossil oligarchy, general commodification, and free trade. Some of the leaders or ex-leaders of these governments – for example, Donald Trump, Jair Bolsonaro, Scott Morrison (Australia) – have been openly ecocidal climate deniers. The other 'reasonable' ones set the tone at the annual COP (Conference of the Parties) meetings, which feature vague 'green' rhetoric and total inertia. The most successful was COP 21, in Paris, which concluded with solemn promises from all participating governments to reduce emissions – promises not kept, except by a few Pacific islands. Scientists calculate that even with adherence to the goals set, the temperature would still increase by 3.3°.

The recent COP 26 (Glasgow, 2021), was another spectacular failure. While the participating governments agreed that 1.5° warming is a limit not to be superseded, the decisions taken at the Conference are in no way suited to achieve this objective. Instead of concrete measures in the next five to ten years – according to scientists a crucially necessary timespan for avoiding runaway global warming – we had beautiful promises of 'carbon neutrality' (a very misleading concept) in 2050 or even 2070 (in India). Instead of a commitment to an immediate halt to the exploitation of new sources of fossil energy, we had vague promises to 'reduce' their consumption.

## VI.

'Green capitalism', 'carbon markets', 'compensation mechanisms', 'carbon offsets', and other inventions of the so-called 'sustainable market economy' proposed by governments, international conferences, and financial institutions have proven perfectly useless.

Quoting a resolution by the Episcopal Conference of Bolivia, Pope Francis writes:

> The strategy of buying and selling 'carbon credits' can lead to a new form of speculation which would not help reduce the emission of polluting gases worldwide. This system seems to provide a quick and easy solution under the guise of a certain commitment to the environment, but in no way does it allow for the radical change which present circumstances require. Rather, it may simply become a ploy which permits maintaining the excessive consumption of some countries and sectors (§171).

While 'greenwashing' continues, emissions are skyrocketing and the 'red line' of 1.5° continues to approach. There is no solution to the ecological crisis within the framework of capitalism, a system entirely devoted to productivism, consumerism, the ferocious struggle for 'market shares', to capital accumulation, and profit maximisation. Its intrinsically perverse logic inevitably leads to the breakdown of the ecological equilibrium and the destruction of the ecosystems.

## VII.

The only effective alternatives, which would be able to avoid the worst scenarios, are radical ones. 'Radical' means attacking the root of the evil. If the capitalist system is at the root, we need anti-systemic alternatives, i.e., anticapitalist ones, such as ecosocialism, an ecological socialism up to the challenges of the twenty-first century. Other radical alternatives such as ecofeminism, social ecology (Murray Bookchin), André Gorz's political ecology, or degrowth have much in common with ecosocialism: relations of reciprocal influence have developed in recent years.

## VIII.

What is socialism? For many Marxists, it is the transformation of the relationships of production – by the collective appropriation of the means of production – to allow the free and unfettered development of productive forces. Ecosocialism lays claim to Marx but explicitly breaks with this approach and with the productivist and anti-ecological model of what used to be called 'really existing socialism'. Of course, collective ownership is indispensible, but the productive forces themselves must also be transformed: a) by changing their energy sources (renewables instead of fossil fuels); b) by reducing global energy consumption; c) by reducing production of goods ('degrowth'), and by eliminating useless activities (advertising) and harmful ones (pesticides, weapons of war); and d) by putting a stop to planned obsolescence. Ecosocialism also involves transformation, after a process of democratic discussion, of consumption models, forms of transportation, urbanism, and 'ways of life'. In short, it is much more than a change of property forms: it is a *civilisational change*, based on values of solidarity, democracy, equaliberty, and respect for nature. Ecosocialist civilisation breaks with productivism and consumerism in favour of shorter working time, thus more free time devoted to social, political, recreational, artistic, erotic, etc. activities. Marx referred to this goal by the term 'realm of freedom'.

From an ecosocialist perspective, degrowth has to be understood in dialectical terms: many production methods, for example, coal-fired facilities should not only be reduced but suppressed; some products, such as private cars, should be reduced; but others would need development, for example organic agriculture, renewable energies, health and educational services, etc. However, even the most useful activities have to respect the limits of the planet, there can be no such a thing as an 'unlimited' production of any particular good.

## IX.

To achieve the transition towards ecosocialism, democratic planning is required, guided by two criteria: meeting actual needs and respect for the ecological balance of the planet. The people – once the onslaught of advertising and the consumption obsession created by the capitalist market are eliminated – will decide, democratically, what their real needs are. Ecosocialism is a wager on the democratic rationality of the popular classes.

Society itself, and not a small oligarchy of property-owners – nor an elite of techno-bureaucrats – will be able to choose, democratically, which productive lines are to be privileged, and how much resources are to be invested in education, health, or culture. Far from being 'despotic' in itself, planning is the exercise, by a whole society, of its freedom: freedom of decision, and liberation from the alienated and reified 'economic laws' of the capitalist system, which has determined the life and death of individuals and enclosed them in an economic 'iron cage' (Max Weber). Planning and the reduction of labour time are the two decisive steps of humanity towards freedom. A significant increase of free time is in fact a precondition for the participation of the working people in the democratic discussion and management of economy and of society.

The ecosocialist conception of planning is nothing other than the radical democratisation of economy: if political decisions are not to be left to a small elite of rulers, why should not the same principle apply to economic ones?

Ecosocialist planning is therefore based on a democratic and pluralist debate, at all the levels where decisions are to be taken – different propositions are submitted to the concerned people, in the form of parties, platforms, or any other political movements, and delegates are accordingly elected.

## X.

This means a real social revolution. To carry out the ecosocialist project, partial reforms will not suffice. How can such a revolution be defined? We could cite a note by Walter Benjamin in the margins of his theses *On the concept of history* (1940): 'Marx said that revolutions are the locomotive of world history. But things might work out otherwise. It is possible that revolutions are the act by which humans travelling in the train pull the emergency brakes.'[7] Translation in twenty-first century terms: we are all passengers on a suicidal train, which is called Modern Industrial Capitalist Civilisation, a train which is speeding towards an abyss: climate change. Revolutionary action aims to halt it – before it is too late.

## XI.

Ecosocialism is at once a project for the future and a strategy for the struggle here and now. There is no question of waiting for 'conditions to ripen'. It is necessary to bring about a convergence between social and ecological struggles and fight the most destructive initiatives by powers in the service of capital. This is what Naomi Klein called *Blockadia*. Within mobilisations of this type, an anticapitalist consciousness and interest in ecosocialism can emerge during struggles. Proposals such as the Green New Deal are part of this struggle, which in their radical forms – not in those limited to recycling 'green capitalism' – require effectively renouncing fossil energy.

## XII.

Who is the subject in this struggle? The workerist/industrialist dogmatism of the previous century is not adequate to our period. The forces now at the forefront of the confrontation are youth, women, indigenous people, and peasants.

Indigenous communities, for instance in the Americas, from Canada to Patagonia, are at the forefront of the struggle against capitalist destruction of the environment, against the razing of forests and poisoning of waters. They are at the moment the socio-ecological vanguard of humanity, and their fight in defence of the Amazonian forest is of utmost importance for the future of the planet's climate. As Hugo Blanco, well-known Peruvian indigenous leader used to say: 'We have been practising ecosocialism for the last five centuries.' It is a dangerous struggle, as documented by the murder, by military thugs, of Berta Caceres, the leader of the indigenous movement in Honduras.

Women are very present in the formidable youth uprising launched by Greta Thunberg's call – one of the great sources of hope for the future. As the ecofeminists explain to us, this massive women's participation in the mobilisations comes from the fact that women are the first victims of the system's damage to the environment. Labour unions are, here and there, also beginning to get involved. This is important because, *in the final analysis, we cannot overcome the system without the active participation of urban and rural workers, who make up the majority of the population.*

## XIII.

Ecosocialism is a process that begins with concrete actions of ecological transition. These changes do not, in themselves, suppose the overcoming of capitalism, but they go against the logic of the system. A few examples:

- The public appropriation of energy production and the phasing out of fossil energies. However, the closing of coal mines, oil wells, coal-fired power stations, etc., must be followed by guaranteed employment for the workers involved.
- The progressive replacement, with the help of public subsidies, of capitalist agro-industry, based on pesticides and chemical inputs, by agro-ecology, promoted by traditional peasantries and modern cooperatives.
- The substantial reduction of meat production – an important source of carbon emissions – and consumption, particularly in the rich countries.
- The development of free public transportation, and increased space for bicycles and pedestrians, while limiting private car circulation.
- The extension, in de-centralised forms, of green energy production, from wind, sun, and water.
- An end to planned obsolescence; an obligation to produce goods that can be repaired.
- The re-localisation of production and a substantial reduction of the transport of commodities by trucks and ships.
- The funding of the ecological transition by a substantial taxation of financial, industrial, or commercial capitalist profits.
- The abolition of the debt of the Global South and financial support, by the richer countries, for the ecological transition in the poorer countries.

## XIV.

Do we have any chance of winning this battle, before it is too late? Unlike the so-called 'collapsologists' who clamorously proclaim that catastrophe is inevitable and that any resistance is futile, we think the future is open. There is no guarantee that this future will be ecosocialist – this is the object of a wager in the Pascalian sense, in which we commit all our forces, in a 'labour for uncertainty'. But as Bertolt Brecht said, with grand and simple wisdom: 'Those who fight may lose. Those who don't fight have already lost.'

NOTES

1. Karl Marx, *Capital*, vol. I, in Karl Marx and Frederick Engels, *Collected Works*, vol. 35, New York: International Publishers, p. 639.
2. Karl Polanyi, *The Great Transformation: The Political and Economic Origins of Our Time*, Boston: Beacon, 2014 (1944), p. 76.
3. Polanyi, p. 200.
4. Karl Marx, *Capital*, vol. III, New York: Vintage, 1981, pp. 949-950.
5. Marx, *Capital*, vol. I, p. 508.
6. Encyclical Letter *Laudato Si'* of the Holy Father Francis on Care for Our Common Home, <https://www.vatican.va/content/francesco/en/encyclicals/documents/papa-francesco_20150524_enciclica-laudato-si.html>.
7. Walter Benjamin, 'On the Concept of Hisotry', in Howard Eiland and Michael W. Jennings (eds), *Walter Benjamin. Selected Writings*, vol. IV 1938-1940, Cambridge MA: Harvard University Press, 2003; for marginal note see Walter Benjamin, *Gesammelte Schriften,* Frankfurt am Main: Suhrkamp, 1972, vol. I/3, p. 1232.

# Ecofeminism Now

## Anna Saave

Ecofeminism is not a solution for everything, but it is for most things.

Given the contested history of ecofeminism's reception, the proposition that ecofeminism could be a solution is provocative. Some feminist positions have long viewed ecofeminism more as a problem than anything else. Geographer Joni Seager[1] comments on the eventful history of the hotly contested field of research and activism that is ecofeminism with the relieved insight that feminist environmentalism is (finally) coming of age, thereby applauding that the baggage attached to the term ecofeminism seems finally to be left behind. Ecofeminism was first coined as a term by Françoise d'Eaubonne in her book *Le féminisme ou la mort* (Feminism or Death).[2] It emerged as a movement in the 1980s and seemed to be defunct already ten years later: 'too spiritual and in principle unfeminist' are still often voiced objections today. But what makes ecofeminism so contentious?

The approaches located within the label ecofeminism differ greatly, including varying worldviews and theoretical stances, from spiritual and theological reflections,[3] to the empirical treatment of women's roles in agrarian change in the Global South,[4] to a broadening of the conception of human-nature-relations via queer ecologies,[5] and new materialisms.[6] Within this spectrum, major controversies exist especially regarding the underlying understanding of feminism. Terms such as feminist environmentalism are posited as counter-concepts to create distance from ecofeminism while still being able to fundamentally address what concerns all of these approaches: connecting gender and nature relations and a critique of the (de)valuations and forms of oppression that are perpetuated through those relations.

In what follows, I will introduce an ecofeminist political-economy perspective that can inform social-ecological transformation projects and respective societal changes of the early 21$^{st}$ century in the Global North. To this end, I will begin with highlighting a main controversy around ecofeminism, introduce ecofeminism's historical insights, and then focus on ecofeminist political economy in particular and conclude with a remark on the expression of rage.

## For and against ecofeminism

While all ecofeminists agree that systems of oppression have to dismantled, especially patriarchy, the way to do this is a topic of debate. One can distinguish a strand of cultural ecofeminism[7] that wants to uplift women's position in society by enhancing the status of formerly devalued feminine qualities. Part of this project of altering how society values feminine vs. masculine characteristics is to connect the feminine with nature in an affirming way. It is this connection – that is at times formulated in an essentialist way – which is so often contested. And it is exactly this debate around essentialism to which ecofeminism is often reduced.

The core of the accusation from an intersectional feminist viewpoint is that the realities of women's lives become generalised through a link to nature, which leads to the concealment of overlapping relations of domination that affect women in different, sometimes contradictory ways. Moreover, linking the theorisation of the exploitation of women and nature and the accompanying attempt to conceptually give value to these domains is thought to have a spiritual, anti-scientific underpinning. The overall result of this debate has been that ecofeminist writings have been severely marginalised in academic discussion for decades.[8]

To disconnect ecofeminist critique from the allegation of a potentially misled idealisation of the connection of women to nature, feminists have tried to find other concepts that still express ecofeminist critique, such as feminist environmentalism. Feminist environmentalism[9] offers empirical data as well as societal analysis to show how women and nature are connected, not regarding their essence or intrinsic worth, but rather through social practice and material realities. New materialist ecofeminist thinkers on the other hand aim at reconceptualising 'nature in such a way that it can no longer serve as the ground of essentialism, because it is no longer the repository of unchanging truths or determining substances but is itself an active, transforming, signifying, material force'.[10] However, with spiritual practice and discourse gaining force,[11] the place of spirituality and the degree to which one should affirm or work with feminine qualities and women's (or people's) inner connection to nature will possibly remain controversial. Beyond this debate, ecofeminism has, however, contributed highly relevant critical reflections. One of those ground-breaking contributions is the critical analysis of European and Western histories through which a connection between women and nature was established in the first place.

## *The Death of Nature* as a starting point

Carolyn Merchant, in her account of the historical changes in Western European conceptions of nature, shows that nature has been historically conceptualised as female throughout most of Western Europe.[12] Until the 16th century, nature was understood as a living organism, a nourishing mother, and humans were considered a part of this nature. In what followed, this organic world view was replaced by a mechanistic one. To enable this paradigm shift, justification first had to be presented for the idea that nature can be interfered with by force, for example in order to extract mineral resources. In her work *The Death of Nature: Women, Ecology, and the Scientific Revolution*, Merchant establishes that feminine nature finally had to 'die' in the transition to the mechanistic world view and respectively that the conception of nature became separated from the assumption of nature as a living organism while the gendered conception prevailed. After the Renaissance, a masculine-mechanistic worldview replaced the earlier feminine-organic one. Within this transition, nature was subjugated, enabled by legitimation attempts that reinforced nature as feminine. Making nature available and exploitable thus became connected to making feminine-coded things exploitable. Although mostly neglected today, this historical perspective shows that the subjugation of subjects and objects considered feminine is not simply given, but follows a logic of appropriation of nature that first had to be established through historical legitimation efforts. From Silvia Federici[13] we know that the subjugation of women, reproductive practices, and the knowledge that comes with them, was also historically constitutive of capitalism in particular.[14]

What prevails as a legacy of this history until today is the more or less conscious presence of dualisms underlying Western societies and understandings of science, such as culture/nature, masculine/feminine, rational/emotional, etc.[15] Thanks to the insights of ecofeminist works such as Merchant's *Death of Nature* it is now understood that the 'female' and the 'ecological' are devalued and made invisible in similar ways. The unreflected continuation of such dualisms has manifold unsustainable and socially unjust consequences. Thus, dualistic thinking and practice need unpacking and need to be transformed. Ecofeminism offers avenues to tackle both challenges and helps to understand that embeddedness, connectedness, or dependence are not human flaws that need to be overcome to reach full subjectivity, but that they have to be recognised as essential experiences in (human) life. Ecofeminism offers to remedy dualistic abstractions and thus counters a tradition of thought that essentially abstracts from life.

In the following, I will focus on the contributions of ecofeminist radical political economy, being one strand of ecofeminism that is, due to its close interrogation of the economy and economics, particularly well positioned to contribute to the question of a social-ecological transformation. Ecofeminist materialism uses Marxian critiques of capitalism to expose and explain the parallel devaluation of women and nature. While some ecofeminist approaches historically trace the devaluation of women as natural and the devaluation of nature as feminine, such as Merchant does, or foreground empirical analyses for these connections,[16] ecofeminist materialism, by contrast, uses the functional involvement of women and nature, or femininely connoted and naturalised subjects and domains, in the accumulation of capital to explain their devalued status. As Johanna Oksala points out: 'The systemic character of the connection between gender oppression and environmental devastation becomes discernible once we recognize the indispensable function that the naturalization of women's reproductive labour plays in contemporary capitalism.'[17] This approach has particular relevance for socio-ecological transformations because it analyses the ecological, gendered, and racialised material foundations and their profit-enhancing contributions to capital accumulation, which have been omitted in mainstream economics and for a long time also in Marxist theories.[18]

### Ecofeminism as ecofeminist political economy

Socio-ecological transformation is a technical term that refers to what one might sum up as humanity's current central project: staying alive while keeping the planet safe and healthy. We are all aware of climate change as well as other critical processes, such as ocean acidification or the loss of biodiversity around the globe. These developments pose the question: How can we, as individuals, as European nation-states, and trans-European movements and institutions, organise human life on earth in a sustainable and equitable way? In answering this question, ecofeminism is insightful as it especially brings to the table perspectives involving devalued and invisiblised aspects as well as the permanent thinking in terms of power structures. Ecofeminists connect staying alive with the questions of how to live well in and with nature and fellow human beings.

Theorists and activists from this sphere of ecofeminist radical political economy[19] connect the cultural subordination of nature, women, and colonies to the economic devaluation of processes and activities attributed to them.[20] They understand capitalism as a system encompassing both an 'inside' of the capitalist mode of production, in which exploitation of workers for generating profits takes place, as well as an 'outside', in which people's (re)productive capacities as well as natural resources and other ecological services are appropriated for free, thereby enabling profits in markets.[21] This implies differences between the formal economy and things that are perceived to be outside of it. Yet, both realms are connected – a fundamental relation that has to be accounted for when designing projects and policies for socio-ecological transformations.

Feminist analyses have shown how some processes and activities are similarly devalued in and excluded from the formal economy – this applies especially to the work of social reproduction, care work, and ecological processes.[22] These processes and activities, while unpaid or poorly paid, and mostly unrecognised, are not actually separate from the formal economy or from capitalism's 'inside'; they only appear as separate. This is the result of a theoretical neglect in the economics discipline as well as a cultural recognition bias and the absence of the practical valuation of things coded as part of an 'outside'. Overall, this leads to a dis-embedded economy – an economy that seemingly works on its own based on commodity production and wage labour. Through the lens of ecofeminist theories of *appropriation*[23] and *externalisation*[24] this dis-embedding can be identified and critiqued.

## Appropriation

One stream of ecofeminist literature converges around the term 'appropriation' with regard to accumulation. Within this literature, feminist sociologists Maria Mies, Claudia von Werlhof, and Veronika Bennholdt-Thomsen contributed the 'subsistence perspective' in the 1980s and 1990s. Originally, the subsistence perspective was intended as a contribution to the wages-for-housework debate of the 1970s. Taking up the feminist Marxist concern for incorporating unwaged female work into an analysis of capitalism, the subsistence perspective assumed that the capitalist mode of production 'permanently needs new wage workers who are living, healthy, strong, not hungry, washed and clean, as well as sexually satisfied, to be able to suck dry their labour power'.[25] As seen from the subsistence perspective, appropriation occurs when the capitalist mode of production makes use of various resources gratis in order to generate profits. Other scholars refer to similar dynamics, as for example David Harvey, who later used the term accumulation by dispossession.[26] However, the three authors offer a feminist, class- and race-conscious reading of appropriation while connecting their analysis to ecological problems, which makes their contribution stand out.

Shaping a society and an economic system that is not based on the 'exploitation of people and nature'[27] motivated the subsistence approach. Its authors intervened in a discussion taking place since Karl Marx introduced his critique of political economy. Marx used the term original (sometimes called primitive) accumulation to describe the process of the beginning of the capitalist mode of production. For the case he studied, England in the 16th century, original accumulation meant that farmers were separated from their land and possessions. As a consequence, two classes of people within society formed: capitalists, who are defined by owning or controlling the means of production, employing workers and making profits, and wage workers, who ended up owning neither land nor the means of production and thus have to sell their labour power. This results in the antagonism between the profit seeking interests of so-called capitalists and workers. The scholars working from the subsistence perspective agree to a critique of political economy,[28] but – building on the substantial contribution of Rosa Luxemburg to the understanding of accumulation with regard to non-capitalist spheres[29] – they question that there are only two relevant classes. What about farmers working in subsistence agriculture in the Global South? What about housewives, or at a more general level, what about all work that is not wage labour? These subsistence producers are neither completely inside nor outside the wage relation and are thus affected by original accumulation in a specific way: their work is appropriated under capitalist conditions but not through the wage relation.

The authors of the subsistence perspective furthermore transfer the concept of the colony from colonised countries and peoples to women's work and nature. They propose to understand capitalism's 'outside' as three colonies: women, the environment, and subsistence workers in the Global South are alike in their function for the accumulation of capital.[30] The outcomes of housework, production in the colonies, and processes of the natural environment are made use of gratis or merely for a meagre and unsustainable compensation. However, the three colonies serve as an enabling condition for making profits. Women and nature are claimed like colonies for profit maximisation and are 'defined into nature'.[31] It is the specific logic of gaining access to their resources and/or services that makes the three colonies comparable, while appropriation – as either an incorporating or predatory process[32] – is the dynamic that puts the three colonies to use for capitalist accumulation.

Drawing a connection between work/resources that are invisible from the perspective of capitalist markets, but still generate profits on those markets, and showing how these relations are structured and devalued along gendered and racialised lines is the landmark contribution of the subsistence perspective. By pointing to processes of appropriation which do not follow the capitalist-wageworker axis, an ecofeminist perspective contributes to a decentring of the exploitation of wage work and to a more encompassing perspective. It is continually necessary to take into account all things appropriated from capitalism's 'outside' as if they were a colony; otherwise the project of re-embedding economies today cannot succeed.

## Externalisation

A complementary ecofeminist perspective is centred around the concept of externalisation. The term externalisation is often used in the context of microeconomics, where it refers to externalities as unintended consequences of economic actions. In the mainstream view, externalities can exist between two economic actors, for example two businesses,[33] of which at least one produces uncompensated external effects on the other during the production process. The ecofeminist reading goes beyond this narrow interpretation of the concept. From a feminist perspective, it is especially the unwaged work (re)producing workers who become the focus of critiques of externalisation, which already goes beyond the framework of formal 'economic actors' producing unintended externalities. To remain within the terminology of mainstream economics, one could say that workers, people who are willing and able to work, are produced and maintained within households, families, and communities. Workers are often paid a wage that secures their lives, but whatever the level of the wage is, it is a compensation for the present and doesn't cover the 'costs', the time or even the work and skill needed to 'produce' and 'maintain' those workers, as feminists have long pointed out.[34] This means that social reproduction and care work can be interpreted as positive externalities,[35] since businesses, and employers more generally, can actually find people to employ. The 'positive externalities' originating from reproductive work have been a point of intervention for feminist analyses, since this work is not only the basis of our societies, but also enables people to be workers. Yet the bulk of this work does not take place within markets, but is externalised from the formal economy. From a feminist perspective, therefore, the positive 'externalities' of reproductive and care work are not to be misunderstood as events of 'accidental' market failure, but as a structural constellation of capitalism as a system that makes use of a capitalist 'inside' and of its 'outside' in various but complementary ways.[36]

Biesecker and von Winterfeld make another, specific point about externalisation.[37] Externalisation is more than the structural occurrence of external effects and the cost shifting to capitalism's outside. It also takes place through a constant separating of the market economy from traditionally female work, subsistence work, and processes of the natural environment. This separation is visible in economic valuation – some activities and things carry a monetary value while others do not. Biesecker and von Winterfeld emphasise that externalisation as a continued separation is a basic principle of capitalist economies supporting capitalist accumulation because it excludes some activities or things from economic valuation. Externalisation requires categorisations about what is 'truly' economic – this usually only includes trade on markets, waged labour and commodity production.[38] Through this facet of externalisation, which is essentially a separation of aspects/subjects/things included or excluded in the formal market economy, power relations, too, are made permanent, because dualisms like production vs. reproduction are reproduced.[39] What is considered reproductive is further externalised, leading to externalised aspects being perceived as outside of the economic realm and as having no value. Externalisation as a separation principle goes hand in hand with non- or de-valuation that makes externalised parts cheap and cheap to use. Reproductive processes and activities are, however, a condition of possibility for economic activity, argue Biesecker and von Winterfeld and fellow ecofeminists, and their value is thus immense and far from nil. Compared to the externalities framework in mainstream economics, externalisation as seen from an ecofeminist standpoint, does not describe 'single phenomena' of market failure but occurs continuously and structurally. Therefore, the problem of a dis-embedded economy must also be looked at from an externalisation perspective in order to be able to reverse effects caused by it.

The ecofeminist thinker Ariel Salleh interprets externalisation as debt.[40] She points out that in the context of re-embedding market economies people usually do not think about debt, precisely because ecological processes and the unpaid human activities of social reproduction and care work are perceived as external to or as separated from the formal market economy. If we combine these perspectives, externalisation as an economic principle has three functions: First, it serves to save costs through making use of the positive externalities stemming from activities of social reproduction, care work, and natural processes. Second, through the principle of externalisation being visible through selective economic valuation and requiring categorisations of having/producing value vs. being valueless we get the perpetuation of societal power relations and dualisms such as the dualism of productive vs. reproductive. And, third, externalisation serves as a practical means to cover up debt – to conceal the fact that the formal market economy is actually indebted to 'women and the environment' and relies on the appropriation of their contributions.

## The challenge of speaking up/being heard

The ecofeminist disentanglement of both appropriation and externalisation dynamics in the context of capitalist utilisation has been available for many decades now, but it has still hardly trickled down into realpolitik. While this is true for many left-oriented forms of societal critique due to the hegemony of (neo)liberal thought, I want to highlight specific challenges for ecofeminist critiques to be voiced and heard.

Environmental problems are an expression of a crisis of society-nature-relations.[41] From the point of view of social-ecological research, it does not make sense to consider social and environmental problems as independent of each other. Since the 1970s, ecofeminists have emphasised this by critically describing relations between the individual, society, and nature, showing that *gendered and racialised* society-nature-relations underlie the sustainability problems we experience today.[42] However, adding the layer of gender and race to society-nature-relations seems to be a step that is too provocative, or even too complex for Western societies, and so this has not reached a larger audience. Revealing gendered patterns of socio-environmental problems was never an easy thing to do, as the story of Rachel Carson exemplifies.

In her book *Silent Spring*,[43] Carson pointed early on to the connection of the ways in which both nature and women have been neglected and devalued in economics, politics, and science.[44] As she showed in her seminal work and also through the tragedies that affected her own biography, societies tend to look away from the socio-ecological disasters they cause. Carson highlighted the dangers of toxic rain caused by industrial emissions that would harm bird life and forests, possibly in a way that forests would become silent, with no more birdsong to be heard. The toxic substances in the rain were also likely to affect humans similarly and in subtle ways. During her lifetime, Carson, who was a well acclaimed ecologist, kept her own illness secret – she suffered from breast cancer. Carson remained silent about her illness because she did not want others to doubt her professional judgement on the matter of the ecological crisis and the dangers to bird life by appearing to be personally affected by the toxic outcomes of the industrial production that she criticised. Carson chose to be silent to be able to communicate the message of the danger of a silent spring to the public. Today, more than five decades later, we know that toxic substances carried in rain not only affect sensible bird species but can also cause cancer.[45] Carson's story exemplifies that speaking up from the position of someone who is experiencing a socio-ecological disaster that calls for ecofeminist critique is harder than criticising symptoms separately. Combined with the open misogyny at her time, she had to conceal that she was affected as a woman to be listened to as a scientist.

Up to the present day, it has remained a challenge to speak up from the experience of a woman – not only since, up to the present, speaking as a woman does not equal speaking as a human being but also since the notion of the unity of all women has become contested (for good reasons!). These challenges remain exacerbated for women of colour and indigenous women, who face prejudice in multiple ways and thus often have to work even harder to be heard. The difficulty of being heard might explain to some extent why the voicing of ecofeminist critique is sometimes delivered as if it were an academic performance rather than a societal critique that is also informed by personal experience. Yet some branches of ecofeminism challenge the male-mode of academic critique, for example when Donna Haraway[46] advocates for a 'storytelling for earthly survival', or when Susan Griffin[47] communicates through an affect-centred and poetic mode of critique in her book *Women and Nature. The Roaring Inside Her* the insidious ways in which patriarchy exerts violence and covers up that violence, thereby sparking a roaring, almost tangible rage within the reader.

## The place and power of rage

As a final step, let me point out the importance of rage in bringing ecofeminism to the table. Like many other feminisms, ecofeminism has been a field in which people, women like Susan Griffin, felt it necessary to express rage. This aspect might seem like a leap of scale – from socio-economic structures to the realm of personal expression and psychology – but it is actually essential. Rage is an emotion that is often misunderstood as purely negative. However, feeling rage shows the individual when a boundary is crossed. For those in society who are usually expected to absorb tension, mediate difficult emotions and serve as a scapegoat, this means especially for women, people of colour, and other subjects socially positioned as inferior, that rage is an emotion that serves to create distance to oppressive dynamics. Sensing and expressing rage can be used as an emancipatory tool that first creates space within the individual and then in groups and societies as a whole – space needed to critically examine and take action against the current mode of production and consumption. Rage can be pacified, mostly through shame. And shaming the expression of female rage still functions as the main vehicle for keeping patriarchy in place.[48] Therefore, ecofeminists of all genders should lead with rage – a rage that supersedes buying into the logic of externalisation-appropriation, a rage that is a signifier showing that the re-centring of life-creating work and processes is necessary. I am talking about a rage that is directed against economic and societal structures, not against individuals. Rage helps to feel and to embody the truth that we all need to be more free of racist, heterosexist patriarchy and of the belief that humans are a more important species. This inner motivator is a force that can carry the project of crafting an 'ecofeminism as politics'[49] for the 21st century. Yet, too often the open and enraged confrontation of patriarchy is perceived as so odd that women are likely to refuse supporting the one speaking up and are quick to distance themselves from the scene of conflict in order not to have to deal with their own patriarchal wounds and possible complicity. It is time for all of us to confront patriarchy jointly and to work towards social movements that go beyond single issues.[50] One way of doing this is to support ecofeminist whistle-blowers such as Rachel Carson.

## Conclusion: What to keep in mind for Europe's transformation challenges

If one combines the two perspectives mentioned earlier – externalisation and appropriation – in their ecofeminist reading, one thing becomes clear: The externalisation of costs combined with the drawing of a boundary between productive and reproductive realms, and the capitalist appropriation of those aspects of life that have been defined as reproductive, are two sides of the same coin. Appropriation and externalisation are functionally intertwined, and ecofeminism is uniquely positioned to grasp this relation, as its main project is to make visible the oppression of women, nature, and racialised people – all of them being the object of capitalist appropriation and efforts at externalisation. The dynamics of appropriation and externalisation both function as means to keep costs low, first by externalising some parts and then by appropriating them at next to zero cost. This double mechanism serves as a condition of possibility for the goal of realising profits in markets under capitalist circumstances. And it serves to preserve power relations that continue accumulation on the basis of externalisation and appropriation into the future.

The question remains of how this knowledge can be used to re-embed the economy and work towards socio-ecological transformations. I already mentioned Salleh's interpretation of the appropriation of contributions from externalised parts of society as debt. The capitalist global economy works because at some points debt is created and never paid back. Salleh's interpretation raises the question whether the whole debt needs to be repaid. Would it be possible and helpful to repay this debt? In my opinion, this is not what one should aim for and it is not even possible. It is not possible to repay the debt created because making profits is only possible precisely because there is this debt. We can never redistribute all the profits created by the few to make up for the debt experienced in many quarters and environments because those profits are a fiction. Profits in the market economy only appear as profits if one chooses to eliminate ecological processes, social reproduction, and care work as well as production in the colonies completely from the picture – to externalize them. At the same time, profits in the formal economy are very real and allow a small segment of the global population to use up large parts of nature at the expense of many others. The important note here is to not fall into the 'trap of capitalist valuation'.[51] Instead, the (eco)feminist idea would be not to value reproductive work for the ability to produce profit or its contribution to the production of workers, but rather to enhance the capacities for producing and reproducing life and also to abolish arrangements that continually produce and rely on the production of negative externalities affecting the (re)production of life.

Being aware of the partly fictitious character of profits, what follows from this feminist perspective if we still want to socio-ecologically transform the economy? First and foremost, the illusion has to be revealed, that profits originate from market economies alone. Pretending that the capitalist mode of production and therefore most enterprises and national economies are not indebted to nature and social reproduction has to stop right now. This disillusion is the necessary first step for an ecofeminist re-structuring of European societies. Politicians, economists, and civil society have to begin to ask the question: How can we create another economy that doesn't need to rely on the fiction of profits and the cover-up of debts? How can we provide for the needs of individuals and societies without relying on the uncompensated appropriation and cost-saving externalisation of work, both across global value chains and (especially via the appropriation of reproductive work) also amidst European societies?

Only if all take part in the project of creating an emancipatory socio-ecological transformation that is aware of the debt-relationships around the capitalist mode of production and the double mechanisms of externalisation-appropriation, can we provide space for real alternatives to come to life. Only when we are aware of those relations can we support and empower the people who live in the complex niches striving for change which are neither inside nor outside the capitalist mode of production. Only if we free economic thinking from the fiction of profits being generated on markets alone can a social-ecological transformation take place, which does not block what so many individuals and movements are already struggling to create. To say it in the words of Rachel Carson: Ours is 'an era dominated by industry, in which the right to make a dollar at whatever cost is seldom challenged'.[52] Ecofeminist insights call for the challenging of this right and thus critically inform the societal project of a socio-ecological transformation.

As Fraser points out, we cannot be satisfied anymore with 'single-issue' social movements.[53] Although ecofeminism, by the components in its name – 'eco' and 'feminism' –, only includes two themes, it actually encompasses manifold struggles in its tradition of thought and social movement practice. Ecofeminism also includes an expanded view of labour. Possibly the future will see labour movements of earthcare[54] – one of many inspirations which arose from ecofeminism. Ecofeminism realised that reproductive labour holds a certain potentiality,[55] which resists capitalist industrial modernity and the 'master model' of humanity.[56] The political outcome of recentring around this potentiality is not predetermined, but has to be crafted step by step by social and political movements from the left, including ecofeminism. It is a false story backed by a specific social organisation of work that leads one to believe that only the productive forces create wealth and are able to feed people and enable a modern society even though they free-ride on reproductive forces. Ecofeminism helps – because it helps us adopt a worldview that is not based on externalisation, on the conscious/unconscious not-knowing of the basis of creating life. It thus helps not to ruin the planet and in this process to struggle for equal relationships and transnational solidarity.

Donna Haraway once said that all movements and eras need a good slogan, which is a bit peculiar for a scientist, as producing slogans is often understood as the opposite of pure and neat academic analyses. Taking up this pragmatic-provocative approach, ecofeminists call the radical left to re-examine their practice through ecofeminist eyes and in so doing join our enraged and engaged movement: 'Ecofeminism is not a solution for everything, but it is for most things.'

NOTES

1   Joni Seager, 'Rachel Carson Died of Breast Cancer: The Coming of Age of Feminist Environmentalism', *Signs: Journal of Women in Culture and Society* 28,3 (2003): 945–972.
2   Francoise D'Eaubonne, *Le Féminisme Ou La Mort*, Paris: Payot, 1974.
3   Winona LaDuke, 'The Indigenous Women's Network: Our Future, Our Responsibility', Estelle B. Freedman (ed.), *The Essential Feminist Reader*, New York: Random House, 2007, pp. 405–408; Rosemary Ruether, 'Religious Ecofeminism: Healing the Ecological Crisis', Roger S. Gottlieb (ed.), *The Oxford Handbook of Religion and Ecology*, Oxford: Oxford University Press, 2009.
4   Bina Agarwal, 'The Gender and Environment Debate: Lessons from India', *Feminist Studies* 18,1 (1992): 119-158.
5   Catriona Mortimer-Sandilands, 'Unnatural Passions?: Notes Toward a Queer Ecology', *Invisible Culture* 9,9 (2005): 1–22.

6 Donna Haraway, *Primate Visions: Gender, Race, and Nature in the World of Modern Science*, New York: Routledge, 1989; Donna Haraway, *Staying with the Trouble: Making Kin in the Chthulucene*, Durham, London: Duke University Press, 2016; Stacy Alaimo, 'Ecofeminism without Nature?', *International Feminist Journal of Politics* 10,3 (2008): 299–304.

7 Kathryn Miles, 'Ecofeminism', *Encyclopedia Britannica*, 2018.

8 Seager, 'Rachel Carson Died of Breast Cancer'; Greta Gaard, 'Ecofeminism Revisited: Rejecting Essentialism and Re-Placing Species in a Material Feminist Environmentalism', *Feminist Formations* 23,2 (2011): 26–53; Ariel Salleh, *Ecofeminism as Politics: Nature, Marx and the Postmodern*, London: Zed Books, 1997.

9 Seager, 'Rachel Carson Died of Breast Cancer'.

10 Alaimo, 'Ecofeminism without Nature?', 302.

11 J. Santamaría-Dávila et al., 'Women's Ecofeminist Spirituality: Origins and Applications to Psychotherapy', *Explore (NY)* 15,1 (2019): 55–60.

12 Carolyn Merchant, *The Death of Nature: Women, Ecology and the Scientfic Revolution*, London: Wildwood House, 1982.

13 Silvia Federici, *Caliban and the Witch*, Brooklyn, NY: Autonomedia, 2004; Silvia Federici, *Aufstand aus der Küche. Reproduktionsarbeit im globalen Kapitalismus und die unvollendete feministische Revolution*, Münster: edition assemblage, 2012.

14 See Maria Mies, *Patriarchy and Accumulation on a World Scale: Women in the International Division of Labour*, London: Zed Books, 1986; Salleh, *Ecofeminism as Politics*.

15 SeeVal Plumwood, *Feminism and the Mastery of Nature*, London and New York: Routledge, 1993.

16 Seager, 'Rachel Carson Died of Breast Cancer'; Agarwal, 'The Gender and Environment Debate'.

17 Johanna Oksala, 'Feminism, Capitalism, and Ecology', *Hypatia* 33, no. 2 (2018), p. 220.

18 Nancy Fraser, 'Behind Marx's Hidden Abode', *New Left Review* 86 (2014), 55–72.

19 Mies, *Patriarchy and Accumulation on a World Scale*; Salleh, *Ecofeminism as Politics*; Anna Saave, *Einverleiben und Externalisieren. Zur Innen-Außen-Beziehung der kapitalistischen Produktionsweise*, Bielefeld: transcript, 2021.

20 Veronika Bennholdt-Thomsen, Maria Mies, and Claudia von Werlhof, *Frauen, Die Letzte Kolonie. Zur Hausfrauisierung Der Arbeit*, Reinbek bei Hamburg: Rowohlt-Taschenbuch-Verlag, 1988.

21 Saave, *Einverleiben und Externalisieren*.

22 Adelheid Biesecker and Uta von Winterfeld, 'Extern? Weshalb und inwiefern moderne Gesellschaften Externalisierung brauchen und erzeugen', *Working Paper Der DFG-KollegforscherInnengruppe Postwachstumsgesellschaften*, no. 2 (2014), pp. 1–16.

23 Claudia von Werlhof, *Was haben die Hühner mit dem Dollar zu tun?*, München: Verlag Frauenoffensive, 1991; Maria Mies, 'Hausfrauisierung, Globalisierung, Subsistenzperspektive', in Marcel van der Linden and Karl Heinz Roth (eds.), *Über Marx Hinaus,* Hamburg: Assoziation A, 2009, pp. 255–290; Saave, *Einverleiben und Externalisieren*.

24 Biesecker and von Winterfeld, 'Extern?'; Salleh, *Ecofeminism as Politics*; Anna Saave-Harnack, 'Die Care-Abgabe. Ein Instrument Vorsorgenden Wirtschaftens?', in David Johannes Petersen et al. (eds), *Perspektiven einer Pluralen Ökonomik*, Wiesbaden: Springer VS, 2019, pp. 367–393.

25 Mies, 'Hausfrauisierung, Globalisierung, Subsistenzperspektive', p. 263.
26 David Harvey, *The New Imperialism*, Oxford and New York: Oxford University Press, 2003.
27 Bennholdt-Thomsen, Mies, and von Werlhof, *Frauen, Die Letzte Kolonie*, p. III.
28 Mies, 'Hausfrauisierung, Globalisierung, Subsistenzperspektive'; von Werlhof, *Was haben die Hühner mit dem Dollar zu tun?*
29 Rosa Luxemburg, *Die Akkumulation Des Kapitals. Ein Beitrag Zur Ökonomischen Erklärung Des Imperialismus, Gesammelte Werke Band 5. Ökonomische Schriften,* Berlin: Dietz Verlag, 1990, pp. 5–411.
30 Oksala, 'Feminism, Capitalism, and Ecology', p. 223.
31 Maria Mies, *Patriarchat und Kapital*, München: bge-verlag, 2015, p. 130.
32 Saave, *Einverleiben und Externalisieren*.
33 Or a company and its customers, for example by reducing the staff of a call centre, which increases the wait time to be connected.
34 Mariarosa Dalla Costa and Selma James, *Die Macht der Frauen und der Umsturz der Gesellschaft*, Berlin: Merve, 1973.
35 Saave-Harnack, 'Die Care-Abgabe'.
36 Fraser, 'Behind Marx's Hidden Abode'; Saave, *Einverleiben und Externalisieren*.
37 Biesecker and von Winterfeld, 'Extern?'.
38 Adelheid Biesecker and Uta von Winterfeld, 'Wertlos? Zur Ausgrenzung Natürlicher Produktivität und Weiblicher Arbeit bei John Locke und Adam Smith', *Bremer Diskussionspapiere zur institutionellen Ökonomie und Sozial-Ökonomie*, no. 58 (2004), p. 29.
39 Biesecker and von Winterfeld, 'Extern?'; Adelheid Biesecker and Sabine Hofmeister, *Die Neuerfindung des Ökonomischen: Ein (re)produktionstheoretischer Beitrag zur sozial-ökologischen Forschung*, München: oekom Verlag, 2006.
40 Salleh, *Ecofeminism as Politics*.
41 Egon Becker and Thomas Jahn, *Soziale Ökologie: Grundzüge einer Wissenschaft von den gesellschaftlichen Naturverhältnissen*, Frankfurt: Campus Verlag, 2006.
42 Maria Mies and Vandana Shiva, *Ökofeminismus. Beiträge zur Praxis und Theorie*, Zürich: Rotpunkt-Verlag, 1995.
43 Rachel Carson, *Silent Spring*, Boston: Mifflin, 1962).
44 Seager, 'Rachel Carson Died of Breast Cancer'.
45 Song Wu et al., 'Substantial Contribution of Extrinsic Risk Factors to Cancer Development', *Nature* 529,7584 (2016): 43–47.
46 For example, Haraway, *Staying with the Trouble: Making Kin in the Chthulucene*.
47 Susan Griffin, *Woman and Nature: The Roaring Inside Her*, New York: Harper & Row, 1978.
48 Bethany Webster, *Discovering the Inner Mother. A Guide to Healing the Mother Wound and Claiming Your Personal Power*, New York: Harper Collins, 2021.
49 Salleh, *Ecofeminism as Politics*.
50 Nancy Fraser, 'Climates of Capital. For a Trans-Environmental Eco-Socialism', *New Left Review* 127 (2021): 94–127.
51 Stefania Barca, *Forces of Reproduction: Notes for a Counter-Hegemonic Anthropocene*, Cambridge: Cambridge University Press, 2020.
52 Carson, *Silent Spring*, p. 13.
53 Fraser, 'Climates of Capital'.

54  See Barca, *Forces of Reproduction*.
55  See Ariel Salleh, 'The Meta-Industrial Class and Why We Need It', *Democracy & Nature* 6,1 (2000): 27–36.
56  Plumwood, *Feminism and the Mastery of Nature*; see also Christel Neusüß, *Die Kopfgeburten der Arbeiterbewegung oder die Genossin Luxemburg bringt alles durcheinander*, Hamburg: Rasch und Röhring Verlag, 1985.

European Country Reports

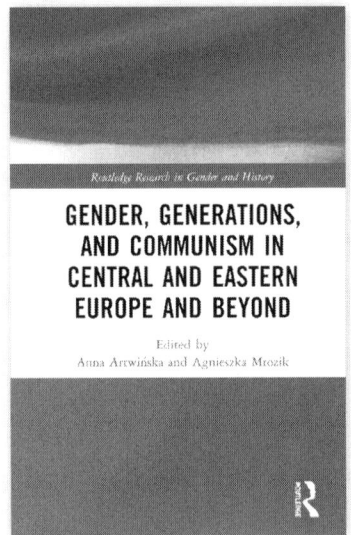

# Gender, Generations, and Communism in Central and Eastern Europe and Beyond

edited by Anna Artwińska, Agnieszka Mrozik

Publisher: Routledge
(July 2020)
Language: English
ISBN-10: 0367423235
ISBN-13: 978-0367423230

The book aims to go beyond the narrative about a totalitarian nature of communism in twentieth-century Europe, and provide an alternative framework to describe the communist past. This reframing is possible thanks to the concepts of generation and gender, which are used in the book as analytical categories in an intersectional overlap. The publication covers twentieth-century Poland, Czechoslovakia/Czech Republic, the Soviet Union/Russia, former Yugoslavia, Turkish communities in West Germany, Italy, and Cuba (as a comparative point of reference).

# Neoliberal Hysteresis: Lessons from Bulgaria's Abortive Vaccination Campaign

## Jana Tsoneva

On a cold December morning in 2020, the dry ice boxes containing the long awaited first batches of mRNA vaccines landed in Bulgaria. They were met with a stately delegation, but soon solemnity turned into farce when a fridge truck owned by a popular wurst factory showed up to take the jabs on the last leg of their journey. Denying the shots the respect they deserve triggered near-universal indignation and accusations that the government did not take Covid-19 and the few tools available to fight it seriously. (It also gave rise to popular jokes. 'Q: What is common to jabs and wieners? A: That we don't know what's inside them.')

Now a year after the first vaccines were received, Bulgaria tops all excess mortality charts in Europe while trailing behind most countries in vaccine coverage with barely 20% of its population fully vaccinated (and a thriving market for fake certificates which skews these statistics); and a group of rabid anti-vaxxers attacked a vaccination point in the city of Varna in late September. How can we explain the abysmal failure of the Covid vaccination campaign in a country that has traditionally seen little to none of the general anti-vaxx phenomenon plaguing public healthcare in the West; a country that mandates a plethora of vaccines for all children that people mostly accept without questioning? In this article I venture some hypotheses, grounded in empirical research conducted among 'vaccine sceptics' in Bulgaria.

My aim is not to excuse scepticism of the advances in modern medical technology but to understand it in order to better counter it. But I also regret that the discussion around vaccination has drawn attention away from non-pharmacological means of combating the virus, such as lockdowns. As usual, technology (whether apps or vaccines) substitutes for a politics of elimination for the sole reason that it does not hurt business interests.

## The survey

In an attempt to gain insight into vaccine hesitancy, I drafted a survey and circulated it among one of the largest anti-vaxx groups on Facebook. It was filled out by 27 people before an admin took it down to de-escalate a row over the 'methodology'. I do not claim that the survey is in any way representative except for a tiny section of the denizens that filled it out. In any case, it gathered data on what makes people anxious about vaccines, which is worth exploring. The survey gathered basic demographic data (age, income, education) and probed users on a variety of questions concerning vaccines (not only against Covid) and their experience with the Bulgarian healthcare system. It also cross-checked these opinions with positions users take on other polarising political issues, such as the Istanbul Convention on Preventing and Combating Violence Against Women and Domestic Violence and sexual education in schools, to see if there is any overlap between popular conservative positions and the anti-vaxx sentiment.

The survey's backdrop was an article profiling the 'typical' anti-vaxxer published in the largest liberal online news outlet, *Dnevnik*, which triggered a wave of indignation among group members. The article, based on a Eurobarometer survey, argued that the 'typical' anti-vaxxer is a poorly educated working-class mother of two in her 30s and 40s.[1] (It did not include the intriguing discovery resulting from our survey that the less educated a person is, the more he or she believes that getting inoculated against Covid-19 is a civic duty.) This framing reflects a widespread faultline in current Covid debates pitting 'uneducated, tabloid-soaked populists' against the 'responsible, informed, and trusting citizens', often of liberal persuasion, opting for vaccines. Yet the Facebook group members claimed the article does not represent them adequately and cited high educational qualifications and career achievements behind their hesitancy. In my survey almost 50% defined themselves as 'middle-class', with 7.4% and 11% belonging to the entrepreneurial class and the intelligentsia, respectively. 25% own their business and only 3 respondents engage in menial (or unskilled) labour. A sizable 60% have a university degree (of them more than 20% have more than one degree). This makes for an interesting 'tension' or 'rift' in the official 'anti-anti-vaxx' discourse in Bulgaria which needs to be explored. While the majority of Bulgarians are not vaccinated, and the majority in every country tend to be the class living from labour, it is worthwhile exploring more 'elitist' (at least by self-definition) misgivings about inoculation.

What then inclines an informed and critical citizen to reject the Covid-vaccine? Liberals tend to explain the problem away with the notion of 'trust' (and the lack thereof) in elites, which leads them to denunciations of the populism of anti-vaxxers (because 'populism' is understood strictly as anti-elite sentiment). In fact, at the outset of the pandemic, the influential political scientist Ivan Krastev trumpeted 'the return of the expert', optimistically announcing the beginning of the end of the pernicious 'populism' plaguing the liberal public sphere and political life. Less than a year into the pandemic, the raging anti-vaxx sentiment makes that declaration at best hasty. Yet, there is a degree of truth to the 'populist' hypothesis inasmuch as Bulgarians indeed have little trust in their elites, as manifested in the ever-diminishing electoral turnout from one apathetic election to the next. Only the spectacular and short-lived outbursts of new 'populist' parties shake up this apathy, then to disappear into oblivion shortly afterwards, bringing in their wake even more resignation. In fact, with three caretaker governments in a row, 2021 will go down in history as the most politically eerie year, in that for the first time in history, there was no regular government for such an extended period of time to deal with the multiple crises looming on the horizon: Covid, the asset-price bubble, historic inflation, and utilities price hikes, along with the political crisis proper. However, is the issue of trust a symptom of rejection of all elites or can it be better understood as an intra-elite conflict, a counter-elite offensive against vaccines and measures-advocates among the elite?

## Some hypotheses

First, the so-called 'populism' of anti-vaxxers does not reject the elite *tout court* but has its own 'high-brow' and elite centres of ('alternative') scientific and political authorities. In Bulgarian public space, professors and doctors are among the most visible sources of Covid vaccine hesitancy. Second, far from being a break with the traditions of the rational liberal public sphere, Covid vaccine hesitancy weaponises key liberal tenets and tools, creating its own 'critical' public sphere, with educated authorities at the apex. Relatedly, far from being a self-styled rebellion of 'the people' rising up against a putative elite conspiracy, my vaccine-hesitant respondents tend to be educated, middle-class professionals enjoying good income and standing in society. If this is 'populism', then it can only be a libertarian populism of individualists consciously defining and defending their inalienable rights (sometimes at gunpoint, as the recent tragic killing of a cashier in Germany by an anti-masker demonstrates). Fourth, their movement indicates less the much awaited break with neoliberalism but rather the latter's *social* resilience even in the face of an unprecedented global health crisis which calls for nothing less than aggressive state intervention in literally every sphere of life, especially in the economy. In that sense, it is a discourse about the state, which radicalises foundational neoliberal prescriptions or models for state-society relations. Finally, understanding how neoliberalism 'lingers on' is crucial to devising new strategies for undoing it. To this end, the left needs not only a radical turn in the realm of ideas and party programmes but a deeper understanding of the unshakable inertia of the neoliberal hold on the public imagination, rooted in practical experience with it in the last decades. This is what the notion of 'hysteresis', which I borrow from Pierre Bourdieu, who in turn borrowed it from physics, captures. Namely, effects can linger on long after their cause has disappeared, and as the case of Covid vaccine hesitancy demonstrates, can shine all the brighter precisely in the abrupt absence of their cause.

Let us unpack each of these hypotheses in relation to the survey in turn.

## Anti-vaxxers, education and science

The survey inquired about respondents' general inoculation status. I intuited that the rejection of Covid vaccines need not be a rejection of all vaccines and the survey confirmed my suspicion. Nearly 70% of the respondents make sure their children are up to date on the national immunisation schedule (with only 11% of these selectively opting for some vaccines). While worryingly high at 18% in a country where vaccination is mandatory and access to care services like kindergarten is obligatory, the number of people not inoculating their children is still over three times less than those who do. Similarly, 77.8% of respondents are themselves vaccinated, although the majority of them do not get boosters regularly (the present author also does not, without harbouring any vaccine scepticism). 7.4% get their boosters regularly and 14.8% are not vaccinated at all, the latter consisting of 3 men and a woman, middle-aged. Only one does not have tertiary education and is above 60 (works in construction); the rest are owners of private businesses or highly educated professionals, and all of them enjoy higher than average incomes (the upper bracket was set at over 3000 BGN corresponding to the national social insurance contribution cap). Naturally, we cannot seek the reasons for their vaccination status in their present circumstances since their parents must have made the decision for them and the survey could not inquire into family history and path dependencies.

This shows that vaccine hesitancy targets specifically Covid inoculation rather than all vaccines and it might be useful to look for the reasons, say, in the way the media covered these vaccines or in the government's actions, rather than in a general rejection of science and vaccination ('populism'). And indeed the respondents' reasons for not getting a jab point in this direction. As a middle-aged judge stated, 'I was sick and I have a high level of protective antibodies. Besides, the relentless pro-jabs propaganda is counterproductive', while at least three respondents feel that the problem with vaccines is not the science but the *insufficient* science proving their efficacy. This is a version of the theory that they are still in the experimental phase and we do not know enough about their long-term effects. It is pointless to argue that science indeed proves the efficacy of the vaccine (if only for a short period); the point here is to notice the predilection for sound science, as opposed to the common misconceptions about anti-vaxxers' blanket rejection of science in general.

This leads us to the next point which concerns the sources of anti-vaxx sentiments. These are to be found in the media. The Bulgarian case clearly shows that far from 'the (anonymous) middle-aged mother of two', the most visible sources of vaccine hesitancy are professors and medical professionals. Of the list with examples of 'your trusted experts on Covid', 100% of respondents selected the names of associate professor Atanas Mangarov, the head of the pediatric ward in Bulgaria's biggest infectious disease hospital and a failed MP candidate; professor Andrei Chorbanov, head of immunology at the Bulgarian Academy of Sciences and an MP from a new, Covid-sceptical party; and Dr. Antonia Parvanova, a liberal politician, former MEP, and pediatrician. Nobody selected the passionate and tireless defenders of vaccination Dr. Asparouh Iliev (University of Bern), Dr. Georgi Markov (University of Oxford), and mathematician Petar Velkov, let alone the representative of the left-wing side of the debate and zero-Covid advocate, Stanford geneticist Georgi K. Marinov. Less than a quarter of the respondents opted for the 'I absolutely do not trust anyone' answer, showing once again that Covid hesitancy is less a generalised rejection of science but rests on its own ('alternative') scientific foundations. Its perniciousness is all the worse that science (even the flawed and dodgy versions of people like Mangarov and Chorbanov) still enjoys universal legitimacy that even the politicisation of Covid hardly erodes.

Survey respondents get their information on Covid mostly from Facebook and internet sites, followed by national and foreign official media. Therefore the public sphere populated mostly by commercial mass media bears a great responsibility. Public rows and passionate 'debates' over inoculation are more profitable than relaying to the public the dry recommendations of the Ministry of Health. In this sense, far from being a guarantor of truth and rational debate in the simplistic Habermasian accounts of the public sphere, the quest for 'transparency' and the belief in 'the equal value of all viewpoints' amplifies the misinformation and scepticism, buttressed by the profit-seeking behaviour of most outlets. Far from being a problem specific to private media, the public channels are also culpable because they too are forced to operate as utility- and profit-maximising market actors. Paradoxically, the first outbreaks of Covid were met with detailed and harrowing reports about the first few victims of the virus, sometimes straight from the ICUs; today, in the meantime, between 100 and 150 people die per day but the media shows no comparable compassion and interest in their fate. Death by Covid seems completely normalised. By contrast, each casualty of the extremely rare vaccine-caused thrombosis is conveyed by the tabloids to the grieving public in the most intimate and personalised detail imaginable, creating the impression that the fix is deadlier than the virus. Not to mention the plethora of blogs, vlogs, Telegram chat-rooms, and social network groups, doubling as 'alternative public spheres' (whose popularity sometimes rivals that of mainstream channels) where anti-vaxx 'science' thrives.

Liberal moralists underestimate the unpalatable trust in these doctors and professors and let the political elite off the hook by blaming an imaginary inherent superstition the Bulgarian populace is supposedly beholden to. They forget that the vaccine roll-out occurred in the most volatile year for Bulgarian political life to date. Four elections (three general and one presidential) made the political class extremely cautious when it comes to vaccines, with tiny exceptions. Most candidates have feared that unequivocal endorsement of mass inoculation will alienate potential voters and espouse 'moderate' positions on the issue. Yet it is precisely in this way that they pander to the most extreme (and numerically insignificant) anti-vaxxer groups, thus inflating their influence. Others are not so shy about exploiting the issue. A whole new anti-establishment party, which swept the snap elections this spring, ran an explicit anti-vaxx campaign; all the while its leadership secretly got their vaccines, as became clear later.

## Neoliberal hysteresis

One striking result of the survey was that a whopping 100% of respondents answered the question whether responsibility for health should be personal or collective (that is, the task of the state). This does not mean that people always act on their stated beliefs: 52% say they take care of themselves, eat healthy, do sports, do not smoke, etc., while 48% believe in predestination ('whatever is in the cards'). Interestingly, the 52% engaging in conscious self-care position themselves in the upper echelons of the class structure: 'middle class', 'intelligentsia', and 'the rich', proving Pierre Bourdieu's tenet that one of the signs of 'middle-class' belonging is taking care of one's health, doing sports, avoiding becoming overweight, and seeing a doctor at the outset of symptoms rather than waiting until one is no longer able to engage in physical work, which is often the case with working-class people for lack of disposable money and time. In fact, among the respondents who said they rush to the doctor right away, only one identified as working-class. In that sense, we can say that 'having a stake in a long and healthy life' is a reliable predictor for belonging to the dominant classes.

The firmly held belief that health is purely a matter of personal responsibility makes Bulgaria somewhat of an outlier in Europe. According to the Eurobarometer Survey mentioned above, 40% of Europeans agree with the statement "vaccination is a civic duty" compared to only 13% of Bulgarians. The ratio among those who disagree is similarly skewed: 16% of Europeans disagree with the statement while in Bulgaria this percentage is twice as high: 34%. These data led to self-orientalising analyses in the liberal press blaming 'a cultural gap' between Europe and Bulgaria, 'since at least Ottoman times'.[2] Such mentalist or culturalist analyses firmly position Bulgaria in the 'backward' end of an imaginary temporal map of 'European progress' and in doing so are completely blind to the possibility that rather than being stuck in a putative 'Ottoman' past (or communism in similar interpretations), Bulgaria might actually already be living the dystopian future nightmare of triumphant neoliberalism, of the victory of the self-reponsibilising logic driving extreme individualisation and the disintegration of the 'moral fabric' (what sociologists since Durkheim refer to as 'the social glue'). Unfortunately, the neoliberal approach to health also seems dominant among healthcare professionals, as a survey conducted among doctors by Dr. Alexander Simidchiev, one of the more visible public advocates for vaccination, demonstrates. In it, 69% say that private citizens bear the biggest responsibility for *public* health. The results are shocking for the doctor who is also an MP from a small neoliberal party rooting for privatisation of the healthcare system, but the irony of his position seems lost on him.

The wildly disappointing approach to a public health crisis of unseen proportions with the worn-out recipes of 'personal responsibility' speaks volumes about the tenacity of neoliberalism. The onset of the pandemic gave rise to many a hasty declaration about the 'death of neoliberalism' (including by the present author) and an outpouring of public expenditure; prohibitions on state intervention in the economy, previously thought unshakable, were lifted. All this inclined commentators to underestimate the inertia of neoliberalism or what can be called 'neoliberal hysteresis' As mentioned, hysteresis is the presence of an effect long after its cause is gone and we see this in the tenacious, self-regenerating legitimacy of austerity even in the face of a crisis requiring unprecedented levels of public spending. Thus more punitive cuts are demanded because of the very negative experiences with the public system brought about by punitive cuts to begin with. For example, increased waiting time at public institutions' front desks because of 'budget optimisation and streamlining' lead to tensions with the remaining staff, who, by dint of being frontline workers, bear the brunt of disgruntled 'customers'' ire. The latter in turn demand more punitive cuts, which were what worsened the service in the first place. This is the logic of 'more of the same' which persists even when the conditions that gave rise to it in the first place have changed beyond recognition. The same applies to the 'neoliberalism from below' in the response to the pandemic: having been accustomed not to expect good service (60% of survey respondents) and to the ever-increasing share of co-payments in the public healthcare system (40% of respondents have had to pay out of pocket expenses for healthcare, 50% nation-wide), people are suddenly lavished with free and high-quality vaccines, free prescriptions for Covid meds, the suspension of the social insurance model for Covid patients and other perks of the long-abandoned Socialist model of free-at-the-point-of-use healthcare (also the NHS model, under neoliberal fire in the past decade). Can we blame them for distrusting the sudden turn away from the hitherto dominant necropolitical model in healthcare? (In the meanwhile, with Covid making free healthcare once again possible, if only for a single disease and its complications, we clearly need to seize the opportunity to demand the extension of free care and treatment to all other health issues.)

This durably entrenched neoliberalism was buttressed right from the start by the EU's 'consumerist' approach to vaccination. In Bulgaria the jabs' arrival was couched in a rhetoric of 'guaranteed free choice' even though initially the government bet on the cheaper AstraZeneca vials. Eventually, in the wake of reports on the rare thrombosis caused by this vaccine, the government ordered more batches from Pfizer/BioNTech. The 'free choice' approach put the vaccination effort squarely on the wrong footing – as if we were choosing among toothpaste brands – forcing people to read up on things they have insufficient competence to understand. This is not the case with conventional vaccines whose availability is predetermined and which most parents readily accept on the discretion of the pediatrician, as opposed to the 'informed consent' approach shaping societal attitudes to the Covid vaccines. Vaccination should have followed in the footsteps of the conventional vaccines (at least in frontline and care sectors) because the very option of giving people 'a choice' over something they lack the tools to understand makes it look suspicious.

Vaccine mandates would only be effective in an altogether different context of a more interventionist state, which the reigning neoliberal orthodoxy radically precluded in the Bulgarian case.

Which leads us to the next hypothesis:

## Vaccine hesitancy as social reproduction anxiety and a symptom of the souring of state-society relations

One popular narrative concerning the vaccines among conspiracy theorists is that they sterilise the inoculated. We may speculate whether this is a 'Chinese whispers'[3] echo from the debates surrounding the jabs' purported sterilising effect, warped beyond recognition, or the result of a malignant conspiracy by nefarious (and named) sources. At any rate, it is a significant fear, one that has deep historical roots and ties to popular insurrections. We may draw a parallel here with the stories from the fascinating book *The Vanishing Children of Paris: Rumour and Politics before the French Revolution*, by Arlette Farge, Jacques Revel, and Claudia Miéville, detailing the fraught relationship between subjects and monarchy in the 1750s and heralding the revolutionary tremors to come. In a nutshell, the book tells the history of rumours percolating in the Parisian working-class quarters that the police were stealing children, leading to frequent riots and clashes. The original meaning of the word 'proletariat' is those who have property only over their children. The ostensible child abductions thus marked people with a deep sense of being robbed not only of their livelihoods in the nascent exploitative capitalist relations, but also of their posterity and future. Even though it is about a specific French case, the book teaches us that even in other contexts, vast progress has been made in re-founding state-society relations on a less exploitative and oppressive basis. It took no less than two world wars and the welfare/socialist revolutions of the twentieth century to change ordinary people's sense of the state from being a parasitic predator that sucks them dry through taxes and takes their children to die in far-flung and incomprehensible dynastic wars, without giving them anything back, to modern relations of citizen-soldiers (in Charles Tilly's sociology of the state), sacrificing themselves but also demanding from the state care, protection, and dignity in return. We should appreciate the change from fearing the state will steal one's children to voluntarily sending them to state-provided daycare and education institutions (and even fighting for their expansion and affordability).

What vaccine hesitancy and the reproduction anxiety it belies tell us is that this deep trust in the goodwill of the state, forged with the bloodshed of countless revolutions, is now under immense pressure and probably has already begun to disintegrate. Far from being a mere effect of a lack of education, this deep mistrust has roots in the very practical experiences of people trying to survive in Bulgaria. Charles Tilly famously defined citizenship as claims-making on the state. However, after several decades of neoliberal rollback of the state, we see that having learned to expect little from the state, ordinary people also stop making claims on it. The survey I conducted shows that nobody received any meaningful economic help but they did not expect to get much help to begin with, although they would have liked to, at least during the intermittent lockdowns. The severance of the ties with the state is also behind the mass disenchantment with politics and the self-elimination from elections. In the survey, 74% expressed disinterest in politics, only 44% voted regularly (this corresponds to the national averages), with the overwhelming majority voting irregularly or not at all, and admitting to casting mostly protest votes as opposed to finding true representation on the electoral market.

## Geopolitical divides?

The pandemic bifurcated the afflicted societies early on but it continues to consolidate the divisions. In the beginning it was Covid-deniers vs. 'covidiots'; maskers vs. anti-maskers; today new boundaries divide us, turning into borders within our very bodies: between being vaccinated and unvaccinated. These are unfortunate divisions obfuscating the real faultline: between ordinary people left to be ravaged by the virus and the corporate-government nexus unwilling to stop the virus lest capitalist accumulation grind to a halt.

However, no matter how artificial, to a degree these new divides correspond to and map themselves onto pre-existing divides. For example, my survey probed the respondents on other 'hot' and divisive social issues such as the Istanbul Convention (only one person admitted to its relevance and necessity, 63% are against it while 33.3% have no opinion on the issue) and sex-ed in schools (55.6% against, 37% for, 7.4% don't know). Cross-checking overlap with conservative positions on other issues is useful but should not be taken as determinate because opposition to masking, measures, and vaccines is also rife among the left, as the outburst of 'Querdenken' protests in Germany show.

In an influential study, Ivan Krastev and Mark Leonard also focus on the novel and Covid-engendered new divisions within Europe, giving rise to what they call a tale of 'two pandemics' and 'two Europes'.[4] While mostly framing these divisions and the experiences of the pandemic they correspond to as 'generational' (young vs. old) and 'geopolitical' (South vs. North), Krastev and Leonard nevertheless give a useful clue as to the readiness of society to accept state-imposed measures against the disease, namely, that those who were economically affected by the pandemic are least predisposed to accept the measures. What does it mean to be economically affected? Obviously, that the social safety nets were too porous or that the state did not do enough to cushion the economic impact of the virus and the measures taken against it. In other words, observing and accepting the measures as a necessary 'evil' for the wider social good is conditioned less on education, culture, civic ethos, and even 'civilisational stage', as critics of the anti-maskers assume, but on a state which actively cares for its population as opposed to only demanding unidirectional sacrifices from it.

Why Bulgaria is not such a state has been belaboured elsewhere. Suffice it to say that the state could not follow a straightforward policy on Covid throughout each wave, abruptly toggling in and out of quarantine with no logical plans and reliable indicators as to when to expect closures (i.e., full lockdown on days with a couple of victims daily at the beginning of the pandemic, and no lockdown until the death rate climbed to over 150 a day later into the pandemic); it did not offer sufficient economic help for the affected workers (businesses were better taken care of, although they also had their reasons to complain), except for cynical measures such as interest-free loans for workers and a pitiful increase in child benefits.

The erratic behaviour of the state (where the only certain thing was that nobody should expect much help) is a clear source of mistrust, also visible from the survey where an impressive 77% of respondents received no state assistance whatsoever. Thankfully, most of them did not suffer from acute Covid and claim they are generally in good health, which spares them unnecessary encounters with the dysfunctional healthcare system. Which brings me to the next point: Bulgarian healthcare is one more reason to suspect the good intentions of the state. Let us see why.

## The long-durée of neoliberal healthcare

The respondents' past experiences with the healthcare system holds another clue to understanding the widespread mistrust of the Covid vaccines. A middle-aged female university lecturer with autoimmune disorder and at higher risk of thrombosis who vaccinates her children, rejects the Covid vaccine by saying that she is not sure the overall aim of the vaccination effort is to protect people's lives. Her experiences at public hospitals have been extremely unpleasant and she considers the widespread co-payments to be prohibitive. She is not satisfied with her GP and when asked to clarify, she writes the following: 'because they abandoned people and "treated" us on the phone. They showed complete lack of concern, and carelessness. That's why hospitals were full — because GPs weren't doing their job.' This has in fact been a recurring complaint, giving rise to misguided diagnoses over the phone, as in the case of death by untreated peritonitis at the beginning of the pandemic. There is anecdotal evidence that GPs did not properly inform themselves about the benefits and risks of the vaccines, turning many people away (such as pregnant women who are a particularly high-risk group).

Almost a third of respondents (29%) deny the existence of the coronavirus and frame it as a hospital conspiracy in which the death of patients is wrongly attributed to Covid so that the hospital can earn more money from the Health Insurance Fund. This is a popular conspiracy narrative which is really a distorted critique of the commercial model Bulgarian healthcare has been based on since the market reforms in 1998. To cut a long, tragic story short, the reforms in question redefined all hospitals as commercial entities responsible for their own cash inflows, substituted a social insurance system, with access to care now pegged to employment (along the German model), for the previous universal and free healthcare, and introduced the 'voucher' system of 'money follows the patient', creating a fierce competition between hospitals for patients, alongside incentives for fraudulent hospitalisations, unnecessary surgeries, and other daily horrors pouring in from the system, including the largest share of co-payments and out-of-pocket expenses in the EU (nearly 50%). The overall result from two decades of relentless market reforms has sent healthcare professionals abroad in droves, cut access to healthcare outside large urban centres, and hollowed out the system, leaving the country abysmally ill-prepared for the Covid disaster. As a result, in each wave Bulgaria tops mortality charts in Europe – which it had already topped in general; Bulgaria gets habitually declared as 'the world's fastest shrinking country' and Covid inherited and accelerated these tendencies. Is it surprising that people harbour mistrust for the system especially in a crisis when there is an increased need for it? Many have sought refuge in 'alternative' medical practices (the combined result of respondents seeking such treatments 'often' and 'sometimes' is a little over 50%), all the while trusting the Covid-sceptical doctors based in the same healthcare system.

What are the take-aways for the left in this rather hopeless situation of self-perpetuating mistrust, suspicion, misplaced accusations, and moralising? First, offering bold new ideas breaking with the neoliberal orthodoxy is not enough. The neoliberal hysteresis is an implicit and even embodied sense rooted in the decades-long practices of self-coping with abandonment. As such it cannot easily be undone on the level of ideas. This was also shown by the failure of the US and UK left in the last elections, even with their different outcomes, to turn the tide in the face of the twin crises in public health and climate change, despite offering more adequate solutions than the right. In inclining people to seek more of the same, the self-responsibilisation effects of neoliberal austerity is a 'bad infinity' (Hegel), engendering its own conditions of possibility. Because as public services deteriorate, so does people's desire to avail themselves of them. It will take many years and a social revolution to undo the damage and refound the state on a radical care basis. The multiple and mutually reinforcing crises of Covid, climate change, and escalating inequalities demand no less if the worst is to be averted.

NOTES

1   <https://www.dnevnik.bg/bulgaria/2021/09/21/4255787_profil_antifaksur_kakvo_pokazvat_sociolozite_za_tazi/>.
2   <https://www.dnevnik.bg/analizi/2021/09/28/4257914_kakvo_ni_otlichava_ot_evropeicite/>.
3   The game also known in US English as 'telephone'.
4   <https://ecfr.eu/publication/europes-invisible-divides-how-covid-19-is-polarising-european-politics/>.

# Decisive Elections and the Future of the Left in Germany

## Mario Candeias

Die LINKE in Germany is living through a critical period; confronted with the pandemic and coming struggles over the financing and distribution of the costs of that crisis and with a new party leadership, the party has to deal with a devastating result in the federal elections and a disadvantageous position in negotiating the new coalition between itself, the Social Democrats, and the Greens in the federal city-state of Berlin. It had been a testing ground for the strategic concept the party had developed and tried to follow in the last 13 years – the concept of the 'connective party'. Let us take a look at the concept and the practice before we discuss the current political conjuncture, the disadvantageous political constellation, the strong counter forces, the inner conflicts, and the stagnation of Die LINKE – and the outcome of the general elections.

### The idea of the connective party

No part of the plural left, no party, no trade union, and no left vanguard can still claim a leadership role today. At the same time, however, we have to prevent plurality from turning into division. This is also the idea behind Mimmo Porcaro's concept of the *partito connettivo* (the 'connective party'), which he developed as a fellow of Rosa Luxemburg Foundation. Porcaro was one of the important intellectuals of Rifondazione Comunista in the late 1990s when the party was the hope for a new left in Europe, with Fausto Bertinotti as its general secretary. The concept 'is intended to overcome the idea of the classical mass party'.[1] The connective party was designed as a 'union of different (political) subjects in forms that do not want to eliminate the existing differences'[2] but rather unite them in a Gramscian sense as a societal party of a new type.

In a nutshell, decades of neoliberal reorganisation of social relations resulted in a kind of unmaking of the working class, its fragmentation, creating new class segments – a growing precariat in insecure living and working conditions, a cybertariat, highly educated and trained, although many of them also in precarious conditions – which coexist of course with the old segments of a shrinking industrial working class. With the ongoing transnationalisation, organised labour was put on the defensive, even before the collapse of state socialism in Eastern Europe. Thus, the base for the old social democratic as well as radical left parties has been shrinking, or at least rapidly changing.

On the other hand, there was never a lack of social mobilisation on the left. There were always a great many different new movements and organisations. But the subaltern, often divided, lacked a common language or an understanding of common interests. We were confronted with a multitude of political movements and demands that could not be translated into one another. The so-called multitude was precisely an expression of this.

In Italy, at the high point of the alterglobalisation movement and during the formation of Rifondazione after the transformation of the old Italian Communist Party into a sad social democratic party, a new alliance, together with the country's largest trade-union confederation, the left-wing CGIL, was created, representing the new plurality, a mosaic left. But the ties were weak and superficial, and this 'alliance' amounted to little more than a discourse without a common strategic project.

Moreover, even if it was possible to involve a great many activists and union staff, they only represented a minority in society with the time and resources for political engagement and could not be seen as an 'expression of the population' and as representing the working class. A left party also needs to reach out to groups that are often difficult or impossible to reach, that may have turned away from politics for good reason, and this is a very difficult task. Anchoring oneself in and connecting with the active parts of the population as well as a variety of left organisations and movements is not enough if one is no longer anchored in the popular classes.

When a new Berlusconi government absolutely had to be prevented, Rifondazione joined a centre-left coalition government. But the links between the different parts of this mosaic left were weak; it was not ready for the overwhelming forces that tear apart a left not rooted in real class action. The left was unable to implement social reforms or avert entry into the Iraq war. The result was an almost complete annihilation of the party form of the radical left in Italy up to the present day.

Or as Porcaro himself put it: A loose network as a 'movement of movements' is not enough. The idea that 'social change consists in the progressive and linear growth of a movement' has proven to be wrong.³ 'The creation of a counter-hegemonic movement cannot succeed as an additive process'⁴ or through cooperation between separate organisations on a case-by-case basis.⁵ Strategic leadership is required in order to generate qualitative leaps and effective breaks, otherwise initiative fizzles out or threatens to drift away in a sectarian manner.

However, there is no longer a privileged locus of leadership, let alone a 'leader'. What is therefore needed and possible is a kind of 'distributed leadership'. Depending on the political situation and strategic necessity, the leadership of the whole subject passes from one part to another, from one part of the movement or union to another, to a party or even to a left-wing government, from the government back to the movement, etc. Every transition of the leadership function from one part of the overall subject to another highlights a new point of condensation, a change in strategy and a realignment of mobilisation.

## The connective party becomes reality

The events in Greece following the 2008/9 financial crisis are a good example of this. Countless riots, demonstrations and general strikes were important symbolic actions at the beginning of the protests since 2009. But they quickly exhausted themselves. Leadership shifted from unions to movements, more or less spontaneously. The crucial point came, following the occupations of central squares in North Africa and Spain, with the occupation of Syntagma Square in Athens. This is where the rise of Syriza began, for instead of advertising their party with the usual symbols and flags, they instead participated as individuals in the occupation and the debates, and resisted together with other activists the attempts of the radical right to infiltrate the squares movement. Syriza provided an infrastructure for the squares – and, above all, they listened. They managed to pick up on moods, passions, and political messages. Syriza symbolised a condensation point that translated civil-society self-organisation and protest into the perspective of the taking of government power. And beyond being seen as political activists, for many they represented the spirit of protest, not least among the lower social classes.

The party combined this with far-reaching changes in the political structure of its own organisation and developed close institutional, even organic connections with movements: The Solidarity4all network was founded together with movements in order to network and strengthen solidarity structures across the country; all MPs paid a substantial part of their salary into the Solidarity4all fund, at least one person among each MP's assistants was assigned to work specifically in the movement, etc. So, there was a very deep connection of the party with the movements. The party was enormously important as an infrastructure for building solidarity movements, movements that not only protested but engaged in direct self-help, political education, and building everyday counter-structures. Although Syriza was admittedly never deeply rooted in organised labour, it did reach out to the precarious sections of the class.

Syriza was itself permeated by the movements. Many of its simple members, but also party functionaries, have been active in movements and struggles for years. Syriza was present in the movements but never tried to control them. It thus stood for a new type of party that could best be characterised by the concept of 'connective party'. The different partners of the connective party fulfilled different roles and functions and each partner 'can become the leader of the entire front'.[6] And this alliance treated the 'social and cultural divisions between and within the subaltern classes as the explicit object of political analysis and strategy formation to overcome fragmentation'.[7]

Later, however, Syriza did not manage to provide for a path of impulses proceeding from the movements to the party, as it did during the occupation of Syntagma Square. 'We have not maintained an active relationship with society;' after entering government there was 'hardly any difference from ND or PASOK in how we functioned', summarises the former Secretary General Tassos Koronakis (also a fellow at our institute) in a debate in 2015.[8]

Although the indispensable role of social movements and struggles on the left is widely recognised, the notion of a linearly ascending political organisational process is still prevalent: at the beginning, there is protest and the movement, followed by the formation or reorganisation of a new left party, which finally competes to win elections, seize power, and implement its policy. In this traditional view, movements have their place, but its sense of conquering power remains old-fashioned, parliament-centred, étatist – 'we'll just make it happen'. At any rate, this traditional relation between movements and government is no longer sustainable.

From today's perspective, it should be clear that the moment of takeover of institutional power is not the time to replace the momentum of movements. With the taking over of government, the activity of the movements, including trade-union activism, needs to be intensified still more, with the strengthening of self-organisation in all areas. New connective practices linking the different functions of government, party, movement, and the various mutual-aid organisations and cooperatives would have to be developed – rather than just acting on behalf of the movements and the voters and calling on the movements on a case-by-case basis to mobilise for the government. Repeated mobilisation from case to case without real participation leads to disappointment, distancing, withdrawal, and division – this was what happened after the OXI referendum, when Syriza decided to sign a new Memorandum and then tried to govern as well as possible under the crushing heel of the Troika.

So, this concrete attempt of a connective party failed, due of course to the overwhelming power of the Troika, but also due to the strategic failure of the left in Greece and Europe.

## A brief look at Spain: Between populism and municipalism

A similarly somewhat old-fashioned understanding of the relation between movements and party was at the centre of Podemos's rise in Spain. In fact, Podemos understood its role simply as a movement party, confusing the two different functions and logics, or as the instrument for active translation of movements into institutional politics. Podemos was able to seize the right moment. However, there never was an *organic* connection with the movements or with the popular classes, but rather a representative one, plus an intelligent use of populist discursive strategies. But once the massive material interventions of movements and neighbourhood organisations weakened, this kind of discursive populism became rather empty. The party became disconnected from the base that once had brought it into being.[9] And it never developed ties with organised labour or the different regional national movements that are so important in Spain. Once in government, it has been unable to implement visible social reforms and put pressure on the dominant social democratic partner. The pandemic made things worse, Pablo Iglesias stepped down as a minister to engage in a regional election, and lost.

The experience of municipalism in Spain, made most famous by Barcelona's mayor Ada Colau, was different. The municipalist movement in many cities of Spain was very clear about the need to transform politics as such, and to find a new connection between self-organisation of the people and government, opening up the institutions for new forms of participation. There is no space here to look more deeply at this experience, but there is much to learn from it. At the beginning its success was huge in changing many things. But in the end it lacked an organisational structure, a real party, and enough forces to perform all the necessary tasks. And at the same time, it absorbed too many activists into institutional politics, weakening the pressure that needed to be exerted on the institutional obstacles from outside.

## Two types of party-movement form

For some ten years we have been discussing a great many new types of relations between party and movement in Europe (and the US). The relevant discourse often refers to Jeremy Corbyn and the organisation Momentum, to Bernie Sanders's election campaign, La France Insoumise, Podemos, and, looking slightly further back, Syriza. Despite the heterogeneity of these examples, we can learn a lot from their achievements and errors.[10] Typologically we can roughly differentiate two different methods of approach, which in practice are combined in different ways.

The *organic-popular option* (in line with Gramsci) builds on a close, everyday cooperation with the movements and mutual structures of solidarity as an organising force, promoting the self-activity and self-representation of the Many to represent further parts of the population that cannot or do not want to engage in active participation. This is achieved by actively connecting the Many across different organisations via direct, practical interventions that have their roots in specific social conditions. Examples are the struggle for housing rights or the collective bargaining movement (Tarifbewegung) for good care work and more staff. Individual interests are jointly formulated and connected. The primary goal is to create a social counterforce and social movements for immediate improvements in everyday life, and to shape new social connections and self-relations. With enough momentum, this popular approach could potentially grow to become a destitutive and constitutive power that unites transformation of the self and, in the long run, of society as a whole.

The *populist option* (in line with Laclau) pursues a strongly media-oriented approach, to interlink the many different groups and demands, identities, and cultures, and condense them into the same narrative. This is achieved through a very sharp polarisation of the political, particularly in the media. The different interests are taken up, absorbed, passively represented, and connected via discursive manoeuvres. The goal is to unify the Many in support of a populist project in which they feel represented. In this sense, the populist project does not focus too much on real-life social movements or initiatives and their everyday engagement, but rather attempts to give the respective demands a louder and more effective voice, thus enhancing their visibility. The goal is to achieve a shift in social discourses and political power structures in order to seize governmental power.

None of these alternatives exist in their pure state, but must, instead, be combined in practice. Both can and must reinforce one another. In my opinion, however, the organic-popular option ought to predominate – not in every instance but as an overall goal and cause. Historically, it has been the movements themselves that have pushed social change forward. The government can play an important role by expanding fields of action, codifying social changes or institutionalising improved relations of power beyond their initial momentum, movement, or social mobilisation.[11] A popular counterforce is further needed to truly empower, promote, and correct a potential government of the left.

To be clear, though, it is also not a matter of becoming categorised as a 'movement party'. The misunderstanding repeatedly arises that if the party anchors itself strongly in left-wing movements it also anchors itself in the popular classes and wins its votes. Unfortunately, this is not the case. Rather, the party must also reach out to the passive parts of popular classes, actively developing its representative function as a party. This could also mean winning back those very groups which, though fundamentally open to left-wing positions, currently feel drawn towards the radical right. (How this could work is, admittedly, quite controversial).[12] It is not enough to simply connect with and focus solely on the politically active parts of society, left-wing organisations, and movements.

Instead, it is necessary to combine both options in a strategic manner. A populist momentum could be used to amplify, spread, and promote any given popular project, promoting self-activity and self-representation rather than simple political representation. In the case of an existing large-scale social momentum, a populist polarisation could further consolidate, strengthen, and promote that project's activities. When that kind of social momentum is absent, a populist polarisation could make the project's delicate potential for self-organisation and progress more visible. This would provide a groundwork and infrastructure for a society-based counterforce that is rooted in the concrete activities of the Many, rather than in ephemeral compliance with the media and the electorate.

However, the weaker the organic-popular momentum becomes in relation to the populist momentum, the greater the danger of the latter developing its own independent course. This would herald a return to an authoritarian charismatic leadership, hierarchical structures, and political representation instead of self-representation. The result would be an insufficient basis for power, limited to merely parliamentary majorities and the media that back them. The voter base would remain volatile at best, leading to immediate electoral losses should the anticipated improvements fail to materialise. But, we must admit, the organic-popular momentum requires time and a long-term perspective, which is not compatible with the kind of quick reaction sometimes required in volatile political situations. The (necessary) combination of both options has, in fact, never been achieved anywhere.

Actually, the two have often been opposed to one another, manifesting in harsh conflicts, within a party (for instance in Syriza but also in Die LINKE) or between left parties (for instance between La France Insoumise and the PCF). This has led to divisions, paralysed party development, and limited the potential for a stronger anchoring in the population and better electoral results. As a result, the real influence of the left has remained limited, with both leadership charisma and practical value dwindling.

## New class politics

Until the last elections, Die LINKE was one of the most stable radical left parties in Europe. In the beginning, the party was a role model for a mosaic left of very diverse old and new left segments, radical activists, high-ranking trade union members, and left social democrats, from both Eastern and Western Germany. In 2009 we reached nearly 12% of votes in general elections, in 2013 our percentage fell to 8.6%, in 2017 it rose in 9.2%. Of course, we have had ups and downs, and many problems, but in the last years more than 30,000 young people have joined the party (while at the same time we lost 25,000 due to aging and death). Now we have more than 60,000 members in total, and a large number of activist members. Moreover, we try to learn from other experiences, not only the ones mentioned above, such as in Spain, Portugal, La France Insoumise, but also from Labour under Corbyn or the Sanders campaign, etc. We have close connections to all of these, having co-organised numerous exchanges and training sessions.

In sum, in the last ten years we have been developing the concept of new or connective class politics. The notion of class politics can help clarify what a socialist class perspective would be in specific political fields:

a) It helps in formulating a clear relation to the opponent, to the leading classes 'above' one and to the radical right.

b) It can reformulate the social question in a sharper way, more precisely class-oriented, and thus contrast it to the generic (social democratic) talk of social justice. It is new in part because it attempts to free the class question from its fixation on the old, often male-centred, predominantly industrial working class and integrate a feminist and ecological class politics and a class-conscious anti-racism; at the same time, it can help to give the latter movements a more clearly left, even antagonistic profile against capital and the ruling classes.

c) It can thus overcome the false opposition between the social question and (so-called) identity politics. Feminism, ecology, and anti-racism are not just something for 'the elite' – they are centrally important to class antagonism.

In this process of clarification, projects and practices must be developed that go beyond the usual suspects of left activists and reach out to the popular classes – with or without a migrant background. This especially involves those formally less qualified, precarious parts of the class living in disadvantaged neighbourhoods, who as a rule are not politically organised and go to the polls less often, but many of whom could potentially vote left. Here, outreach work is about overcoming exclusions due to spatial segregation, classifications, and respectability boundaries, doing simple things that seem so hard to do – such as going from door to door, listening, engaging in conversation with these people, and initiating a process of forming a (self-)organising leadership among these groups. These practices are the litmus test of connective class politics.

The party as such has to become an organising tool, engaged in everyday material struggles within the popular classes, not just debating good programmes and concepts or working on their media presence. Resources have to be used for systematic training and structures of transformative organising.

Die LINKE has trained thousands of party and movement activists in transformative organising methods, in canvassing and campaigning. We have reached out to disadvantaged neighbourhoods, developed projects to organise around rent issues, health, or basic social needs. We have supported the self-organisation of refugees and migrants, bringing them together with the other initiatives with a view to forging common campaigns. In this way we have attracted a mass of young activists who have joined the party as well as people from the lower classes who have become leaders of these campaigns.

In fact, Die LINKE has the highest proportion of workers in its membership of all parties in Germany, just ahead of the SPD, which has many more members. It is also the party with the most members from the so-called 'lower class' (34 per cent), and by a large margin. By contrast, the Greens have one of the lowest worker memberships among German parties.

So, new class politics can act as a kind of 'connective antagonism' that brings together different groups, class segments, and movements across different issues, with a common orientation and *conflict*-oriented in relation to concrete opponents, without negating the differences between the different parts of the class. These are – extremely condensed – the core ideas of connective class strategy.

## Working on exemplary conflicts

Beyond protest, demands, or a good programme, it is crucial to identify a few projects that are able to produce what we call *exemplary conflicts*. Just two years ago, we would not have thought that a campaign for the expropriation of big real-estate groups in Berlin could be successful. The long and continued strikes together with a civil society campaign with patients and social initiatives over staffing at Berlin hospitals also had an enormous impact (with a strong engagement of our foundation and Die LINKE), after which labour disputes and alliances at many other clinics throughout the country followed.

We have seen that such conflicts create visibility, inspire, and motivate. They offer the opportunity for concretely connecting previously fragmented initiatives and organisations. Campaigns like these can shift the social discourse, expand the scope of possibilities, and increase the ability to assert other demands as well. The campaign to 'Expropriate Deutsche Wohnen & Co', Germany's biggest real-estate group, has not only improved the possibility of talking about a 'rent cap' in Berlin, but has also initiated more radical demands in other areas, such as the return of hospitals, energy production, transport, water supply, education, and generally social infrastructure to the public sector or the municipalities. Expropriation and socialisation became *fashionable* again! Even in the industrial sector. We must therefore locate the three or four central social questions suitable for developing such a conflict in a way that promotes the objectives of the left and increases its power.

These central issues should start with everyday needs, aim at immediate improvements for the many, and create a dynamic for next steps and further perspectives for radical shifts. This includes disruptive practices such as acts of disobedience, strikes, occupations, blockades, as well as referendums – and nearly always the question of ownership. Self-empowerment and a long-term perspective are central to expanding the scope of possibilities. However, even on a small scale we see that conflicts can actually be fun in the neighbourhood organisations when a campaign is fruitful, connecting with others, and making one feel part of something bigger. This organising on the ground is central to growing numbers and power.

The tenants' movement has become a real class movement, multi-racial and post-migrant[13] and female, because migrants, women, and children are the most affected by increasing rents, poor housing conditions, and discrimination on the housing market. In addition, however, these conflicts also radiate a new attractiveness for those who do not want to *or* cannot become active themselves. They can see that here someone is struggling for them by confronting powerful interests in order to achieve something for everyone. This is more than a populist strategy, it is a *popular* strategy in the Gramscian sense with organic ties between the different parts of the working class. Or at least it can be.

## The Berlin case

We can take Berlin as an example of the extent to which left movements and Die LINKE are capable of learning how to enable an€ effective division of labour, solidarity-based criticism, and, above all, shared successes. The fact that in the Berlin coalition government between Social Democrats, Greens, and Die LINKE no large party any longer dominates the (two) smaller parties, because electoral results for the three parties have become much more similar, truly facilitates cooperation at the same level. Moreover, the fact that we chose certain concrete conflicts was crucial for success.

For instance, with a bold 5-year rent cap, landlords, especially the bigger ones, were frantic, running media campaigns against us, against this dangerous example of socialism. Nevertheless, more than a million people directly benefited from this law while it was in effect. People have saved anywhere between €150 and €500 a month. This is not only helpful for the lower classes but also for the middle class which has had serious difficulties in paying the increasing rents. Was the cap legal? We really didn't know; we simply passed it. This is a feature of 'rebellious government', that is, to test the rules and disobey if necessary.

Up to that point, rent laws were considered a federal responsibility. But the federal government did not assume responsibility. Of course, we worked not only with the movements on this issue but with a team of legal experts outside of the ministries, which are full of SPD and CDU civil servants, so that we could not rely on the administration. We won the first rounds in court, while the rent cap already became a reality. The legal struggle was continued. But up to this moment, the conflict not only shaped society's power relations – even media campaigns against us did not work – but it also shifted power relations within juridical debates. As I have said, state intervention is becoming popular again, even amongst lawyers.

Right now we are drafting a law to expropriate real-estate firms that own more than 3,000 apartments in Berlin, which means that we are talking about expropriating 240,000 apartments. This also is a result of the long-term connection to the movements. The movement is organising the referendum with hundreds of thousands of signatures, while Die LINKE is not only translating this into a draft law, but thousands of our activists have joined the ranks of the initiative, collecting signatures, campaigning, and ringing doorbells. All the small initiatives that we launched in the disadvantaged neighbourhoods joined the campaign. The Institute for Critical Analysis of the Rosa Luxemburg Stiftung organised a legal assessment of how to justify compensation far below market value, only a little higher than the purchase price. At the same time, we are removing entire buildings from the market, one by one, comprising thousands of flats. The city constructed some 30,000 new apartments and planned for another 160,000 – so that Berlin will become the 'new Vienna' in terms of public and cooperative housing. For this to become a reality, we are trying to establish a city-owned construction company so that we do not have to hire the high-price private monopolies.

We have used this strategy – organising popular conflicts along with active alliance building with civil society initiatives in many different areas – for mobility laws, anti-discrimination laws, healthcare and social provisions, etc. In every instance, long-term cooperation with movements was crucial, even in the legal process. Moreover, we founded new institutions to open up the administration to civil society and the people, for real participation and control. This has involved a tenacious struggle within the administration.

It is also crucial that the party and our Berlin government officials play different roles. The party is pushing for further measures, even if our government officials are restricted by the coalition rules. This strengthens their position in negotiations with their coalition partners. Although this produces tension from time to time, the party and the movements have developed a kind of supervision and constant exchange. *Ciudades rebeldes* (rebel cities) is the Spanish term we adopted for our practice.

It follows that at the federal level too we need to clearly state our strategic goal: not simply a red-red-green (R2G) coalition, because it is arithmetically possible, or opposition, because government is useless; rather, Die LINKE should stand up for a decidedly *left* government that can count on a strong civil society to be its critical partner. A minority government is also conceivable, since this can sometimes be an advantage for the left (see Portugal's first socialist government, in close cooperation with radical left parties, although the second term after the elections in 2019 did not pan out).[14]

Either way, we can no longer afford to only make small corrections. We go into government only when a change of direction is possible – that is the key prerequisite for an enduring politics of hope. We have already defined a number of central projects, minimum conditions for government participation that also generate productive conflicts and create visibility, specifying projects we will promote.

Without such a mobilised party, without the commitment of initiatives and social movements, a left government will not accomplish much and will be unable to hold out in the long term. The opposing forces within society are too strong.

Therefore, in sum, the slogan of this approach could be: 'organising and conflict', or 'organising popular class conflicts'.

## A disadvantageous political constellation, strong counter forces, inner conflicts, and stagnation

Despite considerable successes in party building, organising, strengthened social movements (Fridays for Future, the rent movement, Black Lives Matter, anti-police-law movements, etc.), and a few beacons of left-wing government, shortly before the 2021 elections Die LINKE was stagnating at 7% in surveys, 2% less than in the 2017 elections (with the actual results a true disaster – see below)

Even before the pandemic, it was not easy to generate visibility for Die LINKE, in view of a threefold polarisation between the ruling neoliberal 'centre', the radical right, and the Greens as AfD's liberal-ecological counterpart. The result was that Die LINKE could hardly break into the media and was almost invisible. The pandemic made the situation even more difficult, because crises of this kind always privilege the executive branch of government and many left-wing activities are suspended (strikes, demonstrations, neighbourhood organising, door-to-door visits, or just meetings of different groups and levels).[15]

In particular it was difficult to come up with a distinctive position for pandemic management; in part, Die LINKE felt obliged to support tough government measures against the spread of the virus, while the pole of total opposition was occupied by AfD and the so-called 'Querdenker' (a confused amalgam of esoteric, anthroposophy, and hippie types, open to right-wing allies). A sensible and solidary intermediate position was once again marginalised in the (media) discourse or disparaged as 'unclear'.

In sum, Die LINKE is increasingly better organised and networked in the active parts of the movements and civil society, but it has insufficient reach in the other parts of the population (including some of its own electoral base). The new practice of connective class politics has not yet been sufficiently generalised to fully bear fruit, and the old form of the party as an 'anti-neoliberal movement' gathering different parts of the population from the Agenda 2010 period has long since been exhausted in the face of new social lines of conflict. In this way, the party increasingly represents the active rather than the passive groups of voters once open to the left – an effect that the class political orientation ought to have been able to counteract, if the party had had enough time to fully unfold its policies – but in the end time was too limited.[16]

In this context, the defeat of the Berlin rent cap was particularly harmful. On 15 April 2021, the conservative Second Senate of the Federal Constitutional Court (BVerfG) struck it down. The capitalist class and the conservative parties had lost the struggle on the level of public opinion and popular support, and were far from any parliamentary majority in the parliament of the Berlin city state. But the state within capitalism is organised in such a way that the bourgeoisie can hold several defence lines – in this case a juridical class struggle to stop any transformative step pushed forward by the left and to abrogate even popular laws (in the face of other juridical options in favour of the rent cap). In fact, the BVerfG's argument was purely formal: that the state of Berlin does not have the right to draft such a law because the issue of imposing restrictions on rent levels is purely the competence of the federal government. The true goal of this decision was to bring down the 'rebellious' Berlin government. This is extremely problematic not only for tenants in Berlin and elsewhere but also for Die LINKE itself, as the rent cap was the most popular project the party had mounted in recent years, which created visibility and credibility.

Although this has stimulated a 'now more than ever' spirit among the activists and large parts of the population, strengthened the idea of a nationwide rent cap, and spurred the initiative for a referendum on the expropriation of large real-estate companies, it also led to too much disappointment and bitterness. The inability of an elected government to implement even a law voted by the parliament because a conservative constitutional court denies its authority (contrary to a multitude of differently argued legal opinions and official reports) leads to widespread fatalism: 'Die LINKE means well, but in the end they are not allowed or able to change anything.' The result was that the party lost 1.5% of votes in Berlin but remained strong with 14% – enough to continue the government with the Green Party and the Social Democrats.

In addition, on the federal level there were simmering intra-party conflicts whose flames were gratefully fanned by the media and intentionally deployed against Die LINKE – even by representatives of Die LINKE who were involved in the inner-party power struggle. It is true that 'identity and class politics do not constitute a contradiction in terms but to secure one's own influence, this supposed conflict is constantly fueled,' as Daniel Reitzig writes in *Jacobin*.[17] This line of conflict of false oppositions cannot be explicated here,[18] but it does lead to a situation in which sections of potential left voters and activists are turning away from Die LINKE because of the verbal attacks on anti-racist, feminist, queer, and ecological practices from within the party, and other voters because they believe the constant critique that the party no longer represents the interests of the workers and those left behind. For both reasons people are cancelling their party membership – not in huge numbers, but the frustration is enough to stop membership growth.

Another closely related conflict within the party is how to deal with the ecological question. For the majority in the party, the social and ecological questions are inseparable. And this is precisely where the difference with the Greens is marked. But for a minority, sufficiently powerful because of the involvement of prominent persons with good media access, the party with its radical ecological programme is only tailgating the Greens and distracting from the actual core social issues. This also leads to a perception that the party is undecided: Although in the eyes of relevant sections of the environmental associations and the climate movement, it has the most progressive social-ecological programme in the country, the party's credibility suffers when some of its leading representatives and above all some in the parliamentary fraction repeatedly question the programme in the media. It is all the more damaging that in polls of Die LINKE's electorate, the ecological question always ranks high, in second place behind the social question. Perhaps the party can no longer attract a relevant number of Green voters, but it can still lose large numbers of its own voters to the Greens, as every election in recent years shows. This is another example of how social contradictions are not mediated in such a way as to be progressively resolved (keywords here are 'socio-ecological system change' or 'left Green New Deal') but remain stuck in false opposites, splitting the party's own base.

With an ambiguous polyphony of mixed messages, the party unsettled voters and activists and thus missed historical windows of opportunity at least twice, first in view of the refugee movement from 2015 on[19] and then with the start of Fridays for Future from 2018 and the escalation of the climate crisis. The party had the right programmes but was unable to represent them with credibility in the face of the fierce inner battles.

Moreover, there is no organic connection between (very good) concepts and programme, a wider socialist perspective, credible (media) figures, and everyday-life practice – at the workplace and in the movements. Our strongest political issues such as housing and health policies are no longer represented by our leading figures, or only partially. Socio-ecological and climate issues are most important in the programme and in resolutions, but not with our leading public figures. Regarding climate and peace issues, dissonance prevails in our communication. This is true even for social issues, when important representatives of the party time and again declare in the media that Die LINKE no longer represents social issues. Thus, in terms of the core issues of the party, the different elements fall apart. Representation fails and at the same time counteracts organisational and movement-oriented work – which in turn reaches its limits.

In addition, there are specific regional aspects. The strength of Die LINKE, and previously the PDS, in the East was a large (albeit old and often passive) membership and a core electorate that was very much identified with the party, made up of former SED staff and their environment. That generation will completely fall away as members and voters within the next ten years. This process is leading to a diminishing anchoring on the ground. Either the party gains new members and voters, or it is approaching its end as a generational project in the East. In addition, there are homemade mistakes (in terms of the approval in the Brandenburg government of police laws, as well as failed financial policies, not exiting from coal, etc.) and a political style that focuses on small reforms, better governance or better opposition, on the politics of small steps, especially in parliamentary space. There was no 'spirit of distinction' (Gramsci) in the East, that relies on a clear distinction and a recognisable and sharp profile vis-à-vis other parties. Nevertheless, in recent years more young people have joined the party in the East too. New members cannot compensate for the loss caused by the older generation, but as with the national average, they are predominantly young and active – against the right, against an overall development perceived as threatening, for left-wing politics on the ground, together with the population. Here the party has a real chance of becoming the opposite pole of the AfD; at least in Thuringia it has already achieved this.

In sum, this results in a mélange of demographic, organisational, and political problems, and unresolved intra-party conflicts with an overall political constellation that makes it difficult to become visible as an important force – and even if the party succeeds in becoming visible, it faces overpowering opponents.

## The elections in 2021 and a future for the Die LINKE

The result was a devastating defeat in the last federal election. Die LINKE is only represented in the Bundestag due to a special feature of electoral law that enables the formation of a parliamentary group even without passing the 5% hurdle if three or more direct mandates are won. (Every eligible voter can cast two votes: one for a party list and one for an individual candidate – a direct mandate.) With three direct mandates (two in Berlin, one in Leipzig) the party was able to enter the Bundestag with a full parliamentary group of 39 members, although it remained below the 5% threshold at 4.9%. This means not only a loss of 30 MPs and hundreds of parliamentary staff members as well as a million euros less in state funding for the party, but due to the tight election the party is acting 'on probation', as party co-leader Susanne Hennig-Wellsow puts it, with one last chance to redeem itself.

Against the background of inner-party conflicts, the dynamics of the election campaign led to an (even) less favourable situation: This election was, on the one hand, primarily about the decisive competition for chancellorship between the CDU and the SPD. On the other hand, it was an urgent 'climate election' in which there was a felt imperative that the Greens should be a strong component of any future government. Many potential LINKE voters therefore voted tactically and opted for the SPD or the Greens. Actually, the party's voter potential shows a particularly high proportion of precarious and poorer class segments with exceptionally high rates of electoral abstention, and a large proportion of highly qualified and urban class segments with an especially strong tendency to tactical swing voting (particularly the high-income voters earning over 3,500 € / month) with large overlaps with the SPD and the Greens. Die LINKE therefore creates neither an identity nor a milieu, or only does so to a very limited extent not sufficient for a stable voter base that secures more than five percent of the vote.

However, such a political constellation can translate into a dynamic that endangers the existence of the party. It is precisely this – and not the mistakes that are routinely made – that characterises the precarious situation that the SPD (through its own fault) had gotten into for a long time (and worked itself out of) and which Die LINKE can now also enter. Understanding political constellations is important in order to correctly assess problems and opportunities and to avoid a destructive and defeatist mood. Time and again in parts of Die LINKE, we come across an attitude in which the organisation itself is disparaged, with internal disagreements becoming more important than the actual external opponents. Discussions are not about what we have in common but about what separates us, and in which each is accused of a lack of strategy. However, a party that loses its courage will find itself in dire straits. So, a culture of a connective form of debate is necessary, in which differences are debated and respected and critique is encouraged while the production of what is common remains the main focus.

Perhaps Die LINKE has arrived at a turning point. It once had brought together the very disparate left milieus of the East and the West of Germany against the common enemy – neoliberalism and the so-called Agenda 2010 (the famous workfare programme). But this is over; for young voters Agenda 2010 is a (lost) fight belonging to past history (if they remember it at all), and neoliberalism is still here, but weakened. At present there is a struggle over the recomposition of the power bloc, a different constellation with new lines of social conflict, of which there are at least three: the socio-economic, the ecological, and the cultural-political conflict (regarding the Kulturkampf between the radical right and progressives around migration, gender issues, the pandemic, etc.).

Against this background of social transformations Die LINKE has the long-term problem of divergent groups of voters within its base (and partially also of divergences within its own membership, including a strong generational contrast). This has strategic consequences that have not yet been discussed. Is it possible to reunite these divergent groups in a joint project? Theoretically yes. But can this happen in the context of the current social and media dynamics with a severely weakened party? This is where our strategy of connective class politics reaches its limits.

In the period of Die LINKE's upswing, the common interest in success and the focus on socio-political issues and anti-neoliberal politics could tie the divergent parts together. In the current situation, the question arises whether the party, given the centrifugal dynamics of the divergent voters, members, and inner-party power groups, and without a strong renewal movement (which always needs an impulse from outside), is still able to achieve sufficient cohesion with the common goal of stabilising the party.

The long postponed decision on the party's direction is therefore inevitable. What then could be a new role for Die LINKE?

The Social Democrats understand that they must try not to make the mistake of committing another neoliberal crime in the form of an 'Agenda 2030' and instead act more wisely as a guardian of social guarantees in this new coalition – of course, heavily braked by the neoliberal coalition partner FDP. In that case, a left position reduced to 'we want more' demanding for example a 13 Euro instead of a 12-Euro hourly minimum wage would fall flat. At the same time, the Greens will leave us plenty of room for left-wing ecological positions. Unsurprisingly, the task of the left should not be a defensively oriented demand for 'more social policies' and 'no burden of climate policies on the working class', but the productive taking on of social and ecological class politics with a concrete perspective for real reconstruction and transformation. Do we want to play the role of a defensive *social* party or do we want to be a progressive and thoroughly socialist party for a new socio-ecological economic and societal model that generates equitably distributed wealth – with very concrete projects, and including the critique of a new green capitalism, along with a clear socialist attitude and perspective? In my view, due to the coming social transformations and upheavals, this last option would better suit the circumstances.

The new government coalition between Social Democrats, The Greens, and the (neo)liberal Free Democrats is certainly not the best solution for the social and ecological problems in Germany and in Europe – but ironically it is actually the best one for Die LINKE. This paradox is not intended to be a small consolation after a dramatically poor electoral result for our party, but a sober description of possibilities. The new government has no common project. The different interests represented in it are too contradictory for this. So it will act in a way falling far short of voters' expectations and mainly of the societal challenges ahead. (In the meanwhile, the radical right has been weakened by a conservative party that has moved to the right.) That leaves a lot of leeway for the only opposition to the left of the government – Die LINKE – if we know how to take advantage of this opportunity. There is no automatism here, but a real opportunity to get back on our feet, to fill a specific role.

This simultaneity of disadvantageous constellations, deep social transformations, including the electorate and the membership, and inner conflicts over strategic problems is not only a problem of Die LINKE, but of all radical left parties in Europe. The left populist project of Podemos, La France Insoumise, or #aufstehen (notwithstanding their strong differences), has reached strict limits (or failed), as have the popular upheavals of a renewed social democracy under Corbyn and Sanders (but the latter, after all, was able to move US politics to the left), or the plural, 'connective' left parties such as Syriza, Die LINKE, or the Scandinavian sister parties. Neither representatives of a strategy of opposition nor those of a left-wing government, of reform or of radical class-political or socialist strategies, can claim to have found the right 'recipe' in the *interregnum* beginning with the great crisis of 2009.[20] The adequate form of party-movement for a period of a lost neoliberal hegemony, the rise of the radical right and authoritarian forces, and a green capitalism has not yet been found. The problem is not really one of analysis, for programmatically a lot of things point in the right direction, and the political left largely has the right answers to the challenges but not yet the necessary practices nor a powerful organisation – neither of Die LINKE nor of the left as a whole. Without this, it will be crushed between the other forces. Let us hope that the end of the interregnum will see a relevant and strong left.

NOTES

1  Mimmo Porcaro, 'Partei in der Krise. Chancen für eine Rifondazione?', *Luxemburg* I (2010), 71-75.
2  Porcaro, ,Partei in der Krise' 73.
3  Mimmo Porcaro, 'Linke Parteien in der fragmentierten Gesellschaft. Partei neuen Typs – die "verbindende Partei"', *LuXemburg* IV (2011): 73.
4  Christina Kaindl and Rainer Rilling, 'Eine neue "gesellschaftliche Partei"? Linke Organisation und Organisierung', *LuXemburg* IV (2011): 26.
5  Mario Candeias, 'Von der fragmentierten Linken zum Mosaik', in: *LuXemburg* III (2010), <www.zeitschrift-luxemburg.de/von-der-fragmentierten-linken-zum-mosaik/>.

6   Mimmo Porcaro, 'Occupy Lenin', *Luxemburg* I (2013): 132-138, <www.zeitschrift-luxemburg.de/occupy-lenin/>; see also Porcaro, 'Linke Parteien'.
7   Jan Rehmann, 'Verbindende Partei oder zurück zum "Bewegungskrieg"?', *LuXemburg* I (2013): 139-42, here 139f.
8   Tassos Koronakis, 'Linkspartei auf dem Syntagma-Platz', *LuXemburg* IV (2011): 36–41.
9   For more details see César Rendueles and Jorge Sola, 'Strategic Crossroads. The Situation of the Left in Spain', Rosa-Luxemburg-Stiftung, Madrid, 2018, <www.rosalux.de/fileadmin/rls_uploads/pdfs/engl/SPAIN-EN-DIGI-RGB.PDF>.
10  For details see Mario Candeias, 'Populist Momentum? Learning from Corbyn, Sanders, Mélenchon and Iglesias: an indirect reflection on the #aufstehen campaign in Germany', Rosa-Luxemburg-Stiftung, June 2018, <www.rosalux.de/publikation/id/39654/populist-momentum/>.
11  Momentum is meant to indicate a suitable moment, a 'window of opportunity' for change; a movement is understood as an organised but fluid force around particular issues but still an (active) minority in the population; while social mobilisation implies a societal movement encompassing majorities or at least major sections of the population.
12  We have to be aware that it is much more difficult to win people back once they become part of a radical right project in seeking to lend coherence to their everyday consciousness with a radical right view of the world and a racist modus vivendi. But many such people are aware that the radical right will not solve their everyday problems of manifold insecurity, are uncomfortable, and have a guilty conscience for having voted right. See Mario Candeias, 'Understanding the Rise of the Radical Right', in: *Socialist Project, The Bullet*, 25 October 2018, <socialistproject.ca/2018/10/understanding-the-rise-of-the-radical-right/> and <www.rosalux.de/en/publication/id/39421/understanding-the-rise-of-the-radical-right/>; also at *Transform! Europe*, <www.transform-network.net/en/focus/overview/article/radical-far-and-populist-right/understanding-the-rise-of-the-radical-right-dimensions-of-a-generalized-culture-of-insecurity/>.
13  Post-migrant in the sense of immigrants who became German decades ago, with children who have grown up as Germans.
14  Mario Candeias, 'Portugal: Regierung gegen die Austerität. Bilanz zum Ende des Tolerierungsmodells', Rosa-Luxemburg-Stiftung, Berlin 2022, <www.rosalux.de/fileadmin/images/Ausland/Europa-Nordamerika/1-22_Onl-Publ_Portugal.pdf>.
15  Institut für Gesellschaftsanalyse & Friends, 2020, 'A Window of Opportunity for Leftist Politics? How to Continue in and After the Corona Crisis?', *LuXemburg-Special*, April 2020, <www.rosalux.de/fileadmin/rls_uploads/pdfs/LUXEMBURG/RLS_LUX_Mini_CORONA_EN_FINAL.pdf>.
16  Mario Candeias, 'Left Party ... Now What? Three suggestions for a discussion upon strategy', in: *Transform! Europe*, <www.transform-network.net/es/enfoque/overview/detail/strategic-perspectives-of-the-european-left/left-party-now-what/>.
17  Daniel Reitzig, 'Der Linksruck, der keiner war', *Jacobin*, 29 July 2021, <jacobin.de/artikel/der-linksruck-der-keiner-war-spd-saskia-esken-norbert-walter-borjans-kevin-kuehnert-olaf-scholz-agenda-2010-gerhard-schroeder-seeheimer-kreis/?fbclid=IwAR3SpTHZXj9adWAdWRJKDaWV32PYbK58rlG_Ni193Ac8Kefb9Oy_8W4M_-E>.

18   Bernd Riexinger, 'Für eine plurale LINKE mit sozialistischem Kompass', *LuXemburg* online, June 2021, <www.zeitschrift-luxemburg.de/fuer-eine-plurale-linke-mit-sozialistischem-kompass-einspruch-gegen-sahra-wagenknechts-projekt/>; Mario Candeias, 'Die Theorie kann uns nur ein Kompass sein', preface to Klaus Dörre (ed.), *Projekt Klassenanalyse Jena*, Frankfurt/M (soon to be published).
19   Mario Candeias, 'Eine Frage der Haltung. Über Streit in der Linkspartei, eine fortschrittliche Migrationspolitik und einen "lebendigen" Internationalismus', *LuXemburg*, May 2018, <www.zeitschrift-luxemburg.de/eine-frage-der-haltung/>.
20   Candeias, 'Populist Momentum?'.

# Pandemic De-socialisation in Austria

## Claudia Krieglsteiner

*For more than a year now a large part of the world, Europe, including Austria, has been in crisis mode due to the Covid-19 pandemic. To limit the spread of the virus within the population it was and still is necessary to reduce physical social contact. The crisis is multi-faceted – at the beginning it was a health crisis, with the closing of major areas of public life, such as schools, commerce, and art and cultural institutions. The pandemic and the containment measures led, among other things, to an economic and to a psycho-social crisis. It intensified social and societal divisions along different fault lines. People with lower socioeconomic status were harder hit, both by unemployment and harsher working conditions. In many families we saw a marked re-traditionalisation of gender relations. Care work and tending to children in home schooling was to a great extent taken over by women. There is a sharp difference between conditions for children and youth. While the former had adequate space, rest, and support, the latter fared worse; there was no compensatory effect via school or learning spaces. While togetherness was possible for many families, in others there were increased tensions, leading in some cases to psychological and physical violence. With the prolongation of the crisis, the divisions in society are widening at an increasing rate.* – Johanna Mückenhuber.[1]

The present article is, beginning with the Covid crisis, concerned with a long-term tendency toward de-socialisation that appeared in European Union countries at the latest with the Treaty of Maastricht, as a legal requirement. The failed strategies for coping with this have had massive effects on society and every individual. Most notably, young people are growing up in a de-socialised society.

Three theses will be discussed here, which involve the social aspect of our society in a general sense, the development of the political right wing, and the 'young generation'. We need, first of all, to remember that *the* youth does not exist. Children and young people also live within conditions structured by their family's social position, class position, by their gender, ethnic origin, etc. whose individual overcoming, while possible, is empirically improbable.

Here, as a rule, 'our society' refers to Austria, although very similar processes are occurring in other European countries.

## First Thesis

**The de-socialisation of our society is a long-term process that has been both triggered and accompanied by neoliberal restructuring. Neither the financial crisis of 2008-09 nor the Covid pandemic are causes of this development but have acted as turbines within it.**

The term 'de-socialisation' is meant to suggest the connection between neoliberal restructuring and the processes of privatisation of public property and social services, which has an impact on every individual. The injunction issued to everyone to 'self-management', to an independent and individually responsible mode of life, this individualisation and the greatly increased competitive pressure characterise our lives. It is no longer only adults who are affected but now also the socialisation of children and youth.

An article in the online edition of *Die Zeit*, for example, relates that in autumn 2021 there were 2,700 pupils, amounting to 90 complete classes, in Berlin for whom there were no slots in schools.

> In the district of Pankow there were no places in public school for almost 19% of students. Although a school-construction campaign had been announced in 2016, only four of the sixty planned schools could be completed. Due to the tense situation, fifth-grade pupils are already under enormous pressure to get the highest possible marks. 60% of pupil slots are distributed according to grade-point averages, 10% are assigned to hardship cases and siblings, and the remaining 30% are assigned by drawing lots. Especially popular preparatory schools are only assigned to children with a maximum grade-point average of 1,1.[2]

The *Die Zeit* article also quotes the Berlin psychologist and education researcher Bettina Hannover who feels that it makes pedagogical sense to impress on children and young people the connection between their own effort and the intended result but considers it fatal that despite having laboured hard to obtain good results they can still be rejected. 'This can kill their motivation and, in the worst case, even tip over the pupils' self-image.'[3] While this is certainly true, nevertheless children for whom a grade-point average of 1.1 is out of reach have no place in this perspective.

Up to the mid-1960s it was the church (the Catholic Church in Austria), the state, and institutions of civil society, as well as the educational system that looked after the 'correct life'. Ethically normative models were established not least through families, and the social system was expanded as a safeguard (and against deviance). The real achievements resulted from the needs of the Fordist world of labour, on the one side, and the implemented demands of the labour movement, on the other. A central experience of a large part of the youth of my generation was that movements in various spheres of society were successful in their opposition to authoritarian life and educational models that rigidly pre-formed people's lives and inhibited learning; schools and universities, as well as psychiatry and prisons, were reformed.

There had already been first steps taken in our mothers' generation before us, but at the end of the 1960s and in the 1970s revolutions occurred in women's lives. Organising, defending oneself, and constructively fighting for something produced results. These movements arose alongside the labour movement. Their positions were in part mutually contradictory and in many respects remained alien to each other. Many of the slogans and initiatives of this period's emancipatory struggles turned into weapons of neoliberalism in the mid-1990s, as discourses were take up and re-valorised in different frames of reference. A crass example is the 'women's movement' at the beginning of the 1990s as legitimation for the war in Afghanistan in view of the dramatic dead ends of this neo-colonial intervention. The others who opposed it were delegitimised by being denounced simply as antiquated.

Similarly, criticism of Fordist paternalism became the knockout argument against the 'social'. Consequently, there was and still is hardly any effective, differentiated debate over the further development of social standards. Among the majority of the population, ostracism or instrumentalisation of separate elements of the movements accompanied the assertion of neoliberal thinking.

As a result of the major social changes of the last 30 years, social integration is increasingly failing in a fundamental sense, beginning in childhood.

A German study based on the accounting data of doctors' services between 2009 and 2017 shows a steady rise in mental disorders among children and youth. In 2017, 28% of this age group had this diagnosis; in at least two quarter years 16% of adolescents, and in all four quarters 6%, were diagnosed with mental disorders. Developmental disorders made up the largest part of the diagnoses.[4]

Integration disorders are rapidly growing. Increasingly more people are completely or temporarily failing to see themselves as whole, unified individuals able to act as such.

Each age has its illnesses. It is especially mental illnesses that reflect the burdens and deficits of the prevailing mode of life. Many arc increasingly losing the capacity to act, as a precondition for managing daily life. This has to do with the way in which people exist in the world, position themselves in the world, and see and shape themselves, specifically today with the deficits in socialisation; and it also certainly has equally to do with the makeup of everyday life.

Since the onset of the pandemic, the Donau-Universität of Krems has been investigating the mental health of people who live in Austria. Christian F. Freisleben writes: 'The first results of April 2020 showed that depression, states of anxiety, and sleep disturbances increased nearly fivefold, all of which was confirmed by follow-up inquiries in June and September. This means that 26% of the population are experiencing depressive moods, 23% have anxiety symptoms, and 18% sleep disturbances.'[5] In particular, people between 18 and 24 years old are affected, as a German study shows.

> 71% of children and youth and 75% of parents felt strained by the first wave of the pandemic. By contrast with pre-pandemic times children and youth spoke of a diminished quality of life, the share of children and youth with a psychological disorder has approximately doubled, and their health behaviour has worsened. Socially disadvantaged children experienced the strain of the pandemic especially strongly. Two-thirds of parents wished to have support in dealing with their children's problems.[6]

## Almost two years of foregoing socialisation

Beginning with this already problematic situation, the closings of schools and Kindergartens not only brought many parents – especially single parents – to the financial and psychological breaking point; many children and young people exhibit, alongside knowledge and skill gaps, enormous deficits in socialisation.

Contact with one's contemporaries is, depending on a child's or young person's stage of development, a crucial factor in growing up and in the acquisition of social capacities (or in failing to do so) as well as an integrated self-image. The experience of competition and cooperation and each person's own balancing of these aspects of interpersonal relations cannot be learned and tested with and among adults alone, however helpful this may be, although one of course cannot say this of all adults. Even though families with several children offer better conditions in this regard, developmental opportunities are often in short supply due to lack of space in apartments, financial hardship, and lack of access to educational institutions.

The general insecurity – also spread by the media and politics – hit children and youth especially hard above all in the first lockdown of 2020, because their parents were themselves forced into a position of helplessness and could only fulfil their role as acting and orienting agents in a very limited way. The prohibition on contact with one's closest family members made supportive relations impossible in both directions. Grandparents could not help with childcare, and children and grandchildren could not help their older family members in managing everyday life.

Especially, the commonly held idea at the beginning of the pandemic that children, although themselves not becoming ill, would substantially contribute to the spread of the disease and the frequent reference to 'Grandma who has her grandchild on her conscience' traumatised children. Despite all the urgent need, it was precisely in this acute phase that neither counselling institutions nor psychological or psychiatric support was available.

A child psychiatrist from Vienna's General Hospital, which has the largest children's psychiatric department in Austria, said in a fall 2020 interview in ORF radio that on one particular day she had to send several children home who were diagnosed as suicidal although she was not sure whether these children could cope with home. She simply had no available beds, and said this was also a form of triage. While the record of this interview was removed from public access the discussion of the problem is continuing both in Germany and Austria. A 19 May 2021 press release from the dgkjp, the German Society for Child and Youth Psychiatry, Psychosomatics, and Psychotherapy, vehemently denied that there was triage in children's and youth psychiatry wards, although it was admitted that there were shortages.[7]

## Long-term consequences of the measures

Austria has given itself a timeline of from now to 2032 in which to achieve ten health goals. Goal No. 6 is: the best possible shaping and supporting of healthy growth for all children and youth. For example, a research team has analysed four chains of effects from which we can expect to see long-term impacts on the health of 1- to 19-year-olds.[8]

Regarding the 'psychological-health' chain of effects it was determined that '56% of over-14-year-olds presented depression symptoms with almost as many having anxiety symptoms. The frequency of these conditions increased five- to tenfold. As much as 16% even had suicidal thoughts.'[9]

The long-term consequences of the 'exercise' chain of effects were also regarded as dramatic. The months-long closings of all sports facilities and public playgrounds and the suspension of club activities are not only resulting now in a lack of movement and in overweight but are also influencing the future behaviour of today's youth.

The educational chain of effects involved the already mentioned dramatic health consequences: 'People with higher educational qualifications live longer and spend more years of their lives in good health. In Austria, the life expectation of women having completed compulsory education is 82.8 years, and those with higher-education degrees 85.6 years; that for men having completed compulsory education is 76.5 years, and those with higher-education degrees 83.3 years.'[10]

This gap will widen. During the lockdown, teachers had more difficulty in reaching children from disadvantaged families, who often did not have the requisite technical equipment and living conditions to enable home schooling.

In 'teaching and work', the fourth chain of effects, enormous negative consequences have also been observed:

> In the last year, unemployment among 15 to 24-year-olds increased sharply. In January 2021, 28.4% more people were unemployed than in the previous year. […] Current estimates assume 10,000 jobs lost in the course of the pandemic. […] In the long term, 20% of people remain unemployed even five years after the termination of an apprenticeship. […] Austrians with an apprenticeship certificate live five years longer (men) and ten years longer (women) in good health than those with only a compulsory school degree.[11]

## Generation party – locked down

Beate Grossegger is the scientific director of the Institute for Research in Youth Culture in Vienna. In a March 2021 interview for the Swiss *Migros Online Magazine* she answered Ralf Kaminski's question as to whether there are commonalities shared by all youth: 'Not a lot, but this was always the case. Certainly, there are themes and phenomena that are characteristic of generations, but this was never unitary – there never was a youth culture that included everyone. In the 1960s and 1980s, for example, there were highly-politicised, engaged young people but also many for whom consumerist and leisure culture were more important. It is always about the same question: Where do I belong and from what do I differentiate myself?'[12]

She considers the attitude of the older generations towards young people to be problematic in several respects:

> At first view they indeed seem very sympathetic and open and want to do everything well and correctly. But at the same time they have enormous expectations of the upcoming generation and so put it under pressure. In the 1980s this was still different. Then youth was a phase in which people were allowed to find themselves; there was a protected period between childhood

and the seriousness of an adult life. Certainly, many adults did not like what young people were doing but they said to themselves: 'okay, they have to sow their wild oats, they'll grow out of it and will come out fine.' There was much more tolerance and trust in the growing up process.[13]

## Growing up in the pandemic?

Instead of being able to differentiate oneself during puberty from one's parents and take steps in one's developments together with people of one's own age, young people in 2020/2021 were often locked in with their parents around the clock. Distance learning instead of school, no sports facilities, no shopping centres nor even park benches – which were controlled by the police – were available. There were no first love relationships and sexual experiences with the other or one's own gender. Concerts and festivals, in which getting to know possible partners is often just as important as the cultural offerings themselves, were cancelled one after the other.

It is no wonder then that young people feel as if they have lost two years of their lives, also losing their trust especially in politics.

This is also described by the Austrian youth researcher Bernhard Heinzlmaier in his new book, *Generation Corona*. In an interview with *eXXpress* he has said: 'In Austria the debate around corona was always very alarmist and exaggerated. This resulted in a situation in which barely 33% of young people trusted the government.' By contrast, the statements of the German government were much more objective, with the result that 50% of young people in Germany still trust the government. In this Heinzlmaier sees that: 'Communication also makes it possible to do a lot of wrong things.' Meanwhile, 70% of those under 30 no longer feel that politics represents them. In terms of the isolation from people of their own age, Heinzlmaier notes: 'Now they are at the mercy only of their parents; there is stronger parental control and they are suffering from this.'[14]

## Second Thesis

**The problems connected with the organisation of daily life are growing. This was not necessarily predictable, since people would assume that progress and technological development would ease daily life.**

### Daily life – gainful employment

Work pressure, fear of unemployment, underemployment, the pressure of overtime work, overextension, temporary, precarious, undignified, and underpaid work that is hazardous to health without providing a livelihood.

Constant pressure (also from the media) hostile to the rights of labour and rights to services, rhetoric about 'privileges', pressure directed against pensioners – all of this is experienced as a breathtaking pushback of historically won gains, which is of a piece with the multi-faceted decline of influence of the labour movement, that is, the new neoliberal orientation of the Social Democratic Party and of a good part of the trade unions it dominates.

As a result there has been, on the one side, the recent mass unemployment and, on the other side, conditions in many sectors that make (wage) work more strenuous, exhausting, and unrewarding.

The coping strategies specifically of young people vary greatly. Precarious life situations can also be experienced as freedom, 'work on demand' as flexibility freed from the clock, that is, as long as care duties with children or care-dependent adults do not stand in the way of the (co)shaping of work time and the workplace. Against this backdrop the conditions for a 'beautiful new world of work' often lead to the re-establishment of a gender-hierarchical division of labour in young families.

Especially dramatic are the effects of the labour market's exclusionary mechanisms on young people who – at least temporarily, though still for long periods – find absolutely no entry points into gainful employment. They are the so-called NEETS – Not in Education, Employment, or Training. According to Statistik Austria, in 2020 9% of all people between 14 and 25 years old were in this category. They are neither in school nor had a trainee position, work, or a qualification certificate that benefits them. And yet this is not a 'corona figure', since the percentage was also 9% in 2004, when statistics were first established for this social problem. From 2005 to 2019 various measures were able to lower this figure to 7%, but this improvement was reversed in 2020/2021.[15]

At the EU level, according to official figures, 14% of young people between 14 and 29 years old are in the NEETS category. If we bear in mind that the numbers of the 14 to 18-year-olds look somewhat better because this age group still contains a big share of students, we can imagine what social upheavals are being produced year after year. Although the European Union has been dealing with the problem of NEETS since 2003, nothing about this problem has decisively changed qualitatively or quantitatively.[16]

The neoliberal changes, however, effected a far-reaching de-politicisation of labour relations. Previously in the labour movement the conditions under which one was required to enter into a job relationship were understood as objects of struggles by actors with opposed interests. Trade unions, factory council members, socialist and communist parties were both tools and the results of these struggles. They were also the spheres in which democracy was learned and could be practiced within people's everyday lives.

With neoliberal thinking entrenched among so many who live from some form of work or are dependent on social transfers, work relations are accepted as being completely unpolitical and purely objective/technical. There is no longer a perception that they are defined by capital and its actors. In any case, in a depoliticised world of work there is nothing that can be opposed to the (apparently) self-acting capitalist logic.

Clearly our question is how, despite this, resistance can arise. Or: How can the idea of resistance and its possible efficacy re-emerge? Here socialists and communists have to begin anew – and, despite the given inadequate and often frustrating circumstances, appreciate and take possession of workforce representation in private enterprises, employee representation in the public sector, and trade-union functions, as loci of politics and democracy. This does not mean thinking within the old white male labour stereotypes, but instead conceiving of wage work and the reproductive work of society and life as a whole, and acting accordingly.

## Reproduction and consumption in everyday life

Precarisation also prevails in the everyday processes of reproduction and consumption. The provision of public services is becoming tighter, more expensive, and more exclusive. We are already used to dealing with television, internet, and telephone as constant challenges to one's organisational talents, both in terms of the equipment and service; by contrast most people still hesitate to constantly change between electricity and gas providers.

Along with organising one's communications technology, the degree of individual self-responsibilisation now required of people extends to the provision of ecologically justifiable food, although to achieve this individually one would have to hire domestic workers. And last but not least one is responsible for honing one's body to a perfect state of fitness and work readiness in order to be marketable.

If, in the 1970s, large sections of youth were still politicised via the critique of 'consumerist terror' and in the rebellion against bourgeois conformity, there is pressure among today's young people to not even go to an anti-racist demonstration in the wrong brand of clothing. It is not that dress codes have not always been important for youth culture but in left milieus they were not connected to expensive brand fetishism.

## Everyday life with children

For millennia, living together with and having responsibility for children has always been a social, and in the narrow sense collective, task. It is only in the last less than two hundred years that the idea has taken hold that this could be the mostly individual task of a small family and, for perhaps a quarter century now, increasingly the work only of single parents. And nowadays these parents have to listen to supposed quality media journalists tell them that they are benefiting from 'disproportionate' tax advantages. In reality, children drastically increase the risk of poverty.

In contrast to what is assumed to be the normal living situation, many thousands in Austrian cities live under conditions that need to be seen to be believed. In reality, however, the re-emergence of poverty diseases, which are – shamefully – attributed to immigration, has exclusively to do with the concrete living conditions in each country in which immigrants are often forced to live. Moreover, child poverty results not from the low-income situation of parents alone but also from lack of access to public services in the spheres of education and healthcare. Insecurity in the parenting of most adults, the loss of life plans, which are the 'inner models' to which behaviour can tend to be oriented – even the progeny of well-to-do parents with educational ambitions founder on these obstacles ever more frequently. This is confirmed by the increase in behavioural disorders and mental illnesses among children in recent years.

Even if during the pandemic home schooling generated manifold problems for families, children, and youth, nevertheless 'school' as such had been increasingly perceived as a burden and locus of exclusion. Under the radar of public perception the selection machinery of the educational system fixed generations in place, socially excluded at the margins of society. Naturally, there are always individual examples of people who have fought their way in, and individual biographies are never completely determined by origin; however, it is liberal hypocrisy to maintain that an individual's industriousness is what determines whether the given conditions can be overcome.

Even if one grants that every generation does and thinks things that appear frightful and subversive to the preceding generation, we still see an alarming picture of the disintegration of organised possibilities of experience and the lack of fundamental socialisation for a not small section of youth. On International Literacy Day, 20 September 2020, it was determined that in Carinthia, the southernmost Austrian federal state with 63,000 people, every sixth person over compulsory schooling age was a functional illiterate.[17]

We are not speaking here about an impending loss of knowledge of world literature because this is not transmissible via text messages, or through facebook, Instagram, and the like – although this too is grounds for concern. We are pointing to a functional handicap that operates within a person's work life.

## Third Thesis

**Right-wing extremism on the political level is always tied to the deep processes of authoritarianism and has three 'sources and components' in Austria.**

In Austria right-wing extremism has historical roots that operate across generations. It did not begin with National Socialism, but its stereotypes, modes of operation, and personal cliques, which are alive today, can be directly tied to National Socialism. Anti-Semitism, anti-Slavism, and anti-communism of various stripes are its essential elements. This poses a serious obstacle for the emergence of a broad left because it is embedded in the form of often unconscious prejudiced attitudes linking the – above all social democratic – left to the (extreme) right. The tendency to subjugate everything to a market condition and thus to the competitive drives of 'free forces', which characterises neoliberalism, requires at once the authoritarian setting of parameters (which are enforced internationally including by means of war) and the permanent monitoring of compliance.

Together with the identity deficits experienced as insecurity and flaws and the lack of an 'inner model' for self-regulation, these two tendencies are becoming a fundamental current in the country that makes right-wing extremism and neo-fascism dangerous.

The political mainstream – which has been completely detached from the everyday experiences of people – hardly bothers anymore with the actual life circumstances of people, increasingly not even on election day. And the alternative appears to be the – mostly no longer practiced – paternalist social democratic policies that fix people in their limited capacity to act precisely through this authoritarianism.

With ever more radical slogans, right-wing opinion leaders proffer the denigration and ostracising of entire population groups, mostly ranked according to nationality, and legislation and policies fortify racist prejudices through objective, factual confirmation. Alongside other functions that racism has in society, it superficially stabilises injured identities.

Today racism is often the only field in which policy is still promised. There seems to be not only disenchantment with politics on the part of voters; still worse is this disenchantment on the part of those politicians who do not surf on the waves of right-wing extremism or have not already fallen into the populism trap. 'There is nothing to be done about it,' they say, 'the decisions do not belong to politics but to the economy, responsibility lies with the EU, or the USA, or with globalisation,' etc. – these are the answers frequently given by Austrian politicians.

## What is to be done?

First, we need to own up to the fact that all the above-described difficulties of precarisation have also touched our parties and movements. Precarious life – that is, trying to get by with less money and still less time, or inversely less time and still less money, the atomisation of social ties and capacities, and processes of isolation and individualisation render all kinds of cooperation more difficult.

By contrast, we communists and left socialists can say that we have never fallen into neoliberal temptations and have no need to back-pedal in this regard – which, by contrast, we in fact did learn to do in relation to 'actually existing socialism'. By contrast, we maintain – together with social movements – that another world, a solidary society, is possible. We aim to make available a well worked out, pluralistic and therefore undogmatic identity.

It makes sense to emphasise activities and political demands aimed at enabling or expanding the capacity to act. This also means that people come together to make it possible to speak about and reflect on oneself and one's situation – and to create proposals in which people can participate. It means going back more resolutely to those places in which, due to social conditions, people cooperate in an organised fashion; with the goal of together making these places into political places, that is, places of discussion and confrontation: offices, schools and universities, factories and municipalities.

And it means putting forward demands that contribute to giving people more scope of action in everyday life. For example, an adequate level of unemployment benefits and an extension of the entitlement period to the duration of the job-searching process can mitigate the enormous psychological and financial pressure on an increasing number of unemployed who in any case need to have been previously employed and have paid into the social security fund. This also means effectively counteracting the 'family-with-child' poverty risk by making transfer payments available to families. A 'basic energy insurance for all' could be a first step to basic income that guarantees survival and combats poverty and mitigate social exclusion.

NOTES

1 Johanna Mückenhuber, 'Editorial', *soziales_kapital: wissenschaftliches journal österreichischer fachhochschul-studiengänge soziale arbeit* 25 (2021),
< http://www.soziales-kapital.at/index.php/sozialeskapital/article/view/739/1362.pdf>.
2 Susanne Grautmann, 'Der Kampf um einen Schulplatz ist ein Vollzeitjob', *Zeit online*, 16 August 2021.

3   Grautmann.
4   Annika Steffen, Manas K. Akmatov, Jakob Holstiege, and Jörg Bätzing, 2018, 'Diagnoseprävalenz psychischer Störungen bei Kindern und Jugendlichen in Deutschland: eine Analyse bundesweiter vertragsärztlicher Abrechnungsdaten der Jahre 2009 bis 2017', versorgunsatlas.de, <https://www.versorgungsatlas.de/fileadmin/ziva_docs/93/VA_18-17_Bericht_PsychStoerungenKinderJugendl_V2_2019-01-15.pdf>. In the International Classification of Diseases, 10th edition, 06, or F, indicates Mental, behavioural, or neuro-developmental disorders.
5   Christian Freisleben, 'Völlig überfordert', *Das österreichische Gesundheitswesen ÖKZ* vol. 62, no. 6-7 (May 2021): 10, 11.
6   Ulrike Ravens-Sieberer et al., 2021, 'Seelische Gesundheit und psychische Belastungen von Kindern und Jugendlichen in der ersten Welle der COVID-19-Pandemie - Ergebnisse der COPSY-Studie', *Bundesgesundheitsblatt*, 3 March 2021, at <https://link.springer.com/article/10.1007/s00103-021-03291-3>.
7   <https://www.news4teachers.de/2021/05/kinderpsychiater-widersprechen-kinderaerzten-es-gibt-keine-triage-bei-therapien-schuloeffnungen-sind-nicht-die-loesungen-fuer-psychiatrische-probleme/>.
8   Raphael Hengl, Felizia Kreczi, Kathrin Maier, Niklas Stockreiter, and Martin Sprenger, 'Langzeitfolgen, Was die Maßnahmen zur Eindämmung der Pandemie für das weitere Leben der Kinder und Jugendlichen bedeuten', *Das österreichische Gesundheitswesen ÖKZ* vol. 62,6-7 (2021): 15-17.
9   Hengl et al.: 15.
10  Hengl et al.: 16.
11  Hengl et al.: 16,17.
12  Beate Grossegger, <https://www.migros.ch/de/Magazin/2021/03/beate-grossegger-jugendforscherin.html>.
13  Grossegger.
14  Bernhard Heinzlmaier, 'Die Politik hat in der Corona-Pandemie die unteren zwei Drittel der Bürger vergessen', Interview with eXXpress editor-in-chief Richard Schmitt, 10 September 2021, <https://exxpress.at/soziologe-heinzlmaier-corona-debatte-fand-aus-sicht-des-oberen-drittels-statt/>.
15  <https://www.statistik.at/web_de/statistiken/menschen_und_gesellschaft/bildung/bildungsindikatoren/nichterwerbstaetige_jugendliche/index.html>.
16  For a particularly helpful analysis see Massimiliano Mascherini, 'Origins and future of the concept of NEETs in the European policy agenda', in Jacqueline O'Reilly, Janine Leschke, Renate Ortlieb, Martin Seeleib-Kaiser, and Paola Villa (eds), *Youth Labor in Transition: Inequalities, Mobility, and Policies in Europe*, Oxford: Oxford University Press, 2018, <https://www.universitypressscholarship.com/view/10.1093/oso/9780190864798.001.0001/oso-9780190864798-chapter-17>.
17  <https://www.ktn.gv.at/Service/News?nid=31747>.

# Portugal: Time Is Running Out

## Francisco Louçã

The 2015 election of a new government headed by the Socialist Party (SP – a centrist social democratic party) that depended on parliamentary support from the Left Bloc and the Communist Party, ushered in an impressive array of progressive economic policies, after a long period in which the economy and, indeed, politics more broadly were dictated by the Troika (the European Commission (EC), the European Central Bank (ECB) and the International Monetary Fund (IMF)) and the right-wing parties, which imposed an austerity agenda. It should be said that economic policy after 2015 was aided by a number of additional favourable circumstances, including the external depreciation of the euro, the relatively low price of oil, economic growth in the main export destinations, Portugal's rise as a tourist destination partly as a consequence of the political turmoil and instability in Northern Africa, and the ECB's accommodating monetary-policy stance, which contributed to a significant reduction in interest rates and a reduction in public debt outlays. The changes in economic policy orientation raised disposable income, re-established confidence, and fuelled a remarkable economic recovery. Unemployment has fallen substantially, poverty and inequality have decreased, and, in contrast to what occurred in most years since 1999, real GDP has grown slightly faster than the EU and the eurozone averages between 2016 and 2018, and yet at the same time Portugal has managed to run a current account surplus – a particularly rare combination. The government did this while refraining from any major confrontation with the EU authorities and rules, which in any case accepted these internal changes in Portugal, since they could not risk a major political shock after what had happened to Greece.

Portugal thus became both the poster child for the alternative to austerity and an apparent proof of the possibility of successfully implementing progressive economic policies within the existing legal, institutional, and political framework of the European Union. However, this is an oversimplification, for the Portuguese economy remains significantly constrained by the same structural vulnerabilities that brought on the recession of the last decade, and its fiscal policy has been severely hamstrung during this period by the eurozone's fiscal rules, which meant that fiscal policy has failed to adequately support economic growth and has practically no chances of doing so in the future. At the end of the mandate, a new election was held by October 2019, after which the SP rejected the renewal of the pact with the left parties, preparing a political crisis and a new election (January 2022) that gave it, for the first time since 2005, an absolute majority in parliament. A brief overview of the major political and economic decisions of the last years is presented in what follows.

## The two lost decades after the euro[*]

The post-2015 policy turn was particularly welcome since Portugal, like other peripheral countries, had suffered a setback imposed by the euro and its rules. Indeed, between 1975 and 1998, Portuguese GDP grew at an average annual real per capita rate of 3.2%. The public debt was then 51.8% of GDP. The rate of growth declined during the first euro decade to 1.2% and then, in the second decade, 2008-2018, to 0.5% (despite a sharp recovery in 2017 and 2018). Unemployment, which had on average been 7.4% between 1976 and 2008, went up to 11.6% in the last decade, but these figures are understated, as they do not account for the fall in the active population. (In 2012, after a year's implementation of the Troika programme, real unemployment eventually reached over 18%, when non-declared unemployment and subemployment are considered).

In any case, Portugal's change in policy orientation after 2015 unquestionably led to positive results in many spheres. The progressive income policy and the reestablishment of economic confidence gave a significant boost to domestic demand: real private consumption grew slightly above 2% per year between 2016 and 2018; nominal investment grew by 13.8% in 2016 and by 9.0% in 2017 (although from the low levels of the previous recession years). At the same time, the favourable external circumstances, especially a relatively depreciated real effective exchange rate since around 2014 and the expansion in Portugal's main export markets, boosted the country's nominal exports by 2.7% in 2016, by 11.6% in 2017, and by 6.0% in 2018, a process which, together with Portugal's extraordinary tourist boom in recent years, improved Portugal's balance of payments. Taken together, these developments combined to bring about a real GDP growth of 2.0%

---

[*] This section is based on Francisco Louçã, Ricardo Cabral, Alexandre Abreu, Andrea Peniche, Vicente Ferreira (2019), *The economic evolution of Portugal: Possibilities and limits for a progressive economic program*, Berlin: Rosa Luxemburg Foundation.

in 2016, 3.5% in 2017, and 2.4% in 2018, in all three years allowing for real convergence relative to the EU-28 and the eurozone averages – which is exceptional for Portugal since it joined the euro (Figure 1).

*Figure 1: Evolution of the Portuguese economy pre- and post-2015*

Evolution of economic indicators between 2011 and 2014 (Troika adjustment programme)

|  | 2011 | 2012 | 2013 | 2014 |
|---|---|---|---|---|
| Real GDP growth rate (%) | -1.7 | -4.1 | -0.9 | 0.8 |
| Budget balance (% GDP) | -7.7 | -6.2 | -5.1 | -7.4 |
| Gross public debt (% GDP) | 114.4 | 129 | 131.4 | 132.9 |
| Unemployment rate (%) | 12.7 | 15.5 | 16.2 | 13.9 |
| Total expenditure (% GDP) | 50 | 48.9 | 49.9 | 51.7 |
| Total revenue (% GDP) | 42.4 | 2.5 | 2.2 | 2 |
| Total revenue (% GDP) | 42.4 | 42.7 | 44.8 | 44.4 |
| Gross fixed capital formation, general government (% GDP) | 3.5 | 2.5 | 2.2 | 2 |

Evolution of economic indicators between 2015 and 2019

|  | 2015 | 2016 | 2017 | 2018 | 2019 |
|---|---|---|---|---|---|
| Real GDP growth rate (%) | 1.8 | 2.0 | 3.5 | 2.8 | 2.5 |
| Budget balance (% GDP) | -4.4 | -1.9 | -0.9 | -0.3 | 0.1 |
| Gross public debt (% GDP) | 131.2 | 131.5 | 126.1 | 121.5 | 117.2 |
| Unemployment rate (%) | 12.4 | 11.1 | 8.9 | 7.0 | 6.5 |
| Underemployment rate (%) | 21.3 | 19.6 | 16.5 | 13.7 | 12.7 |
| Total expenditure (% GDP) | 48.2 | 44.8 | 45.4 | 43.2 | 42.7 |
| Total revenue (% GDP) | 43.8 | 42.9 | 42.4 | 42.9 | 42.7 |
| Gross fixed capital formation, general government (% GDP) | 2.3 | 1.5 | 1.8 | 1.8 | 1.9 |

Source: Istituto Nacional de Estatística (INE)

Also impressive was the evolution of employment and unemployment. From a record high of 16.4% in 2013 (official figures – real unemployment was higher), and still 12.6% when the SP government took office in 2015, the unemployment rate kept falling in subsequent years reaching around

6% in 2019. The total employed population increased from a low of 4.4 million in 2013 and 4.5 million in 2015 to 4.9 million in 2019 through 2022, an evolution unaltered by the pandemic. The negative migration balance was halted and reversed. Also notable is the reduction of the high level of underemployment, although it is still double the figures of officially recognised unemployment.

These positive labour-market developments, despite their shortcomings (on which more below), along with the improvements in the coverage and levels of several social transfers, contributed to the at-risk-of-poverty rate falling from 19.5% in 2015 to 17.3% in 2018, while income inequality, as measured by the Gini coefficient, fell from 34.0 in 2015 to 32.1 in 2018.

## Some major obstacles for a democracy in combating inequality

Despite the rejection of IMF and EC-imposed austerity since 2015, major obstacles remain for the development of a left orientation and solution to the structural problems of inequality, exploitation, and poverty. First, one of the secrets of reconciling the government's progressive income policy with budgetary orthodoxy has been massive cuts to public investment, which have often left public services in disarray; this, alongside private investment also at perilously low levels, limits the prospects for future economic progress and structural change, especially as the space for bouncing back from the recession may well have been exhausted. This has stoked intense discussions between the SP government and the left parties. Second, the remarkably favourable set of external circumstances which contributed to the outcome of the last few years is unlikely to remain intact. Third, the volume of foreign and public debt remains among the highest in the world, constituting a significant risk factor in the event of a change of circumstances. Fourth, Portugal's newly-found 'Florida model' of job-intensive, low-productivity growth with considerable prominence of the tourism sector and a policy of attracting wealthy foreign pensioners has not only not resulted in a structural upgrading of the productive sector but has also had some serious negative consequences for working people, especially the drastic increase of housing costs in the major cities. And fifth, the progressive content of especially the 2019-2021 Costa government's policies has some serious limitations, most notably with regard to labour-market policy.

Indeed, a major limitation of Portugal's post-2015 economic trajectory is the quality of employment, namely the high and growing level of temporary, short-term and precarious jobs. The first consequence of this is stagnant labour productivity; GDP per hour worked has remained virtually unchanged since 2015, reflecting the fact that GDP growth has been entirely of an extensive character and based on employment creation, but also on dismantling labour relations, rather than on productivity gains. Furthermore, this seems to reflect a tendency to the reallocation of employment towards low value-added sectors. Certainly, most employment creation in the last few years has taken place in restaurants, housing, retail commerce, and temporary-work sectors, which tend to be characterised by low labour productivity and low median wages.

*Figure 2: GDP per hour worked index (2010=100), 2002-2018*

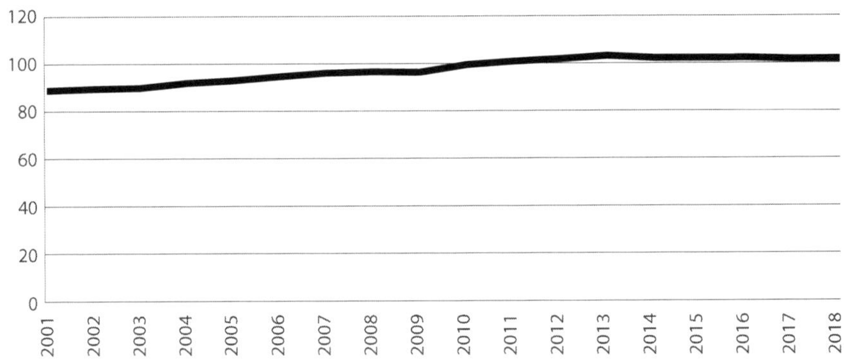

Source: Istituto Nacional de Estatística (INE)

As already said, the common dimension related to these structural difficulties is the precarious character of employment contracts, an issue that has been the object of considerable debate. The government has argued that new permanent contracts account for a large proportion – more than 90% – of net employment creation since the SP government took office. Critics, on the other hand, have pointed out that new permanent contracts have accounted for a much smaller proportion of gross employment creation, reflecting continuing high levels of precarious job rotation, and especially that the share of temporary employment in total employment, which is one of the highest in the EU, has remained unchanged in the last few years – 22.0% in 2019, the same level as in 2015. Yet, this was much worse among under-25-year-olds, amounting to more than 60% in this age cohort; among those between 25-34 years it was 35%. This is a social disaster, and the figures are getting worse.

More fundamentally, left critics of the SP government have pointed to labour legislation as the single most important area in which the SP government has proven to be a barrier to progressive change, rather than an agent of it. On such issues as mandatory paid vacation days, the amount of dismissal compensations, the rules governing overtime work, and the rules promoting and governing collective bargaining agreements, all of which were used effectively by the Troika and the conservative government to bring down the cost of labour, the SP government has chosen to preserve the status quo as established under the Troika and has systematically turned down the left parties' attempts to restore a balance of forces in industrial relations more favourable to labour. Arguably, this is one of the reasons why, in a context of significant economic recovery and robust employment creation, the wage share in national income has barely recovered during the SP government's terms in office from the sharp drop that it experienced during the crisis and Troika years. This retention of the kind of labour laws typifying the Troika period became one of the major points of confrontations between the SP government and the left parties from 2019 to 2022.

The problems of job insecurity and relatively stagnant wages for the low and middle classes have been compounded by the crisis in the housing market, which has been felt most acutely in the urban centres. Several factors have come together to bring about this crisis: the liberalisation of the rental market by the previous conservative government (which the SP government has refrained from reversing), Portugal's tourism boom, the ultra-low interest rate given the monetary expansion by the ECB, and a couple of more specific policy measures like the 'golden visa' scheme introduced in 2012 and the extraordinarily favourable tax regime for expatriate workers and retirees. All of these have combined to bring about a dynamic of skyrocketing valorisation and speculation in the (purchase and rental) housing market, into which significant amounts of capital, including from outside the country, have flowed in recent years. For example, in 2018, according to the National Institute of Statistics, average housing prices rose 10.3% while rents per square meter rose 9.3%, with prices and rents in metropolitan areas, particularly Lisbon, rising faster than in the rest of the country. This dynamic has added to the income of some Portuguese families (those who invested their savings in the housing market and those employed in related sectors, like the short-term rental industry) and helped sustain the physical renewal of urban areas, but it meant a dramatic increase in the cost of home rental and ownership for the vast majority and the expulsion of the low- and middle-income population, older residents, and the young from central urban areas.

## A setback since 2019

A major change occurred with the October 2019 general election campaign, as the SP decided to abandon its agreement with the left parties, fighting for an absolute majority that would favour a government with no obligations to the left. Although some polls suggested this could be possible, it was a difficult gamble, since there was widespread mistrust in the country of the absolute power of a single party, including among the very supporters of the governing Socialist Party. And, as in the end the election re-established the same balance of power as in 2015, the break from the previous cooperation had its price. Despite the Left Bloc's offer to negotiate a platform for the following years, if it included major changes in the labour laws and strategies for public services, the SP was not willing to do so and rejected the platform. From then on, and particularly after 2020, it depended solely on the parliamentary support of the Communist Party and persisted in rejecting any correction to the labour markets and its tendency to precarisation.

Some measures still pointed in the direction of redistribution (the plan was for the minimum wage to increase by almost 50% in four years, for instance), but social inequality is still among the worst in Europe.

All these factors have led to social discontent and, specifically, to the emergence of a new extreme right, benefiting from the promotion of xenophobia (in particular, against Roma, despite these communities having lived in the country for many centuries) and a general discourse against the 'system', on the model of Salvini and Abascal.

The 2022 general election confirmed these trends. Provoking an artificial crisis, the SP obtained an absolute majority with 42% of the popular vote, while the left parties suffered a defeat, losing votes and seats (the Left Bloc was reduced to 4.46% and the Communist Party 4.39% of the popular vote, with, respectively, 5 and 6 MPs in the 230-seat parliament), just as the traditional right-wing alternative party lost some of its influence (falling to 28%) and the right wing emerged as a new force (7%).

## Challenges of the post-pandemic period

The pandemic aggravated some of these problems and created new ones. By the end of summer 2021 the percentage of infected in the total population reached ca. 10%, and the death toll among those registered as infected amounted to 1.7%. Although the vaccination process has been one of the most efficient in Europe and the world, the total impact on health was worse than in other European countries. The economic consequences were also damaging, with a 7.6% reduction of GDP in 2020. Yet, as this corresponds partially to depressed consumption, the relative recovery was quick in 2021 as far as total internal demand is concerned. The same did not occur, as could be expected, in exports and tourism revenues, which did not recover in 2021. Two other consequences were the burden on health services and the intensification of precarisation and platformisation, as well as the general deterioration of labour conditions. Indeed, as already mentioned, before the pandemic the percentage of precarious and temporary labour was already 22%, the highest in the OECD.

## Challenges for the left

It follows that there are three main challenges the left, now from a position of opposition, needs to address in the next months and years.

The first is the struggle to reduce precarity and change the labour laws, re-establishing contracts and negotiations with trade unions as a pillar of social relations. It is crucial to incorporate young workers and professionals into movements that represent their collective interests, renewing or transforming the current trade unions, which lost some of their capacity for initiative and the ability to concentrate the hopes and action of the popular masses.

The second major task is to elaborate and propose a fair tax system, taxing profits and dividends and closing tax-evasion loopholes, and to push for freedom from the rules and constraints that prevent the use of fiscal expansion in order to create jobs, increase public investment, pay for high-quality social services, and finance the productive system's adaptation to the climate emergency, so that democracy can be lived by the people as access to common goods and social security.

Third, strong political representation is required, with increased capacity for mobilisation and unitary orientation on the part of left parties. Only if the political balance of forces is shifted to favour the emerging demands of the popular sectors will it be possible to sustain an alternative to austerity or EU-oriented liberal strategies. This implies reorganising the left's political influence and projecting a new vision of climate and social and economic alternative policies suited to youth, workers', and pensioners' struggles.

Anniversary

# The Contested Legacy of Derry's Bloody Sunday

## Daniel Finn

Fifty years after Bloody Sunday, it may seem as if there is little new to say about what happened in Derry on 30 January 1972. The massacre has attracted more attention than any other single episode of the conflict that ravaged Northern Ireland for almost three decades. There have been millions of words devoted to the subject in every conceivable format, from books and newspaper articles to feature films and official inquiries. The British government has formally acknowledged that the fourteen men killed by soldiers from the Parachute Regiment were civilians taking part in a civil rights march whose deaths had no justification. Does this mean that controversy has now given way to consensus?

While few people now dispute the basic facts, we cannot say the same about the political context in which the massacre took place. The killings were not simply the result of choices made by soldiers and their immediate commanding officers on the day. They were the predictable outcome of decisions taken at the highest levels of government in the months and years leading up to the march in Derry. If Britain's state managers had opted for a different course during that crucial period, they could have avoided not only the deaths on Bloody Sunday, but thousands more over the decades that followed.

## Challenging Stormont

In 2006, the British Army published a document with the title *Operation Banner: An Analysis of Military Operations in Northern Ireland*. It sought to anatomise the Army's campaign in Northern Ireland – 'Operation Banner' – which had been directed primarily against the Irish Republican Army (IRA).

The report described the experience of Northern Ireland's Catholic-nationalist minority under Protestant-unionist majority rule after Britain partitioned the island in 1921:

> All important posts were held by Protestants, and local elections were manipulated to ensure a Protestant advantage. For example, in Londonderry 19,000 Protestants controlled eight of the 12 wards, leaving only four for 36,000 Catholics. This gave the minority effective and permanent control of the city council. By the early 1960s discrimination had become institutionalised. It was not that legislation was discriminatory in itself, but rather that the way it was applied in practice discriminated against the Catholic minority. In 1969 Londonderry was the most deprived city in the United Kingdom. 33,000 of the 36,000 Catholics were crowded into the Victorian slums of the Creggan and the Bogside. Unemployment in Londonderry was the highest in the UK. A similar pattern applied in Belfast (with a population of 385,000) and many of the other towns throughout Northern Ireland.[1]

Gerrymandering was essential to maintain unionist control in local government districts such as Derry where there was a nationalist preponderance. There was no need to manipulate electoral boundaries for the regional parliament at Stormont: it had a guaranteed unionist majority, so long as Protestants continued to vote for the Unionist Party. Anyone who tried to challenge the Northern Irish system outside these channels could fall foul of the Special Powers Act, which gave Stormont the authority to intern suspects without trial for an indefinite period of time.

Nationalist discontent crystallised in the late 1960s around the Northern Ireland Civil Rights Association (NICRA), partly inspired by the example of the civil rights movement in the US. Although support for NICRA came overwhelmingly from the nationalist community, the group did not call for an end to partition, and its list of demands amounted to a plea for equal status as British citizens. A NICRA demonstration in Derry on 5 October 1968 proved to be the first major flashpoint after police attacked the marchers. This inaugurated a cycle of protest and reaction in which Derry played a decisive role.

Under pressure from the British government, the Unionist leadership offered reforms that merely angered their own supporters without going far enough to satisfy NICRA. The policing of civil rights demonstrations by the Royal Ulster Constabulary (RUC) became a major point of contention in its own right. Matters came to a head in August 1969 when a unionist organisation, the Apprentice Boys, went ahead with a march through the centre of Derry, despite pleas from local nationalists to call it off.[2] Clashes between Derry Catholics and the RUC erupted into a full-scale confrontation known as the 'Battle of the Bogside'. At the same time, disturbances in Belfast resulted in eight deaths, including five Catholics who had been shot dead by the RUC, and the expulsion of several hundred Catholic families from their homes.

## Part of the problem

The events of August 1969 brought two new military forces into the equation: the British Army and the IRA. Harold Wilson's Labour government sent in troops to restore order in Derry and Belfast. Although most people assumed that their function was to protect the Catholic minority from attack, their actual mandate was to support the 'civil power', i.e. the administration at Stormont. This would become a highly significant point as the politics of the crisis worked themselves out.

Wilson and Edward Heath, the Conservative politician who replaced him as Britain's Prime Minister in June 1970, did want the local government to carry out reforms. But they also wanted to keep that government in place for as long as possible, instead of taking full responsibility into their own hands by imposing direct rule from Westminster. The nature of the political system meant that any viable Stormont premier would have to come from the Unionist Party.

Unionist leaders demanded that the British Army act decisively to impose 'law and order' after the unrest of 1968–69. In remarks that he prepared for a staff conference in October 1969, the Army commander Ian Freeland translated that call into what he understood to be its true meaning: 'Why didn't the Army counter the resistance of the Roman Catholics behind their barricades by force of arms and reduce this minority to their original state of second-class citizenship?'[3]

The Army's *Operation Banner* report spelled out the implications of allowing the regional administration to carry on:

> In 1969 the British Cabinet saw much of the problem of Northern Ireland as being Stormont's responsibility. However, given its composition, Stormont was most unlikely to take substantive action. Indeed it would probably have seen that as being contrary to its own interests. Stormont was part of the problem and could have been so recognised at the time.[4]

British politicians might have been less reluctant to impose direct rule if they had grasped what was happening on the nationalist side of the political fence, and what its long-term consequences would be. IRA members had been involved in the civil rights movement, but the IRA itself was effectively dormant as a military force in 1968–69. Its Dublin-based leadership had no plans to start a fresh insurgency against British rule after the failure of the 1956–62 Border Campaign.

Following the arrival of British troops, a group of traditional republicans who distrusted the movement's left-wing political turn came forward to accuse the IRA leadership of having left nationalist areas defenceless in August 1969. They set up a new organisation called the Provisional IRA (Provos for short) that soon won over much of the existing republican base in Belfast. Their former comrades became known as the Official IRA. Meanwhile, some of the politicians who had taken part in the civil rights protests set up a new political organisation, the Social Democratic and Labour Party (SDLP), as a vehicle for reformist, parliamentary nationalism.

The Provos wanted to launch a full-scale campaign of guerrilla warfare against the British Army, but they needed the right political conditions to make that possible. If the British government had suspended the local parliament and imposed a package of sweeping reforms to address the grievances that had fuelled the civil rights movement, the Provisional IRA would have been a marginal force within the nationalist community, incapable of getting its campaign off the ground. Instead, its leaders had a rich seam of political discontent into which they could tap. The SDLP's commitment to legal and non-violent methods of struggle now faced a real challenge from those who favoured the bullet over the ballot.

In July 1970, the Army launched a search operation in the nationalist Lower Falls district of Belfast, at a time when neither the Provos nor the Officials, who were the larger group in the area, had carried out any attacks on British soldiers. After the troops met with a hostile response from stone-throwing youths, they imposed a full curfew and killed four civilians. As the *Operation Banner* report acknowledged, the Falls Road curfew was a disaster for British security policy:

> It handed a significant information operations opportunity to the IRA, and this was exploited to the full. The Government and Army media response was unsophisticated and unconvincing. The search also convinced most moderate Catholics that the Army was pro-loyalist. The majority of the Catholic population became effectively nationalist, if they were not already. The IRA gained significant support.[5]

By the spring of 1971, the Provos felt confident enough to begin shooting directly at British troops. The Army suffered its first casualty at the hands of the IRA in February of that year. The Northern Irish premier James Chichester-Clark stepped down soon afterwards and was replaced by Brian Faulkner.

Faulkner immediately began pressing the British government for permission to intern suspects without trial. With an IRA bombing campaign gathering momentum, Edward Heath finally gave Faulkner the green light for the operation, which went ahead on 9 August 1971. The Army's account of the conflict dismissed the publicly stated rationale for these mass arrests as a rhetorical cover story:

> Internment was introduced largely as a result of pressure from unionist politicians. The British Prime Minister stated that it was a political decision for Stormont that could not be justified on security grounds. The consequences were severe.[6]

## Civil resistance

Instead of reducing the violence, as Faulkner claimed that it would, internment resulted in a massive escalation. There had been 34 deaths in Northern Ireland during the first seven months of 1971; within two days, there were 17 more, with 140 to follow by the end of the year.[7] Soldiers from the Parachute Regiment shot ten civilians dead in Ballymurphy, a nationalist area in west Belfast, over the course of thirty-six hours; in May 2021, a coroner's report found that all of the victims had been killed 'without justification'.[8]

The two republican groups were still perfectly capable of operating despite the fact that some of their members were now in custody while others had gone on the run. Both Provos and Officials did everything in their power to carry out lethal attacks on British soldiers, assisted by an influx of new recruits. Many of those arrested had no connection to either IRA faction; that contributed to the sense of outrage among nationalists, as did the reports of brutal interrogation methods that began filtering out from the prison camps.

However, there was a wider reason for the failure of internment to restore stability. Most nationalists believed that Faulkner's goal was to prop up the Unionist Party and coerce the minority into accepting the status quo, perhaps combined with a few cosmetic reforms that would not address the core issues of exclusion and discrimination. They had good reason for believing this to be the case. Even if all the people arrested on 9 August had been IRA members, there would still have been a popular backlash against the operation and the political agenda that stood behind it.

On the first day of internment, an emergency bulletin from NICRA's Belfast branch called for 'total withdrawal by non-Unionists from every governmental structure, rent and rates strikes by the people, barricades for defence where necessary and total non-cooperation with a regime which has been stigmatised by the British establishment itself'.[9] Nationalists quickly turned this blueprint into a reality. Although this campaign of mass civil resistance has not attracted the same interest from historians as the shootings and bombings of republican guerrillas, it had a huge impact on the course of events.

A rent-and-rates strike by council tenants won solid backing among working-class nationalists. By the end of September, there were 26,000 households on strike, representing one-fifth of the 135,000 local authority tenants. Participation rates were particularly high in certain areas, such as Strabane (87 per cent of tenants) and Belfast's Divis estate (almost 100 per cent).[10] Faulkner's government claimed that republicans had coerced tenants into withholding payments. In private, his civil servants recognised 'the great mass of sincere and immediate support from the rank and file' that lay behind it: 'The relative success of the campaign from the beginning is probably due less to any organisation behind it, which can only have been minimal, than to the conviction of individual participants that their cause was just.'[11]

In tandem with the strike, nationalist anger expressed itself in the form of 'no-go areas' in Derry and Belfast where it was no longer safe for British troops to enter. A confidential briefing at the end of 1971 described the challenge facing the authorities in Derry:

> At present neither the IRA nor the military have control of the Bogside and Creggan areas, law and order are not being effectively maintained and the Security Forces now face an entirely hostile Catholic community numbering 33,000 in those areas alone.[12]

The SDLP had already withdrawn from Stormont in July 1971 after the killing of two young nationalists by the Army in Derry, and there was no question of that boycott now being reversed. When the Irish civil servant Eamonn Gallagher paid a visit to Northern Ireland, he found that 'moderate leaders' on the nationalist side were close to despair: 'Even the most pacific of them have now begun to say that they have a vested interest in the continuance of violence for as long as Stormont exists.'[13] Gallagher's boss, the Irish premier Jack Lynch, urged his British counterpart Edward Heath to recognise that internment had simply increased the IRA's popularity:

'Urban guerrilla warfare can only work if there is cooperation from the people. This cooperation certainly exists because the minority are looking to the Provisionals for protection.'[14]

## Back to the streets

This was the context in which some of those who had organised the civil rights protests of 1968–69 decided to revive the tactic of street marches at the end of 1971. The Derry activist Eamonn McCann later described their political motivation for doing so:

> The faction most in favour of marching, almost as a matter of principle, was the left within the broad civil rights movement. The argument was that none of the other forms of protest provided a way for the mass of working-class people to become actively involved in the fight. The rent-and-rates strike had its attractions, but it was a passive sort of activity. The armed struggle could, of its nature, involve only a few, while rioting was appropriate mainly to the energetic young.[15]

The left-wing current that McCann had in mind was not represented by a single organisation. By this stage, the dominant political forces in NICRA were the Official republicans and the Communist Party of Ireland. Although the Official IRA had begun carrying out attacks on British soldiers as the crisis intensified, its leadership team stressed the need for political action as a complement to guerrilla warfare. This set them apart from the Provos, who saw armed struggle as the main priority and tended to dismiss other forms of activity as a wasteful diversion.

However, NICRA did not have a monopoly on the organisation of street marches. People's Democracy (PD), a small group inspired by New Left ideology, had peeled away from NICRA because of political differences, and now helped establish a campaigning front called the Northern Resistance Movement (NRM). PD was keen to involve the Provos in political mobilisations and persuaded them to endorse the NRM. In principle, every shade of nationalist opinion endorsed the new wave of street marches, from SDLP politicians to IRA guerrillas, although that appearance of consensus masked some profound divisions over tactics and strategy. Some of those who joined the marches would have been happy to accept reforms within the existing constitutional framework, while the Provos and their allies would settle for nothing less than a British withdrawal.

In the final weeks of 1971, Brian Faulkner suddenly had to grapple with an upsurge of protest. On Christmas Day, the NRM led an anti-internment march that reached the gates of the prison camp at Long Kesh. On the first weekend of January 1972, NICRA organised a demonstration on the Falls Road, attended by five thousand people. SDLP spokesmen insisted that there could be no talks with the British government until it released all the internees.[16] These protests posed a direct challenge to Stormont's authority, as Faulkner had imposed a six-month ban on all street processions to coincide with internment, which he extended in January.

NICRA raised the stakes again on 22 January by organising a march to Magilligan, just north of Derry, where the authorities had recently opened another camp for internees. Soldiers of the Parachute Regiment prevented the marchers from reaching the camp by firing rubber bullets and striking freely with their batons. One soldier was heard remarking to his officers: 'I thought we were here to stop them, not massacre them.'[17] NICRA then announced its intention to defy the ban once more with a demonstration in Derry on 30 January.

The local branch of Ian Paisley's Democratic Unionist Party promised to hold a counter-protest, then called it off at the last minute, claiming to have received assurances that the security forces would stop the marchers 'by force if necessary'.[18] The local RUC commander, Frank Lagan, also wanted to minimise the danger of a violent confrontation. According to Brendan Duddy, who acted as an intermediary between Lagan and the two IRAs, he received assurances from both the Provos and the Officials that their members would not bring weapons on the march or use it as an opportunity to attack the British Army. The Army commander Robert Ford ignored Lagan's advice and decided to use the protest as the occasion for mass arrests, aiming to 'scoop up as many hooligans as possible'.[19]

Ford chose the Paras – known to be the most aggressive of all the regiments stationed in Northern Ireland, with the killings in Ballymurphy already on their record – as the agent of his plan. By one reporter's estimate, 20,000 people joined the demonstration as it made its way towards the city centre of Derry.[20] When the marchers reached the Army barricade, the Paras went into action, cheered on by Ford. By the time they were finished, the soldiers had shot thirteen civilians dead; another victim later died of his wounds.

## From Widgery to Saville

Journalists quickly established that every known fact and every available eyewitness contradicted the Army's version of events. But the British Home Secretary Reginald Maudling still used that account as the basis for his speech in the House of Commons, claiming that the soldiers had acted in self-defence after coming under sustained fire from republican guerrillas.

Edward Heath appointed Britain's most senior judge, Lord John Widgery, to conduct an official inquiry. Two months after Bloody Sunday, the British ambassador in Dublin passed on an advance copy of Widgery's report to the Irish government. The civil servant who received the ambassador observed that Widgery's account appeared to be 'a rather one-sided interpretation' and wondered 'how those in Derry, who were fully familiar with what had happened, would take the report'.[21]

This was a classic case of diplomatic understatement. The Widgery Report did almost as much to inflame nationalist fury as the massacre itself. Its author held the organisers of the march responsible for what had happened, expressed 'strong suspicion' that some of the victims had been 'firing weapons or handling bombs', and found 'no reason to suppose that the soldiers would have opened fire if they had not been fired upon first'.[22] Eamonn McCann published a devastating critique of the report in 1992, showing the ways in which Lord Widgery had ignored clear evidence that discredited the claims of the Army:

> At the time of Widgery's appointment it was argued by many that he would be unable to examine what had happened in Derry on 30 January objectively, that he would, automatically and perhaps unconsciously, view the events through a prism of class and national prejudice and thus gain a distorted impression. But this is altogether too generous. The inconsistencies, illogicalities and untruths in the report cannot be attributed to an *inability* to discover and tell the truth. The distance between the report and the reality yawns far too widely for that. It is a politically-motivated unwillingness to tell the truth, not an inability to see the truth, which explains the Widgery Report.[23]

The British authorities no longer consider Widgery's conclusions to be defensible. In 2010, Lord Mark Saville published a new report on Bloody Sunday after hearing testimony from eyewitnesses for several years and sifting through the documentary record. Saville concluded that none of the victims was 'posing a threat of causing death or serious injury' and that the use of lethal force by the Paras was 'unjustifiable'. He blamed the soldiers and their commanding officer Derek Wilford for the killings. The British Prime Minister David Cameron immediately accepted the report's findings and apologised to the families of the victims.

The contrast between the Widgery and Saville reports is readily apparent to anyone who has read the two documents. However, this does not mean that the second report was free of the political bias that had characterised its predecessor. Widgery and Saville both reflected the needs of the British state and its ruling class in their conclusions. Those needs had shifted dramatically between 1972 and 2010.

In the immediate aftermath of Bloody Sunday, it was essential for Widgery to hold the line and deliver a comprehensive whitewash in defiance of logic and evidence. By the time Saville completed his report, the British state had established a new political framework in Northern Ireland based on power-sharing between unionist and nationalist politicians, including former members of the IRA. It would have been entirely counter-productive for Saville to repeat the approach of the Widgery report. Instead, he took a more subtle approach, glossing over the role played by officers such as Derek Wilford's superior Robert Ford, who had taken the decision to send in the Paras, and his adjutant Mike Jackson, who later became the Army's chief of staff. If Saville had given Ford and Jackson their due share of attention, it would have been much harder for David Cameron to endorse his findings without discrediting the Army as an institution.[24]

## The end of the beginning

For supporters of the Provisional IRA, Bloody Sunday had sounded the death knell for the tactic of unarmed protest: from now on, force would have to be met with force. That was certainly the view of the young men and women who flocked to join the Provos after the massacre. However, the civil resistance campaign actually entered its most intense phase in the weeks that followed. On 6 February, a NICRA demonstration in Newry attracted more than 50,000 people, despite warnings that the violence in Derry might be repeated and threats of mass arrest broadcast to the marchers from a low-flying helicopter.[25]

Sympathy for northern nationalists in the southern Irish state began to assume organised form for the first time, with protest committees springing up and trade unionists calling for a general strike, hastily rebranded as a day of national mourning by Jack Lynch's government. In his statement to the Irish parliament, the Dáil, Lynch demanded the withdrawal of British troops from the Catholic ghettoes, and promised to fund 'peaceful action by the minority in Northern Ireland, designed to obtain their freedom from Unionist misgovernment'.[26] An angry crowd in Dublin burnt the British embassy to the ground as police stood by helpless. The no-go areas were consolidated, the rent-and-rates strike strengthened. With the SDLP still boycotting Stormont and refusing to negotiate while internment continued, Brian Faulkner and Edward Heath now faced a nationalist population united in rejection of their authority.

When Faulkner refused to hand over security powers to Westminster, Heath imposed direct rule on 24 March, ending half a century of Unionist Party rule. British civil servants began putting out feelers for a new political initiative that might bring the SDLP and the Irish government back onside and isolate the republican guerrillas. Divisions within the nationalist community that had been papered over since internment began to resurface. The Official IRA called a ceasefire in May 1972, after which they gradually wound down their armed wing. This made it easier for the Provos to call a ceasefire of their own the following month.

Heath's secretary of state for Northern Ireland, William Whitelaw, invited the Provisional leadership for secret talks on the region's future. The Provos insisted that Britain should declare its intention to withdraw all troops by the end of 1974 and allow the island's future to be determined by an all-Ireland poll. This was much more than the British government was prepared to concede. With no possibility of agreement between the two sides, the truce soon broke down and the Provos decided to launch a major bombing offensive. But the mood in the nationalist community had shifted since Bloody Sunday. Many Catholics were glad to see the end of Stormont and now wanted to find out what Heath's reform proposals would amount to in practice.

The Provisional offensive served only to isolate their movement. On 21 July 1972, IRA members planted twenty-one bombs in Belfast's city centre, killing nine people and injuring more than 130. Although the IRA had phoned in warnings, there were too many devices for the security forces to cope with at once. 'Bloody Friday' was a propaganda disaster for the Provos, and it gave William Whitelaw the opportunity to launch a major military operation ten days later that swept aside the no-go areas in Belfast and Derry. Civil resistance never reached the same heights again.

The British state learnt an important lesson from Bloody Sunday and its aftermath. It never drove all sections of nationalist opinion into full-blown opposition to its policy again – although Margaret Thatcher's government came close during the republican hunger strikes of 1981. This comparatively subtle approach ensured that the Provos could only win support from a minority of nationalists, as Sinn Féin's electoral performances in the 1980s demonstrated. The IRA ultimately called a ceasefire in the 1990s, having come to recognise that victory was beyond its grasp. But it would never have been able to sustain an armed campaign for over two decades if the British government had not embarked on such a disastrous course in the early 1970s.

NOTES

1. *Operation Banner: An Analysis of Military Operations in Northern Ireland*, July 2006, 2–2. 'Londonderry' was the preferred unionist title for the city.
2. Niall Ó Dochartaigh, *From Civil Rights to Armalites: Derry and the Birth of the Irish Troubles*, Basingstoke: Palgrave Macmillan, 2005, pp. 103-4.
3. Simon Prince and Geoffrey Warner, *Belfast and Derry in Revolt: A New History of the Start of the Troubles*, Newbridge: Irish Academic Press, 2012, p. 221.
4. *Operation Banner*, 8-2.
5. *Operation Banner*, 2-5, 6.
6. *Operation Banner*, 4-2.
7. Henry Patterson, *Ireland Since 1939: The Persistence of Conflict*, London: Penguin Books, 2007, p. 221.
8. Rory Carroll, 'The Ballymurphy shootings: 36 hours in Belfast that left 10 dead', *Guardian*, 11 May 2021. Another Ballymurphy resident died of a heart attack after an altercation with a group of soldiers who, according to the dead man's family, stuck an unloaded gun in his mouth and pulled the trigger.
9. Rosa Gilbert, 'No Rent, No Rates: Civil Disobedience Against Internment in Northern Ireland, 1971-1974', *Studi irlandesi: A Journal of Irish Studies* 7 (2017), p. 27.
10. Gilbert, 'No Rent, No Rates', pp. 27-29.
11. Gilbert, 'No Rent, No Rates', p. 28.
12. Patterson, *Ireland Since 1939*, p. 222.
13. National Archives of Ireland, D/T/2002/8/843.
14. National Archives of Ireland, DFA/2003/13/6.
15. Eamonn McCann, *Bloody Sunday in Derry: What Really Happened*, Dingle: Brandon Books, 1992, p. 62.
16. *United Irishman*, January 1972.
17. *Irish Times*, 24 January 1972.
18. *Irish Times*, 31 January 1972.
19. Ó Dochartaigh, *From Civil Rights to Armalites*, pp. 279-84.
20. *Irish Times*, 31 January 1972.
21. National Archives of Ireland, DFA/2003/13/22.
22. *Bloody Sunday, 1972: Lord Widgery's Report of Events in Londonderry, Northern Ireland, on 30 January 1972*, London: The Stationery Office, 2001, pp. 97-100.
23. McCann, *Bloody Sunday in Derry*, p. 129.
24. Eamonn McCann, 'Twisting the truth about Bloody Sunday', *Socialist Worker*, 16 June 2011.
25. *Irish Times*, 7 February 1972.
26. National Archives of Ireland, DFA/2003/17/284.

# Authors and Editors

**Nidžara Ahmetašević** is an independent researcher and journalist from Sarajevo. Her work has been featured in various media in the Balkans, as well as *The New Yorker*, *Al Jazeera English online*, *The Observer*, *The Independent on Sunday*, the *International Justice Tribune*, and *The Guardian*. She has received the AHDA Columbia University Fellowship, the UNICEF Keizo Obuchi Award and the Annenberg – Oxford Summer Media Policy Summer Institute Fellowship.

**Katerina Anastasiou** is the facilitator of the chapters Migration and Global Strategy at transform! europe. Her work covers peace and security, as well as European migration politics and policies. She is active in various grassroots antiracism groups in Austria and Europe with a focus on organisational practices and communication. She is currently also a District Councilwoman in Vienna's Fifteenth District, elected on the coalition slate of the Austrian Communist Party (KPÖ) and Links. She is KPÖ Federal Spokesperson.

**Ricardo Antunes** is a Full Professor of Sociology at the University of Campinas, Brazil, and author of several books, including *Farewell to Work?*, *The Meanings of Work*, *Viraler Kapitalismus*, and *Il privilegio della servitù*. He was Visiting Professor at University Ca' Foscari in Venice, Visiting Researcher at University of Sussex, and has for several decades collaborated with social movements, trade unions, and left parties in Brazil, Latin America, and Europe.

**Walter Baier** is an economist in Vienna, was National Chairman of the Communist Party of Austria (KPÖ) from 1994 to 2006, an editor of the Austrian weekly *Volksstimme* and from 2007 to 2020 Political Coordinator of the network transform! europe. His books include *Linker Aufbruch in Europa?* (2015) and *Unentwegte – ÖsterreichsKommunist_innen 1918-2018* (2018).

**Loren Balhorn** is a contributing editor at *Jacobin* magazine and co-founder of the magazine's German-language edition, as well as a Historical Materialism Book Series board member. He is currently based in Brussels, where he works as lead editor of the Rosa Luxemburg Foundation's English-language website.

**Étienne Balibar** has held positions at Paris-Nanterre, Kingston University London, UC Irvine, and Columbia University. He is the author of *Reading Capital* (1965, with Louis Althusser); *Race, Nation, Class: Ambiguous Identities* (1991, with Immanuel Wallerstein); *Politics and the Other Scene* (2002); *Violence and Civility* (2015); *Citizen Subject: Foundations for Philosophical Anthropology* (2017); *Secularism and Cosmopolitanism* (2018); and *On Universals: Constructing and Deconstructing Community* (2020).

**Jan Campbell** is a German citizen whose professional activities include the management of the European Union's programme for support to the former states of the USSR (CU TACIS). He has been a senior consultant to the World Bank, the United Nations Development Programme, and the Asian Development Bank. He is a foreign member of the Russian Academy of Natural Sciences. In 2014 he was awarded the gold medal Zlatýbiate and in 2020 was appointed Chairman of the Academic Board of the Institute of the Czech Left.

**Mario Candeias** is a political economist, director of the Institute for Critical Social Analysis at the Rosa Luxemburg Foundation in Berlin, and Co-Editor of the journal *LuXemburg*. His most recent publications are *Klassentheorie: Vom Making und Remaking* (Argument, 2021) and *Spurwechsel: Studien zu Mobilitätsindustrien, Beschäftigungspotenzialen und alternativer Produktion* (VSA, 2022).

**Eric Canepa** is a music historian and co-editor of the *transform! yearbook*. From 2001 to 2006 he was the Coordinator of the Socialist Scholars Conference/Left Forum in New York and from 2008 to 2012 Co-coordinator of the Rosa Luxemburg Foundation's project North-Atlantic Left Dialogue.

**Luciana Castellina** is a founder of the Italian newspaper *Il Manifesto* and of the Partito di Unità Proletaria, a past Member of the European parliament, where she was president of its Culture and Education and Foreign Economic Relations committees, several times a Deputy to the Italian Chamber of Deputies, former president of Italy's academy of motion pictures Italcinema, author of numerous books and one of the leading figures of Italy's Left continuously from the 1970s to the present day. Her latest books are *Mannuale antiretorico dell' UE* (2017) and *Amori comunisti* (2018).

**Donatella della Porta** is Director of the PhD programme in Political Science and Sociology at the Scuola Normale Superiore in Florence, where she also leads the Center on Social Movement Studies (Cosmos). In 2021, she received the Research Award of the Alexander von Humboldt Stiftung. She is the author or editor of numerous books, journal articles, and contributions in edited volumes. Among her more recent publications are: *Social Movements: An introduction* and *Can Social Movements Save Democracy?*

**Daniel Finn** is from Dublin. He received his doctorate in Irish history from University College Cork. He is the author of *One Man's Terrorist: A Political History of the IRA* (Verso Books, 2019) and has contributed to publications such as the *London Review of Books*, *Le Monde Diplomatique*, *Foreign Affairs*, and *The Guardian*. He is features editor for *Jacobin* and a member of the *New Left Review* editorial board.

**Aníbal García Fernández** has a masters in Latin American Studies from the Universidad Autónoma de México and is member of the Centro Estratégico Latinoamericano de Geopolítica (CELAG), whose latest publication is 'Manufacturing Consent? U.S. Influence in Latin America's Media'(*NACLA Report on the Americas* 53, (2021)).

**Haris Golemis** is a Greek economist who worked at the Research Department of the Bank of Greece, was scientific advisor to the Federation of Greek Bank Employees, and consultant to the United Nations Centre on Transnational Corporations. From 1999 to 2017 director of the Nicos Poulantzas Institute, he is now a member of the Editorial Committee of the Greek newspaper *Epohi*, Scientific and Strategic Advisor to the Board of transform! europe, and co-editor of the *transform! europe yearbook*.

**Margareta Gruber is** a Franciscan sister and Chair of New Testament Exegesis at the Vinzenz Pallotti University in Vallendar, Germany. From 2009 to 2013 she held the Chair of Biblical and Ecumenical Theology at the Dormition Abbey in Jerusalem as a long-term DAAD-lecturer in Israel. She is on the board of the International Journal of Theology, *Concilium*. Her field of research covers the Gospel of John, the Book of Revelation, Intertextuality, Exegesis and Biblical Spirituality and the Bible in interreligious contexts.

**Claudia Krieglsteiner** is a social worker who has been active in probationary and youth services and in various social and feminist initiatives. She is a member of the national board of the Communist Party of Austria (KPÖ) and a city councilwoman in Vienna's Fifth District.

**Tamara Lajtman** is a member of the Centro Estratégico Latinoamericano de Geopolítica (CELAG) and coordinates the Working Group on Geopolitics, Regional Integration and World System at the Latin American and Caribbean

Social Science Council (CLACSO). Its latest publication is 'Manufacturing Consent? U.S. Influence in Latin America's Media' (*NACLA Report on the Americas* 53, (2021)). Her publications cover democracy theory, state theory, political Islam, the Western Balkans, political economy, and methodology in the social sciences.

**Dunja Larise** holds a Ph.D. in political theory from the University of Vienna and has been a postdoctoral researcher at the European University Institute (EUI) in Florence, at the Center for International Studies and Research (CERI), at Sciences Po in Paris, and the MacMillan Center for International and Area Studies at Yale University. She has been a visiting fellow at the Institute of Public Goods and Policies (IPP) at the Spanish National Research Council (CSIC) and the Faculty of Political Science in Belgrade.

**Steffen Lehndorff** is a Research Fellow at the Institut Arbeit und Qualifikation (Institute for Work, Skills and Qualification / IAQ), University of Duisburg/Essen, Germany. Before his retirement in 2012, he was Head of the Department on Working-Time and Work Organisation at IAQ. His areas of research include problems of European integration, trade unions, and industrial relations in the EU, as well as strategies of socio-ecological transformation in Germany.

**Francisco Louçã** is professor of economics at Lisbon University. His most recent book, with Michael Ash, is *Shadow Networks* (OUP, 2019) on shadow finance and liberalism. He has co-authored, with Mariana Mortágua, a Handbook of Political Economy (2021, Bertrand, in Portuguese) and was a member of the Portuguese Parliament (1999-2012) and coordinator of the Left Bloc until 2012.

**Michael Löwy** was born in Brazil and has lived in Paris since 1969. He is Emeritus Research Director at the Centre National de la Recherche Scientifique, Paris. His books and articles have been translated into thirty languages. Among his main publications are: *Georg Lukacs: From Romanticism to Bolchevism*; *Fire Alarm: Reading Walter Benjamin's 'On the Concept of History'*, and *Ecosocialism: A Radical Alternative to Capitalist Catastrophe*.

**Gerassimos Moschonas** is Professor of Comparative Politics at Panteion University, Athens. He has held visiting positions at Free University of Brussels, SciencesPo-Paris, University of Leicester, Princeton University, Yale University, University of Paris 8, Montpellier 1 University, and the University of Paris II. Author of *In the Name of Social Democracy – The Great Transformation: 1945 to the Present* and *La Social-démocratie de 1945 à nos jours*, his research includes the radical left, the European left, the European Union and political parties, Europarties, elections, and Greek politics.

**Leigh Philips** is a science writer and a political journalist. His work has appeared in *Nature, New Scientist, Science, The Guardian, The Telegraph, The New Republic*, and *Jacobin*, amongst other outlets. He is the author of *Austerity Ecology & the Collapse-Porn Addicts* (Hunt, 2014).

**María Eugenia Rodríguez Palop** is member of the European Parliament, First Vice-President of the Committee on Women's Rights and Gender Equality (FEMM), and a member of the Committee on Employment and Social Affairs and the Commission on Agriculture and Rural Development (AGRI). She is also part of the Mexican and Chilean delegations of EuroLat, a professor of Philosophy of Law at the UC3M (Madrid), an ecofeminist, and a specialist in human rights and women's rights.

**Silvina Romano** is a researcher with the Consejo Nacional de Investigaciones Científicas y Técnicas (CONICET) in Argentina and coordinator of the Unidad de Análisis Geopolítico and the Observatorio de Lawfare of the Centro Estratégico Latinoamericano de Geopolítica (CELAG) whose latest publication is 'Manufacturing Consent? U.S. Influence in Latin America's Media' (*NACLA Report on the Americas* 53, (2021)).

**Axel Ruppert** is Project Manager at the Rosa Luxemburg Stiftung Brussels Office. His work covers issues of peace, security, and disarmament as well as EU militarisation and the European arms industry. He holds degrees in Political Science and European Studies and has previously worked in the field of anti-racism and equality advocacy.

**Anna Saave** is a feminist political economist with a background in sustainability economics. She works as a postdoctoral researcher at the Institute of Sociology at Friedrich-Schiller-University Jena. Her forthcoming *Appropriating and Externalizing: The Inside-Outside-Relation of the Capitalist Mode of Production* focuses on the interconnections of care, reproductive work, ecological processes, and capitalism. Further academic interests are feminist economics, degrowth, and socio-economic higher education.

**Ariel Salleh** is a member of the Global University for Sustainability; a Visiting Professor in Humanities at Nelson Mandela University; former Honorary Associate in Political Economy, University of Sydney; and a Fellow in Post-Growth Societies, Friedrich Schiller University Jena. Her positions are developed in *Ecofeminism as Politics: Nature, Marx and the Postmodern* (2017/1997), *Eco-Sufficiency & Global Justice: Women Write Political Ecology* (2009), and some 250 chapters and articles in various publications.

**Donald Sassoon** is Emeritus Professor of Comparative European History, Queen Mary University of London. His works include: *One Hundred Years of Socialism*, *The Culture of the Europeans*, *Mussolini and the Rise of Fascism*, and, more recently, *The Anxious Triumph. A Global History of Capitalism, 1860-1914*. He has been the organiser of the festival La Storia in Piazza (Genoa) and is the recipient of the Deutscher Memorial Prize, the Premio Acqui Storia, the Premio Napoli, and the 2021 Premio Altiero Spinelli.

**Seraphim Seferiades** is Professor of Political Science at the Panteion University, Athens, Life Member in Politics and History at the University of Cambridge (CLH), and Director of the Laboratory on Contentious Politics. Author of many books and articles, he has been Senior Member at the University of Oxford (St Peter's College), Fellow and Tutor in the Arts at the University of Cambridge (CHU), Jean Monnet Fellow at the European University Institute, and Hannah Seeger Davis Fellow at Princeton University.

**Veronika Sušová-Salminen** is a comparative historian specialising in the modern history of Central and Eastern Europe and Russia. She graduated from Charles University in Prague, Czech Republic (with degrees in General and Comparative History and in Anthropology). She is also Editor-in-Chief of the webzine *!Argument* and author of dozens of academic articles and essays, as well as two books.

**Jana Tsoneva** is an Assistant Professor at the Institute of Philosophy and Sociology of the Bulgarian Academy of Sciences and a founding member of the Association KOI (Collective for Social Interventions), a progressive NGO and publishing house.

**Asbjørn Wahl** is a Norwegian trade-union adviser, political writer, and activist. A past President of the Urban Transport Committee of the International Transport Workers' Federation (ITF) and Leader of the ITF Working Group on Climate Change, he is now on the Global Advisory Group of the Trade Unions for Energy Democracy network as well as a Research Fellow of Canada's Parkland Institute. He has published widely on politics, social, and labour questions and is the author of *The Rise and Fall of the Welfare State* (Pluto Press, 2011).

# transform! european network for alternative thinking and political dialogue

office@transform-network.net
Gusshausstraße 14/3
1040 Vienna, Austria

## Austria

Institute of Intercultural Research and Cooperation - IIRC★
www.latautonomy.com

transform!at
www.transform.or.at

## Cyprus

Research Institute PROMITHEAS★
www.inep.org.cy

## Czechia

The Institute of the Czech Left (Institut české levice)★
www.institutcl.cz

Society for European Dialogue - SPED
e-mail: malek_j@cbox.cz

## Denmark

transform!danmark
www.transformdanmark.dk

## Finland

Left Forum
www.vasemmistofoorumi.fi

Democratic Civic Association - DSL
www.desili.fi

## France

Espaces Marx
www.espaces-marx.fr

Foundation Copernic★
www.fondation-copernic.org

Foundation Gabriel Péri★
www.gabrielperi.fr

Institut la Boétie
institutlaboetie.fr

## Germany

Journal Sozialismus
www.sozialismus.de

Rosa Luxemburg Foundation RLF
www.rosalux.de

Instituute for Social, Ecological and Economic Studies – isw
www.isw-muenchen.de

## Greece

Nicos Poulantzas Institute - NPI
www.poulantzas.gr

## Hungary

transform!hungary★
www.balmix.hu

## Italy

transform! italia
www.transform-italia.it

Cultural Association Punto Rosso (Associazione Culturale Punto Rosso)
www.puntorosso.it

Fondazione Claudio Sabattini★
www.fondazionesabattini.it

## Lithuania

DEMOS. Institute of Critical Thought★
www.demos.lt

## Luxembourg

Transform! Luxembourg

## Moldova

Transform! Moldova★
e-mail: transformoldova@gmail.com

## Norway

Manifesto Foundation★
www.manifestanalyse.no

## Poland

Foundation Forward / Fundacja Naprzód
www.fundacja-naprzod.pl

## Portugal

Cultures of Labour and Socialism - CUL:TRA
e-mail: info@cultra.pt

## Romania

Association for the Development of the Romanian Social Forum★
e-mail: pedroxma@yahoo.com

## Serbia

Center for Politics of Emancipation - CPE★
www.pe.org.rs

## Slovenia

Institute for Labour Studies - IDS★
www.delavske-studije.si

## Spain

Alternative Foundation (Catalonia)
www.fundacioalternativa.cat

Europe of Citizens Foundation - FEC
www.lafec.org

Foundation for Marxist Studies - FIM
www.fim.org.es

Instituto República y Democracia★
www.instituto25m.info

Iratzar Foundation (Basque Country)★
www.iratzar.eus

**Sweden**

Center for Marxist Social Studies
www.cmsmarx.org

**Turkey**

Sol Siyaset★
http://solsiyaset.org/

Social Investigations and Cultural Development Foundation – TAKSAV★
www.taksav.org

**UK**

The World Transformed - TWT★
www.theworldtransformed.org

Transform! UK – A Journal of the Radical Left
www.prruk.org

★*Observers*